About "POLYGONS"

Over the past 30 years, I have been an Exhibitor at over 600 Woodworking Shows around the United States. While driving the Show circuit for about 25 years, my wife Betty and I drove over 1 million miles that took us all over the country (a lot of times).

When we first started doing the shows, many of our customers would ask questions like *"if I want to make an Octagon 14" wide, how long do I need to make the sides"* or *"how do I cut an 8 sided panel that fits into the back"*? I didn't have the answers to their questions. I was a mediocre Geometry student in High School, and quite truthfully wasn't very interested in a bunch of formulas (that I really didn't understand) for something that I knew I wouldn't want to do, anyway.

I felt that I owed it to my customers to give them answers, and bought my first laptop. I was hoping that if I learned a "drawing program", I might be able to write a booklet to help them. *The first time I sat down at the computer, I felt what the human equivalent of a monkey sitting at piano was like!! So* many keys, and no idea what to do with them.

I'm still pretty incompetent on a computer, and admit the book isn't all that pretty. What "POLYGONS" has is a tremendous amount of information that will provide you with basically everything you need to know, to build just about any shape you wish, to any size you want it to be...the first time you do it. Simply choose the shape you want, determine what you want it to look like, figure the size you want it, and look at the charts to see how wide to make the material, and how long the sides need to be. It's also simple enough that your children can learn to use it if you want to get them involved in Woodworking, one of the most rewarding activities there is.

"POLYGONS" took over 3 years to complete, occupying most of my spare time. The pictures in the Illustrations are photos that I took as we traveled around this great country, my wife, our grand kids, and our dogs.

What's In "POLYGONS"?

"REGULAR" POLYGONS:	5,6,7,8,9,10,12,14, and 16 Sided Shapes.
SCALE ILLUSTRATIONS:	Illustrations showing all shapes above, changing material width. This allows you to see what your finished project will look like (before you start to build it).
DIMENSION CHARTS:	Allow you to determine the project size, width of material needed, side lengths, and the total amount of material required for the project.
FORMULAS:	Allow you to calculate dimensions for a project not included in the Dimension Charts.
RABBETED AREA CHART:	Show you rabbet dimensions for standard picture sizes, and tell you how much material will be cropped from the picture.
ADDED WIDTH AND LENGTH CHARTS:	Pre-calculated Charts that allow you to determine the outside side length based on the rabbet length and width of the material (outside the rabbet).
"CREATIVE" POLYGONS:	6,8,10,12,14, and 16 Sided Shapes.
SCALE ILLUSTRATIONS:	Illustrations showing how to change side lengths to make creative shaped frames.
RABBET AREA CHART:	Pre-calculated Charts that allow you to make creative frames for most popular picture sizes, with minimal cropping of the picture required.
FORMULAS:	Allow you to calculate dimensions for a project not included in the Dimension Charts.

Woodworking projects don't need to be difficult if you have the right tools and the knowledge of how to build the project. I hope "POLYGONS" will become a reference that will use regularly to simplify the process of building your projects.

If you would like a visual presentation about how "POLYGONS" is intended to be used, a "POLYGONS" techniques DVD is available through IN-LINE Industries. We also have free video segments and a few articles available for you to view on our web site. For more information, please visit us at: **www.in-lineindustries com.**

"Happy Woodworking"

Jerry Cole

TABLE OF CONTENTS

PAGE: **SUBJECT:**

1   THE RIGHT TOOLS AND A LITTLE KNOWLEDGE DO MAKE A DIFFERENCE

2   MY "DUMMIES" APPROACH TO POLYGONS

3   "THE BASICS" OF POLYGONS

4   SIMPLIFYING PROJECTS BY CONVERTING DIMENSIONS

6   CONVERSION CHARTS

7   PLANNING FRAMES USING RABBET AREA DIMENSIONS

10   EXAMPLES OF POLYGON BOX PROJECTS

11   GETTING CREATIVE AS YOU FINISH YOUR PROJECTS

12   EXAMPLES OF TURNED POLYGON PROJECTS

13   SHOW OFF YOUR ARTWORK WITH CREATIVE FRAMES

14   GETTING CREATIVE WITH MULTI-SIDED FRAMES

15   CREATIVE 8, 12, AND 16 SIDED FRAME SAMPLES

17   CREATIVE 6, 10, AND 14 SIDED FRAME SAMPLES

19   CREATIVE FRAME FORMULAS AND INFORMATION

26   "CATHEDRAL STYLE" FRAMES

30   USING THE INFORMATION IN THE CHARTS AND ILLUSTRATIONS

32   5 SIDED PROJECT INFORMATION

42   6 SIDED PROJECT INFORMATION

56   7 SIDED PROJECT INFORMATION

72   8 SIDED PROJECT INFORMATION

88   9 SIDED PROJECT INFORMATION

104   10 SIDED PROJECT INFORMATION

120   12 SIDED PROJECT INFORMATION

138   14 SIDED PROJECT INFORMATION

154   16 SIDED PROJECT INFORMATION

172   PROJECT WORKSHEETS

173   PROJECT MATERIAL "CUT-LIST"

174   PROJECT MATERIAL "CALCULATIONS"

THE RIGHT TOOLS AND A LITTLE KNOWLEDGE DO MAKE A DIFFERENCE

Like most Woodworkers, I experienced about every problem you can encounter while trying to build a project. The majority of the time, the main issue was the pieces that I had cut for the project weren't perfect, and as a result they didn't fit together correctly.. I went through the normal routine that many Woodworkers go through with after-market miter gauges, "chop"saws, and dedicated "one-cut" sleds, with all of them giving me less than perfect results.

I don't intend to use this book to "push" a product at you, but I do want to help people who would like to find a better way to work. If you don't have our "**POLYGONS**" DVD, I suggest that you go to our web site at **www.in-lineindustries.com** and watch some of the free video clips that we have on building the different project shapes that we have in this book. What you will see is that these projects aren't only possible, they are actually quite easy, and will fit together perfectly the first time you do them.

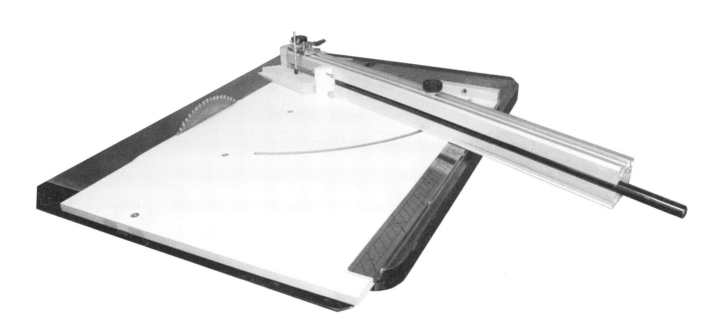

MY "DUMMIES" APPROACH TO POLYGONS

I had a terrible time with Geometry in High School, so when I started Woodworking I had to teach myself a way to build different "Multi-Sided" (Polygon) projects. Since I'm not smart enough to over-complicate something, I came up with a very simple way to approach them. I approach Polygons depending on the number of sides, and show them below in 3 different groups (with each group having similar characteristics). The information given below is based on all of the sides of the project being equal length.

On Projects with 8, 12, and 16 Sides, every side is parallel to another side, and each side has 2 sides square (90°) to it. The distance between each pair of parallel sides is equal, and the height and width of the project is equal. Note the Illustrations below.

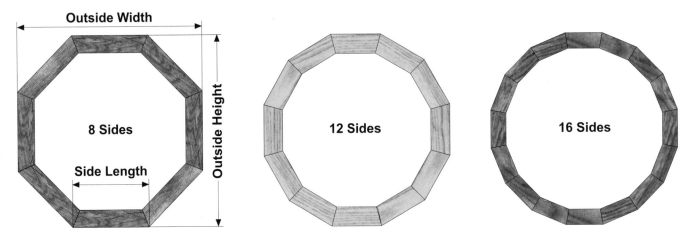

On Projects with 6, 10, and 14 Sides, every side is parallel to another side, but no sides are square (90°) to one another. The height and width of the project are unequal, as the point-to-point distance (shown below as the project width) is longer than the side-to-side distance (shown below as the project height). Note the Illustrations below.

On Projects with 5, 7, and 9 Sides, no sides are parallel to another side, and no sides are square (90°) to one another. The height and width of the project is unequal, as the point-to-point distance (shown below as the project width) is longer than the side-to-point distance (shown below as the project height). Note the Illustrations below.

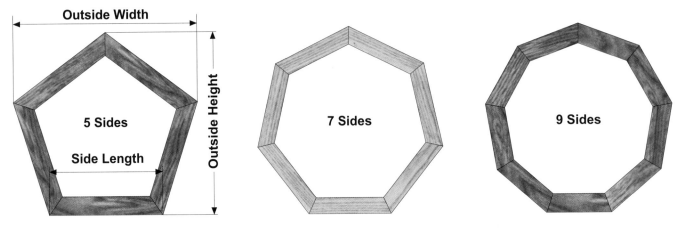

"THE BASICS" OF POLYGONS

One of the first things I learned when I started Woodworking was that when I made angle cuts, I should always cut with the inside edge of the material being forward toward the saw blade. By cutting from the inside edge to the outside edge of the material, I always cut the material with the grain. This means I never have problems tearing out the inside corners of the material, which are the most difficult joints to correct as you assemble your project.

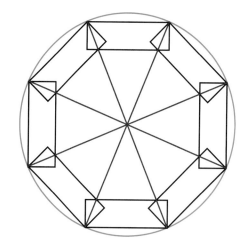

To build a perfect Polygon (regardless of the number of sides) the total of the angles (on material removed from the inside edges of the sides) must total exactly 360° (the total angles of a circle). The angled cut must radiate from the exact center of the shape, and you need consistency in the angle of the cuts. In the Illustration to the right, you can see this on what will be an Octagonal frame. You should note that the angled (red) lines that would represent the required angle cuts intersect with the 8 pieces where both the inside and outside edges would be cut. Note that each of the sides would need to be cut twice.

What this Illustration (hopefully) shows you is a simple way to calculate the required angle formula needed for any shape we want to build:

Formula: 360 ÷ (Number of sides x 2) = Miter Angle
Example: 360 ÷ (8 sides x 2 = 16) = 22.5°

If all of the angle cuts are accurate and all of the side lengths are equal, the project should fit together perfectly, as shown in the Illustration to the right. If the mitered angles aren't perfect, one of two things will happen, as shown in the Illustrations below. This information is based on the material being cut with the inside (rabbeted) edge of the molding being forward, the molding being cut from the inside edge toward the outside edge, and all sides being equal length.

Gaps on the inside, as shown in the Illustration below left, indicate the miter angle is too sharp. (Too much material is cut off the inside edge).

Gaps on the outside, as shown in the Illustration below right, indicate the miter angle is not sharp enough. (Not enough material is cut off the inside edge).

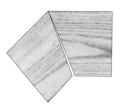   

One of the things that I enjoy is building projects that would be difficult (if not impossible) for many other Woodworkers, as long as I can keep it simple. A good example of this would be something like the Octagonal frame shown in the Illustration to the right.

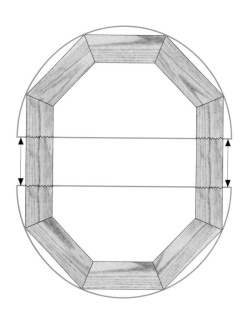

On "even number sided" Polygons, it is really quite easy to change the shape of the project, by just changing the length of a few of the sides. As you can see in the Illustration, all we have done is "split" the circle at the center of the parallel vertical sides, and moved the halves of the frame (and circle) apart. (Note the dimension lines at the vertical sides).

By then making the 2 vertical sides longer than the other sides, the Octagonal frame (shown above-right) is transformed into a frame (shown right) that is not only attractive, but would also eliminate a lot of cropping on a picture.

I have tried to emphasize in the written articles in this book how you can get creative with the projects you build. If you take the time to read these articles and use the information provided, I guarantee the way you approach a project will change dramatically.

SIMPLIFYING PROJECTS BY CONVERTING DIMENSIONS

On the Frame Illustration pages, the Illustrations are drawn (in scale) to outside dimensions. To draw them to specific sizes for the different sizes of pictures would not only require more work than I could do in a lifetime, but would also require a complete series of books to provide all of the information that would be involved.

I thought that a more practical approach in "**POLYGONS**" would be to show you how to plan your project(s) to size first. Then you can use the Frame Illustrations and Dimension Charts to see what your project will look like, and also how much material would be required. By working in this way, there should never be a case where you will be disappointed with the results of your efforts.

As mentioned in other articles in "**POLYGONS**", the size of the frame must be planned according to the size of the object(s) that will be placed into the rabbeted area of the frame. Since the rabbet is the most difficult dimension to cut accurately, (since it is not on the inside or outside edge of the molding) I wanted to find a way that would allow you to work easier. I call this method of calculations "**ADDED WIDTH AND LENGTH**".

For planning purposes, the molding width (shown in black) is the total of 2 dimensions:
The rabbet width (shown in green) is the desired width of the rabbet in which the object(s) being framed will be positioned.
The Width outside the rabbet (shown in red) is the dimension determined by subtracting the rabbet width from the overall width of the molding. It is this dimension that will control not only the outside length(s) of the sides of your projects, but also the amount of material required to build them.

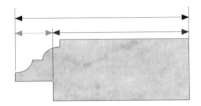

In each section of "**POLYGONS**" we have included "**FRAME INFORMATION**" articles that provide you with the Formulas, Charts, and even a "**RABBET AREA DIMENSION CHART**" that has pre-calculated rabbet dimensions for most sizes of frames. In these articles, you will also find a Chart for "**ADDED WIDTH AND LENGTH**". You should find this chart in particular to be very helpful. To allow you to see how these charts were designed, I have compiled all of the Illustrations used to design the Charts for the Polygons Illustrated in this book in the Section below. The Illustrations show the changes in length according to the changes in width for each Polygon. We have also included the calculations determined by each Illustration. You may find it easier to reference the following information as a "quick reference" when planning your projects.

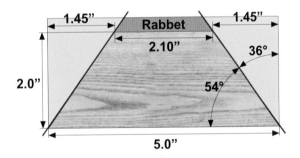

Polygon Name:	Pentagon
Number of Sides:	5
Miter Angle:	36°
Resulting Angle:	54°
Length Change per 2" Change in Width:	2.90"
Calculation: Added Length ÷ Added Width = Multiplier	
Conclusion: Added Length = Added Width x 1.45	

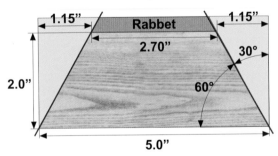

Polygon Name:	Hexagon
Number of Sides:	6
Miter Angle:	30°
Resulting Angle:	60°
Length Change per 2" Change in Width:	2.30"
Calculation: Added Length ÷ Added Width = Multiplier	
Conclusion: Added Length = Added Width x 1.15	

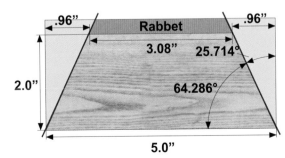

Polygon Name:	Heptagon
Number of Sides:	7
Miter Angle:	25.714°
Resulting Angle:	64.286°
Length Change per 2" Change in Width:	1.92"
Calculation: Added Length ÷ Added Width = Multiplier	
Conclusion: Added Length = Added Width x .96	

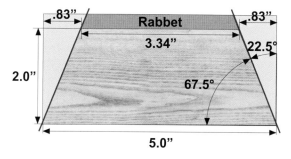

Polygon Name:	Octagon
Number of Sides:	8
Miter Angle:	22.5°
Resulting Angle:	67.5°
Length Change per 2" Change in Width:	1.66"
Calculation: Added Length ÷ Added Width = Multiplier	
Conclusion: Added Length = Added Width x .83	

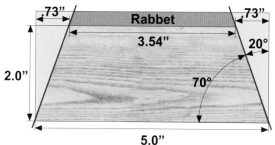

Polygon Name:	Nonagon
Number of Sides:	9
Miter Angle:	20°
Resulting Angle:	70°
Length Change per 2" Change in Width:	1.46"
Calculation: Added Length ÷ Added Width = Multiplier	
Conclusion: Added Length = Added Width x .73	

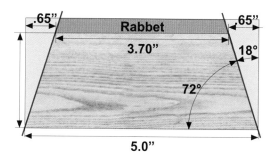

Polygon Name:	Decagon
Number of Sides:	10
Miter Angle:	18°
Resulting Angle:	72°
Length Change per 2" Change in Width:	1.30"
Calculation: Added Length ÷ Added Width = Multiplier	
Conclusion: Added Length = Added Width x .65	

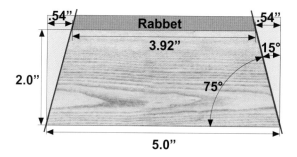

Polygon Name:	Dodecagon
Number of Sides:	12
Miter Angle:	15°
Resulting Angle:	75°
Length Change per 2" Change in Width:	1.08"
Calculation: Added Length ÷ Added Width = Multiplier	
Conclusion: Added Length = Added Width x .54	

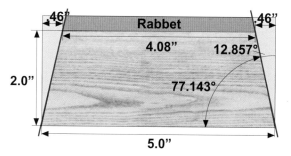

Polygon Name:	Tetradecagon
Number of Sides:	14
Miter Angle:	12.857°
Resulting Angle:	77.143°
Length Change per 2" Change in Width:	.92"
Calculation: Added Length ÷ Added Width = Multiplier	
Conclusion: Added Length = Added Width x .46	

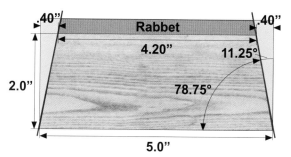

Polygon Name:	Hexadecagon
Number of Sides:	16
Miter Angle:	11.25°
Resulting Angle:	78.75°
Length Change per 2" Change in Width:	.80"
Calculation: Added Length ÷ Added Width = Multiplier	
Conclusion: Added Length = Added Width x .40	

CONVERSION CHARTS

To help with the formulas for your projects, Conversion Charts are provided. The Charts within the different Sections on Polygons are formatted in 16ths, and if you work closely to these fractions when building your projects, your results should turn out very well. The main thing you should remember is that if your measurements aren't perfect, *make sure your pieces will be slightly long*.

DECIMAL TO FRACTION CONVERSION CHART

Decimal	Fraction	Decimal	Fraction	Decimal	Fraction	Decimal	Fraction
.0156	1/64	.2656	17/64	.5156	33/64	.7656	49/64
.0312	1/32	.2812	9/32	.5312	17/32	.7812	25/32
.0469	3/64	.2969	19/64	.5469	35/64	.7969	51/64
.0625	1/16	.3125	5/16	.5625	9/16	.8125	13/16
.0781	5/64	.3281	21/64	.5781	37/64	.8281	53/64
.0937	3/32	.3437	11/32	.5937	19/32	.8437	27/32
.1094	7/64	.3594	23/64	.6094	39/64	.8594	55/64
.1250	1/8	.3750	3/8	.6250	5/8	.8750	7/8
.1406	9/64	.3906	25/64	.6406	41/64	.8906	57/64
.1562	5/32	.4062	13/32	.6562	21/32	.9062	29/32
.1719	11/64	.4219	27/64	.6719	43/64	.9219	59/64
.1875	3/16	.4375	7/16	.6875	11/16	.9375	15/16
.2031	13/64	.4531	29/64	.7031	45/64	.9531	61/64
.2187	7/32	.4687	15/32	.7187	23/32	.9687	31/32
.2344	15/64	.4844	31/64	.7344	47/64	.9844	63/64
.2500	1/4	.5000	1/2	.7500	3/4	1.0000	**

** Decimal value 1.000 is equivalent to any fraction where the numerator (number above the line) and denominator (number below the line) are equal. Examples: 2/2, 4/4, 8/8, 16/16, 32/32, 64/64, etc.

The **LEAST COMMON DENOMINATOR CHART** is included to help those of you who may be relatively new to the hobby, or not familiar with tape measures. When you determine a measurement, follow the numbers in that row to the right to find the least common denominator for that specific measurement.

LEAST COMMON DENOMINATOR CHART

1/32nds	1/16ths	1/8ths	1/4ths	1/2s	1/32nds	1/16ths	1/8ths	1/4ths	1/2s
1/32					17/32				
2/32	1/16				18/32	9/16			
3/32					19/32				
4/32	2/16	1/8			20/32	10/16	5/8		
5/32					21/32				
6/32	3/16				22/32	11/16			
7/32					23/32				
8/32	4/16	2/8	1/4		24/32	12/16	6/8	3/4	
9/32					25/32				
10/32	5/16				26/32	13/16			
11/32					27/32				
12/32	6/16	3/8			28/32	14/16	7/8		
13/32					29/32				
14/32	7/16				30/32	15/16			
15/32					31/32				
16/32	8/16	4/8	2/4	1/2	32/32	16/16	8/8	4/4	2/2

PLANNING FRAMES USING RABBETED AREA DIMENSIONS

The size of a frame is normally controlled by the size of the object(s) that will be placed inside it, not by the inside or outside dimensions of the frame. By learning the following techniques, you will understand how to build multi-sided frames by working with the dimensions that will enable you to make frames to fit the picture. This will eliminate unnecessary cropping of the picture or re-trimming all of the sides on a frame that was made to the wrong size. Though working "inside-out" may be a little confusing at first, with the information we have provided and a little practice, you should be able to build any shape of frame you want with little or no difficulty. I don't mean to keep repeating myself, but for every shape of Polygon (multi-sided shape) illustrated in this book, you will find the formulas and charts that you need to make any frame you wish, (right to size) the first time you build it.

The first thing you need to understand is that on projects with 8, 12, and 16 sides the width and the height will be equal dimensions, providing all sides are the same length. On all other shapes shown in this book, the width and height will be slightly different. On any frame you build, what I call the "controlling" dimension will always be the smaller dimension on the object being framed. On an object that is taken in a "Portrait" format, where it is taller than it is wide, the width would be the controlling dimension. In a "Landscape" format, where it is wider than it is tall, the height would be the controlling dimension.

As an example of how these formulas will help us, lets say that we want to make a 5 sided frame for the picture of my friend Joe Spurlock's pet squirrel "Friday". For our example, we'll say it measures 8" x !0" in the "Landscape" format.

As you can see, when a 5 sided shape is placed over the picture, there is a lot of material that will need to be cropped from the width of the picture, where there would need to be no cropping off the top or the bottom.

We know that the height of our 5 sided picture will be 8". Now we need to calculate what we need to do to build a frame that will allow us to use the picture without needing to crop the height.

Helpful Hint: Professional Picture Framers will almost always make the inside opening of their frames 1/8" larger than the object(s) being placed into the openings. This is done to allow for movement of the frame and also the object(s) being placed into the frame. By allowing for this, it is very unlikely that you'll build your frame, and then need to do unnecessary trimming (cropping) of the picture. (Most Professionals also "float" the picture so it doesn't make contact with the glass on the frame).

As mentioned above, for every shape of frame illustrated in this book, we have included formulas and charts to assist you as you build your frames. Since we are using 5 sides as our example, you would refer to the "**5 SIDED FRAME FORMULAS**", as shown below.

5 SIDED FRAME FORMULAS		
WIDTH	**HEIGHT**	**SIDE LENGTH**
Width = Side Length x 1.620	Height = Side Length x 1.539	Side Length = Width x .618
Width = Height x 1.053	Height = Width x .950	Side Length = Height x .650

We know only the desired height (8 1/8") of our 5 sided frame opening. To calculate the desired rabbet length, use 2 simple steps:

Step 1. Using a calculator and the **DECIMAL TO FRACTION CONVERSION CHART** provided, refer to the (bright yellow) highlighted section **"SIDE LENGTH"** chart above.

Step 2. Multiply the desired 8 1/8" height (decimal equivalent is 8.125) by .650. The product (total) is 5.281. Using the chart, we find that .281 is slightly less than 9/32nds of an inch. This tells us how long (5 9/32") the sides need to be *at the rabbeted (notched) edge of the molding*.

Though the information above is helpful, it would still require a lot of trial and error (and wasted material) to build a 5 sided frame. The following information should be helpful as you learn how to use our formulas and charts as you build your different shapes of frames.

When a board is cut at an angle, there will be a "constant" change in length for every "constant" change in width. The sharper the angle, the larger the change between the inside and outside length will be. In the top Illustration on the next page, we show a piece of wood that is 1.5" (1 1/2") wide. You will notice that on a 22.5 cut (shown in red) for every .375 (3/8") change in width there is a

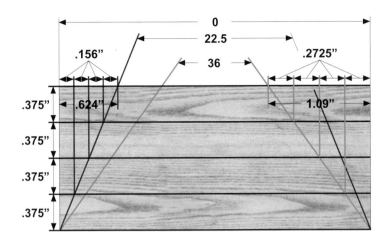

.156" (5/32") change in length. Over the width of the board, the length change is .624" (approximately 5/8") on one end. Since we would cut both ends of the piece, the inside edge would be 1.248" (approximately 1 1/4") shorter than the outside edge.

On the 36 degree cut (shown in green) for every 3/8" of width, the length changes .2725" (17/64"), and across the width the change on each end would be 1.09" (1 3/32'). Since we would cut both ends of the piece, the inside edge would be 2.18" (approximately 2 3/16") shorter than the outside edge.

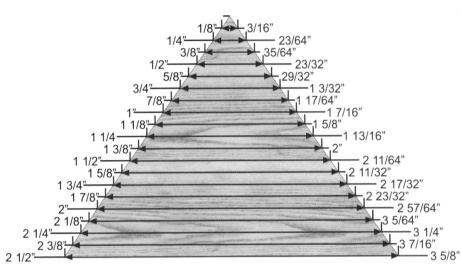

The next steps that should be done are to calculate how wide you want the molding to be, and how much material you need. In the Illustration to the left, you see one piece of a 5 sided frame that has been cut (at 36°) to a point on the inside. The numbers down the left side (black) show the width change in 1/8" increments. Down the right side, (red) they show the increase in the side length for every 1/8" increase in width.

By using the charts provided for each of the shapes illustrated in this book, you will be able to determine the outside lengths you will need to build your frames.

The Chart shown below is the "**5 SIDED FRAME ADDED WIDTH AND LENGTH CHART**." As you can see, for every 1/8" of width that is added to the width of the molding (from 1/8" to 5") it shows you how much length would be added to the side length of the frame side <u>at the rabbet</u>. This does not allow for the width of the molding that will be used for the rabbet. Let's say that you want to use 1 3/8" wide material for the frame, and install a 1/4" rabbet on the molding. This would give you 1 1/8" of molding to the outside of the rabbet. As you can see in the chart below, this would give us 1 5/8" (1 20/32") of extra length. This would be added to the 5 9/32" length needed for the rabbet measurement, for an outside length of 6 29/32". By looking at the Dimension Charts and Frame Illustration pages, we can see that the finished frame will be similar to **Illustration C** on the 5 Sided Frame Illustrations.

5 SIDED FRAME ADDED WIDTH AND LENGTH CHART									
Added Width	Added Length	Added Width	Added Length	Added Width	Added Length	Added Width	Added Length	Added Width	Added Length
2/16	3/16	1 2/16	1 10/16	2 2/16	3 1/16	3 2/16	4 9/16	4 2/16	6
4/16	6/16	1 4/16	1 13/16	2 4/16	3 4/16	3 4/16	4 11/16	4 4/16	6 3/16
6/16	9/16	1 6/16	2	2 6/16	3 7/16	3 6/16	4 14/16	4 6/16	6 6/16
8/16	12/16	1 8/16	2 3/16	2 8/16	3 10/16	3 8/16	5 1/16	4 8/16	6 8/16
10/16	15/16	1 10/16	2 6/16	2 10/16	3 13/16	3 10/16	5 4/16	4 10/16	6 11/16
12/16	1 1/16	1 12/16	2 9/16	2 12/16	4	3 12/16	5 7/16	4 12/16	6 14/16
14/16	1 4/16	1 14/16	2 12/16	2 14/16	4 3/16	3 14/16	5 10/16	4 14/16	7 1/16
1	1 7/16	2	2 14/16	3	4 6/16	4	5 13/16	5	7 4/16

By using the information provided, we know that the finished frame will look like the Illustration on the next page before we start to build it. If we are satisfied with the appearance of the frame, the next step would be to calculate how much material would be required to complete it. Obviously we don't want to waste material, so we would use the information provided in the Section on 5 Sided Frames to determine how much molding we need for our project. In the Dimension Charts for the frames, we have calculated the amount of material required for each frame, allowing 1/4" of waste for each frame side. As you start getting used to working with the methods we describe, you may want to allow for a little more waste as you design your projects.

Helpful Hint: I prefer to use my table saw almost exclusively for my crosscut and mitering work. By using a home made "right angle stop" against the rip fence as you do the "rough cuts" on the frame sides, it is easy to cut the sides for any shape of frame with virtually no wasted material. On our frame, we know that each of the sides should be 6 29/32" long (decimal equivalent is 6.906") when cut to a finished length. We also know that we need 5 sides cut to this length, so we multiply the length (6.906") by 5. We find that the total length required for the 5 sides of the frame is 34.53" (34 1/2") .

The length above (34 1/2") doesn't allow for the material that will be removed as we make the cuts. Most woodworkers use 1/8" wide blades on their saws. As a result, at *a very minimum*, you should add 1/4" per side to allow for the 2 cuts that would me made on each side.

With 1/4" waste per side, the minimum amount of waste on our frame (5 x 1/4") would be 1 1/4".

If we add this to our length required for the frame sides, *the absolute minimum* amount of material required to build our frame would be 35 3/4".

NOTE: The Illustration below is to scale, and has been reduced to approximately 5/8" of the actual size to fit within the page margins.

NOTE: Friday is the "Shop Buddy" of my friend Joe Spurlock, and is about 5 years old. He lives in Joe's shop, and loves it when Joe cuts walnuts in half on his bandsaw. He also loves Root Beer, but insists that it "goes flat" first.

EXAMPLES OF POLYGON BOX PROJECTS

Though most of the articles in "**POLYGONS**" speak of building frames, the same principles apply to other types of woodworking projects. I though some of the readers of this book might find it interesting to see some of the different ways that woodworkers have applied different techniques to build their multi-sided projects.

The 2 Photos below show an Octagonal (8 sided) Box that was built by Joe Spurlock. In the process of building this box, instead of laying the pieces down (as we would do to build a frame), Joe stood the material (on which he had routed the top outside edge and cut a dado groove for the bottom panel) up, with the inside face of the stock forward, toward the saw blade. As he cut the 8 pieces to the same length, he created the carcass of the box. He then cut the lid and bottom pieces, routed the edge of the lid, and rabbeted the bottom edge of the lid so it would lock into the box. The result is an extremely attractive project that we are very proud to display.

The Photo below shows one of 2 Dodecagon (12 sided) boxes that I built. One was for my wife Betty, and the other was for my Mother. This was one of the projects I designed when I wrote 6 articles for a woodworking magazine a few years ago. The box was fairly simple to build, as I used 1 length for the front and back sides and another length for the 10 short sides

Since the design of the box was fairly plain, I glued together bloodwood and lacewood strips before I planed the pieces for the sides and lid panel. The dado for the box bottom was cut in the inside face of the long pieces for the sides before the sides were cut to length. Since the lid overhangs the box, the only routing done on the project was on the top outside edge of the lid.

I think the project turned out fairly well, and was proud to give the boxes as gifts. It also made me proud to give my Mom a copy of the magazine that showed her box on the front cover.

GETTING CREATIVE AS YOU FINISH YOUR PROJECTS

The way you finish your projects can have a dramatic impact on the final appearance, and the projects on this page should be a good example of what I am trying to get across.

Until about 8 years ago, I wouldn't even consider making a project that I thought I would like to see painted. It was about then that my wife Betty got interested in Decorative Painting.

The 2 boxes to the left are identical in size and design, though the angle the photos were shot at may make them appear to be a little bit different. These were both built for an article I wrote for a Magazine. The top one was built by Rob Joseph, as he followed my article to make sure I hadn't "goofed things up." He used Mahogany for the carcass and lid of the box.

The bottom box was the prototype that I built as I wrote the article. Since we wanted it painted, I used Poplar for all of the stiles, rails, and lid trim. For all of the raised panel stock, I used a lightweight MDF.

The boxes measure 15 1/4" wide x 11 1/4" deep x 5 3/4" high. The painted box (in my opinion) would be a great sewing box or something that is just out on display as a conversation piece.

Regardless of how you decide to finish your project, I would think you would be proud to display (or give away) a project such as these.

The 2 "Heart Shaped" boxes are another example of how we change the appearance by changing the finish.

Again, these are from a project article I wrote. The painted box was the prototype I built as I wrote the article, The box was painted by Linda Hendry.

The Purple Heart box was built by Rob Joseph as he checked out my article.

Again, I would think you would be pleased with the project, regardless of how you decided to finish it.

EXAMPLES OF TURNED POLYGON PROJECTS

As I mentioned in the "POLYGONS" DVD, I have a lot of respect for Woodturners, especially those that have the creativity to convert some simple segmented rings into beautiful projects.

Below are some of the pieces that Betty & I have been given by some of our customers (and friends). I must admit I'm envious of these guys (since I don't have the talent to build projects like these). We would like to thank them for these beautiful projects, and are proud to display them in our home. I wish you could see these "first hand" as the photos below don't do these projects justice.

It's amazing how some simple techniques can give beautiful results. On the project to the right and the project below, the gluing together of different species of wood and assembling in different patterns resulted in 2 outstanding projects.

The project to the right was masterfully crafted by our friend Don Riggs. By laminating the mahogany and maple pieces face-to-face before he cut the pieces for the 2 sections that have the "ring patterns", hc was able to expose the ovals as he turned the segmented rings round.

The lid and "zig-zag" ring really make this project stand out. There are 2 very narrow strips of Osage Orange wood that are between the Mahogany and Satinwood strips, which make the lid pattern outstanding.

Don's technique made this a beautiful project that we cherish, and the 8" wide x 6 ½"high project shows 241 pieces of wood.

The project to the left is a perfect example of what you can do with domestic woods.

On this project, our friend D. J. Dolan used walnut, maple, and oak to create this beautiful bowl. By gluing the maple to the walnut before cutting the ring segments, the maple ovals were created as the bowl was turned.

One thing that I really like about this project is how he placed the walnut pieces between the oak pieces on the top ring of the bowl, as it really makes the project stand out. The bowl is 10" x 4", has 75 pieces of wood, and was done using 9 sided rings.

The Satinwood and Bloodwood bowl to the right is a perfect example of how attractive a project can be, even if it's simple.

The bowl to the right is a project of "combined efforts". I cut the 12 sided rings for the piece, which were then assembled and turned by Lloyd Johnson.

SHOW OFF YOUR ARTWORK WITH CREATIVE FRAMES

Though there are a few sizes of canvas projects that are square, most objects we build frames for are rectangular. In other words, the width will usually be different than the height. In a Portrait format, the height is the larger dimension, and in a Landscape format, the width is the larger dimension. Though we can build some very attractive rectangular frames (which we cover in our first book "**The Picture Frame Guide**"), building more "creative" frames using different Polygons can give you an extremely attractive project.

In the next Section, we have included a lot of information that will allow you to build some very unusual frames, without it becoming a major project. For those of you who would like some visual assistance in building these types of frames, you should go to our web site at **www.in-lineindustries.com** to check out the "**POLYGONS**" DVD that we offer to help you build creative frames simply.

Below you will see just a few frame styles that can be (easily) done on multi-sided frames. One of the things you will appreciate is that these shapes can all be built to the specific size of the object being framed, so you won't need to crop any of the height of width of the object. Charts in each section will show you the specific dimensions of rabbet lengths needed for most popular sizes of pictures.

We hope you find the information helpful, and know you will be proud to display frames like these. They can transform a regular photo into a real "work of art".

To give you an idea of how you can get creative with your projects, we've included photos of some of the frame styles we built in the "**POLYGONS**" DVD.

The picture to the right is of our Yorkie "Chewy" (who is really a "Mommy's boy" and a bundle of fun)! The frame is a creative Octagon (8 sides in Landscape) using 2 different side lengths.

The frame below-left is a Dodecagon (12 sides in Portrait) using 3 different side lengths. That's our Yorkie "Sam". Other than my wife Betty, Sam is probably the best friend I've ever had. I thought she deserved a special place in this book, so I built this type of frame (which is one of my most favorite frames to build) for her picture.

The picture below-right is an abandoned farmhouse that Betty & I saw in Winterville, Maine. I'll bet there were a lot of memories created in this place. The frame is a Hexadecagon (16 sides in Landscape) using 2 different side lengths. If you are looking for a "fixer-upper, I'd bet you could get a real deal on this property!

GETTING CREATIVE WITH MULTI-SIDED FRAMES

This information is based on the rabbeted areas of the frames. In each section on "even sided" frames, you will find the formulas (which are quite simple) that will enable you to build frames that are not only unique, but fairly simple to do. I recommend that you read and understand the principles in the "**PLANNING FRAMES USING RABBETED AREA DIMENSIONS**" article. It should help you understand what you need to do not only to use the formulas, but also build the perfect frame on the first attempt.

On frames with an odd number of sides, it can be quite a challenge if you try to make something "unique", as the mathematics can be very difficult. This is because on odd numbers, there are no parallel sides on the frame. As a result, if you try to change the length on any of the sides, you will need to have at least 3 different lengths of sides for the frame to fit together. It is also questionable about what the final shape of the frame will be as you are building it.

On frames with an even number of sides, the possibilities of building a fairly unique frame are pretty much unlimited (providing you have all of the information you need to make the needed calculations). For each (even sided) shape illustrated in this book, you will find the information that you need to make many unique frames(right to size) for the object you are framing.

Though it wouldn't be practical to show every possible variation that can be made on the different shaped frames, we have tried to include a variety of samples to help you understand how making a few changes in the length on some of the sides will allow you to be quite creative while building your projects.

One of the first things that you should consider when building a creative frame is how much of the picture you want to eliminate when you frame it. Most objects we frame (pictures, paintings, etc.) have 4 sides, and are either square or rectangular. To make them into creative frames, the object being framed will be trimmed (cropped) to fit inside the frame. To help you learn how to make creative frames and keep it as simple as possible, we will first discuss the easiest shapes to work with; 8, 12, and 16 sided frames.

On frames with 8, 12, and 16 sides, there are sides on the frame that are parallel to the 4 sides of the picture being framed. This is because these shapes are all multiples of 4. As a result, this will give us quite an advantage when working with these 3 shapes, as it allows us to modify the shape and keep the math pretty simple to calculate.

The Illustrations to the right should help you to understand why 8, 12, and 16 sided frames are the easiest shapes to work with when building creative frames. In each of the Illustrations, (which are all partial Illustrations of the "A" Illustrations on the next page), you can see where the top of each shape is parallel to the top of the picture.

You should also notice on the Illustrations on the next page:

The yellow areas on each Illustration show the material that would be cropped from the picture. Each Illustration is drawn to scale, and the yellow area represents a picture either 8" x 10", 16" x 20", or 24" x 30".

On an 8 sided frame, it takes 1 side to connect the top and vertical side on each corner.

On a 12 sided frame, it takes 2 sides to connect the top and vertical side on each corner.

On a 16 sided frame, it takes 3 sides to connect the top and vertical side on each corner.

On the "**A**" Illustrations, the top and sides of the frame (all shown in red) that connect with the two vertical sides are all the same length.

On the "**B**" Illustrations, the top (shown in green) is long, and the sides (shown in red) that connect the top with the vertical sides are shorter. On the 12 and 16 sided shapes, these sides (shown in red) are the same length within each Illustration.

On the "**C**" Illustrations, the top (shown in green) is short, and the sides (shown in red) that connect the top with the vertical sides are longer. On the 12 and 16 sided shapes, these sides (shown in red) are the same length within each Illustration.

In the top right corner of each Illustration, you will see that the horizontal and vertical dimension lines (inside the circles in the Illustrations to the right) are the same length. The reason for this is since the sides that connect the top to the vertical sides (regardless of how many are used) are the same length. The distance from the outside corners of the picture (to where the picture will need to be cropped) will be the same to the end of the top, and he top of the side on the object being framed.

8 SIDED FRAMES

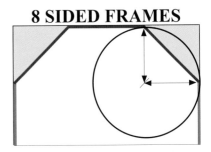

12 SIDED FRAMES

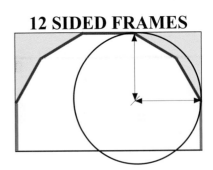

16 SIDED FRAMES

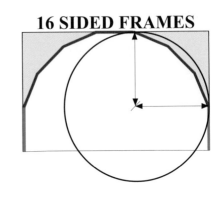

CREATIVE 8, 12, and 16 SIDED FRAME SAMPLES

8 SIDED FRAMES

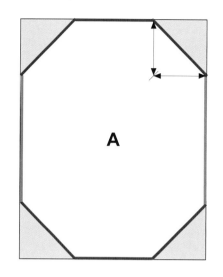

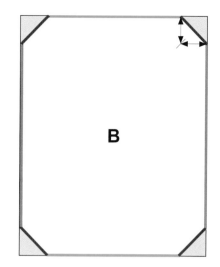

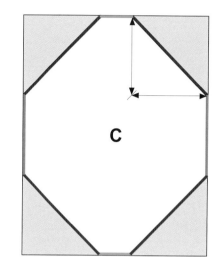

12 SIDED FRAMES

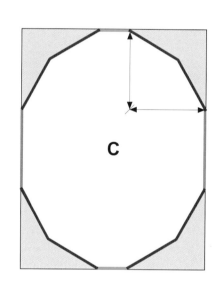

16 SIDED FRAMES

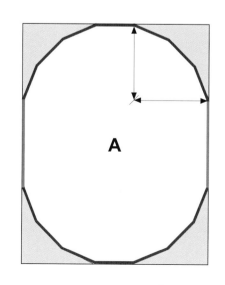

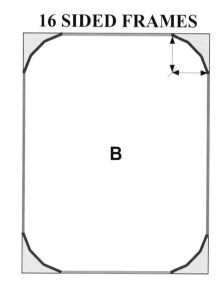

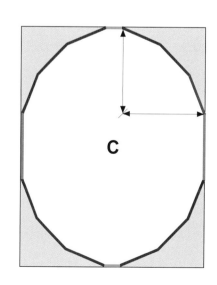

On frames with 6, 10, and 14 sides, you will have points on the frame that point toward one pair of parallel sides of the picture, and one pair of frame sides that are parallel to the other 2 sides of the picture. This will tend to make the mathematics of these frame more difficult than 8, 12, and 16 sided frames, but by no means beyond your capability to make (if you use the information we've included in each section on even sided frame shapes*).*

In the Illustrations below, you should be able so see why there are differences in building these shapes of frames. In each of the Illustrations, (which are partial Illustrations of the "**A**" Illustrations on the next page) you can see that there points on each shape at the top of the picture. ***These points will always meet at the center of the picture***.

6 SIDED FRAMES

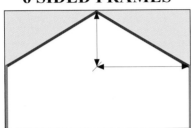

10 SIDED FRAMES

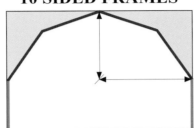

14 SIDED FRAMES

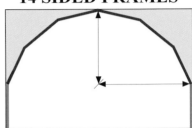

The first things you should notice are the points at the top of the frames, and that the dimension lines on the frames are not the same lengths in any of the pictures. This is the reason these shapes are more difficult than the 8, 12, and 16 sided frames (to build to specific dimensions).

You should also notice on the Illustrations on the next page:

On a 6 sided frame, it takes 1 frame side to connect the top and vertical sides of the picture.

On the "**A**" Illustration, the longest frame sides (shown in blue) are parallel to the vertical sides of the picture.

On the "**B**" Illustration, the top and bottom frame sides are parallel to the top and bottom of the picture, and the long sides (shown in red) are the longest sides.

On the "**C**" Illustration of a 6 sided frame, the picture has been rotated to a Landscape format. The top (shown in blue) and bottom sides (shown in black) are parallel to the sides of the picture. The 2 sides (shown in red) connect the top with the vertical sides. The short bottom corners(shown in green) connect the vertical sides of the picture to the bottom of the picture. The bottom is parallel to the bottom of the picture. If this sounds a little complicated, it is. To make a frame this shape fit a specific dimension, it takes 4 different lengths of sides. Though it can be done, I wouldn't recommend this frame as a learning project, and it will not be discussed further in this article. The next thing I would like to do is show you how we develop the formulas that help determine dimensions.

Illustration 1 to the right is a partial (to scale) drawing of an 8" x 10" sheet. It represents the top (8") side in a portrait format (or if rotated 90°, the vertical side in a landscape format) for Illustration "**A**". As you can see, the sheet has been divided in half across the width of the sheet, with 4" to each side of the center line (**C/L**). Note the 4" lines above the sheet. On the sheet, you can see the same 4" lines, each rotated 30°, which is the miter angle in a Hexagon. As you see, when we join these lines at the center line, they are too short to join with the vertical sides of the sheet.

Illustration 1

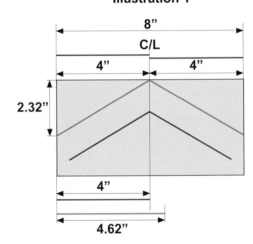

To start determining the formulas required on Hexagons, I duplicated the 30° lines, (made them blue), and stretched them to meet with the vertical sides of the sheet. By doing this, I determined that the required length of these 2 sides would be 4.62" (approximately 4 5/8"). This information is what I need to make a formula for the "pointed" side lengths, but I also need to determine how to also use this information to help calculate what the side lengths parallel to the sheet sides would be.

On the left side of the Illustration, you can see (where the blue line meets with the edge of the sheet) dimension lines and a 2.32" (approximately 2 5/16") dimension. This dimension tells us how far down from the top (and bottom) of the sheet these sides meet with the sheet sides. By multiplying this dimension by 2 (since it happens on both the top and bottom of the sheet) we can determine that we would take 4 5/8" (2 5/16" x 2) from the 10" height of the picture. This would give us side lengths (along the rabbeted edge of the molding of 5 3/8". This gives us the information for our formula, but I will confirm them by checking in landscape format.

CREATIVE 6, 10, and 14 SIDED FRAME SAMPLES

6 SIDED FRAMES

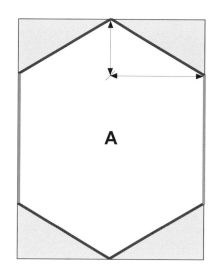

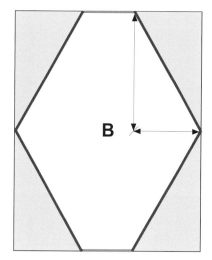

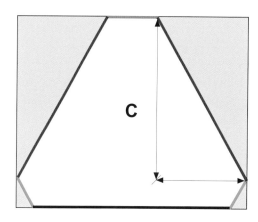

10 SIDED FRAMES

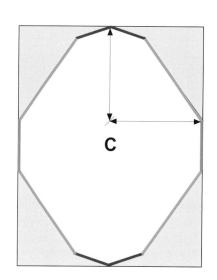

14 SIDED FRAMES

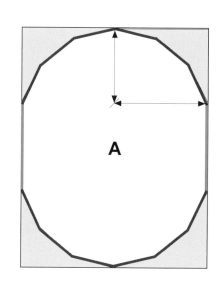

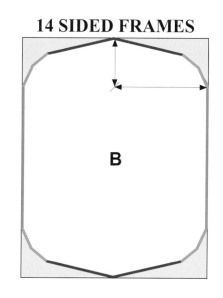

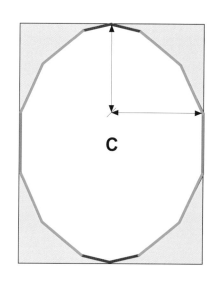

Illustration 2 to the right is also a partial (to scale) drawing of an 8" x 10" sheet, this time representing the long (10") side. It represents the top side in a landscape format (or if rotated 90°, the vertical side in a portrait format) for Illustration "B".

Using the same technique that was used in the previous Illustration, it was determined that with a 5" dimension representing one half of the sheet width, the "pointed" side lengths would be 5.78", and the dimension down the side of the sheet are 2.90".

Now that we have 2 samples to work with, we will use some basic division and multiplication techniques to determine whether the samples both give us consistent results. If they do, we can use them to develop the charts we will use in the section on 6 sided frames.

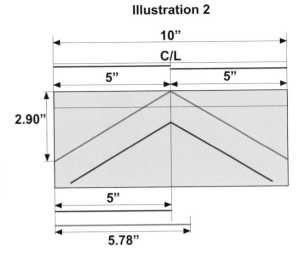

Illustration 2

CALCULATIONS FOR ILLUSTRATION 1			
Side Lgth.	Function	1/2 Width	Total
4.62	Divide by	4.00	1.16
1/2 Width	Function	Side Lgth.	Total
4.00	Divide by	4.62	0.87
Side Crop	Function	Width	Total
2.32	Divide by	8.00	0.29
Width	Function	Side Crop	Total
8.00	Divide by	2.32	3.45
Vert. Size	Function	Crop x 2	Vert. Side
10.00	Subtract	4.64	5.36

CALCULATIONS FOR ILLUSTRATION 2			
Side Lgth.	Function	1/2 Width	Total
5.78	Divide by	5.00	1.16
1/2 Width	Function	Side Lgth.	Total
5.00	Divide by	5.78	0.87
Side Crop	Function	Width	Total
2.90	Divide by	10.00	0.29
Width	Function	Side Crop	Total
10.00	Divide by	2.90	3.45
Vert. Size	Function	Crop x 2	Vert. Side
8.00	Subtract	5.80	2.20

The red outlined sections represent the length of the sides that point toward the sheet sides.
The blue outllined sections represent the length of the sides that are parallel to the frame sides.

To determine if the formulas above work, I laid out (to scale) a sheet that measures 11" x 14" in the portrait format. I then made the following calculations using the following technique(s).

I multiplied 5.5" (One half of the 11" width) by 1.16, as shown in the top formula on Illustration 1. This gave a side length (for the sides that make a point at the top and bottom of the frame) of 6.38" (approximately 6 3/8"). I created the red sides (for the points) using this dimension.

To determine the length of the vertical sides, I multiplied the width of the sheet (11") by .29. This gave me a dimension of 3.19", which is the distance down from a corner where the vertical side would start. Since we need to allow for this at both the top and bottom of the vertical side, I multiplied that dimension by 2, which gave me a result of 6.38".

I then subtracted the 6.38" from the 14" height of the sheet to get a 7.62"length for the blue vertical sides of the frame.

The Illustration to the right shows the results the calculations gave me. As a result, I know the formulas are accurate.

These same techniques will be used to help you on each (even number sided) shape in this book.

CREATIVE FRAME FORMULAS AND INFORMATION

On 6 and 8 sided shapes, creativity is fairly limited since there is only one side on the frame that connects the top and bottom of the sheet with the sides of the sheet (on each corner of the object you are framing). With the other even numbered shapes illustrated in this book, you are fairly unlimited as to how creative you can be. This is because there are a minimum of 2 sides that connect the top and bottom of the sheet with the sides of the sheet. By changing the lengths on these sides, you can dramatically make a difference in the appearance (and also the shape) of the frame.

To help you as much as possible, we will provide charts that will enable you to make frames for most popular sizes of pictures. The Charts are only applicable on frames in which you keep the lengths for the sides (that connect the top of the sheet with the sides of the sheet) the same length.

The information we provide is using dimensions on the rabbeted edge of the molding. You will need to use the **ADDED WIDTH AND LENGTH CHART** for the shape you are building to determine the outside lengths needed for the frame sides.

6 SIDED FRAMES

As I mentioned earlier, the 6 sided frame is not a very easy shape to get creative with. We are pretty much limited to the 2 formats as shown to the right. In the left Illustration, the "red sides" meet at a point at the narrow side of the sheet. In the right Illustration, the "red sides" meet at the long side of the sheet. In either case, a lot of cropping of the picture will need to be done.

The 6 sided frame is the easiest shape in this book to build, because all angle cuts for the project are done at 30°.

The Chart below will provide you with the information you need to work with the most popular standard sizes of pictures.

A

B

RABBET AREA DIMENSIONS FOR CREATIVE 6 SIDED FRAMES									
FOR ILLUSTRATION "A" TYPE LAYOUT					FOR ILLUSTRATION "B" TYPE LAYOUT				
Object Width	Object Height	Red Side Length	Side Crop Length*	Blue Side Length	Object Width	Object Height	Red Side Length	Side Crop Length*	Blue Side Length
4	5	2 5/16	2 5/16	2 11/16	4	5	2 14/16	2 14/16	1 2/16
5	7	2 14/16	2 14/16	4 2/16	5	7	4 1/16	4 1/16	15/16
6	8	3 7/16	3 8/16	4 8/16	6	8	4 10/16	4 10/16	1 6/16
8	10	4 10/16	4 10/16	5 6/16	8	10	5 12/16	5 13/16	2 3/16
8 1/2	11	4 15/16	4 15/16	6 1/16	8 1/2	11	6 6/16	6 6/16	2 2/16
10	14	5 12/16	5 13/16	8 3/16	10	14	8 1/16	8 2/16	1 14/16
11	14	6 6/16	6 6/16	7 10/16	11	14	8 1/16	8 2/16	2 14/16
12	16	6 15/16	6 15/16	9 1/16	12	16	9 4/16	9 4/16	2 12/16
16	20	9 4/16	9 4/16	10 12/16	16	20	11 9/16	11 10/16	4 6/16
18	24	10 6/16	10 7/16	13 9/16	18	24	13 14/16	13 15/16	4 1/16
20	24	11 9/16	11 10/16	12 6/16	20	24	13 14/16	13 15/16	6 1/16
24	30	13 14/16	13 15/16	16 1/16	24	30	17 5/16	17 6/16	6 10/16

* Side Crop Length is the total amount of material removed (from both sides of the sheet) that determine the "Blue Side" length.

For any other picture sizes or non-standard sizes of frames, the formulas that you would use are shown below.

DIMENSION FOR:	ILLUSTRATION "A"	ILLUSTRATION "B"
Red Side Length =	Sheet Width x .578	Sheet Height x .578
Side Crop =	Sheet Width x .580	Sheet Height x .580
Blue Side Length =	Sheet Height - Side Crop	Sheet Width - Side Crop

8 SIDED FRAMES

On an 8 sided frame, it's pretty easy to get creative without losing a lot of the picture to the "cropping knife".

The main advantage of this shape is that two sides of the frame will be parallel to the top and bottom of the object being framed, and two sides of the frame will be parallel to the other two sides of the object. There is only 1 ("red") frame side that will connect two adjacent sides of the picture.

Your options on this shape are to make the 6 "red sides" all the same length (**Illustration A**) or to make the top ("green") side longer than the "red sides" (**Illustration B**).

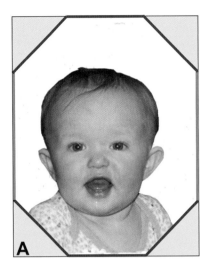

If you plan to make the 6 "red sides" the same length, the Chart below will provide you with the information you need to work with the most popular standard sizes of pictures.

Object Width	Object Height	Red Side Length	Side Crop Length*	Blue Side Length	Object Width	Object Height	Red Side Length	Side Crop Length*	Blue Side Length
4	5	1 10/16	2 6/16	2 10/16	11	14	4 9/16	6 7/16	7 9/16
5	7	2 1/16	2 15/16	4 1/16	12	16	4 15/16	7 1/16	8 15/16
6	8	2 8/16	3 8/16	4 8/16	16	20	6 10/16	9 6/16	10 10/16
8	10	3 5/16	4 11/16	5 5/16	18	24	7 7/16	10 9/16	13 7/16
8 1/2	11	3 8/16	5	6	20	24	8 4/16	11 12/16	12 4/16
10	14	4 2/16	5 14/16	8 2/16	24	30	9 15/16	14 1/16	15 15/16

RABBET AREA DIMENSIONS FOR CREATIVE 8 SIDED FRAMES

* <u>Side Crop Length</u> is the total amount of material removed (from both sides of the sheet) that determine the "Blue Side Length".

If you plan to build a frame for an object size not shown above, and want to keep the "red sides" equal lengths, you should refer to the Chart below. You would multiply the Object Width by .413 to determine the "red side" length. <u>NOTE</u>: This formula does not allow for changes in dimensions in Length. You would need to adjust the "blue side" lengths as needed to build a creative frame.

8 SIDED FRAME FORMULAS		
WIDTH	**HEIGHT**	**SIDE LENGTH**
Width = Side Length x 2.42	Height = Side Length x 2.42	Side Length = Width x .413
Width = Height x 1.00	Height = Width x 1.00	Side Length = Height x .413

If you want to build a creative 8 sided frame and use 3 different lengths for the sides, as shown above in **Illustration B** the Chart below should prove helpful.

CREATIVE 8 SIDED FRAME FORMULAS			
RED SIDE LENGTH	**GREEN SIDE LENGTH**	**BLUE SIDE LENGTH**	**SIDE CROP**
(Width-Green Side) x .705 or (Height-Blue Side) x .705	Width - Side Crop	Height - Side Crop	Width - Green. Side or Height - Blue Side

One very important thing to remember is that on an 8 sided frame, the angle change between adjoining sides is 45°. This means the change in dimension on the top and sides of the frame will be equal. To determine the lengths at the rabbeted edge on the 4 diagonal corners, you would multiply the "Side Crop" dimension by .705 to determine the lengths at the rabbeted edge of the molding on these sides of the frame. I would recommend that you read the "**EXAMPLE OF GETTING CREATIVE (WITH AN 8 SIDED FRAME)** article to help you understand these principles.

EXAMPLE OF GETTING CREATIVE (WITH AN 8 SIDED FRAME)

To help you understand the principles of working with creative frames, we'll "walk through" a fairly simple project. Hopefully, the information you will be given will allow you to see how easy (what appear to complicated) projects can be.

For our example, let's say I want to make a frame for the picture of our twin Granddaughters (Katherine on the left and Victoria on the right) when they were about 5 months old. *(It's hard to believe they're twins, huh!)* We'll say the picture (which is drawn to scale) is an 11" x 14" in the landscape format, as shown in the top- right Illustration.

The frame we will build for the picture will be 8 sided (an Octagon) but to make it unique, let's say that we'll use 3 different lengths for the sides, somewhat like Illustration "**B**" of the "**8 SIDED FRAMES**".

In the center-right Illustration, I've made a layout of what I want the picture to look like. I plan on cropping 2 inches on both ends of the top, bottom, and vertical sides of the picture. On an Octagon, the angle change from one side to the next is 45

You can see that when we subtract 4" (2" on each corner) from the width of the picture, the top and bottom sides need to be 10" lengths along the rabbeted edge of the molding. You can also see that when we subtract 4" from the height of the picture, the sides need to be 7" lengths along the rabbeted edge of the molding.

What we need to determine at this point is what the length along the rabbeted edge of the molding would be on the 4 short sides that join with the top, bottom, and vertical sides of the frame. For this, we need to use the information provided for the diagonal sides in the **8 Sided Frame Information** in the section on 8 Sided Frames.

As seen in the information mentioned above, the diagonal length will be the result of multiplying .705 by the desired change (in this case 4") from what would be the outside corners of the rectangular picture. This gives us a length of 2.82" (approximately 2 27/32") along the rabbeted edge of the molding on the 4 short diagonal frame sides.

Now that we know the rabbet lengths, we need to pick a width for the molding. For the Illustration, I chose 1 1/4" wide material. With a 1/4" rabbet, this gives us 1" outside the rabbeted area on the molding.

In the "**8 Sided Frame Added Width & Length Chart**", we find that we need to add .828" (27/32") at 1" added width to the rabbet length to determine the outside lengths we need for the frame sides.

By adding 27/32" to the rabbet lengths, we get the following results:

The outside length for top and bottom sides should be 10 27/32".
The outside length for the vertical sides should be 7 27/32".
The outside length for the 4 short diagonal sides should be 3 11/16".

Using this information, we know that the finished frame should look like the frame in the Illustration to the right.

Though this may seem complicated, I think that once you try this technique a couple of times you will find it to be a very fun and accurate way to work. In this book we have provided the information, charts, and formulas you need to build most shapes you'll ever want to do. The data in each section is simple, and is there to help you learn.

I honestly feel that almost anyone who has he desire to learn and is willing to spend some "training time" in the shop will be amazed how simple these techniques are to use.

10 SIDED FRAMES

Creative 10 sided frames can be relatively easy, if you build them like the frame shown in **Illustration A** (shown to the right), with the 8 "red sides" being of equal length.

Where things get pretty complicated is when we try to build a frame like **Illustration B** on which we try to use 2 different lengths for the sides that connect the top of the frame to the vertical sides of the frame. The reason this type of frame is so difficult is that these sides (red and green) will have a different formula. Therefore, we must calculate them in such a way that the totals for the formulas add up to the exact size for the object width that we will build the frame for.

If you plan to make the 8 "red sides" the same length, the Chart below will provide you with the information you need to work with the most popular standard sizes of pictures.

RABBET AREA DIMENSIONS FOR CREATIVE 10 SIDED FRAMES								
Object Width	Object Height	Red Side Length	Side Crop Length*	Blue Side Length	Object Width	Object Height	Red Side Length	Side Crop Length*	Blue Side Length
4	5	1 5/16	2 15/16	2 1/16	11	14	3 9/16	8	6
5	7	1 10/16	3 10/16	3 6/16	12	16	3 15/16	8 12/16	7 4/16
6	8	1 15/16	4 6/16	3 10/16	16	20	5 3/16	11 10/16	8 6/16
8	10	2 10/16	5 13/16	4 3/16	18	24	5 14/16	13 2/16	10 14/16
8 1/2	11	2 12/16	6 3/16	4 13/16	20	24	6 8/16	14 9/16	9 7/16
10	14	3 4/16	7 4/16	6 12/16	24	30	7 13/16	17 8/16	12 8/16

* Side Crop Length is the total amount of material removed (from both sides of the sheet) that determine the "Blue Side Length".

If you plan to build a frame for an object size not shown above, and want to keep the "red sides" equal lengths, you should refer to the Chart below. You would multiply the Object Width by .310 to determine the "red side" length. NOTE: This formula does not allow for changes in dimensions in Length. You would need to adjust the "blue side" lengths as needed to build a creative frame.

10 SIDED FRAME FORMULAS		
WIDTH	**HEIGHT**	**SIDE LENGTH**
Width = Side Length x 3.23	Height = Side Length x 3.075	Side Length = Width x .310
Width = Height x 1.05	Height = Width x .952	Side Length = Height x .325

The Illustration to the right shows the top of a creative 10 sided frame on an 8" wide sheet. As you can see, the 2 "red sides" come out 3" to each side of the center line of the sheet, and the 2 "green sides" extend 1" to meet with the sheet sides. You should also notice that the end of the "red side" is .996" from the top of the sheet, and the " green side" meets the side of the sheet 1.31" from where it meets with the "red side". If this sounds a little confusing...it is! Hopefully, I can make it a little simpler by showing you how to approach a frame like this. Remember that in this explanation we are talking about the rabbet lengths. You still need to use the **10 Sided Frame Added Width and Length Chart** to get outside lengths.

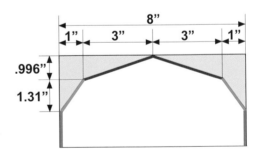

The first step in planning this frame would be to decide how far from the center line of the frame you want each of the "red sides" to extend to meet with a "green side". (In the Illustration above, 3" was used for this dimension). I will call this measurement the "Horizontal Length from Center". You would refer to the **CREATIVE 10 SIDED FRAME FORMULAS** Chart on the next page, and multiply this dimension by 1.049 to determine the length for each of the "red sides". For the Illustration above, this would make the "red side" length 3.147". You should then multiply this length by .3165 to determine the Vertical Crop Dimension (Distance down from the top of the sheet) for the "red side" end. For the Illustration, this measurement is .996", which confirms our Formula.

The next step would be to determine the "green side" length. For the Illustration on the previous page, you would multiply the Horizontal Distance from Edge (in this case 1") by 1.684 to determine the "green side" length. For the Illustration, this would make the "green side" length 1.684". You should then multiply this measurement by .778 to determine the Vertical Crop for the "green side". For the Illustration, this measurement is 1.31" which again confirms our Formula.

CREATIVE 10 SIDED FRAME FORMULAS	
RED SIDE	**GREEN SIDE LENGTH**
Length = Horizontal Length from Center x 1.049	Length = Horizontal Distance from Edge x 1.684
Vertical Crop = Red Side Length x .3165	Vertical Crop = Green Side Length x .778

Now that we have the formulas developed for this shape, let's apply what we have to finish the dimensions for our frame. Since we used an 8" width for our Illustration, let's say that the sheet size is an 8" x 10".

We know that (for our Illustration) the Vertical Crop of the "red side" is .996" and the Vertical Crop of the "green side" is 1.31". If we add these dimensions together, this tells us that the ends of the "green sides" will meet with the ends of the "blue sides" 2.306" from the top and bottom of the sheet. Since this happens on both ends, we would multiply this dimension by 2. The total (4.612") is then subtracted from the sheet height (10") to give us a "blue side" length of 5.388". <u>Remember that these dimensions are at the rabbeted edge of the molding.</u> You would then refer to the **10 Sided Frame Added Width and Length Chart** to determine the outside lengths for the frame sides.

12 SIDED FRAMES

Another example of a shape that can be a very pretty frame is 12 sided. Whether you keep it simple and make all of the "red sides" the same lengths, as shown in **Illustration A**, or make the "red sides" shorter to save the picture from the "cropping knife" as shown in **Illustration B**, the result is an attractive frame.

Like the Octagon, the Dodecagon (12 sided) frame will have 4 sides that are parallel to the 4 sides of the object being framed.

As a result, the 12 sided frame is a simple to build project that is (almost) guaranteed to give you a frame you'll be proud to display.

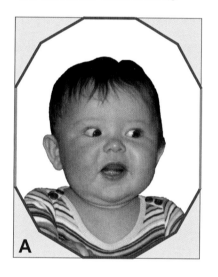

If you plan to make the 10 "red sides" the same length, the Chart below will provide you with the information you need to work with the most popular standard sizes of pictures.

RABBET AREA DIMENSIONS FOR CREATIVE 12 SIDED FRAMES									
Object Width	Object Height	Red Side Length	Side Crop Length*	Blue Side Length	Object Width	Object Height	Red Side Length	Side Crop Length*	Blue Side Length
4	5	1 1/16	2 15/16	2 1/16	11	14	3	8 2/16	5 14/16
5	7	1 6/16	3 11/16	3 5/16	12	16	3 4/16	8 13/16	7 3/16
6	8	1 10/16	4 7/16	3 9/16	16	20	4 5/16	11 12/16	8 4/16
8	10	2 3/16	5 14/16	4 2/16	18	24	4 14/16	13 4/16	10 12/16
8 1/2	11	2 5/16	6 4/16	4 12/16	20	24	5 6/16	14 12/16	9 4/16
10	14	2 11/16	7 6/16	6 10/16	24	30	6 8/16	17 11/16	12 5/16

* <u>Side Crop Length</u> is the total amount of material removed (from both sides of the sheet) that determine the "Blue Side Length".

If you plan to build a frame for an object size not shown above, and want to keep the "red sides" equal lengths, you should refer to the Chart on the next page. You would multiply the Object Width by .270 to determine the "red side" length. <u>NOTE</u>: This formula does not allow for changes in dimensions in length. You would need to adjust the "blue side" lengths as needed to build a creative frame.

12 SIDED FRAME FORMULAS		
WIDTH	**HEIGHT**	**SIDE LENGTH**
Width = Side Length x 3.75	Height = Side Length x 3.75	Side Length = Width x .267
Width = Height x 1.00	Height = Width x 1.00	Side Length = Height x .267

If you want to build a creative 12 sided frame and use 3 different lengths for the sides, as shown above in **Illustration B** shown on the previous page, the Chart below should prove helpful.

CREATIVE 12 SIDED FRAME FORMULAS			
RED SIDE LENGTH	**GREEN SIDE LENGTH**	**BLUE SIDE LENGTH**	**SIDE CROP**
(Width-Green Side) x .366 or (Height-Blue Side) x .366	Width - Side Crop	Height - Side Crop	Width - Green Side or Height - Blue Side

14 SIDED FRAMES

Of the even numbered frames illustrated in this book, without a doubt the 14 sided frame is the most difficult to work with, especially if you are trying to make a creative frame.

Not only are we dealing with a frame that has points toward two sides of the sheet, we also have the most difficult miter angles (12.857°) to work with of all of the shapes we have discussed. There are also some very difficult angles (25.714° and 38.571°) when cutting the panel that would become the back panel for the frame.

With that said, the 14 sided frame can be done, (with the right tools and the knowledge of how to do it) so we will explain how to make a creative frame with this unique shape. The only way that makes sense to build it (because of the complex mathematics) is to use 1 length for all 12 of the "red sides" and another length for the 2 "blue sides".

If you plan to make the 12 "red sides" the same length, the Chart below will provide you with the information you need to work with the most popular standard sizes of pictures.

A

RABBET AREA DIMENSIONS FOR CREATIVE 14 SIDED FRAMES									
Object Width	Object Height	Red Side Length	Side Crop Length*	Blue Side Length	Object Width	Object Height	Red Side Length	Side Crop Length*	Blue Side Length
4	5	15/16	3 3/16	1 13/16	11	14	2 8/16	8 12/16	5 4/16
5	7	1 2/16	4	3	12	16	2 12/16	9 9/16	6 7/16
6	8	1 6/16	4 12/16	3 4/16	16	20	3 11/16	12 12/16	7 4/16
8	10	1 13/16	6 6/16	3 10/16	18	24	4 2/16	14 5/16	9 11/16
8 1/2	11	1 15/16	6 12/16	4 4/16	20	24	4 9/16	15 14/16	8 2/16
10	14	2 5/16	7 15/16	6 1/16	24	30	5 8/16	19 1/16	10 15/16

* Side Crop Length is the total amount of material removed (from both sides of the sheet) that determine the "Blue Side Length".

If you plan to build a frame for an object size not shown above, and want to keep the "red sides" equal lengths, you should refer to the Chart below. You would multiply the Object Width by .270 to determine the "red side" length. NOTE: This formula does not allow for changes in dimensions in Length. You would need to adjust the "blue side" lengths as needed to build a creative frame.

Though rather complicated to build, this shape does make a very attractive frame that you will be extremely proud to display.

14 SIDED FRAME FORMULAS		
WIDTH	**HEIGHT**	**SIDE LENGTH**
Width = Side Length x 4.37	Height = Side Length x 4.49	Side Length = Width x .229
Width = Height x .973	Height = Width x 1.027	Side Length = Height x .223

16 SIDED FRAMES

One of my favorite frames to build is 16 sided. Whether you keep it fairly simple and make all of the "red sides" the same lengths, as shown in **Illustration A**, or make the "red sides" shorter, as shown in **Illustration B**, the result is an attractive frame.

Like both the Octagon and Dodecagon, the Hexadecagon (16 sided) frame will have 4 sides that are parallel to the 4 sides of the object being framed.

As a result, the Hexadecagon frame is fairly simple, and is a project that is guaranteed to give you a frame you'll be proud to display. (As long as the sides fit together properly).

If you plan to make the 14 "red sides" the same length, the Chart below will provide you with the information you need to work with the most popular standard sizes of pictures.

RABBET AREA DIMENSIONS FOR CREATIVE 16 SIDED FRAMES									
Object Width	Object Height	Red Side Length	Side Crop Length*	Blue Side Length	Object Width	Object Height	Red Side Length	Side Crop Length*	Blue Side Length
4	5	13/16	3 3/16	1 13/16	11	14	2 3/16	8 12/16	5 4/16
5	7	1	4	3	12	16	2 6/16	9 8/16	6 8/16
6	8	1 3/16	4 12/16	3 4/16	16	20	3 3/16	12 11/16	7 5/16
8	10	1 10/16	6 6/16	3 10/16	18	24	3 10/16	14 5/16	9 11/16
8 1/2	11	1 11/16	6 12/16	4 4/16	20	24	4	15 14/16	8 2/16
10	14	2	7 15/16	6 1/16	24	30	4 13/16	19 1/16	10 15/16

* Side Crop Length is the total amount of material removed (from both sides of the sheet) that determine the "Blue Side Length".

If you plan to build a frame for an object size not shown above, and want to keep the "red sides" equal lengths, you should refer to the Chart below. You would multiply the Object Width by .199 to determine the "red side" length. NOTE: This formula does not allow for changes in dimensions in Length. You would need to adjust the "blue side" lengths as needed to build a creative frame.

16 SIDED FRAME FORMULAS		
WIDTH	HEIGHT	SIDE LENGTH
Width = Side Length x 5.02	Height = Side Length x 5.02	Side Length = Width x .199
Width = Height x 1.00	Height = Width x 1.00	Side Length = Height x .199

If you want to build a creative 16 sided frame and use 3 different lengths for the sides, as shown above in **Illustration B** shown on the previous page, the Chart below should prove helpful.

CREATIVE 16 SIDED FRAME FORMULAS			
RED SIDE LENGTH	GREEN SIDE LENGTH	BLUE SIDE LENGTH	SIDE CROP
(Width-Green Side) x .250 or (Height-Blue Side) x .250	Width - Side Crop	Height - Side Crop	Width - Green Side or Height - Blue Side

In the Chart above, the most important information is in the **RED SIDE LENGTH** block. Since we should always calculate for the shortest sides of the object being framed as a first step, subtracting the "green side" length from the picture width will automatically determine the "side crop" measurement. NOTE: The information above pertains to the pictures in a "portrait" format. If you want to do the frame in a "landscape" format, the height would become the shortest dimension on the picture. In this case, you would use the formula for **RED SIDE LENGTH: (Height-Green Side) x .250** as the "green side" would be on the short side of the picture.

"CATHEDRAL STYLE" FRAMES

Special mementos can mean a lot to many of us, and the Illustration of Christ below is a good example. I took a photo of a gift that was given to my wife Betty by her mother about 40 years ago. Though the original was a rectangular picture, I think the image inside a Hexadecagon (the top of the frame is based on 16 sides) Cathedral Frame would be perfect to display. If the frame was designed as we describe later in this article, you could have images back-to-back, and it could be viewed from both sides.

BUILDING "CATHEDRAL STYLE" FRAMES

One of the demonstrations that attendees at the Woodworking Shows are most fascinated by is when I change angles in the middle of a project, and build what I call a "Cathedral Style" frame. I call them this because I really couldn't think of any other appropriate name, and (depending on how many sides you use) they look close to the shape of the stained glass windows found in churches. Regardless of their "proper" name, if you try one of these frames, you will call it really fun to build, and will find they are no harder than making any other of the other creative frames.

To help you understand the technique of building this style of frame, I have made an Illustration (to the right) of an 8" x10" sheet (in portrait format) that overlays a regular 12 sided frame. We will say that the frame is face down, and the dark brown area around the inside of the frame represents the rabbet.

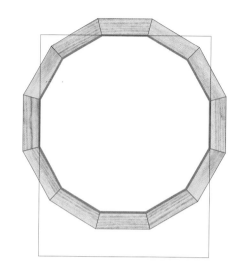

It's obvious that we would end up cropping a large part of the picture away if we used this shape.

Our first option would be to increase the lengths of the two vertical sides, and create an oval shaped frame to keep from losing so much of the picture

A second option would be to take part of the first option, (increase the lengths of the two vertical sides) but extend their length so the rabbet on these sides ends at the bottom of the picture. We could then miter the bottom ends of these sides at 45° and make squared corners on the bottom of the frame. What this would give us a frame that is rounded on the top, and square on the bottom. This may seen very complicated, but it is not as difficult as it may sound.

The first step (after you make your molding) would be to refer to the **RABBET AREA DIMENSION CHART** for 12 Sided Frames. You will find that for the top 5 sides of the frame, the rabbet length would be 2 3/16" for an 8" wide picture. You would then go to the **ADDED WIDTH AND LENGTH CHART** to find the length needed for the molding you made. You should then cut the top 5 sides to length.

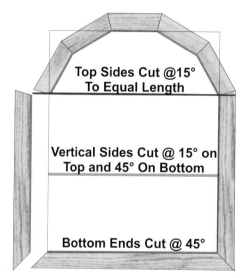

Top Sides Cut @15°
To Equal Length

Vertical Sides Cut @ 15° on
Top and 45° On Bottom

Bottom Ends Cut @ 45°

The next step would be to make the 2 vertical sides. You can see on the side (to the left) of the Illustration that the top is cut at the same angle as the top pieces (15°) and the bottom is cut at 45°. To determine the length along the rabbet for these, we need to take a few different steps:

Step 1: In the **RABBET AREA DIMENSION CHART FOR CREATIVE 12 SIDED FRAMES**, we see the **Side Crop Length** for an 8" x 10" is 5 14/16". In these Charts, the Side Crop is calculated for both ends of the frame. We divide this by 2 since we are only "rounding" 1 end of the frame. This gives us a Side Crop of 2 15/16" on one end of the frame.

Step 2: Subtract the Side Crop from the picture height. **(10" - 2 15/16" = 7 1/16")**

Step 3: To be able to work with an outside length, we must add the lengths of the molding outside the rabbets on both ends of the vertical sides. For this Illustration, we'll say the width outside the rabbet on the molding is 1". In the "Simplifying" article, you see an Illustration for a side of a 12 Sided Shape. Note that on one end of the side, we have a .54" change in length over a 2" change in width. Since on our project we have 1" outside the rabbet, we would divide the length change by half, which would give us an added length of .27" (a little over 1/4") on the top cut.

For the bottom cut on the side, since it is at 45°, we would add 1". (On a 45° cut, the change in length is always the same as the change in width). This means we would add 1 1/4" (the length change for both ends of the sides) to the 7 1/16" rabbet length for an outside length of 8 5/16". (I'd make these a little long the first time you do this). *When you cut these sides*, remember to cut one of the sides "face up" and the other side "face down" so you don't end up with a pair of the same frame side.

The Bottom side of the frame should be cut to exactly the same outside dimension as you have where the "rounded" part of the frame meets with the vertical sides.

I know this may seem a little confusing, but it really isn't as complicated as it may seem. The main thing you need to pay attention to when you make the cuts on the 2 long vertical sides is that you "reverse the procedure" as you cut them. I would recommend that you place these pieces with the inside faces together, and mark the ends that need to be cut at 45°. Then you will see that when you cut these sides, one will be cut with the front face up and the other with the front face down as you cut these pieces.

One of the things I like about "Cathedral" frames is that they can give us a lot of options of how to display them. Let's say you have a special picture that you would like to display, and just don't have the wall space. By making the molding more of a "shadow box" style (where the frame is "deep") it is very easy to make the frame in such a way that it is free standing. This means we can place it almost anywhere where we have a flat surface for it to stand on. This style of frame does have some issues, however, depending on how you design your moldings.

When I first started building "Cathedral" frames, I normally made my molding similar to the molding shown in the Illustration to the right. Approaching it like a conventional frame, I put the rabbet for the frame on the back side of the molding. On these frames, I normally put the routed profile on the inside of the frame. This is just my personal preference, you should design the molding the way you like it.

Normally I would cut the frame and glue it together, then I would install the back. One of the things I didn't like was on these frames is the back of the frame is visible, (since the frame doesn't have a wall behind it) and most often the back of a frame is pretty unattractive. After a little thought, I came up with a better solution.

On these frames, if you display them on a shelf or table, the only side that can't be seen is the bottom. If the vertical sides are parallel to each other, we can glue the top joints of the frame together, but leave the bottom loose. This would allow us to install the picture by sliding it into a dado groove from the bottom, and then attach the bottom side of the frame with screws, as shown in the Illustration to the right.

This design makes these frames a lot neater in appearance, as no one will see the screws that hold the frame together, and there are no unsightly screws holding in the back of the frame.

The molding will need to be designed differently for the "bottom install" frames, but is no harder than making a conventional type of molding.

By eliminating the rabbet toward the back edge of the molding, and installing a dado groove for the objects (back, picture, mat, glass, etc.) being placed in the frame, we no longer need to have screws showing on the back of the frame.

A second advantage to this method is that if the back panel is not cut perfectly, it would not be noticeable, because the edges of the back panel are all hidden in the dado groove in the molding.

I think the most unique "Cathedral" frame style I've done takes very little extra effort, and is really an eye catching project. You should first center the dado groove on the inside of the molding. Instead of routing just one edge on your molding, do both edges. Now we can build a frame that has no unsightly back, as we can display pictures on both sides of the frame. This is really a project you'll be proud to display...try it!

Another thing you may want to try is to make a base to mount under the bottom frame side. Rout all the way around the base, and glue (or screw) the bottom frame side to the base. Then screw through the base into the vertical frame sides to assemble the frame. I think you will be extremely happy with the results.

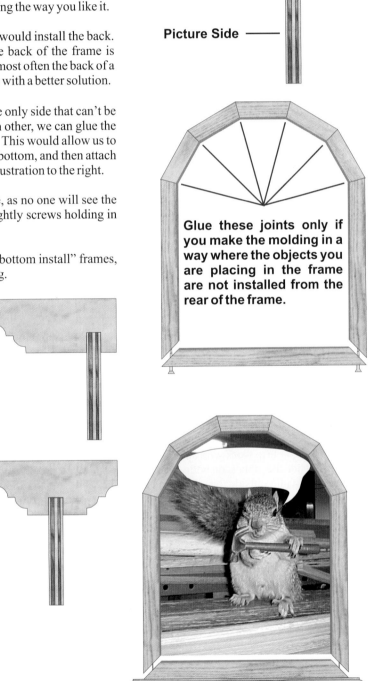

Picture Side ——

Glue these joints only if you make the molding in a way where the objects you are placing in the frame are not installed from the rear of the frame.

To help you decide which "Cathedral Style" frame you would like to build, an Illustration is shown below for all "even number sided" frames Illustrated in this book. All Illustrations are drawn to size for an 8" x 10" object. The "**Sides**" designation in the frames indicates how many sides the frame would have had if we had not squared the bottom corners.

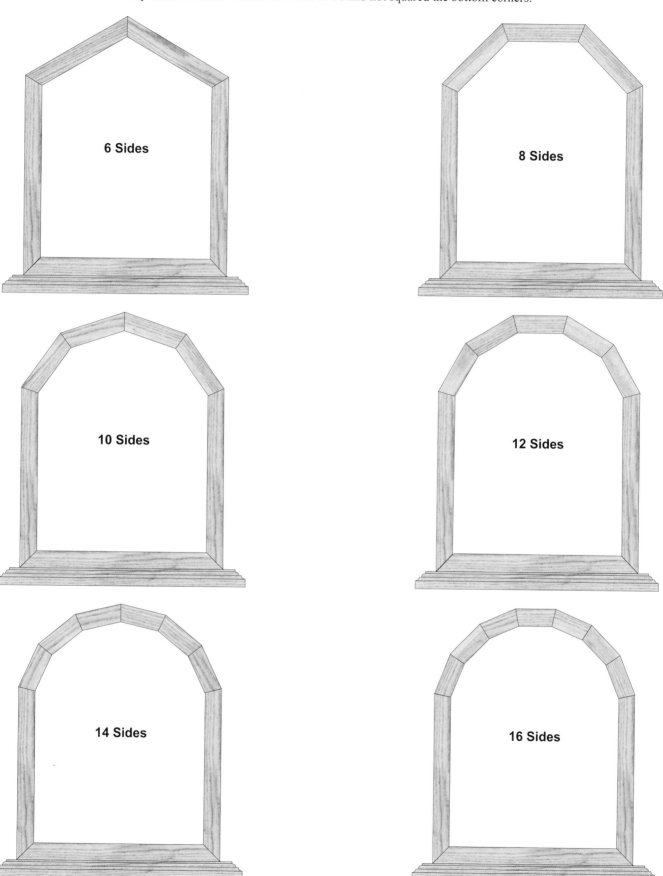

6 Sides

8 Sides

10 Sides

12 Sides

14 Sides

16 Sides

USING THE INFORMATION IN THE CHARTS AND ILLUSTRATIONS

For the first few years in the hobby, it seemed like I ended up with as much "creative kindling" as I had in the material in my projects. A lot of the wasted material was caused by the fact that I didn't cut the pieces for my projects right, and out of frustration I just threw the entire project out. Most of the remaining waste was created because I hadn't planned the project properly, and made a lot more material than I really needed for the project. (My first invention was a game that I called *"I'll just make em' long to start with"*).

You will notice that in each section of shapes in this book, there are 2 pages that start the section that have the information you need to plan building that particular shape. The majority of the text from one section to another is almost identical. This was done intentionally, since the same principles apply to building our projects. Only the mathematics change in our planning process for the different shapes. I'm a firm believer in *"the more you do it, the better you get"* concept, and I really want this book to make your Woodworking faster, easier, and more fun.

In the previous articles, we covered "Creative" frames. In the different sections that follow, we cover "Regular" Polygons, where all of the sides on the projects are equal lengths. To give you an idea of how we would use the information in each of the sections, we will say that we have a photo that is 8" x 10" in size. We don't mind cropping part of the photo, and would like to put it into an 8 sided frame, where all sides are equal length. We'll say for planning purposes that we would like the rabbeted opening on the frame to be 1/8" oversize to make sure that if the glass that's cut for the frame isn't perfect, we will still be able to fit it into the opening. We will make the rabbet width on the molding 1/4" wide, because we don't want to hide a lot of the photo in the rabbet. We will say that we like the look of Illustration "**H**" below (shown on page 44) with the photo of "Friday". (*Yes, he really is holding that sign*)! I changed the woodgrain pattern on this Illustration to better show the red lines which represent the rabbeted area on the frame.

We will first show you the planning procedure, and then show you how you would apply these steps to build your project.

8 1/8"

H

PROJECT PLANNING PROCEDURE

Step 1. Select the Project you want to build.

Step 2. Use the "FRAME FORMULAS" Chart to determine the required rabbet length for the project.

Step 3. Use the "ADDED WIDTH AND LENGTH Chart to determine the inside length of the project sides.

Step 4. Use the Dimension Chart to determine the outside length of the "Reference Frame".

Step 5. Determine the "Constant" needed to build the project.

Step 6. Multiply the Constant x the Reference Frame side length to determine outside length for project.

Step 7. Multiply the Constant x the Reference Frame side width to determine material width for project.

Step 8. Determine how much material is needed for the project.

We know that we want the rabbeted opening (which is shown in the Illustration in red) to be 8 1/8", but to simplify building the project, we would want to be able to work using outside dimensions. To make this simple for you, we have included formulas and charts for your reference within each section that apply to that particular shape.

To determine what the rabbet length needs to be for your frame, you would refer to the **8 SIDED FRAME FORMULAS**, which are shown on the next page. In the **SIDE LENGTH** formula, we see that we would multiply **Width x .413** to determine the **Side Length**. Since the width of the rabbeted opening is 8 1/8", we would multiply it (8.125") by .413 to determine the rabbet length needed on the sides. You would use a calculator and enter: **8.125 x .413 = 3.3556**

You would then refer to the **DECIMAL TO FRACTION CONVERSION CHART** on page 6. You will find that .3556 is slightly less than 23/64" (1/64" of an inch less than 3/8"). As we are only .019" (about 1/50th of an inch) shorter than 3/8", I would "round this up" and use 3 3/8" as the rabbet dimension. It is better to make your projects a little bit on the "strong" side and re-trim the lengths rather than make them small and need to re-cut the rabbets or cut the picture down.

8 SIDED FRAME FORMULAS		
WIDTH	**HEIGHT**	**SIDE LENGTH**
Width = Side Length x 2.42	Height = Side Length x 2.42	Side Length = Width x .413
Width = Height x 1.00	Height = Width x 1.00	Side Length = Height x .413

Now that we know the rabbet length, we need to calculate what the dimensions (width and length) each of the sides need to be. The first thing I would recommend is determine the <u>inside length</u> on each side.

If you refer to the **8 SIDED FRAME ADDED WIDTH AND LENGTH CHART** on page 555, you will notice that if we add the 1/4" (4/16") rabbet width, we would add 3/16" in length. <u>Since we are determining the inside length of the side pieces, we would subtract the same measurement</u> (3/16") from the rabbet length to determine the inside length on the side pieces. When we subtract 3/16" from the 3 3/8" rabbet length, this would give us an inside measurement of 3 3/16".

At this point, you should refer to the Dimension Chart that covers Illustration "**H**" on page 66. For this reference, I will refer to the 5" Side Length in the left column of the Chart. If you follow the row over to the "**H Side Width**" Column, you will note that the width of the side is 1 12/16" (1 3/4) at a 5" length.

If we refer back to the **8 SIDED FRAME ADDED WIDTH AND LENGTH CHART** on page 555, we find that at 1 12/16" (1 3/4") change in width, the change in length would be 1 7/16". <u>Since we are determining the inside length of the side pieces, we would subtract the same measurement (1 7/16")</u> from the outside length to determine the inside length on the side pieces. When we subtract When we subtract 1 7/16" from the 5" side length, this would give us an inside measurement of 3 9/16".

Since the inside length of our project pieces is not the same as the reference we used from the Chart, we need to determine a Formula that would allow our project (even though it a different size than our reference) to look exactly like the frame "**H**".

If we divide the 3 3/16" (3.1875") inside length of our proposed project by the 3 9/16" (3.5625") inside length of our reference, the result is .8947, which I would "round up to .895. This is the "Constant" that we will use for our calculations.

If we then multiply the outside length of our reference from the Chart (5") by .895, the outside length of our project sides is 4.475" (4 15/32"+).

If we multiply the side width of our reference from the Chart (1 3/4") by .895, the width of our project sides is 1.5662 (1 9/16"+).

If we allow about 1/4" to each side length for "cutting waste", we would need about 4 3/4" for each side. If we multiply this by 8, our result would be 38", which would be the <u>minimum</u> amount of material needed to complete the project.

To confirm my formulas, I first drew a rectangle using the dimensions above for the outside length and width. This was drawn "full scale" in my computer, and then "shrunk down" to fit in the area available on this page. I then used these same dimensions and drew the red lines which represent the inside and outside lengths (full scale). They were positioned over the rectangular box. I then drew the 2 lines that connect the inside and outside, and rotated them 22.5 degrees (positive and negative) to connect the inside and outside edges of the frame side..

The small woodgrain frame side (top-right) was copied from Illustration "**H**". In the large woodgrain frame side, the small side was magnified over the rectangle, proving that our frame formulas are correct, and that the proposed frame would look exactly like Illustration "**H**".

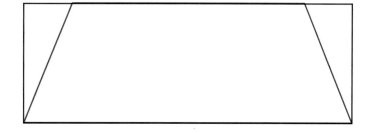

I will admit that these may mot be the most attractive Illustrations, but they are the best way I found to show you how we can use a few simple formulas to greatly simplify building our projects.

In the Illustrations in each Section, we show all of the shapes as regular Frames, round Frames (or rings if you are into segmented Woodturning), and also as Panels.

5 SIDED PROJECT INFORMATION

Geometric Name: Pentagon
Definition: A Polygon having 5 sides
Miter Angle: 36°
Angle Change / Adjoining Sides: 72°

As one of the "odd numbered" shapes Illustrated in this book, the 5 sided shape (Pentagon) is one of the shapes that is pretty difficult to get creative with. With that said, it's still a fun project to build, and in some cases can be the perfect shape for the item you may wish to frame. The one thing that should be considered when using this shape is that for most standard sizes of pictures, a lot of cropping of the picture will be required.

The Illustrations to the right should give you an idea of the amount of cropping that may be required by using a Pentagon as your choice of shape for a frame.

In the left Illustration, you see a scale (shown in red) 8" x 10" sheet in portrait format. The sheet border is slightly outside the rabbeted area (shown in yellow) of the frame. Note the amount of material that would need to be cropped off of the sheet top and/or bottom.

In the right Illustration, you see the same size sheet, but rotated 90° into a landscape format. Note the amount of material that would need to be cropped off of the sheet sides.

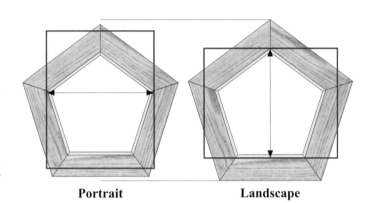

Portrait   **Landscape**

You should note that the frame for the sheet shown in portrait format is also smaller than the frame for the sheet shown in landscape format. This is due to the fact that on a Pentagon, the dimension "point-to-point" is slightly larger than the dimension "point-to-flat. In our **5 SIDED FRAME FORMULAS** below, you will be able to see exactly what the changes between these dimensions will be.

If the project you are building is a frame for a specific size object, you should refer to the **5 SIDED FRAME FORMULAS** Chart below as a first step. On a Pentagon, the height is shorter than the width, and is the controlling dimension for the frame for a picture in landscape format. In landscape format, the picture height would be multiplied by .650 to determine the length of the sides at the rabbeted edge. (See the bottom formula under **SIDE LENGTH** in the Chart below). In a portrait format, the width is the controlling dimension. In portrait format, the width should be multiplied by .618 to determine the lengths of the sides of the rabbeted edge. (See the top formula under **SIDE LENGTH** in the Chart below).

5 SIDED FRAME FORMULAS		
WIDTH	**HEIGHT**	**SIDE LENGTH**
Width = Side Length x 1.620	Height = Side Length x 1.539	Side Length = Width x .618
Width = Height x 1.053	Height = Width x .950	Side Length = Height x .650

Though the information above is very helpful, one of the most time consuming (and frustrating) things about building frames is to try to cut to a dimension that is not measured on either the inside or outside edge of the molding. I like to cut miters from the inside to the outside edges of the molding. This not only allows me to eliminate tear out on the inside corners of the frame since I am cutting into the inside edge, I am also cutting with the grain of the molding. It also allows me to see the outside edge of the material as I cut it. To help you understand how easy it is to convert a dimension along the rabbeted edge into an outside measurement, I will explain how we can use some basic math to help us determine the outside length of our frame sides. The Illustration below should be helpful in showing you how we designed our **5 SIDED FRAME ADDED WIDTH AND LENGTH CHART** on the next page.

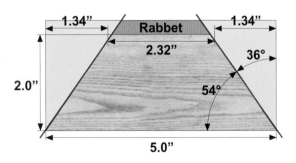

The Illustration to the left represents a piece of wood that is 5" long and 2" wide (to the edge of the rabbet). Note that on the right side that the end of the piece shows the miter angle for a Pentagon (36°) and the resulting angle of the cut (54°).

You should also note that at the rabbet, the 36° cuts shorten each end of the piece by 1.34". Since both ends of the piece are cut, this means that the length at the rabbet is 2.32", which is 2.68" shorter than the outside edge of the molding. What this Illustration tells us is that at a 36° cut, we will add 2.68" to the length at a 2" width. This is the basis of our formula.

If we divide the **Added Length** (2.68") by the **Added Width** (2.0") we end up with 1.34 as our multiplier. In the event that you want to make a frame and need to work in fractions smaller than 1/16 increments, you would multiply the width of the molding outside the rabbet by 1.34. To determine the decimal equivalent of the fractions you need to use, refer to the **FRACTION TO DECIMAL CONVERSION CHART** provided.

If you are able to use 1/16" increments for the mathematics of your frames, you should use the **5 SIDED FRAME ADDED WIDTH & LENGTH CHART** below.

Determine how wide you want the material to be (outside the rabbet). Refer to the Chart below to find this dimension in one of the yellow shaded columns. The added length for that width will be shown in the green shaded block to the right of it. Add this dimension to the side length determined in the first step. You should then add whatever waste you want to allow for each side. This total is then multiplied by 5 to determine how much material is needed to build your project.

\multicolumn{10}{c}{5 SIDED FRAME ADDED WIDTH AND LENGTH CHART}
Added Width	Added Length	Added Width	Added Length	Added Width	Added Length	Added Width	Added Length	Added Width	Added Length
1/16	1/16	1 1/16	1 7/16	2 1/16	2 12/16	3 1/16	4 2/16	4 1/16	5 7/16
2/16	3/16	1 2/16	1 8/16	2 2/16	2 14/16	3 2/16	4 3/16	4 2/16	5 8/16
3/16	4/16	1 3/16	1 9/16	2 3/16	2 15/16	3 3/16	4 4/16	4 3/16	5 10/16
4/16	5/16	1 4/16	1 11/16	2 4/16	3	3 4/16	4 6/16	4 4/16	5 11/16
5/16	7/16	1 5/16	1 12/16	2 5/16	3 2/16	3 5/16	4 7/16	4 5/16	5 12/16
6/16	8/16	1 6/16	1 13/16	2 6/16	3 3/16	3 6/16	4 8/16	4 6/16	5 14/16
7/16	9/16	1 7/16	1 15/16	2 7/16	3 4/16	3 7/16	4 10/16	4 7/16	5 15/16
8/16	11/16	1 8/16	2	2 8/16	3 6/16	3 8/16	4 11/16	4 8/16	6
9/16	12/16	1 9/16	2 2/16	2 9/16	3 7/16	3 9/16	4 12/16	4 9/16	6 2/16
10/16	13/16	1 10/16	2 3/16	2 10/16	3 8/16	3 10/16	4 14/16	4 10/16	6 3/16
11/16	15/16	1 11/16	2 4/16	2 11/16	3 10/16	3 11/16	4 15/16	4 11/16	6 5/16
12/16	1	1 12/16	2 6/16	2 12/16	3 11/16	3 12/16	5	4 12/16	6 6/16
13/16	1 1/16	1 13/16	2 7/16	2 13/16	3 12/16	3 13/16	5 2/16	4 13/16	6 7/16
14/16	1 3/16	1 14/16	2 8/16	2 14/16	3 14/16	3 14/16	5 3/16	4 14/16	6 9/16
15/16	1 4/16	1 15/16	2 10/16	2 15/16	3 15/16	3 15/16	5 4/16	4 15/16	6 10/16
1	1 5/16	2	2 11/16	3	4	4	5 6/16	5	6 11/16

The Chart below is provided to enable you to make 5 sided frames using the mathematics of most popular picture sizes. The Chart is divided into 2 parts; the left section, which shows the sheet sizes in portrait format, and the right section, which shows the sheet sizes in landscape format. In the Charts, the different colored columns represent the following information:

Red: The controlling dimension of the sheet size. (width in portrait, height in landscape)
Gray: The dimension of the sheet size that will need to be cropped.

White: The rabbet length for the frame sides.
Orange: The size of the opening in the direction the picture will need to be cropped.
Blue: The amount of material that will need to be cropped.

\multicolumn{10}{c}{RABBET AREA DIMENSIONS FOR 5 SIDED FRAMES}
\multicolumn{5}{c}{FOR PORTRAIT FORMAT}	\multicolumn{5}{c}{FOR LANDSCAPE FORMAT}
Object Width	Object Height	Rabbet Length	Opening Height	Vertical Crop	Object Width	Object Height	Rabbet Length	Opening Width	Horizontal Crop
4	5	2 9/16	3 15/16	1 1/16	5	4	2 11/16	4 5/16	11/16
5	7	3 3/16	4 14/16	2 2/16	7	5	3 5/16	5 6/16	1 10/16
6	8	3 13/16	5 13/16	2 3/16	8	6	4	6 7/16	1 9/16
8	10	5	7 12/16	2 5/16	10	8	5 5/16	8 9/16	1 7/16
8 1/2	11	5 5/16	8 3/16	2 13/16	11	8 1/2	5 10/16	9 1/16	1 15/16
10	14	6 4/16	9 10/16	4 6/16	14	10	6 9/16	10 11/16	3 5/16
11	14	6 14/16	10 9/16	3 7/16	14	11	7 4/16	11 11/16	2 5/16
12	16	7 8/16	11 8/16	4 8/16	16	12	7 14/16	12 12/16	3 4/16
16	20	9 15/16	15 5/16	4 11/16	20	16	10 8/16	17	3
18	24	11 3/16	17 4/16	6 13/16	24	18	11 13/16	19 1/16	4 15/16
20	24	12 7/16	19 2/16	4 14/16	24	20	13 1/16	21 3/16	2 13/16
24	30	14 15/16	22 15/16	7 1/16	30	24	15 11/16	25 6/16	4 10/16

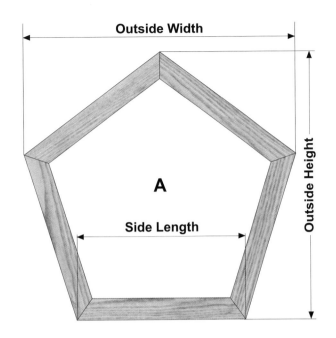

Outside Width

Side Length

Outside Height

A

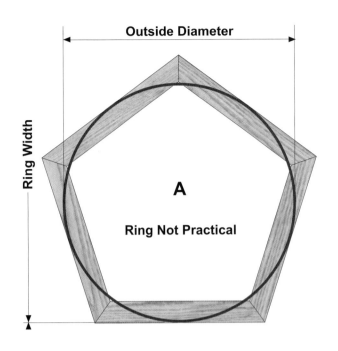

Outside Diameter

Ring Width

A

Ring Not Practical

B

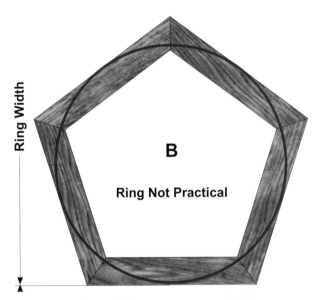

Ring Width

B

Ring Not Practical

C

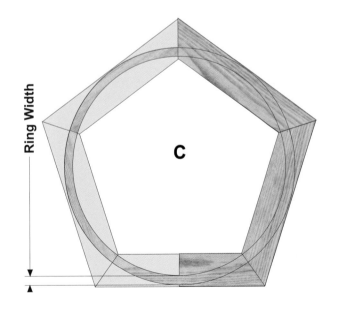

Ring Width

C

Side Length	Frame Width	Frame Height	Ring Max. OD	Material Req'd.	A Side Width	A Ring Width	B Side Width	B Ring Width	C Side Width	C Ring Width
8/16	13/16	12/16	11/16	3 12/16	1/16		1/16		2/16	0
10/16	1	15/16	14/16	4 6/16	1/16		2/16		2/16	1/16
12/16	1 3/16	1 2/16	1	5	2/16		2/16		2/16	1/16
14/16	1 7/16	1 6/16	1 3/16	5 10/16	2/16		2/16		3/16	1/16
1	1 10/16	1 9/16	1 6/16	6 4/16	2/16		3/16		3/16	1/16
1 4/16	2	1 15/16	1 11/16	7 8/16	3/16		3/16		4/16	1/16
1 8/16	2 7/16	2 5/16	2 1/16	8 12/16	3/16		4/16		5/16	1/16
1 12/16	2 13/16	2 11/16	2 6/16	10	4/16		4/16		5/16	1/16
2	3 4/16	3 1/16	2 12/16	11 4/16	4/16		5/16		6/16	2/16
2 4/16	3 10/16	3 7/16	3 1/16	12 8/16	5/16		6/16		7/16	2/16
2 8/16	4 1/16	3 14/16	3 6/16	13 12/16	5/16		6/16		8/16	2/16
2 12/16	4 7/16	4 4/16	3 12/16	15	6/16		7/16		8/16	2/16
3	4 14/16	4 10/16	4 1/16	16 4/16	6/16		8/16		9/16	2/16
3 4/16	5 4/16	5	4 7/16	17 8/16	7/16		8/16		10/16	3/16
3 8/16	5 11/16	5 6/16	4 12/16	18 12/16	7/16		9/16		11/16	3/16
3 12/16	6 1/16	5 12/16	5 2/16	20	8/16		9/16		11/16	3/16
4	6 8/16	6 3/16	5 7/16	21 4/16	8/16		10/16		12/16	3/16
4 4/16	6 14/16	6 9/16	5 13/16	22 8/16	9/16		11/16		13/16	4/16
4 8/16	7 5/16	6 15/16	6 2/16	23 12/16	9/16		11/16		14/16	4/16
4 12/16	7 11/16	7 5/16	6 7/16	25	10/16		12/16		14/16	4/16
5	8 2/16	7 11/16	6 13/16	26 4/16	10/16		13/16		15/16	4/16
5 4/16	8 8/16	8 1/16	7 2/16	27 8/16	11/16		13/16		1	4/16
5 8/16	8 15/16	8 8/16	7 8/16	28 12/16	11/16		14/16		1 1/16	5/16
5 12/16	9 5/16	8 14/16	7 13/16	30	12/16		14/16		1 1/16	5/16
6	9 12/16	9 4/16	8 3/16	31 4/16	12/16		15/16		1 2/16	5/16
6 8/16	10 8/16	10	8 14/16	33 12/16	13/16		1		1 4/16	5/16
7	11 5/16	10 12/16	9 8/16	36 4/16	14/16		1 2/16		1 5/16	6/16
7 8/16	12 2/16	11 9/16	10 3/16	38 12/16	15/16		1 3/16		1 7/16	6/16
8	12 15/16	12 5/16	10 14/16	41 4/16	1		1 4/16		1 8/16	7/16
8 8/16	13 12/16	13 1/16	11 9/16	43 12/16	1 1/16		1 5/16		1 10/16	7/16
9	14 9/16	13 14/16	12 4/16	46 4/16	1 2/16		1 7/16		1 11/16	7/16
9 8/16	15 6/16	14 10/16	12 15/16	48 12/16	1 3/16		1 8/16		1 13/16	8/16
10	16 3/16	15 6/16	13 10/16	51 4/16	1 4/16		1 9/16		1 14/16	8/16
10 8/16	17	16 3/16	14 5/16	53 12/16	1 5/16		1 10/16		2	9/16
11	17 13/16	16 15/16	15	56 4/16	1 6/16		1 12/16		2 1/16	9/16
11 8/16	18 10/16	17 11/16	15 10/16	58 12/16	1 7/16		1 13/16		2 3/16	10/16
12	19 7/16	18 8/16	16 5/16	61 4/16	1 8/16		1 14/16		2 4/16	10/16
13	21 1/16	20	17 11/16	66 4/16	1 10/16		2 1/16		2 7/16	11/16
14	22 11/16	21 9/16	19 1/16	71 4/16	1 12/16		2 3/16		2 10/16	12/16
15	24 5/16	23 2/16	20 7/16	76 4/16	1 14/16		2 6/16		2 13/16	12/16
16	25 15/16	24 10/16	21 12/16	81 4/16	2		2 8/16		3	13/16
17	27 9/16	26 3/16	23 2/16	86 4/16	2 2/16		2 11/16		3 3/16	14/16
18	29 3/16	27 12/16	24 8/16	91 4/16	2 4/16		2 13/16		3 6/16	15/16
19	30 12/16	29 4/16	25 14/16	96 4/16	2 6/16		3		3 9/16	1
20	32 6/16	30 13/16	27 3/16	101 4/16	2 8/16		3 2/16		3 12/16	1 1/16
21	34	32 5/16	28 9/16	106 4/16	2 10/16		3 5/16		3 15/16	1 1/16
22	35 10/16	33 14/16	29 15/16	111 4/16	2 12/16		3 7/16		4 2/16	1 2/16
23	37 4/16	35 7/16	31 5/16	116 4/16	2 14/16		3 10/16		4 5/16	1 3/16
24	38 14/16	36 15/16	32 11/16	121 4/16	3		3 12/16		4 8/16	1 4/16
25	40 8/16	38 8/16	34	126 4/16	3 2/16		3 15/16		4 11/16	1 5/16
26	42 2/16	40 1/16	35 6/16	131 4/16	3 4/16		4 1/16		4 14/16	1 6/16
27	43 12/16	41 9/16	36 12/16	136 4/16	3 6/16		4 4/16		5 1/16	1 6/16
28	45 6/16	43 2/16	38 2/16	141 4/16	3 8/16		4 6/16		5 4/16	1 7/16

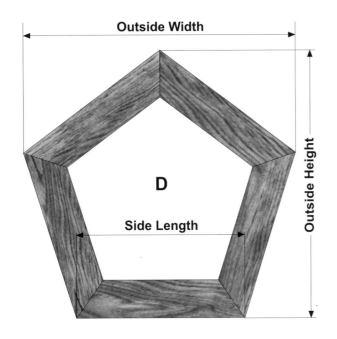

Outside Width

Outside Height

Side Length

D

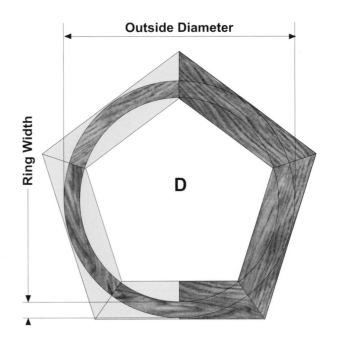

Outside Diameter

Ring Width

D

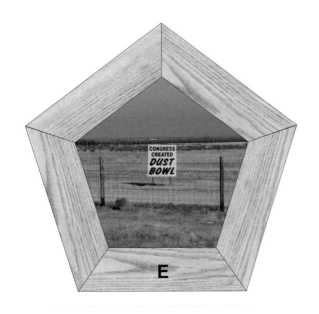

E

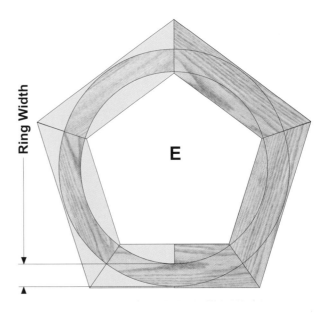

Ring Width

E

F

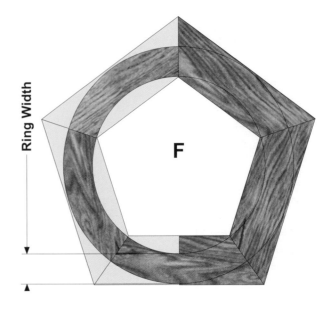

Ring Width

Outside Diameter

F

Side Length	Frame Width	Frame Height	Ring Max. OD	Material Req'd.	D Side Width	D Ring Width	E Side Width	E Ring Width	F Side Width	F Ring Width
8/16	13/16	12/16	11/16	3 12/16	2/16	1/16	2/16	1/16	2/16	1/16
10/16	1	15/16	14/16	4 6/16	2/16	1/16	3/16	1/16	3/16	2/16
12/16	1 3/16	1 2/16	1	5	3/16	1/16	3/16	2/16	3/16	2/16
14/16	1 7/16	1 6/16	1 3/16	5 10/16	3/16	1/16	4/16	2/16	4/16	2/16
1	1 10/16	1 9/16	1 6/16	6 4/16	4/16	1/16	4/16	2/16	5/16	3/16
1 4/16	2	1 15/16	1 11/16	7 8/16	4/16	2/16	5/16	3/16	6/16	3/16
1 8/16	2 7/16	2 5/16	2 1/16	8 12/16	5/16	2/16	6/16	3/16	7/16	4/16
1 12/16	2 13/16	2 11/16	2 6/16	10	6/16	3/16	7/16	4/16	8/16	5/16
2	3 4/16	3 1/16	2 12/16	11 4/16	7/16	3/16	8/16	4/16	9/16	5/16
2 4/16	3 10/16	3 7/16	3 1/16	12 8/16	8/16	3/16	9/16	5/16	10/16	6/16
2 8/16	4 1/16	3 14/16	3 6/16	13 12/16	9/16	4/16	10/16	5/16	11/16	7/16
2 12/16	4 7/16	4 4/16	3 12/16	15	10/16	4/16	11/16	6/16	12/16	7/16
3	4 14/16	4 10/16	4 1/16	16 4/16	11/16	4/16	12/16	6/16	14/16	8/16
3 4/16	5 4/16	5	4 7/16	17 8/16	11/16	5/16	13/16	7/16	15/16	9/16
3 8/16	5 11/16	5 6/16	4 12/16	18 12/16	12/16	5/16	14/16	7/16	1	9/16
3 12/16	6 1/16	5 12/16	5 2/16	20	13/16	5/16	15/16	8/16	1 1/16	10/16
4	6 8/16	6 3/16	5 7/16	21 4/16	14/16	6/16	1	8/16	1 2/16	11/16
4 4/16	6 14/16	6 9/16	5 13/16	22 8/16	15/16	6/16	1 1/16	9/16	1 3/16	11/16
4 8/16	7 5/16	6 15/16	6 2/16	23 12/16	1	7/16	1 2/16	9/16	1 4/16	12/16
4 12/16	7 11/16	7 5/16	6 7/16	25	1 1/16	7/16	1 3/16	10/16	1 5/16	13/16
5	8 2/16	7 11/16	6 13/16	26 4/16	1 2/16	7/16	1 4/16	10/16	1 7/16	13/16
5 4/16	8 8/16	8 1/16	7 2/16	27 8/16	1 2/16	8/16	1 5/16	11/16	1 8/16	14/16
5 8/16	8 15/16	8 8/16	7 8/16	28 12/16	1 3/16	8/16	1 6/16	11/16	1 9/16	15/16
5 12/16	9 5/16	8 14/16	7 13/16	30	1 4/16	8/16	1 7/16	12/16	1 10/16	15/16
6	9 12/16	9 4/16	8 3/16	31 4/16	1 5/16	9/16	1 8/16	12/16	1 11/16	1
6 8/16	10 8/16	10	8 14/16	33 12/16	1 7/16	9/16	1 10/16	13/16	1 13/16	1 1/16
7	11 5/16	10 12/16	9 8/16	36 4/16	1 9/16	10/16	1 12/16	14/16	2	1 3/16
7 8/16	12 2/16	11 9/16	10 3/16	38 12/16	1 10/16	11/16	1 14/16	15/16	2 2/16	1 4/16
8	12 15/16	12 5/16	10 14/16	41 4/16	1 12/16	12/16	2	1 1/16	2 4/16	1 5/16
8 8/16	13 12/16	13 1/16	11 9/16	43 12/16	1 14/16	12/16	2 2/16	1 2/16	2 6/16	1 7/16
9	14 9/16	13 14/16	12 4/16	46 4/16	2	13/16	2 4/16	1 3/16	2 9/16	1 8/16
9 8/16	15 6/16	14 10/16	12 15/16	48 12/16	2 1/16	14/16	2 6/16	1 4/16	2 11/16	1 10/16
10	16 3/16	15 6/16	13 10/16	51 4/16	2 3/16	14/16	2 8/16	1 5/16	2 13/16	1 11/16
10 8/16	17	16 3/16	14 5/16	53 12/16	2 5/16	15/16	2 10/16	1 6/16	2 15/16	1 12/16
11	17 13/16	16 15/16	15	56 4/16	2 7/16	1	2 12/16	1 7/16	3 2/16	1 14/16
11 8/16	18 10/16	17 11/16	15 10/16	58 12/16	2 8/16	1 1/16	2 14/16	1 8/16	3 4/16	1 15/16
12	19 7/16	18 8/16	16 5/16	61 4/16	2 10/16	1 1/16	3	1 9/16	3 6/16	2
13	21 1/16	20	17 11/16	66 4/16	2 14/16	1 3/16	3 4/16	1 11/16	3 11/16	2 3/16
14	22 11/16	21 9/16	19 1/16	71 4/16	3 1/16	1 4/16	3 8/16	1 13/16	3 15/16	2 6/16
15	24 5/16	23 2/16	20 7/16	76 4/16	3 5/16	1 6/16	3 12/16	1 15/16	4 4/16	2 8/16
16	25 15/16	24 10/16	21 12/16	81 4/16	3 8/16	1 7/16	4	2 1/16	4 8/16	2 11/16
17	27 9/16	26 3/16	23 2/16	86 4/16	3 12/16	1 9/16	4 4/16	2 3/16	4 13/16	2 14/16
18	29 3/16	27 12/16	24 8/16	91 4/16	3 15/16	1 10/16	4 8/16	2 5/16	5 1/16	3
19	30 12/16	29 4/16	25 14/16	96 4/16	4 3/16	1 11/16	4 12/16	2 7/16	5 6/16	3 3/16
20	32 6/16	30 13/16	27 3/16	101 4/16	4 6/16	1 13/16	5	2 9/16	5 10/16	3 6/16
21	34	32 5/16	28 9/16	106 4/16	4 10/16	1 14/16	5 4/16	2 11/16	5 15/16	3 8/16
22	35 10/16	33 14/16	29 15/16	111 4/16	4 13/16	2	5 8/16	2 13/16	6 3/16	3 11/16
23	37 4/16	35 7/16	31 5/16	116 4/16	5 1/16	2 1/16	5 12/16	3	6 8/16	3 14/16
24	38 14/16	36 15/16	32 11/16	121 4/16	5 4/16	2 3/16	6	3 2/16	6 12/16	4
25	40 8/16	38 8/16	34	126 4/16	5 8/16	2 4/16	6 4/16	3 4/16	7 1/16	4 3/16
26	42 2/16	40 1/16	35 6/16	131 4/16	5 11/16	2 6/16	6 8/16	3 6/16	7 5/16	4 6/16
27	43 12/16	41 9/16	36 12/16	136 4/16	5 15/16	2 7/16	6 12/16	3 8/16	7 10/16	4 9/16
28	45 6/16	43 2/16	38 2/16	141 4/16	6 2/16	2 9/16	7	3 10/16	7 14/16	4 11/16

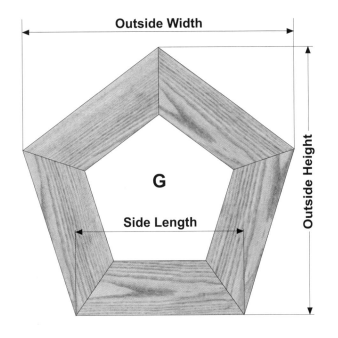

Outside Width

Outside Height

Side Length

G

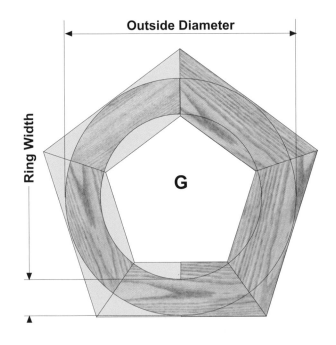

Outside Diameter

Ring Width

G

H

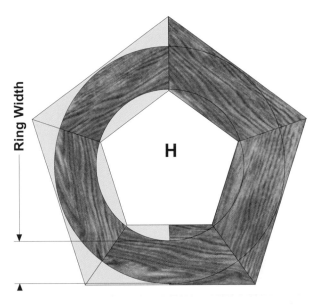

Ring Width

H

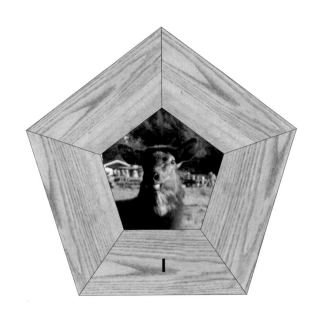

I

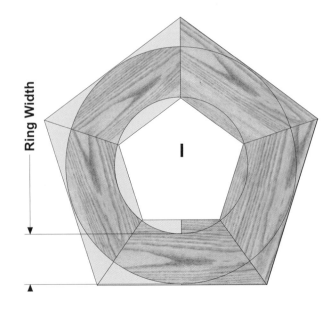

Ring Width

I

Side Length	Frame Width	Frame Height	Ring Max. OD	Material Req'd.	G Side Width	G Ring Width	H Side Width	H Ring Width	I Side Width	I Ring Width
8/16	13/16	12/16	11/16	3 12/16	3/16	2/16	3/16	2/16	3/16	2/16
10/16	1	15/16	14/16	4 6/16	3/16	2/16	3/16	2/16	4/16	3/16
12/16	1 3/16	1 2/16	1	5	4/16	2/16	4/16	3/16	5/16	3/16
14/16	1 7/16	1 6/16	1 3/16	5 10/16	4/16	3/16	5/16	3/16	5/16	4/16
1	1 10/16	1 9/16	1 6/16	6 4/16	5/16	3/16	6/16	4/16	6/16	5/16
1 4/16	2	1 15/16	1 11/16	7 8/16	6/16	4/16	7/16	5/16	8/16	6/16
1 8/16	2 7/16	2 5/16	2 1/16	8 12/16	8/16	5/16	8/16	6/16	9/16	7/16
1 12/16	2 13/16	2 11/16	2 6/16	10	9/16	6/16	10/16	7/16	11/16	8/16
2	3 4/16	3 1/16	2 12/16	11 4/16	10/16	7/16	11/16	8/16	12/16	9/16
2 4/16	3 10/16	3 7/16	3 1/16	12 8/16	11/16	7/16	12/16	9/16	14/16	10/16
2 8/16	4 1/16	3 14/16	3 6/16	13 12/16	13/16	8/16	14/16	10/16	15/16	11/16
2 12/16	4 7/16	4 4/16	3 12/16	15	14/16	9/16	15/16	11/16	1 1/16	12/16
3	4 14/16	4 10/16	4 1/16	16 4/16	15/16	10/16	1 1/16	12/16	1 2/16	14/16
3 4/16	5 4/16	5	4 7/16	17 8/16	1	11/16	1 2/16	13/16	1 4/16	15/16
3 8/16	5 11/16	5 6/16	4 12/16	18 12/16	1 2/16	12/16	1 3/16	14/16	1 5/16	1
3 12/16	6 1/16	5 12/16	5 2/16	20	1 3/16	12/16	1 5/16	15/16	1 7/16	1 1/16
4	6 8/16	6 3/16	5 7/16	21 4/16	1 4/16	13/16	1 6/16	1	1 8/16	1 2/16
4 4/16	6 14/16	6 9/16	5 13/16	22 8/16	1 5/16	14/16	1 7/16	1 1/16	1 10/16	1 3/16
4 8/16	7 5/16	6 15/16	6 2/16	23 12/16	1 7/16	15/16	1 9/16	1 2/16	1 11/16	1 4/16
4 12/16	7 11/16	7 5/16	6 7/16	25	1 8/16	1	1 10/16	1 3/16	1 13/16	1 6/16
5	8 2/16	7 11/16	6 13/16	26 4/16	1 9/16	1 1/16	1 12/16	1 4/16	1 14/16	1 7/16
5 4/16	8 8/16	8 1/16	7 2/16	27 8/16	1 10/16	1 1/16	1 13/16	1 5/16	2	1 8/16
5 8/16	8 15/16	8 8/16	7 8/16	28 12/16	1 12/16	1 2/16	1 14/16	1 6/16	2 1/16	1 9/16
5 12/16	9 5/16	8 14/16	7 13/16	30	1 13/16	1 3/16	2	1 7/16	2 3/16	1 10/16
6	9 12/16	9 4/16	8 3/16	31 4/16	1 14/16	1 4/16	2 1/16	1 8/16	2 4/16	1 11/16
6 8/16	10 8/16	10	8 14/16	33 12/16	2 1/16	1 5/16	2 4/16	1 10/16	2 7/16	1 14/16
7	11 5/16	10 12/16	9 8/16	36 4/16	2 3/16	1 7/16	2 7/16	1 11/16	2 10/16	2
7 8/16	12 2/16	11 9/16	10 3/16	38 12/16	2 6/16	1 9/16	2 9/16	1 13/16	2 13/16	2 2/16
8	12 15/16	12 5/16	10 14/16	41 4/16	2 8/16	1 10/16	2 12/16	1 15/16	3	2 4/16
8 8/16	13 12/16	13 1/16	11 9/16	43 12/16	2 11/16	1 12/16	2 15/16	2 1/16	3 3/16	2 7/16
9	14 9/16	13 14/16	12 4/16	46 4/16	2 13/16	1 14/16	3 2/16	2 3/16	3 6/16	2 9/16
9 8/16	15 6/16	14 10/16	12 15/16	48 12/16	3	1 15/16	3 4/16	2 5/16	3 9/16	2 11/16
10	16 3/16	15 6/16	13 10/16	51 4/16	3 2/16	2 1/16	3 7/16	2 7/16	3 12/16	2 13/16
10 8/16	17	16 3/16	14 5/16	53 4/16	3 5/16	2 3/16	3 10/16	2 9/16	3 15/16	3
11	17 13/16	16 15/16	15	56 4/16	3 7/16	2 4/16	3 13/16	2 11/16	4 2/16	3 2/16
11 8/16	18 10/16	17 11/16	15 10/16	58 12/16	3 10/16	2 6/16	3 15/16	2 13/16	4 5/16	3 4/16
12	19 7/16	18 8/16	16 5/16	61 4/16	3 12/16	2 8/16	4 2/16	2 15/16	4 8/16	3 7/16
13	21 1/16	20	17 11/16	66 4/16	4 1/16	2 11/16	4 8/16	3 3/16	4 14/16	3 11/16
14	22 11/16	21 9/16	19 1/16	71 4/16	4 6/16	2 14/16	4 13/16	3 7/16	5 4/16	4
15	24 5/16	23 2/16	20 7/16	76 4/16	4 11/16	3 2/16	5 3/16	3 11/16	5 10/16	4 4/16
16	25 15/16	24 10/16	21 12/16	81 4/16	5	3 5/16	5 8/16	3 15/16	6	4 9/16
17	27 9/16	26 3/16	23 2/16	86 4/16	5 5/16	3 8/16	5 14/16	4 3/16	6 6/16	4 13/16
18	29 3/16	27 12/16	24 8/16	91 4/16	5 10/16	3 11/16	6 3/16	4 7/16	6 12/16	5 2/16
19	30 12/16	29 4/16	25 14/16	96 4/16	5 15/16	3 15/16	6 9/16	4 11/16	7 2/16	5 6/16
20	32 6/16	30 13/16	27 3/16	101 4/16	6 4/16	4 2/16	6 14/16	4 14/16	7 8/16	5 11/16
21	34	32 5/16	28 9/16	106 4/16	6 9/16	4 5/16	7 4/16	5 2/16	7 14/16	5 15/16
22	35 10/16	33 14/16	29 15/16	111 4/16	6 14/16	4 9/16	7 9/16	5 6/16	8 4/16	6 4/16
23	37 4/16	35 7/16	31 5/16	116 4/16	7 3/16	4 12/16	7 15/16	5 10/16	8 10/16	6 9/16
24	38 14/16	36 15/16	32 11/16	121 4/16	7 8/16	4 15/16	8 4/16	5 14/16	9	6 13/16
25	40 8/16	38 8/16	34	126 4/16	7 13/16	5 3/16	8 10/16	6 2/16	9 6/16	7 2/16
26	42 2/16	40 1/16	35 6/16	131 4/16	8 2/16	5 6/16	8 15/16	6 6/16	9 12/16	7 6/16
27	43 12/16	41 9/16	36 12/16	136 4/16	8 7/16	5 9/16	9 5/16	6 10/16	10 2/16	7 11/16
28	45 6/16	43 2/16	38 2/16	141 4/16	8 12/16	5 13/16	9 10/16	6 14/16	10 8/16	7 15/16

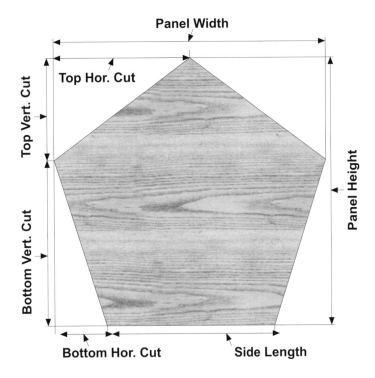

The Chart below shows the formulas that were used in the process of laying out the 5 sided shapes. These are included to assist you if you are designing a project to a size that is not illustrated in the Dimension Charts provided. We hope you find them helpful as you design your projects.

5 SIDED PANEL FORMULAS		
Panel Width =	Panel Height x	1.054
Panel Height =	Panel Width x	0.949
Side Length =	Panel Height x	0.646
Side Length =	Panel Width x	0.620
Top Hor. Cut =	Panel Width x	0.500
Bott. Hor. Cut =	Panel Width x	0.191
Top Vert. Cut =	Panel Width x	0.362
Bott.Vert. Cut =	Panel Width x	0.586

PANEL WIDTH	PANEL HEIGHT	SIDE LENGTH	TOP HOR. CUT	BOTTOM HOR. CUT	TOP VERT. CUT	BOTTOM VERT. CUT
12/16	11/16	7/16	6/16	2/16	4/16	7/16
1	15/16	10/16	8/16	3/16	6/16	9/16
1 4/16	1 3/16	12/16	10/16	4/16	7/16	12/16
1 8/16	1 7/16	15/16	12/16	5/16	9/16	14/16
1 12/16	1 11/16	1 1/16	14/16	5/16	10/16	1
2	1 14/16	1 4/16	1	6/16	12/16	1 3/16
2 4/16	2 2/16	1 6/16	1 2/16	7/16	13/16	1 5/16
2 8/16	2 6/16	1 9/16	1 4/16	8/16	14/16	1 7/16
2 12/16	2 10/16	1 11/16	1 6/16	8/16	1	1 10/16
3	2 14/16	1 14/16	1 8/16	9/16	1 1/16	1 12/16
3 4/16	3 1/16	2	1 10/16	10/16	1 3/16	1 14/16
3 8/16	3 5/16	2 3/16	1 12/16	11/16	1 4/16	2 1/16
3 12/16	3 9/16	2 5/16	1 14/16	11/16	1 6/16	2 3/16
4	3 13/16	2 8/16	2	12/16	1 7/16	2 6/16
4 4/16	4 1/16	2 10/16	2 2/16	13/16	1 9/16	2 8/16
4 8/16	4 4/16	2 13/16	2 4/16	14/16	1 10/16	2 10/16
4 12/16	4 8/16	2 15/16	2 6/16	15/16	1 12/16	2 13/16
5	4 12/16	3 2/16	2 8/16	15/16	1 13/16	2 15/16
5 4/16	5	3 4/16	2 10/16	1	1 14/16	3 1/16
5 8/16	5 4/16	3 7/16	2 12/16	1 1/16	2	3 4/16
5 12/16	5 7/16	3 9/16	2 14/16	1 2/16	2 1/16	3 6/16
6	5 11/16	3 12/16	3	1 2/16	2 3/16	3 8/16
6 4/16	5 15/16	3 14/16	3 2/16	1 3/16	2 4/16	3 11/16
6 8/16	6 3/16	4	3 4/16	1 4/16	2 6/16	3 13/16
6 12/16	6 6/16	4 3/16	3 6/16	1 5/16	2 7/16	3 15/16
7	6 10/16	4 5/16	3 8/16	1 5/16	2 9/16	4 2/16
7 4/16	6 14/16	4 8/16	3 10/16	1 6/16	2 10/16	4 4/16
7 8/16	7 2/16	4 10/16	3 12/16	1 7/16	2 11/16	4 6/16
7 12/16	7 6/16	4 13/16	3 14/16	1 8/16	2 13/16	4 9/16
8	7 9/16	4 15/16	4	1 8/16	2 14/16	4 11/16
8 4/16	7 13/16	5 2/16	4 2/16	1 9/16	3	4 13/16
8 8/16	8 1/16	5 4/16	4 4/16	1 10/16	3 1/16	5

PANEL WIDTH	PANEL HEIGHT	SIDE LENGTH	TOP HOR. CUT	BOTTOM HOR. CUT	TOP VERT. CUT	BOTTOM VERT. CUT
8 12/16	8 5/16	5 7/16	4 6/16	1 11/16	3 3/16	5 2/16
9	8 9/16	5 9/16	4 8/16	1 12/16	3 4/16	5 4/16
9 4/16	8 12/16	5 12/16	4 10/16	1 12/16	3 6/16	5 7/16
9 8/16	9	5 14/16	4 12/16	1 13/16	3 7/16	5 9/16
9 12/16	9 4/16	6 1/16	4 14/16	1 14/16	3 8/16	5 11/16
10	9 8/16	6 3/16	5	1 15/16	3 10/16	5 14/16
10 4/16	9 12/16	6 6/16	5 2/16	1 15/16	3 11/16	6
10 8/16	9 15/16	6 8/16	5 4/16	2	3 13/16	6 2/16
10 12/16	10 3/16	6 11/16	5 6/16	2 1/16	3 14/16	6 5/16
11	10 7/16	6 13/16	5 8/16	2 2/16	4	6 7/16
11 4/16	10 11/16	7	5 10/16	2 2/16	4 1/16	6 9/16
11 8/16	10 15/16	7 2/16	5 12/16	2 3/16	4 3/16	6 12/16
12	11 6/16	7 7/16	6	2 5/16	4 6/16	7 1/16
12 4/16	11 10/16	7 10/16	6 2/16	2 5/16	4 7/16	7 3/16
12 8/16	11 14/16	7 12/16	6 4/16	2 6/16	4 8/16	7 5/16
12 12/16	12 2/16	7 14/16	6 6/16	2 7/16	4 10/16	7 8/16
13	12 5/16	8 1/16	6 8/16	2 8/16	4 11/16	7 10/16
13 4/16	12 9/16	8 3/16	6 10/16	2 8/16	4 13/16	7 12/16
13 8/16	12 13/16	8 6/16	6 12/16	2 9/16	4 14/16	7 15/16
13 12/16	13 1/16	8 8/16	6 14/16	2 10/16	5	8 1/16
14	13 5/16	8 11/16	7	2 11/16	5 1/16	8 3/16
14 8/16	13 12/16	9	7 4/16	2 12/16	5 4/16	8 8/16
15	14 4/16	9 5/16	7 8/16	2 14/16	5 7/16	8 13/16
15 8/16	14 11/16	9 10/16	7 12/16	2 15/16	5 10/16	9 1/16
16	15 3/16	9 15/16	8	3 1/16	5 13/16	9 6/16
16 8/16	15 11/16	10 4/16	8 4/16	3 2/16	6	9 11/16
17	16 2/16	10 9/16	8 8/16	3 4/16	6 2/16	9 15/16
17 8/16	16 10/16	10 14/16	8 12/16	3 5/16	6 5/16	10 4/16
18	17 1/16	11 3/16	9	3 7/16	6 8/16	10 9/16
19	18	11 12/16	9 8/16	3 10/16	6 14/16	11 2/16
20	19	12 6/16	10	3 13/16	7 4/16	11 12/16
21	19 15/16	13	10 8/16	4	7 10/16	12 5/16
22	20 14/16	13 10/16	11	4 3/16	7 15/16	12 14/16
23	21 13/16	14 4/16	11 8/16	4 6/16	8 5/16	13 8/16
24	22 12/16	14 14/16	12	4 9/16	8 11/16	14 1/16
25	23 12/16	15 8/16	12 8/16	4 12/16	9 1/16	14 10/16
26	24 11/16	16 2/16	13	4 15/16	9 7/16	15 4/16
27	25 10/16	16 12/16	13 8/16	5 3/16	9 12/16	15 13/16
28	26 9/16	17 6/16	14	5 6/16	10 2/16	16 7/16
29	27 8/16	18	14 8/16	5 9/16	10 8/16	17
30	28 8/16	18 10/16	15	5 12/16	10 14/16	17 9/16
31	29 7/16	19 4/16	15 8/16	5 15/16	11 4/16	18 3/16
32	30 6/16	19 13/16	16	6 2/16	11 9/16	18 12/16
33	31 5/16	20 7/16	16 8/16	6 5/16	11 15/16	19 5/16
34	32 4/16	21 1/16	17	6 8/16	12 5/16	19 15/16
35	33 3/16	21 11/16	17 8/16	6 11/16	12 11/16	20 8/16
36	34 3/16	22 5/16	18	6 14/16	13 1/16	21 2/16
37	35 2/16	22 15/16	18 8/16	7 1/16	13 6/16	21 11/16
38	36 1/16	23 9/16	19	7 4/16	13 12/16	22 4/16
39	37	24 3/16	19 8/16	7 7/16	14 2/16	22 14/16
40	37 15/16	24 13/16	20	7 10/16	14 8/16	23 7/16
41	38 15/16	25 7/16	20 8/16	7 13/16	14 13/16	24
42	39 14/16	26 1/16	21	8	15 3/16	24 10/16

6 SIDED PROJECT INFORMATION

Geometric Name: Hexagon
Definition: A Polygon having 6 sides
Miter Angle: 30°
Angle Change / Adjoining Sides: 60°

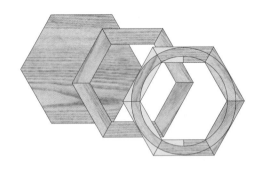

As one of the "even numbered" shapes Illustrated in this book, the 6 sided shape (Hexagon) is one of the shapes that is relatively easy to get creative with, but is pretty limited. With that said, it's a fun project to build, and in some cases can be the perfect shape for the item you may wish to frame. The one thing that should be considered when using this shape (with sides of equal length) is that for most standard sizes of pictures, a lot of cropping of the picture will be required.

The Illustrations to the right should give you an idea of the amount of cropping that may be required by using a Hexagon (with equal length sides) as your choice of shape for a frame.

In the left Illustration, you see a scale (shown in red) 8" x 10" sheet in portrait format. The sheet border is slightly outside the rabbeted area (shown in yellow) of the frame. Note the amount of material that would need to be cropped off the sheet top and/or bottom.

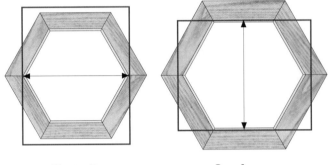

Portrait   **Landscape**

In the right Illustration, you see the same size sheet, but rotated 90° into a landscape format. Note the amount of material that would need to be cropped off the sheet sides.

You should note that the frame for the sheet shown in portrait format is also smaller than the frame for the sheet shown in landscape format. This is due to the fact that on a Hexagon, the dimension "point-to-point" is larger than the dimension "flat-to-flat". In our **6 SIDED FRAME FORMULAS** below, you will be able to see exactly what the changes between these dimensions will be.

If the project you are building is a frame for a specific size object, you should refer to the **6 SIDED FRAME FORMULAS** Chart below as a first step. On a Hexagon, the height (when the Hexagon is positioned as shown above) is shorter than the width, and is the controlling dimension for the frame for a picture in landscape format. In landscape format, the picture height would be multiplied by .650 to determine the length of the sides at the rabbeted edge. (See the bottom formula under **SIDE LENGTH** in the Chart below). In a portrait format, the width is the controlling dimension. In portrait format, the picture width should be multiplied by .618 to determine the lengths of the sides of the rabbeted edge. (See the top formula under **SIDE LENGTH** in the Chart below).

6 SIDED FRAME FORMULAS		
WIDTH	**HEIGHT**	**SIDE LENGTH**
Width = Side Length x 2.0	Height = Side Length x 1.73	Side Length = Width x .500
Width = Height x 1.143	Height = Width x .875	Side Length = Height x .571

Though the information above is very helpful, one of the most time consuming (and frustrating) things about building frames is to try to cut to a dimension that is not measured on either the inside or outside edge of the molding. I like to cut miters from the inside to the outside edges of the molding. This not only allows me to eliminate tear out on the inside corners of the frame since I am cutting into the inside edge, I am also cutting with the grain of the molding. It also allows me to see the outside edge of the material as I cut it. To help you understand how easy it is to convert a dimension along the rabbeted edge into an outside measurement, I will explain how we can use some basic math to help us determine the outside length of our frame sides. The Illustration below should be helpful in showing you how we designed our **6 SIDED FRAME ADDED WIDTH AND LENGTH CHART** on the next page.

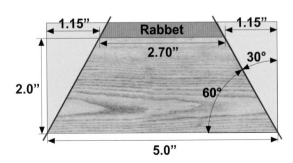

The Illustration to the left represents a piece of wood that is 5" long and 2" wide (to the edge of the rabbet). Note that on the right side that the end of the piece shows the miter angle for a Hexagon (30°) and the resulting angle of the cut (60°).

You should also note that at the rabbet, the 30° cuts shorten each end of the piece by 1.15". Since both ends of the piece are cut, this means that the length at the rabbet is 2.70", which is 2.30" shorter than the outside edge of the molding. What this Illustration tells us is that at a 30°cut, we will add 2.30" to the length at a 2" width. This is the basis of our formula.

If we divide the **Added Length** (2.3") by the **Added Width** (2.0") we end up with 1.15 as our multiplier. In the event that you want to make a frame and need to work in fractions smaller than 1/16 increments, you would multiply the width of the molding outside the rabbet by 1.15. To determine the decimal equivalent of the fractions you need to use, refer to the **FRACTION TO DECIMAL CONVERSION CHART** provided.

If you are able to use 1/16" increments for the mathematics of your frames, you should use the **6 SIDED FRAME ADDED WIDTH AND LENGTH CHART** below.

Determine how wide you want the material to be (outside the rabbet). Refer to the Chart below to find this dimension in one of the yellow shaded columns. The added length for that width will be shown in the green shaded block to the right of it. Add this dimension to the side length determined in the first step. You should then add whatever waste you want to allow for each side. This total is then multiplied by 6 to determine how much material is needed to build your project.

6 SIDED FRAME ADDED WIDTH AND LENGTH CHART

Added Width	Added Length	Added Width	Added Length	Added Width	Added Length	Added Width	Added Length	Added Width	Added Length
1/16	1/16	1 1/16	1 4/16	2 1/16	2 6/16	3 1/16	3 8/16	4 1/16	4 11/16
2/16	2/16	1 2/16	1 5/16	2 2/16	2 7/16	3 2/16	3 9/16	4 2/16	4 12/16
3/16	3/16	1 3/16	1 6/16	2 3/16	2 8/16	3 3/16	3 11/16	4 3/16	4 13/16
4/16	5/16	1 4/16	1 7/16	2 4/16	2 9/16	3 4/16	3 12/16	4 4/16	4 14/16
5/16	6/16	1 5/16	1 8/16	2 5/16	2 11/16	3 5/16	3 13/16	4 5/16	4 15/16
6/16	7/16	1 6/16	1 9/16	2 6/16	2 12/16	3 6/16	3 14/16	4 6/16	5 1/16
7/16	8/16	1 7/16	1 10/16	2 7/16	2 13/16	3 7/16	3 15/16	4 7/16	5 2/16
8/16	9/16	1 8/16	1 12/16	2 8/16	2 14/16	3 8/16	4	4 8/16	5 3/16
9/16	10/16	1 9/16	1 13/16	2 9/16	2 15/16	3 9/16	4 2/16	4 9/16	5 4/16
10/16	12/16	1 10/16	1 14/16	2 10/16	3	3 10/16	4 3/16	4 10/16	5 5/16
11/16	13/16	1 11/16	1 15/16	2 11/16	3 1/16	3 11/16	4 4/16	4 11/16	5 6/16
12/16	14/16	1 12/16	2	2 12/16	3 3/16	3 12/16	4 5/16	4 12/16	5 7/16
13/16	15/16	1 13/16	2 1/16	2 13/16	3 4/16	3 13/16	4 6/16	4 13/16	5 9/16
14/16	1	1 14/16	2 3/16	2 14/16	3 5/16	3 14/16	4 7/16	4 14/16	5 10/16
15/16	1 1/16	1 15/16	2 4/16	2 15/16	3 6/16	3 15/16	4 8/16	4 15/16	5 11/16
1	1 2/16	2	2 5/16	3	3 7/16	4	4 10/16	5	5 12/16

The Chart below is provided to enable you to make 6 sided frames using the mathematics of most popular picture sizes. The Chart is divided into 2 parts; the left section, which shows the sheet sizes in portrait format, and the right section, which shows the sheet sizes in landscape format. In the Charts, the different colored columns represent the following information:

Red: The controlling dimension of the sheet size. (width in portrait, height in landscape)
Gray: The dimension of the sheet size that will need to be cropped.

White: The rabbet length for the frame sides.
Orange: The size of the opening in the direction the picture will need to be cropped.
Blue: The amount of material that will need to be cropped.

RABBET AREA DIMENSIONS FOR 6 SIDED FRAMES

FOR PORTRAIT FORMAT					FOR LANDSCAPE FORMAT				
Object Width	Object Height	Rabbet Length	Opening Height	Vertical Crop	Object Width	Object Height	Rabbet Length	Opening Width	Horizontal Crop
4	5	2	3 8/16	1 8/16	5	4	2 5/16	4 9/16	7/16
5	7	2 8/16	4 6/16	2 10/16	7	5	2 14/16	5 11/16	1 5/16
6	8	3	5 4/16	2 12/16	8	6	3 7/16	6 14/16	1 2/16
8	10	4	7	3	10	8	4 9/16	9 2/16	14/16
8 1/2	11	4 4/16	7 7/16	3 9/16	11	8 1/2	4 14/16	9 11/16	1 5/16
10	14	5	8 12/16	5 4/16	14	10	5 11/16	11 7/16	2 9/16
11	14	5 8/16	9 10/16	4 6/16	14	11	6 4/16	12 9/16	1 7/16
12	16	6	10 8/16	5 8/16	16	12	6 14/16	13 11/16	2 5/16
16	20	8	14	6	20	16	9 2/16	18 5/16	1 11/16
18	24	9	15 12/16	8 4/16	24	18	10 4/16	20 9/16	3 7/16
20	24	10	17 8/16	6 8/16	24	20	11 7/16	22 14/16	1 2/16
24	30	12	21	9	30	24	13 11/16	27 7/16	2 9/16

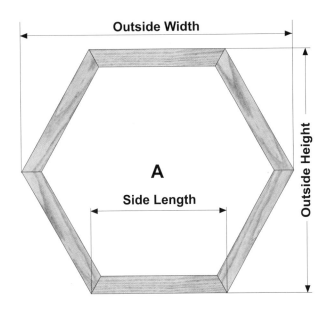

Outside Width

Outside Height

A

Side Length

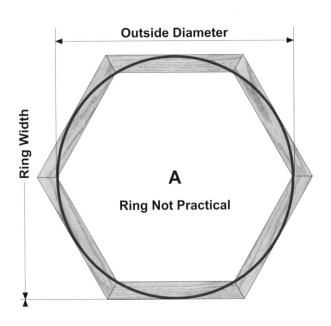

Outside Diameter

Ring Width

A

Ring Not Practical

B

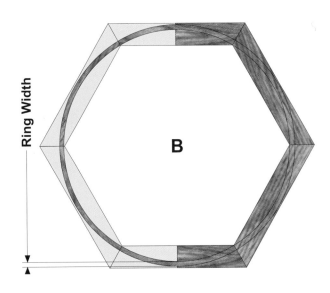

Ring Width

B

C

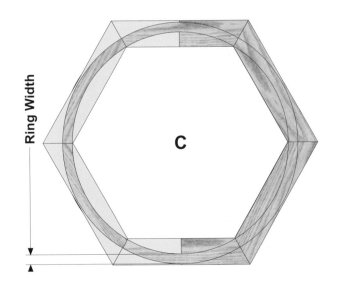

Ring Width

C

Side Length	Frame Width	Frame Height	Ring Max. OD	Material Req'd.	A Side Width	A Ring Width	B Side Width	B Ring Width	C Side Width	C Ring Width
8/16	1	14/16	14/16	4 8/16	1/16		1/16		2/16	1/16
10/16	1 4/16	1 1/16	1 1/16	5 4/16	1/16		2/16		2/16	1/16
12/16	1 8/16	1 5/16	1 5/16	6	2/16		2/16		2/16	1/16
14/16	1 12/16	1 8/16	1 8/16	6 12/16	2/16		2/16		3/16	1/16
1	2	1 12/16	1 11/16	7 8/16	2/16		3/16	1/16	3/16	2/16
1 4/16	2 8/16	2 3/16	2 2/16	9	3/16		3/16	1/16	4/16	2/16
1 8/16	3	2 10/16	2 9/16	10 8/16	3/16		4/16	1/16	5/16	2/16
1 12/16	3 8/16	3	3	12	4/16		4/16	1/16	5/16	3/16
2	4	3 7/16	3 7/16	13 8/16	4/16		5/16	1/16	6/16	3/16
2 4/16	4 8/16	3 14/16	3 14/16	15	5/16		6/16	1/16	7/16	4/16
2 8/16	5	4 5/16	4 4/16	16 8/16	5/16		6/16	1/16	8/16	4/16
2 12/16	5 8/16	4 12/16	4 11/16	18	6/16		7/16	2/16	8/16	4/16
3	6	5 3/16	5 2/16	19 8/16	6/16		8/16	2/16	9/16	5/16
3 4/16	6 8/16	5 10/16	5 9/16	21	7/16		8/16	2/16	10/16	5/16
3 8/16	7	6 1/16	6	22 8/16	7/16		9/16	2/16	11/16	6/16
3 12/16	7 8/16	6 8/16	6 7/16	24	8/16		9/16	2/16	11/16	6/16
4	8	6 15/16	6 13/16	25 8/16	8/16		10/16	2/16	12/16	6/16
4 4/16	8 8/16	7 6/16	7 4/16	27	9/16		11/16	2/16	13/16	7/16
4 8/16	9	7 13/16	7 11/16	28 8/16	9/16		11/16	3/16	14/16	7/16
4 12/16	9 8/16	8 3/16	8 2/16	30	10/16		12/16	3/16	14/16	8/16
5	10	8 10/16	8 9/16	31 8/16	10/16		13/16	3/16	15/16	8/16
5 4/16	10 8/16	9 1/16	9	33	11/16		13/16	3/16	1	8/16
5 8/16	11	9 8/16	9 7/16	34 8/16	11/16		14/16	3/16	1 1/16	9/16
5 12/16	11 8/16	9 15/16	9 13/16	36	12/16		14/16	3/16	1 1/16	9/16
6	12	10 6/16	10 4/16	37 8/16	12/16		15/16	3/16	1 2/16	10/16
6 8/16	13	11 4/16	11 2/16	40 8/16	13/16		1	4/16	1 4/16	11/16
7	14	12 2/16	12	43 8/16	14/16		1 2/16	4/16	1 5/16	11/16
7 8/16	15	13	12 13/16	46 8/16	15/16		1 3/16	4/16	1 7/16	12/16
8	16	13 13/16	13 11/16	49 8/16	1		1 4/16	4/16	1 8/16	13/16
8 8/16	17	14 11/16	14 9/16	52 8/16	1 1/16		1 5/16	5/16	1 10/16	14/16
9	18	15 9/16	15 6/16	55 8/16	1 2/16		1 7/16	5/16	1 11/16	15/16
9 8/16	19	16 7/16	16 4/16	58 8/16	1 3/16		1 8/16	5/16	1 13/16	15/16
10	20	17 5/16	17 2/16	61 8/16	1 4/16		1 9/16	6/16	1 14/16	1
10 8/16	21	18 3/16	17 15/16	64 8/16	1 5/16		1 10/16	6/16	2	1 1/16
11	22	19	18 13/16	67 8/16	1 6/16		1 12/16	6/16	2 1/16	1 2/16
11 8/16	23	19 14/16	19 11/16	70 8/16	1 7/16		1 13/16	6/16	2 3/16	1 3/16
12	24	20 12/16	20 8/16	73 8/16	1 8/16		1 14/16	7/16	2 4/16	1 3/16
13	26	22 8/16	22 4/16	79 8/16	1 10/16		2 1/16	7/16	2 7/16	1 5/16
14	28	24 4/16	23 15/16	85 8/16	1 12/16		2 3/16	8/16	2 10/16	1 7/16
15	30	25 15/16	25 11/16	91 8/16	1 14/16		2 6/16	8/16	2 13/16	1 8/16
16	32	27 11/16	27 6/16	97 8/16	2		2 8/16	9/16	3	1 10/16
17	34	29 7/16	29 1/16	103 8/16	2 2/16		2 11/16	10/16	3 3/16	1 11/16
18	36	31 2/16	30 13/16	109 8/16	2 4/16		2 13/16	10/16	3 6/16	1 13/16
19	38	32 14/16	32 8/16	115 8/16	2 6/16		3	11/16	3 9/16	1 15/16
20	40	34 10/16	34 3/16	121 8/16	2 8/16		3 2/16	11/16	3 12/16	2
21	42	36 5/16	35 15/16	127 8/16	2 10/16		3 5/16	12/16	3 15/16	2 2/16
22	44	38 1/16	37 10/16	133 8/16	2 12/16		3 7/16	12/16	4 2/16	2 4/16
23	46	39 13/16	39 6/16	139 8/16	2 14/16		3 10/16	13/16	4 5/16	2 5/16
24	48	41 8/16	41 1/16	145 8/16	3		3 12/16	13/16	4 8/16	2 7/16
25	50	43 4/16	42 12/16	151 8/16	3 2/16		3 15/16	14/16	4 11/16	2 8/16
26	52	45	44 8/16	157 8/16	3 4/16		4 1/16	15/16	4 14/16	2 10/16
27	54	46 11/16	46 3/16	163 8/16	3 6/16		4 4/16	15/16	5 1/16	2 12/16
28	56	48 7/16	47 14/16	169 8/16	3 8/16		4 6/16	1	5 4/16	2 13/16

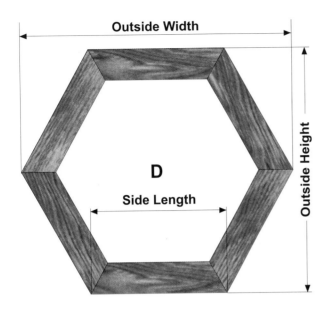

Outside Width

Outside Height

Side Length

D

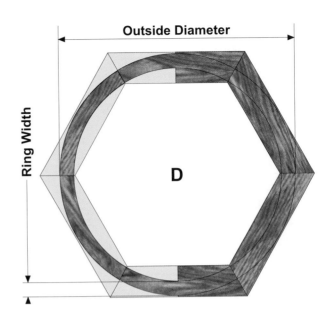

Outside Diameter

Ring Width

D

E

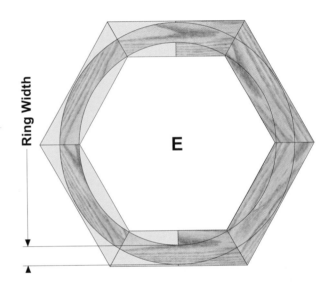

Ring Width

E

F

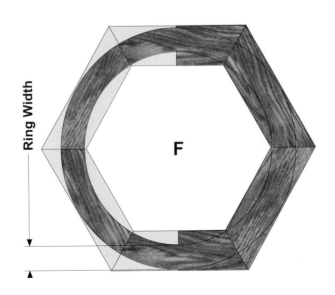

Ring Width

Outside Diameter

F

Side Length	Frame Width	Frame Height	Ring Max. OD	Material Req'd.	D Side Width	D Ring Width	E Side Width	E Ring Width	F Side Width	F Ring Width
8/16	1	14/16	14/16	4 8/16	2/16	1/16	2/16	1/16	2/16	1/16
10/16	1 4/16	1 1/16	1 1/16	5 4/16	2/16	1/16	3/16	1/16	3/16	2/16
12/16	1 8/16	1 5/16	1 5/16	6	3/16	1/16	3/16	2/16	3/16	2/16
14/16	1 12/16	1 8/16	1 8/16	6 12/16	3/16	1/16	4/16	2/16	4/16	2/16
1	2	1 12/16	1 11/16	7 8/16	4/16	2/16	4/16	2/16	5/16	3/16
1 4/16	2 8/16	2 3/16	2 2/16	9	4/16	2/16	5/16	3/16	6/16	4/16
1 8/16	3	2 10/16	2 9/16	10 8/16	5/16	3/16	6/16	3/16	7/16	4/16
1 12/16	3 8/16	3	3	12	6/16	3/16	7/16	4/16	8/16	5/16
2	4	3 7/16	3 7/16	13 8/16	7/16	3/16	8/16	4/16	9/16	6/16
2 4/16	4 8/16	3 14/16	3 14/16	15	8/16	4/16	9/16	5/16	10/16	6/16
2 8/16	5	4 5/16	4 4/16	16 8/16	9/16	4/16	10/16	6/16	11/16	7/16
2 12/16	5 8/16	4 12/16	4 11/16	18	10/16	5/16	11/16	6/16	12/16	8/16
3	6	5 3/16	5 2/16	19 8/16	11/16	5/16	12/16	7/16	14/16	8/16
3 4/16	6 8/16	5 10/16	5 9/16	21	11/16	5/16	13/16	7/16	15/16	9/16
3 8/16	7	6 1/16	6	22 8/16	12/16	6/16	14/16	8/16	1	10/16
3 12/16	7 8/16	6 8/16	6 7/16	24	13/16	6/16	15/16	8/16	1 1/16	11/16
4	8	6 15/16	6 13/16	25 8/16	14/16	7/16	1	9/16	1 2/16	11/16
4 4/16	8 8/16	7 6/16	7 4/16	27	15/16	7/16	1 1/16	10/16	1 3/16	12/16
4 8/16	9	7 13/16	7 11/16	28 8/16	1	8/16	1 2/16	10/16	1 4/16	13/16
4 12/16	9 8/16	8 3/16	8 2/16	30	1 1/16	8/16	1 3/16	11/16	1 5/16	13/16
5	10	8 10/16	8 9/16	31 8/16	1 2/16	8/16	1 4/16	11/16	1 7/16	14/16
5 4/16	10 8/16	9 1/16	9	33	1 2/16	9/16	1 5/16	12/16	1 8/16	15/16
5 8/16	11	9 8/16	9 7/16	34 8/16	1 3/16	9/16	1 6/16	12/16	1 9/16	15/16
5 12/16	11 8/16	9 15/16	9 13/16	36	1 4/16	10/16	1 7/16	13/16	1 10/16	1
6	12	10 6/16	10 4/16	37 8/16	1 5/16	10/16	1 8/16	13/16	1 11/16	1 1/16
6 8/16	13	11 4/16	11 2/16	40 8/16	1 7/16	11/16	1 10/16	15/16	1 13/16	1 2/16
7	14	12 2/16	12	43 8/16	1 9/16	12/16	1 12/16	1	2	1 4/16
7 8/16	15	13	12 13/16	46 8/16	1 10/16	13/16	1 14/16	1 1/16	2 2/16	1 5/16
8	16	13 13/16	13 11/16	49 8/16	1 12/16	13/16	2	1 2/16	2 4/16	1 6/16
8 8/16	17	14 11/16	14 9/16	52 8/16	1 14/16	14/16	2 2/16	1 3/16	2 6/16	1 8/16
9	18	15 9/16	15 6/16	55 8/16	2	15/16	2 4/16	1 4/16	2 9/16	1 9/16
9 8/16	19	16 7/16	16 4/16	58 8/16	2 1/16	1	2 6/16	1 5/16	2 11/16	1 11/16
10	20	17 5/16	17 2/16	61 8/16	2 3/16	1 1/16	2 8/16	1 6/16	2 13/16	1 12/16
10 8/16	21	18 3/16	17 15/16	64 8/16	2 5/16	1 2/16	2 10/16	1 8/16	2 15/16	1 13/16
11	22	19	18 13/16	67 8/16	2 7/16	1 2/16	2 12/16	1 9/16	3 2/16	1 15/16
11 8/16	23	19 14/16	19 11/16	70 4/16	2 8/16	1 3/16	2 14/16	1 10/16	3 4/16	2
12	24	20 12/16	20 8/16	73 8/16	2 10/16	1 4/16	3	1 11/16	3 6/16	2 2/16
13	26	22 8/16	22 4/16	79 8/16	2 14/16	1 6/16	3 4/16	1 13/16	3 11/16	2 4/16
14	28	24 4/16	23 15/16	85 8/16	3 1/16	1 7/16	3 8/16	1 15/16	3 15/16	2 7/16
15	30	25 15/16	25 11/16	91 8/16	3 5/16	1 9/16	3 12/16	2 2/16	4 4/16	2 10/16
16	32	27 11/16	27 6/16	97 8/16	3 8/16	1 11/16	4	2 4/16	4 8/16	2 13/16
17	34	29 7/16	29 1/16	103 8/16	3 12/16	1 12/16	4 4/16	2 6/16	4 13/16	3
18	36	31 2/16	30 13/16	109 8/16	3 15/16	1 14/16	4 8/16	2 8/16	5 1/16	3 3/16
19	38	32 14/16	32 8/16	115 8/16	4 3/16	2	4 12/16	2 11/16	5 6/16	3 5/16
20	40	34 10/16	34 3/16	121 8/16	4 6/16	2 2/16	5	2 13/16	5 10/16	3 8/16
21	42	36 5/16	35 15/16	127 8/16	4 10/16	2 3/16	5 4/16	2 15/16	5 15/16	3 11/16
22	44	38 1/16	37 10/16	133 8/16	4 13/16	2 5/16	5 8/16	3 1/16	6 3/16	3 14/16
23	46	39 13/16	39 6/16	139 8/16	5 1/16	2 7/16	5 12/16	3 4/16	6 8/16	4 1/16
24	48	41 8/16	41 1/16	145 8/16	5 4/16	2 8/16	6	3 6/16	6 12/16	4 3/16
25	50	43 4/16	42 12/16	151 8/16	5 8/16	2 10/16	6 4/16	3 8/16	7 1/16	4 6/16
26	52	45	44 8/16	157 8/16	5 11/16	2 12/16	6 8/16	3 10/16	7 5/16	4 9/16
27	54	46 11/16	46 3/16	163 8/16	5 15/16	2 13/16	6 12/16	3 13/16	7 10/16	4 12/16
28	56	48 7/16	47 14/16	169 8/16	6 2/16	2 15/16	7	3 15/16	7 14/16	4 15/16

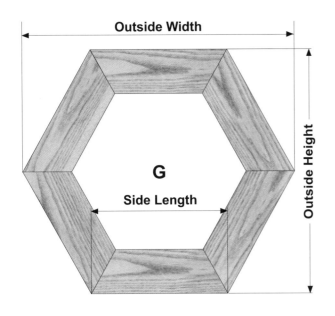

Outside Width

Outside Height

Side Length

G

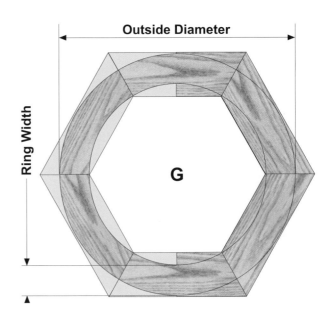

Outside Diameter

Ring Width

G

H

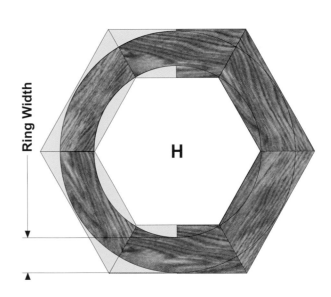

Ring Width

H

I

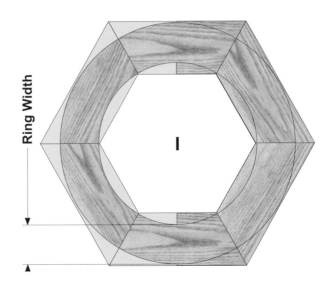

Ring Width

Outside Diameter

I

Side Length	Frame Width	Frame Height	Ring Max. OD	Material Req'd.	G Side Width	G Ring Width	H Side Width	H Ring Width	I Side Width	I Ring Width
8/16	1	14/16	14/16	4 8/16	3/16	2/16	3/16	2/16	3/16	2/16
10/16	1 4/16	1 1/16	1 1/16	5 4/16	3/16	2/16	3/16	2/16	4/16	3/16
12/16	1 8/16	1 5/16	1 5/16	6	4/16	3/16	4/16	3/16	5/16	3/16
14/16	1 12/16	1 8/16	1 8/16	6 12/16	4/16	3/16	5/16	3/16	5/16	4/16
1	2	1 12/16	1 11/16	7 8/16	5/16	3/16	6/16	4/16	6/16	5/16
1 4/16	2 8/16	2 3/16	2 2/16	9	6/16	4/16	7/16	5/16	8/16	6/16
1 8/16	3	2 10/16	2 9/16	10 8/16	8/16	5/16	8/16	6/16	9/16	7/16
1 12/16	3 8/16	3	3	12	9/16	6/16	10/16	7/16	11/16	8/16
2	4	3 7/16	3 7/16	13 8/16	10/16	7/16	11/16	8/16	12/16	9/16
2 4/16	4 8/16	3 14/16	3 14/16	15	11/16	8/16	12/16	9/16	14/16	10/16
2 8/16	5	4 5/16	4 4/16	16 8/16	13/16	8/16	14/16	10/16	15/16	11/16
2 12/16	5 8/16	4 12/16	4 11/16	18	14/16	9/16	15/16	11/16	1 1/16	12/16
3	6	5 3/16	5 2/16	19 8/16	15/16	10/16	1 1/16	12/16	1 2/16	14/16
3 4/16	6 8/16	5 10/16	5 9/16	21	1	11/16	1 2/16	13/16	1 4/16	15/16
3 8/16	7	6 1/16	6	22 8/16	1 2/16	12/16	1 3/16	14/16	1 5/16	1
3 12/16	7 8/16	6 8/16	6 7/16	24	1 3/16	13/16	1 5/16	15/16	1 7/16	1 1/16
4	8	6 15/16	6 13/16	25 8/16	1 4/16	14/16	1 6/16	1	1 8/16	1 2/16
4 4/16	8 8/16	7 6/16	7 4/16	27	1 5/16	14/16	1 7/16	1 1/16	1 10/16	1 3/16
4 8/16	9	7 13/16	7 11/16	28 8/16	1 7/16	15/16	1 9/16	1 2/16	1 11/16	1 4/16
4 12/16	9 8/16	8 3/16	8 2/16	30	1 8/16	1	1 10/16	1 3/16	1 13/16	1 5/16
5	10	8 10/16	8 9/16	31 8/16	1 9/16	1 1/16	1 12/16	1 4/16	1 14/16	1 7/16
5 4/16	10 8/16	9 1/16	9	33	1 10/16	1 2/16	1 13/16	1 5/16	2	1 8/16
5 8/16	11	9 8/16	9 7/16	34 8/16	1 12/16	1 3/16	1 14/16	1 6/16	2 1/16	1 9/16
5 12/16	11 8/16	9 15/16	9 13/16	36	1 13/16	1 3/16	2	1 7/16	2 3/16	1 10/16
6	12	10 6/16	10 4/16	37 8/16	1 14/16	1 4/16	2 1/16	1 8/16	2 4/16	1 11/16
6 8/16	13	11 4/16	11 2/16	40 8/16	2 1/16	1 6/16	2 4/16	1 10/16	2 7/16	1 13/16
7	14	12 2/16	12	43 8/16	2 3/16	1 8/16	2 7/16	1 12/16	2 10/16	2
7 8/16	15	13	12 13/16	46 8/16	2 6/16	1 9/16	2 9/16	1 14/16	2 13/16	2 2/16
8	16	13 13/16	13 11/16	49 8/16	2 8/16	1 11/16	2 12/16	2	3	2 4/16
8 8/16	17	14 11/16	14 9/16	52 8/16	2 11/16	1 13/16	2 15/16	2 2/16	3 3/16	2 6/16
9	18	15 9/16	15 6/16	55 8/16	2 13/16	1 14/16	3 2/16	2 4/16	3 6/16	2 9/16
9 8/16	19	16 7/16	16 4/16	58 8/16	3	2	3 4/16	2 6/16	3 9/16	2 11/16
10	20	17 5/16	17 2/16	61 8/16	3 2/16	2 2/16	3 7/16	2 8/16	3 12/16	2 13/16
10 8/16	21	18 3/16	17 15/16	64 8/16	3 5/16	2 3/16	3 10/16	2 10/16	3 15/16	2 15/16
11	22	19	18 13/16	67 8/16	3 7/16	2 5/16	3 13/16	2 12/16	4 2/16	3 2/16
11 8/16	23	19 14/16	19 11/16	70 8/16	3 10/16	2 7/16	3 15/16	2 14/16	4 5/16	3 4/16
12	24	20 12/16	20 8/16	73 8/16	3 12/16	2 9/16	4 2/16	3	4 8/16	3 6/16
13	26	22 8/16	22 4/16	79 8/16	4 1/16	2 12/16	4 8/16	3 3/16	4 14/16	3 11/16
14	28	24 4/16	23 15/16	85 8/16	4 6/16	2 15/16	4 13/16	3 7/16	5 4/16	3 15/16
15	30	25 15/16	25 11/16	91 8/16	4 11/16	3 3/16	5 3/16	3 11/16	5 10/16	4 4/16
16	32	27 11/16	27 6/16	97 8/16	5	3 6/16	5 8/16	3 15/16	6	4 8/16
17	34	29 7/16	29 1/16	103 8/16	5 5/16	3 9/16	5 14/16	4 3/16	6 6/16	4 13/16
18	36	31 2/16	30 13/16	109 8/16	5 10/16	3 13/16	6 3/16	4 7/16	6 12/16	5 1/16
19	38	32 14/16	32 8/16	115 8/16	5 15/16	4	6 9/16	4 11/16	7 2/16	5 6/16
20	40	34 10/16	34 3/16	121 8/16	6 4/16	4 4/16	6 14/16	4 15/16	7 8/16	5 10/16
21	42	36 5/16	35 15/16	127 8/16	6 9/16	4 7/16	7 4/16	5 3/16	7 14/16	5 15/16
22	44	38 1/16	37 10/16	133 8/16	6 14/16	4 10/16	7 9/16	5 7/16	8 4/16	6 3/16
23	46	39 13/16	39 6/16	139 8/16	7 3/16	4 14/16	7 15/16	5 11/16	8 10/16	6 8/16
24	48	41 8/16	41 1/16	145 8/16	7 8/16	5 1/16	8 4/16	5 15/16	9	6 12/16
25	50	43 4/16	42 12/16	151 8/16	7 13/16	5 4/16	8 10/16	6 3/16	9 6/16	7 1/16
26	52	45	44 8/16	157 8/16	8 2/16	5 8/16	8 15/16	6 7/16	9 12/16	7 5/16
27	54	46 11/16	46 3/16	163 8/16	8 7/16	5 11/16	9 5/16	6 11/16	10 2/16	7 10/16
28	56	48 7/16	47 14/16	169 8/16	8 12/16	5 15/16	9 10/16	6 15/16	10 8/16	7 14/16

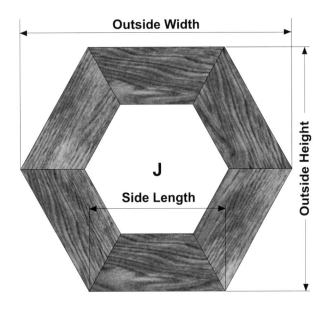

Outside Width

Outside Height

Side Length

J

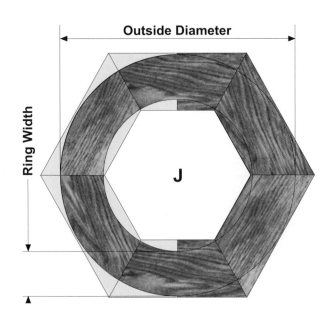

Outside Diameter

Ring Width

J

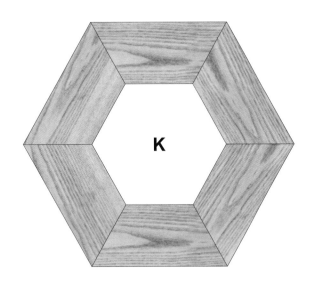

K

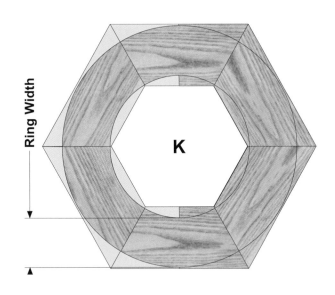

Ring Width

K

L

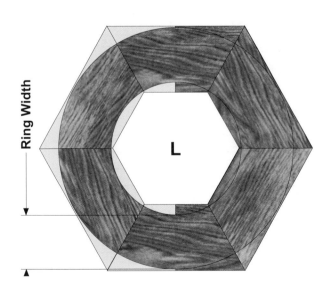

Ring Width

L

50

Side Length	Frame Width	Frame Height	Ring Max. OD	Material Req'd.	J Side Width	J Ring Width	K Side Width	K Ring Width	L Side Width	L Ring Width
8/16	1	14/16	14/16	4 8/16	3/16	3/16	4/16	3/16	4/16	3/16
10/16	1 4/16	1 1/16	1 1/16	5 4/16	4/16	3/16	4/16	4/16	5/16	4/16
12/16	1 8/16	1 5/16	1 5/16	6	5/16	4/16	5/16	4/16	6/16	5/16
14/16	1 12/16	1 8/16	1 8/16	6 12/16	6/16	4/16	6/16	5/16	7/16	5/16
1	2	1 12/16	1 11/16	7 8/16	7/16	5/16	7/16	6/16	8/16	6/16
1 4/16	2 8/16	2 3/16	2 2/16	9	8/16	6/16	9/16	7/16	9/16	8/16
1 8/16	3	2 10/16	2 9/16	10 8/16	10/16	8/16	11/16	8/16	11/16	9/16
1 12/16	3 8/16	3	3	12	11/16	9/16	12/16	10/16	13/16	11/16
2	4	3 7/16	3 7/16	13	13/16	10/16	14/16	11/16	15/16	12/16
2 4/16	4 8/16	3 14/16	3 14/16	15	15/16	11/16	1	13/16	1 1/16	14/16
2 8/16	5	4 5/16	4 4/16	16 8/16	1	13/16	1 2/16	14/16	1 3/16	1
2 12/16	5 8/16	4 12/16	4 11/16	18	1 2/16	14/16	1 3/16	1	1 5/16	1 1/16
3	6	5 3/16	5 2/16	19 8/16	1 4/16	15/16	1 5/16	1 1/16	1 7/16	1 3/16
3 4/16	6 8/16	5 10/16	5 9/16	21	1 5/16	1 1/16	1 7/16	1 2/16	1 8/16	1 4/16
3 8/16	7	6 1/16	6	22 8/16	1 7/16	1 2/16	1 9/16	1 4/16	1 10/16	1 6/16
3 12/16	7 8/16	6 8/16	6 7/16	24	1 8/16	1 3/16	1 10/16	1 5/16	1 12/16	1 7/16
4	8	6 15/16	6 13/16	25 8/16	1 10/16	1 4/16	1 12/16	1 7/16	1 14/16	1 9/16
4 4/16	8 8/16	7 6/16	7 4/16	27	1 12/16	1 6/16	1 14/16	1 8/16	2	1 10/16
4 8/16	9	7 13/16	7 11/16	28 8/16	1 13/16	1 7/16	2	1 9/16	2 2/16	1 12/16
4 12/16	9 8/16	8 3/16	8 2/16	30	1 15/16	1 8/16	2 1/16	1 11/16	2 4/16	1 14/16
5	10	8 10/16	8 9/16	31 8/16	2 1/16	1 9/16	2 3/16	1 12/16	2 6/16	1 15/16
5 4/16	10 8/16	9 1/16	9	33	2 2/16	1 11/16	2 5/16	1 14/16	2 7/16	2 1/16
5 8/16	11	9 8/16	9 7/16	34 8/16	2 4/16	1 12/16	2 7/16	1 15/16	2 9/16	2 2/16
5 12/16	11 8/16	9 15/16	9 13/16	36	2 5/16	1 13/16	2 8/16	2 1/16	2 11/16	2 4/16
6	12	10 6/16	10 4/16	37 8/16	2 7/16	1 15/16	2 10/16	2 2/16	2 13/16	2 5/16
6 8/16	13	11 4/16	11 2/16	40 8/16	2 10/16	2 1/16	2 14/16	2 5/16	3 1/16	2 9/16
7	14	12 2/16	12	43 8/16	2 14/16	2 4/16	3 1/16	2 8/16	3 5/16	2 12/16
7 8/16	15	13	12 13/16	46 8/16	3 1/16	2 6/16	3 5/16	2 10/16	3 8/16	2 15/16
8	16	13 13/16	13 11/16	49 8/16	3 4/16	2 9/16	3 8/16	2 13/16	3 12/16	3 2/16
8 8/16	17	14 11/16	14 9/16	52 8/16	3 7/16	2 11/16	3 12/16	3	4	3 5/16
9	18	15 9/16	15 6/16	55 8/16	3 11/16	2 14/16	3 15/16	3 3/16	4 4/16	3 8/16
9 8/16	19	16 7/16	16 4/16	58 8/16	3 14/16	3	4 3/16	3 6/16	4 7/16	3 11/16
10	20	17 5/16	17 2/16	61 8/16	4 1/16	3 3/16	4 6/16	3 9/16	4 11/16	3 14/16
10 8/16	21	18 3/16	17 15/16	64 8/16	4 4/16	3 5/16	4 10/16	3 11/16	4 15/16	4 1/16
11	22	19	18 13/16	67 8/16	4 8/16	3 8/16	4 13/16	3 14/16	5 3/16	4 5/16
11 8/16	23	19 14/16	19 11/16	70 8/16	4 11/16	3 11/16	5 1/16	4 1/16	5 6/16	4 8/16
12	24	20 12/16	20 8/16	73 8/16	4 14/16	3 13/16	5 4/16	4 4/16	5 10/16	4 11/16
13	26	22 8/16	22 4/16	79 8/16	5 5/16	4 2/16	5 11/16	4 10/16	6 2/16	5 1/16
14	28	24 4/16	23 15/16	85 8/16	5 11/16	4 7/16	6 2/16	4 15/16	6 9/16	5 7/16
15	30	25 15/16	25 11/16	91 8/16	6 2/16	4 12/16	6 9/16	5 5/16	7 1/16	5 14/16
16	32	27 11/16	27 6/16	97 8/16	6 8/16	5 1/16	7	5 11/16	7 8/16	6 4/16
17	34	29 7/16	29 1/16	103 8/16	6 15/16	5 7/16	7 7/16	6	8	6 10/16
18	36	31 2/16	30 13/16	109 8/16	7 5/16	5 12/16	7 14/16	6 6/16	8 7/16	7
19	38	32 14/16	32 8/16	115 8/16	7 12/16	6 1/16	8 5/16	6 12/16	8 15/16	7 6/16
20	40	34 10/16	34 3/16	121 8/16	8 2/16	6 6/16	8 12/16	7 1/16	9 6/16	7 13/16
21	42	36 5/16	35 15/16	127 8/16	8 9/16	6 11/16	9 3/16	7 7/16	9 14/16	8 3/16
22	44	38 1/16	37 10/16	133 8/16	8 15/16	7	9 10/16	7 13/16	10 5/16	8 9/16
23	46	39 13/16	39 6/16	139 8/16	9 6/16	7 5/16	10 1/16	8 2/16	10 13/16	8 15/16
24	48	41 8/16	41 1/16	145 8/16	9 12/16	7 10/16	10 8/16	8 8/16	11 4/16	9 6/16
25	50	43 4/16	42 12/16	151 8/16	10 3/16	7 15/16	10 15/16	8 14/16	11 12/16	9 12/16
26	52	45	44 8/16	157 8/16	10 9/16	8 4/16	11 6/16	9 3/16	12 3/16	10 2/16
27	54	46 11/16	46 3/16	163 8/16	11	8 9/16	11 13/16	9 9/16	12 11/16	10 8/16
28	56	48 7/16	47 14/16	169 8/16	11 6/16	8 15/16	12 4/16	9 15/16	13 2/16	10 15/16

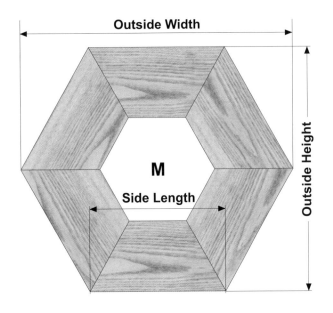

Outside Width

Outside Height

Side Length

M

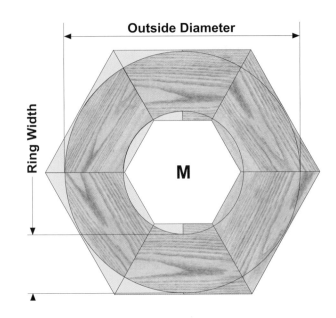

Outside Diameter

Ring Width

M

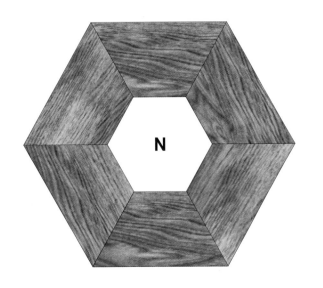

N

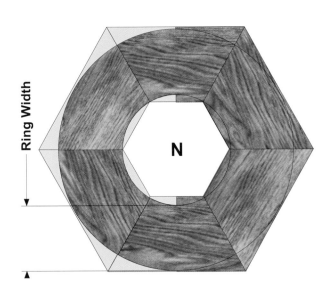

Ring Width

N

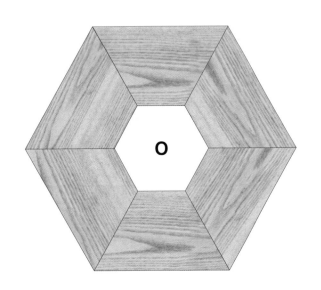

O

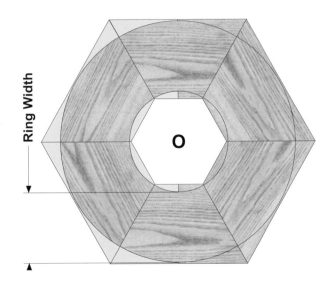

Ring Width

Outside Diameter

O

Side Length	Frame Width	Frame Height	Ring Max. OD	Material Req'd.	M Side Width	M Ring Width	N Side Width	N Ring Width	O Side Width	O Ring Width
8/16	1	14/16	14/16	4 8/16	4/16	3/16	4/16	4/16	5/16	4/16
10/16	1 4/16	1 1/16	1 1/16	5 4/16	5/16	4/16	5/16	5/16	6/16	5/16
12/16	1 8/16	1 5/16	1 5/16	6	6/16	5/16	6/16	6/16	7/16	6/16
14/16	1 12/16	1 8/16	1 8/16	6 12/16	7/16	6/16	7/16	6/16	8/16	7/16
1	2	1 12/16	1 11/16	7 8/16	8/16	7/16	9/16	7/16	9/16	8/16
1 4/16	2 8/16	2 3/16	2 2/16	9	10/16	9/16	11/16	9/16	11/16	10/16
1 8/16	3	2 10/16	2 9/16	10 8/16	12/16	10/16	13/16	11/16	14/16	12/16
1 12/16	3 8/16	3	3	12	14/16	12/16	15/16	13/16	1	14/16
2	4	3 7/16	3 7/16	13 8/16	1	14/16	1 1/16	15/16	1 2/16	1
2 4/16	4 8/16	3 14/16	3 14/16	15	1 2/16	15/16	1 3/16	1 1/16	1 4/16	1 2/16
2 8/16	5	4 5/16	4 4/16	16 8/16	1 4/16	1 1/16	1 5/16	1 2/16	1 7/16	1 4/16
2 12/16	5 8/16	4 12/16	4 11/16	18	1 6/16	1 3/16	1 7/16	1 4/16	1 9/16	1 6/16
3	6	5 3/16	5 2/16	19 8/16	1 8/16	1 4/16	1 10/16	1 6/16	1 11/16	1 8/16
3 4/16	6 8/16	5 10/16	5 9/16	21	1 10/16	1 6/16	1 12/16	1 8/16	1 13/16	1 10/16
3 8/16	7	6 1/16	6	22 8/16	1 12/16	1 8/16	1 14/16	1 10/16	2	1 12/16
3 12/16	7 8/16	6 8/16	6 7/16	24	1 14/16	1 10/16	2	1 12/16	2 2/16	1 14/16
4	8	6 15/16	6 13/16	25 8/16	2	1 11/16	2 2/16	1 14/16	2 4/16	2
4 4/16	8 8/16	7 6/16	7 4/16	27	2 2/16	1 13/16	2 4/16	1 15/16	2 6/16	2 2/16
4 8/16	9	7 13/16	7 11/16	28 8/16	2 4/16	1 15/16	2 6/16	2 1/16	2 9/16	2 4/16
4 12/16	9 8/16	8 3/16	8 2/16	30	2 6/16	2	2 8/16	2 3/16	2 11/16	2 6/16
5	10	8 10/16	8 9/16	31 8/16	2 8/16	2 2/16	2 11/16	2 5/16	2 13/16	2 8/16
5 4/16	10 8/16	9 1/16	9	33	2 10/16	2 4/16	2 13/16	2 7/16	2 15/16	2 10/16
5 8/16	11	9 8/16	9 7/16	34 8/16	2 12/16	2 5/16	2 15/16	2 9/16	3 2/16	2 12/16
5 12/16	11 8/16	9 15/16	9 13/16	36	2 14/16	2 7/16	3 1/16	2 10/16	3 4/16	2 14/16
6	12	10 6/16	10 4/16	37 8/16	3	2 9/16	3 3/16	2 12/16	3 6/16	3
6 8/16	13	11 4/16	11 2/16	40 8/16	3 4/16	2 12/16	3 7/16	3	3 11/16	3 4/16
7	14	12 2/16	12	43 8/16	3 8/16	3	3 12/16	3 4/16	3 15/16	3 8/16
7 8/16	15	13	12 13/16	46 8/16	3 12/16	3 3/16	4	3 7/16	4 4/16	3 12/16
8	16	13 13/16	13 11/16	49 8/16	4	3 6/16	4 4/16	3 11/16	4 8/16	4
8 8/16	17	14 11/16	14 9/16	52 8/16	4 4/16	3 10/16	4 8/16	3 15/16	4 13/16	4 4/16
9	18	15 9/16	15 6/16	55 8/16	4 8/16	3 13/16	4 13/16	4 2/16	5 1/16	4 8/16
9 8/16	19	16 7/16	16 4/16	58 8/16	4 12/16	4 1/16	5 1/16	4 6/16	5 6/16	4 12/16
10	20	17 5/16	17 2/16	61 8/16	5	4 4/16	5 5/16	4 10/16	5 10/16	4 15/16
10 8/16	21	18 3/16	17 15/16	64 8/16	5 4/16	4 7/16	5 9/16	4 13/16	5 15/16	5 3/16
11	22	19	18 13/16	67 8/16	5 8/16	4 11/16	5 14/16	5 1/16	6 3/16	5 7/16
11 8/16	23	19 14/16	19 11/16	70 8/16	5 12/16	4 14/16	6 2/16	5 5/16	6 8/16	5 11/16
12	24	20 12/16	20 8/16	73 8/16	6	5 2/16	6 6/16	5 9/16	6 12/16	5 15/16
13	26	22 8/16	22 4/16	79 8/16	6 8/16	5 8/16	6 15/16	6	7 5/16	6 7/16
14	28	24 4/16	23 15/16	85 8/16	7	5 15/16	7 7/16	6 7/16	7 14/16	6 15/16
15	30	25 15/16	25 11/16	91 8/16	7 8/16	6 6/16	8	6 15/16	8 7/16	7 7/16
16	32	27 11/16	27 6/16	97 8/16	8	6 13/16	8 8/16	7 6/16	9	7 15/16
17	34	29 7/16	29 1/16	103 8/16	8 8/16	7 4/16	9 1/16	7 13/16	9 9/16	8 7/16
18	36	31 2/16	30 13/16	109 8/16	9	7 10/16	9 9/16	8 5/16	10 2/16	8 15/16
19	38	32 14/16	32 8/16	115 8/16	9 8/16	8 1/16	10 2/16	8 12/16	10 11/16	9 7/16
20	40	34 10/16	34 3/16	121 8/16	10	8 8/16	10 10/16	9 4/16	11 4/16	9 15/16
21	42	36 5/16	35 15/16	127 8/16	10 8/16	8 15/16	11 3/16	9 11/16	11 13/16	10 7/16
22	44	38 1/16	37 10/16	133 8/16	11	9 6/16	11 11/16	10 2/16	12 6/16	10 15/16
23	46	39 13/16	39 6/16	139 8/16	11 8/16	9 13/16	12 4/16	10 10/16	12 15/16	11 7/16
24	48	41 8/16	41 1/16	145 8/16	12	10 3/16	12 12/16	11 1/16	13 8/16	11 15/16
25	50	43 4/16	42 12/16	151 8/16	12 8/16	10 10/16	13 5/16	11 8/16	14 1/16	12 7/16
26	52	45	44 8/16	157 8/16	13	11 1/16	13 13/16	12	14 10/16	12 15/16
27	54	46 11/16	46 3/16	163 8/16	13 8/16	11 8/16	14 6/16	12 7/16	15 3/16	13 7/16
28	56	48 7/16	47 14/16	169 8/16	14	11 15/16	14 14/16	12 15/16	15 12/16	13 15/16

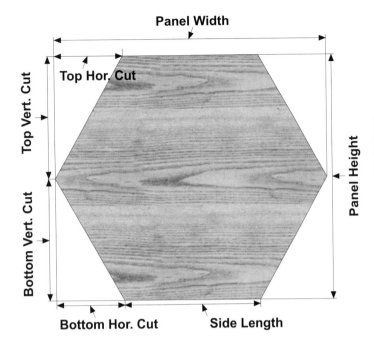

Panel Width

Top Vert. Cut

Top Hor. Cut

Bottom Vert. Cut

Panel Height

Bottom Hor. Cut

Side Length

The Chart below shows the formulas that were used in the process of laying out the 6 sided shapes. These are included to assist you if you are designing a project to a size that is not illustrated in the Dimension Charts provided. We hope you find them helpful as you design your projects.

6 SIDED PANEL FORMULAS		
Panel Width =	Panel Height x	1.149
Panel Height =	Panel Width x	0.870
Side Length =	Panel Height x	0.500
Side Length =	Panel Width x	0.578
Top Hor. Cut =	Panel Width x	0.253
Bott. Hor. Cut =	Panel Width x	0.253
Top Vert. Cut =	Panel Width x	0.500
Bott.Vert. Cut =	Panel Width x	0.500

PANEL WIDTH	PANEL HEIGHT	SIDE LENGTH	TOP HOR. CUT	BOTTOM HOR. CUT	TOP VERT. CUT	BOTTOM VERT. CUT
12/16	10/16	6/16	3/16	3/16	5/16	5/16
1	14/16	8/16	4/16	4/16	7/16	7/16
1 4/16	1 1/16	10/16	5/16	5/16	9/16	9/16
1 8/16	1 5/16	12/16	6/16	6/16	10/16	10/16
1 12/16	1 8/16	14/16	14/16	14/16	12/16	12/16
2	1 12/16	1	1	1	14/16	14/16
2 4/16	1 15/16	1 2/16	1 2/16	1 2/16	1	1
2 8/16	2 3/16	1 4/16	1 4/16	1 4/16	1 1/16	1 1/16
2 12/16	2 6/16	1 6/16	1 6/16	1 6/16	1 3/16	1 3/16
3	2 10/16	1 8/16	1 8/16	1 8/16	1 5/16	1 5/16
3 4/16	2 13/16	1 10/16	1 10/16	1 10/16	1 7/16	1 7/16
3 8/16	3 1/16	1 12/16	1 12/16	1 12/16	1 8/16	1 8/16
3 12/16	3 4/16	1 14/16	1 14/16	1 14/16	1 10/16	1 10/16
4	3 8/16	2	2	2	1 12/16	1 12/16
4 4/16	3 11/16	2 2/16	2 2/16	2 2/16	1 14/16	1 14/16
4 8/16	3 15/16	2 4/16	2 4/16	2 4/16	1 15/16	1 15/16
4 12/16	4 2/16	2 6/16	2 6/16	2 6/16	2 1/16	2 1/16
5	4 6/16	2 8/16	2 8/16	2 8/16	2 3/16	2 3/16
5 4/16	4 9/16	2 10/16	2 10/16	2 10/16	2 5/16	2 5/16
5 8/16	4 13/16	2 12/16	2 12/16	2 12/16	2 6/16	2 6/16
5 12/16	5	2 14/16	2 14/16	2 14/16	2 8/16	2 8/16
6	5 4/16	3	3	3	2 10/16	2 10/16
6 4/16	5 7/16	3 2/16	3 2/16	3 2/16	2 12/16	2 12/16
6 8/16	5 10/16	3 4/16	3 4/16	3 4/16	2 13/16	2 13/16
6 12/16	5 14/16	3 6/16	3 6/16	3 6/16	2 15/16	2 15/16
7	6 1/16	3 8/16	3 8/16	3 8/16	3 1/16	3 1/16
7 4/16	6 5/16	3 10/16	3 10/16	3 10/16	3 2/16	3 2/16
7 8/16	6 8/16	3 12/16	3 12/16	3 12/16	3 4/16	3 4/16
7 12/16	6 12/16	3 14/16	3 14/16	3 14/16	3 6/16	3 6/16
8	6 15/16	4	4	4	3 8/16	3 8/16
8 4/16	7 3/16	4 2/16	4 2/16	4 2/16	3 9/16	3 9/16
8 8/16	7 6/16	4 4/16	4 4/16	4 4/16	3 11/16	3 11/16

PANEL WIDTH	PANEL HEIGHT	SIDE LENGTH	TOP HOR. CUT	BOTTOM HOR. CUT	TOP VERT. CUT	BOTTOM VERT. CUT
8 12/16	7 10/16	4 6/16	2 3/16	2 3/16	3 13/16	3 13/16
9	7 13/16	4 8/16	2 4/16	2 4/16	3 15/16	3 15/16
9 4/16	8 1/16	4 10/16	2 5/16	2 5/16	4	4
9 8/16	8 4/16	4 12/16	2 6/16	2 6/16	4 2/16	4 2/16
9 12/16	8 8/16	4 14/16	2 7/16	2 7/16	4 4/16	4 4/16
10	8 11/16	5	2 8/16	2 8/16	4 6/16	4 6/16
10 4/16	8 15/16	5 2/16	2 9/16	2 9/16	4 7/16	4 7/16
10 8/16	9 2/16	5 4/16	2 11/16	2 11/16	4 9/16	4 9/16
10 12/16	9 6/16	5 6/16	2 12/16	2 12/16	4 11/16	4 11/16
11	9 9/16	5 8/16	2 13/16	2 13/16	4 13/16	4 13/16
11 4/16	9 13/16	5 10/16	2 14/16	2 14/16	4 14/16	4 14/16
11 8/16	10	5 12/16	2 15/16	2 15/16	5	5
12	10 7/16	6	3 1/16	3 1/16	5 4/16	5 4/16
12 4/16	10 11/16	6 2/16	3 2/16	3 2/16	5 5/16	5 5/16
12 8/16	10 14/16	6 4/16	3 3/16	3 3/16	5 7/16	5 7/16
12 12/16	11 1/16	6 6/16	3 4/16	3 4/16	5 9/16	5 9/16
13	11 5/16	6 8/16	3 5/16	3 5/16	5 10/16	5 10/16
13 4/16	11 8/16	6 10/16	3 6/16	3 6/16	5 12/16	5 12/16
13 8/16	11 12/16	6 12/16	3 7/16	3 7/16	5 14/16	5 14/16
13 12/16	11 15/16	6 14/16	3 8/16	3 8/16	6	6
14	12 3/16	7	3 9/16	3 9/16	6 1/16	6 1/16
14 8/16	12 10/16	7 4/16	3 11/16	3 11/16	6 5/16	6 5/16
15	13 1/16	7 8/16	3 13/16	3 13/16	6 8/16	6 8/16
15 8/16	13 8/16	7 12/16	3 15/16	3 15/16	6 12/16	6 12/16
16	13 15/16	8	4 1/16	4 1/16	6 15/16	6 15/16
16 8/16	14 6/16	8 4/16	4 3/16	4 3/16	7 3/16	7 3/16
17	14 13/16	8 8/16	4 5/16	4 5/16	7 6/16	7 6/16
17 8/16	15 4/16	8 12/16	4 7/16	4 7/16	7 10/16	7 10/16
18	15 11/16	9	4 9/16	4 9/16	7 13/16	7 13/16
19	16 8/16	9 8/16	4 13/16	4 13/16	8 4/16	8 4/16
20	17 6/16	10	5 1/16	5 1/16	8 11/16	8 11/16
21	18 4/16	10 8/16	5 5/16	5 5/16	9 2/16	9 2/16
22	19 2/16	11	5 9/16	5 9/16	9 9/16	9 9/16
23	20	11 8/16	5 13/16	5 13/16	10	10
24	20 14/16	12	6 1/16	6 1/16	10 7/16	10 7/16
25	21 12/16	12 8/16	6 5/16	6 5/16	10 14/16	10 14/16
26	22 10/16	13	6 9/16	6 9/16	11 5/16	11 5/16
27	23 8/16	13 8/16	6 13/16	6 13/16	11 12/16	11 12/16
28	24 6/16	14	7 1/16	7 1/16	12 3/16	12 3/16
29	25 4/16	14 8/16	7 5/16	7 5/16	12 10/16	12 10/16
30	26 2/16	15	7 9/16	7 9/16	13 1/16	13 1/16
31	27	15 8/16	7 13/16	7 13/16	13 8/16	13 8/16
32	27 13/16	16	8 2/16	8 2/16	13 15/16	13 15/16
33	28 11/16	16 8/16	8 6/16	8 6/16	14 6/16	14 6/16
34	29 9/16	17	8 10/16	8 10/16	14 13/16	14 13/16
35	30 7/16	17 8/16	8 14/16	8 14/16	15 4/16	15 4/16
36	31 5/16	18	9 2/16	9 2/16	15 11/16	15 11/16
37	32 3/16	18 8/16	9 6/16	9 6/16	16 2/16	16 2/16
38	33 1/16	19	9 10/16	9 10/16	16 8/16	16 8/16
39	33 15/16	19 8/16	9 14/16	9 14/16	16 15/16	16 15/16
40	34 13/16	20	10 2/16	10 2/16	17 6/16	17 6/16
41	35 11/16	20 8/16	10 6/16	10 6/16	17 13/16	17 13/16
42	36 9/16	21	10 10/16	10 10/16	18 4/16	18 4/16

7 SIDED PROJECT INFORMATION

Geometric Name: Heptagon
Definition: A Polygon having 7 sides
Miter Angle: 25.714°
Angle Change / Adjoining Sides: 51.428°

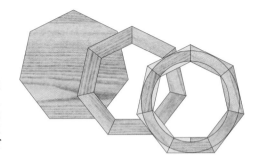

As another one of the "odd numbered" shape Illustrated in this book, the 7 sided shape (Heptagon) is one of the shapes that is pretty difficult to get creative with. With that said, it's still a fun project to build, and in some cases can be the perfect shape for the item you may wish to frame. The one thing that should be considered when using this shape is that for most standard sizes of pictures, a lot of cropping of the picture will be required.

The Illustrations to the right should give you an idea of the amount of cropping that may be required by using a Heptagon as your choice of shape for a frame.

In the left Illustration, you see a scale (shown in red) 8" x 10" sheet in portrait format. The sheet border is slightly outside the rabbeted area (shown in yellow) of the frame. Note the amount of material that would need to be cropped off the sheet top and/or bottom.

In the right Illustration, you see the same size sheet, but rotated 90° into a landscape format. Note the amount of material that would need to be cropped off the sheet sides.

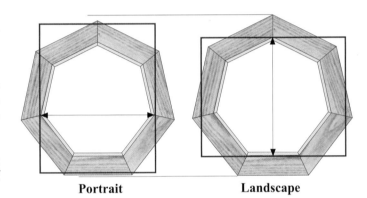

Portrait   **Landscape**

You should note that the frame for the sheet shown in portrait format is also smaller than the frame for the sheet shown in landscape format. This is due to the fact that on a Heptagon, the dimension "point-to-point" is slightly larger than the dimension "point-to-flat. In our **7 SIDED FRAME FORMULAS** below, you will be able to see exactly what the changes between these dimensions will be.

If the project you are building is a frame for a specific size object, you should refer to the **7 SIDED FRAME FORMULAS** Chart below as a first step. On a Heptagon, the height is shorter than the width, and is the controlling dimension for the frame for a picture in landscape format. In landscape format, the picture height would be multiplied by .457 to determine the length of the sides at the rabbeted edge. (See the bottom formula under **SIDE LENGTH** in the Chart below). In a portrait format, the width is the controlling dimension. In portrait format, the picture width should be multiplied by .447 to determine the lengths of the sides of the rabbeted edge. (See the top formula under **SIDE LENGTH** in the Chart below).

7 SIDED FRAME FORMULAS		
WIDTH	**HEIGHT**	**SIDE LENGTH**
Width = Side Length x 2.24	Height = Side Length x 2.19	Side Length = Width x .447
Width = Height x 1.018	Height = Width x .983	Side Length = Height x .457

Though the information above is very helpful, one of the most time consuming (and frustrating) things about building frames is to try to cut to a dimension that is not measured on either the inside or outside edge of the molding. I like to cut miters from the inside to the outside edges of the molding. This not only allows me to eliminate tear out on the inside corners of the frame since I am cutting into the inside edge, I am also cutting with the grain of the molding. It also allows me to see the outside edge of the material as I cut it. To help you understand how easy it is to convert a dimension along the rabbeted edge into an outside measurement, I will explain how we can use some basic math to help us determine the outside length of our frame sides. The Illustration below should be helpful in showing you how we designed our **7 SIDED FRAME ADDED WIDTH AND LENGTH CHART** on the next page.

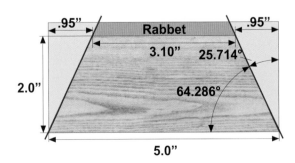

The Illustration to the left represents a piece of wood that is 5" long and 2" wide (to the edge of the rabbet). Note that on the right side that the end of the piece shows the miter angle for a Heptagon (25.714°) and the resulting angle of the cut (64.287°).

You should also note that at the rabbet, the 25.714° cuts shorten each end of the piece by .95". Since both ends of the piece are cut, this means that the length at the rabbet is 3.10", which is 1.90" shorter than the outside edge of the molding. This Illustration tells us is that at a 25.714° cut, we will add 1.90" to the length at a 2" width. This is the basis of our formula.

If we divide the **Added Length** (1.90") by the **Added Width** (2.0") we end up with .95 as our multiplier. In the event that you want to make a frame and need to work in fractions smaller than 1/16 increments, you would multiply the width of the molding outside the rabbet by .95. To determine the decimal equivalent of the fractions you will need to use, refer to the **FRACTION TO DECIMAL CONVERSION CHART** provided.

If you are able to use 1/16" increments for the mathematics of your frames, you should use the **7 SIDED FRAME ADDED WIDTH AND LENGTH CHART** below.

Determine how wide you want the material to be (outside the rabbet). Refer to the Chart below to find this dimension in one of the yellow shaded columns. The added length for that width will be shown in the green shaded block to the right of it. Add this dimension to the side length determined in the first step. You should then add whatever waste you want to allow for each side. This total is then multiplied by 7 to determine how much material is needed to build your project.

7 SIDED FRAME ADDED WIDTH AND LENGTH CHART

Added Width	Added Length	Added Width	Added Length	Added Width	Added Length	Added Width	Added Length	Added Width	Added Length
1/16	1/16	1 1/16	1	2 1/16	1 15/16	3 1/16	2 15/16	4 1/16	3 14/16
2/16	2/16	1 2/16	1 1/16	2 2/16	2	3 2/16	3	4 2/16	3 15/16
3/16	3/16	1 3/16	1 2/16	2 3/16	2 1/16	3 3/16	3	4 3/16	4
4/16	4/16	1 4/16	1 3/16	2 4/16	2 2/16	3 4/16	3 1/16	4 4/16	4 1/16
5/16	5/16	1 5/16	1 4/16	2 5/16	2 3/16	3 5/16	3 2/16	4 5/16	4 2/16
6/16	6/16	1 6/16	1 5/16	2 6/16	2 4/16	3 6/16	3 3/16	4 6/16	4 3/16
7/16	7/16	1 7/16	1 6/16	2 7/16	2 5/16	3 7/16	3 4/16	4 7/16	4 3/16
8/16	8/16	1 8/16	1 7/16	2 8/16	2 6/16	3 8/16	3 5/16	4 8/16	4 4/16
9/16	9/16	1 9/16	1 8/16	2 9/16	2 7/16	3 9/16	3 6/16	4 9/16	4 5/16
10/16	10/16	1 10/16	1 9/16	2 10/16	2 8/16	3 10/16	3 7/16	4 10/16	4 6/16
11/16	10/16	1 11/16	1 10/16	2 11/16	2 9/16	3 11/16	3 8/16	4 11/16	4 7/16
12/16	11/16	1 12/16	1 11/16	2 12/16	2 10/16	3 12/16	3 9/16	4 12/16	4 8/16
13/16	12/16	1 13/16	1 12/16	2 13/16	2 11/16	3 13/16	3 10/16	4 13/16	4 9/16
14/16	13/16	1 14/16	1 13/16	2 14/16	2 12/16	3 14/16	3 11/16	4 14/16	4 10/16
15/16	14/16	1 15/16	1 13/16	2 15/16	2 13/16	3 15/16	3 12/16	4 15/16	4 11/16
1	15/16	2	1 14/16	3	2 14/16	4	3 13/16	5	4 12/16

The Chart below is provided to enable you to make 7 sided frames using the mathematics of most popular picture sizes. The Chart is divided into 2 parts; the left section, which shows the sheet sizes in portrait format, and the right section, which shows the sheet sizes in landscape format. In the Charts, the different colored columns represent the following information:

Red: The controlling dimension of the sheet size. (width in portrait, height in landscape)
Gray: The dimension of the sheet size that will need to be cropped.

White: The rabbet length for the frame sides.
Orange: The size of the opening in the direction the picture will need to be cropped.
Blue: The amount of material that will need to be cropped.

RABBET AREA DIMENSIONS FOR 7 SIDED FRAMES

FOR PORTRAIT FORMAT					FOR LANDSCAPE FORMAT				
Object Width	Object Height	Rabbet Length	Opening Height	Vertical Crop	Object Width	Object Height	Rabbet Length	Opening Width	Horizontal Crop
4	5	1 14/16	4 1/16	15/16	5	4	1 14/16	4 3/16	13/16
5	7	2 5/16	5 1/16	1 15/16	7	5	2 5/16	5 3/16	1 13/16
6	8	2 12/16	6	2	8	6	2 13/16	6 4/16	1 12/16
8	10	3 10/16	8	2	10	8	3 11/16	8 4/16	1 12/16
8 1/2	11	3 14/16	8 8/16	2 8/16	11	8 1/2	3 15/16	8 12/16	2 4/16
10	14	4 8/16	9 15/16	4 1/16	14	10	4 10/16	10 5/16	3 11/16
11	14	5	10 15/16	3 1/16	14	11	5 1/16	11 5/16	2 11/16
12	16	5 7/16	11 15/16	4 1/16	16	12	5 9/16	12 5/16	3 11/16
16	20	7 3/16	15 14/16	4 2/16	20	16	7 6/16	16 7/16	3 9/16
18	24	8 2/16	17 13/16	6 3/16	24	18	8 5/16	18 7/16	5 9/16
20	24	9	19 13/16	4 3/16	24	20	9 3/16	20 8/16	3 8/16
24	30	10 13/16	23 11/16	6 5/16	30	24	11	24 9/16	5 7/16

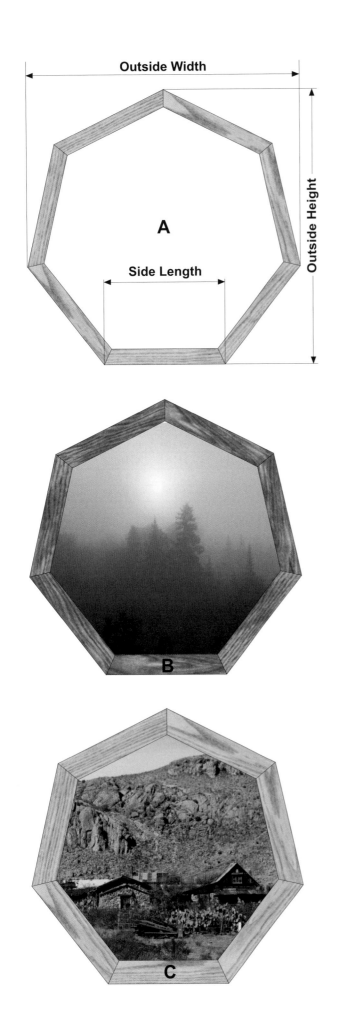

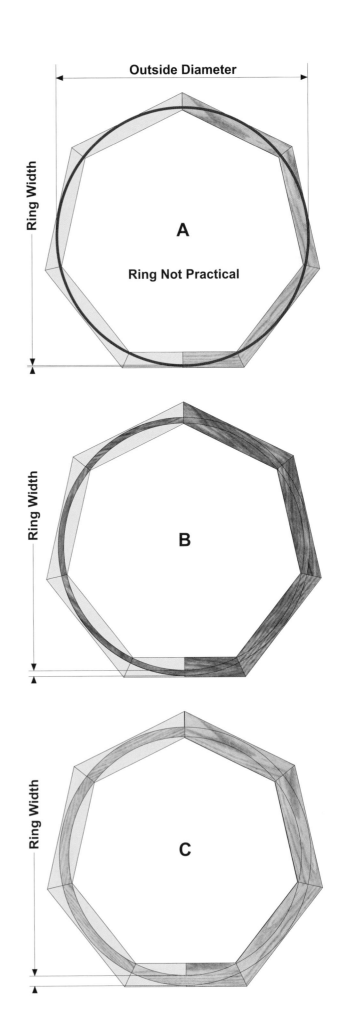

Side Length	Frame Width	Frame Height	Ring Max. OD	Material Req'd.	A Side Width	A Ring Width	B Side Width	B Ring Width	C Side Width	C Ring Width
8/16	1 2/16	1 2/16	1	5 4/16	1/16		1/16		2/16	1/16
10/16	1 6/16	1 6/16	1 5/16	6 2/16	1/16		2/16		2/16	1/16
12/16	1 11/16	1 10/16	1 9/16	7	2/16		2/16	1/16	2/16	1/16
14/16	1 15/16	1 15/16	1 13/16	7 14/16	2/16		2/16	1/16	3/16	1/16
1	2 4/16	2 3/16	2 1/16	8 12/16	2/16		3/16	1/16	3/16	1/16
1 4/16	2 13/16	2 12/16	2 9/16	10 8/16	3/16		3/16	1/16	4/16	2/16
1 8/16	3 6/16	3 5/16	3 1/16	12 4/16	3/16		4/16	1/16	5/16	2/16
1 12/16	3 15/16	3 13/16	3 10/16	14	4/16		4/16	1/16	5/16	2/16
2	4 8/16	4 6/16	4 2/16	15 12/16	4/16		5/16	1/16	6/16	2/16
2 4/16	5 1/16	4 15/16	4 10/16	17 8/16	5/16		6/16	2/16	7/16	3/16
2 8/16	5 10/16	5 8/16	5 2/16	19 4/16	5/16		6/16	2/16	8/16	3/16
2 12/16	6 3/16	6	5 10/16	21	6/16	1/16	7/16	2/16	8/16	3/16
3	6 12/16	6 9/16	6 3/16	22 12/16	6/16	1/16	8/16	2/16	9/16	4/16
3 4/16	7 4/16	7 2/16	6 11/16	24 8/16	7/16	1/16	8/16	2/16	10/16	4/16
3 8/16	7 13/16	7 11/16	7 3/16	26 4/16	7/16	1/16	9/16	3/16	11/16	4/16
3 12/16	8 6/16	8 3/16	7 11/16	28	8/16	1/16	9/16	3/16	11/16	5/16
4	8 15/16	8 12/16	8 3/16	29 12/16	8/16	1/16	10/16	3/16	12/16	5/16
4 4/16	9 8/16	9 5/16	8 12/16	31 8/16	9/16	1/16	11/16	3/16	13/16	5/16
4 8/16	10 1/16	9 14/16	9 4/16	33 4/16	9/16	1/16	11/16	3/16	14/16	6/16
4 12/16	10 10/16	10 6/16	9 12/16	35	10/16	1/16	12/16	3/16	14/16	6/16
5	11 3/16	10 15/16	10 4/16	36 12/16	10/16	1/16	13/16	4/16	15/16	6/16
5 4/16	11 12/16	11 8/16	10 13/16	38 8/16	11/16	1/16	13/16	4/16	1	7/16
5 8/16	12 5/16	12 1/16	11 5/16	40 4/16	11/16	1/16	14/16	4/16	1 1/16	7/16
5 12/16	12 14/16	12 9/16	11 13/16	42	12/16	1/16	14/16	4/16	1 1/16	7/16
6	13 7/16	13 2/16	12 5/16	43 12/16	12/16	1/16	15/16	4/16	1 2/16	7/16
6 8/16	14 9/16	14 4/16	13 6/16	47 4/16	13/16	1/16	1	5/16	1 4/16	8/16
7	15 11/16	15 5/16	14 6/16	50 12/16	14/16	1/16	1 2/16	5/16	1 5/16	9/16
7 8/16	16 13/16	16 7/16	15 7/16	54 4/16	15/16	1/16	1 3/16	5/16	1 7/16	9/16
8	17 15/16	17 8/16	16 7/16	57 12/16	1	2/16	1 4/16	6/16	1 8/16	10/16
8 8/16	19 1/16	18 10/16	17 7/16	61 4/16	1 1/16	2/16	1 5/16	6/16	1 10/16	11/16
9	20 3/16	19 11/16	18 8/16	64 12/16	1 2/16	2/16	1 7/16	7/16	1 11/16	11/16
9 8/16	21 4/16	20 13/16	19 8/16	68 4/16	1 3/16	2/16	1 8/16	7/16	1 13/16	12/16
10	22 6/16	21 14/16	20 9/16	71 12/16	1 4/16	2/16	1 9/16	7/16	1 14/16	12/16
10 8/16	23 8/16	23	21 9/16	75 4/16	1 5/16	2/16	1 10/16	8/16	2	13/16
11	24 10/16	24 1/16	22 10/16	78 12/16	1 6/16	2/16	1 12/16	8/16	2 1/16	14/16
11 8/16	25 12/16	25 3/16	23 10/16	82 4/16	1 7/16	2/16	1 13/16	8/16	2 3/16	14/16
12	26 14/16	26 4/16	24 10/16	85 12/16	1 8/16	2/16	1 14/16	9/16	2 4/16	15/16
13	29 2/16	28 8/16	26 11/16	92 12/16	1 10/16	3/16	2 1/16	9/16	2 7/16	1
14	31 6/16	30 11/16	28 12/16	99 12/16	1 12/16	3/16	2 3/16	10/16	2 10/16	1 1/16
15	33 10/16	32 14/16	30 13/16	106 12/16	1 14/16	3/16	2 6/16	11/16	2 13/16	1 3/16
16	35 13/16	35 1/16	32 14/16	113 12/16	2	3/16	2 8/16	12/16	3	1 4/16
17	38 1/16	37 4/16	34 15/16	120 12/16	2 2/16	3/16	2 11/16	12/16	3 3/16	1 5/16
18	40 5/16	39 7/16	37	127 12/16	2 4/16	4/16	2 13/16	13/16	3 6/16	1 6/16
19	42 9/16	41 10/16	39 1/16	134 12/16	2 6/16	4/16	3	14/16	3 9/16	1 8/16
20	44 13/16	43 13/16	41 1/16	141 12/16	2 8/16	4/16	3 2/16	14/16	3 12/16	1 9/16
21	47 1/16	46	43 2/16	148 12/16	2 10/16	4/16	3 5/16	15/16	3 15/16	1 10/16
22	49 4/16	48 3/16	45 3/16	155 12/16	2 12/16	4/16	3 7/16	1	4 2/16	1 11/16
23	51 8/16	50 6/16	47 4/16	162 12/16	2 14/16	5/16	3 10/16	1 1/16	4 5/16	1 13/16
24	53 12/16	52 9/16	49 5/16	169 12/16	3	5/16	3 12/16	1 1/16	4 8/16	1 14/16
25	56	54 12/16	51 6/16	176 12/16	3 2/16	5/16	3 15/16	1 2/16	4 11/16	1 15/16
26	58 4/16	56 15/16	53 7/16	183 12/16	3 4/16	5/16	4 1/16	1 3/16	4 14/16	2
27	60 8/16	59 2/16	55 8/16	190 12/16	3 6/16	5/16	4 4/16	1 4/16	5 1/16	2 2/16
28	62 12/16	61 5/16	57 8/16	197 12/16	3 8/16	6/16	4 6/16	1 4/16	5 4/16	2 3/16

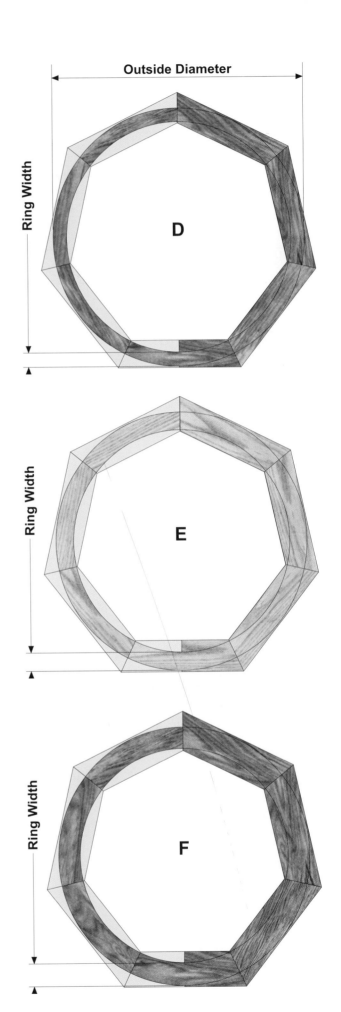

60

Side Length	Frame Width	Frame Height	Ring Max. OD	Material Req'd.	D Side Width	D Ring Width	E Side Width	E Ring Width	F Side Width	F Ring Width
8/16	1 2/16	1 2/16	1	5 4/16	2/16	1/16	2/16	1/16	2/16	1/16
10/16	1 6/16	1 6/16	1 5/16	6 2/16	2/16	1/16	3/16	1/16	3/16	2/16
12/16	1 11/16	1 10/16	1 9/16	7	3/16	1/16	3/16	2/16	3/16	2/16
14/16	1 15/16	1 15/16	1 13/16	7 14/16	3/16	2/16	4/16	2/16	4/16	2/16
1	2 4/16	2 3/16	2 1/16	8 12/16	4/16	2/16	4/16	2/16	5/16	3/16
1 4/16	2 13/16	2 12/16	2 9/16	10 8/16	4/16	2/16	5/16	3/16	6/16	4/16
1 8/16	3 6/16	3 5/16	3 1/16	12 4/16	5/16	3/16	6/16	3/16	7/16	4/16
1 12/16	3 15/16	3 13/16	3 10/16	14	6/16	3/16	7/16	4/16	8/16	5/16
2	4 8/16	4 6/16	4 2/16	15 12/16	7/16	4/16	8/16	5/16	9/16	6/16
2 4/16	5 1/16	4 15/16	4 10/16	17 8/16	8/16	4/16	9/16	5/16	10/16	6/16
2 8/16	5 10/16	5 8/16	5 2/16	19 4/16	9/16	4/16	10/16	6/16	11/16	7/16
2 12/16	6 3/16	6	5 10/16	21	10/16	5/16	11/16	6/16	12/16	8/16
3	6 12/16	6 9/16	6 3/16	22 12/16	11/16	5/16	12/16	7/16	14/16	9/16
3 4/16	7 4/16	7 2/16	6 11/16	24 8/16	11/16	6/16	13/16	8/16	15/16	9/16
3 8/16	7 13/16	7 11/16	7 3/16	26 4/16	12/16	6/16	14/16	8/16	1	10/16
3 12/16	8 6/16	8 3/16	7 11/16	28	13/16	7/16	15/16	9/16	1 1/16	11/16
4	8 15/16	8 12/16	8 3/16	29 12/16	14/16	7/16	1	9/16	1 2/16	11/16
4 4/16	9 8/16	9 5/16	8 12/16	31 8/16	15/16	8/16	1 1/16	10/16	1 3/16	12/16
4 8/16	10 1/16	9 14/16	9 4/16	33 4/16	1	8/16	1 2/16	10/16	1 4/16	13/16
4 12/16	10 10/16	10 6/16	9 12/16	35	1 1/16	9/16	1 3/16	11/16	1 5/16	14/16
5	11 3/16	10 15/16	10 4/16	36 12/16	1 2/16	9/16	1 4/16	12/16	1 7/16	14/16
5 4/16	11 12/16	11 8/16	10 13/16	38 8/16	1 2/16	9/16	1 5/16	12/16	1 8/16	15/16
5 8/16	12 5/16	12 1/16	11 5/16	40 4/16	1 3/16	10/16	1 6/16	13/16	1 9/16	1
5 12/16	12 14/16	12 9/16	11 13/16	42	1 4/16	10/16	1 7/16	13/16	1 10/16	1
6	13 7/16	13 2/16	12 5/16	43 12/16	1 5/16	11/16	1 8/16	14/16	1 11/16	1 1/16
6 8/16	14 9/16	14 4/16	13 6/16	47 4/16	1 7/16	12/16	1 10/16	15/16	1 13/16	1 3/16
7	15 11/16	15 5/16	14 6/16	50 12/16	1 9/16	13/16	1 12/16	1	2	1 4/16
7 8/16	16 13/16	16 7/16	15 7/16	54 4/16	1 10/16	13/16	1 14/16	1 1/16	2 2/16	1 5/16
8	17 15/16	17 8/16	16 7/16	57 12/16	1 12/16	14/16	2	1 3/16	2 4/16	1 7/16
8 8/16	19 1/16	18 10/16	17 7/16	61 4/16	1 14/16	15/16	2 2/16	1 4/16	2 6/16	1 8/16
9	20 3/16	19 11/16	18 8/16	64 12/16	2	1	2 4/16	1 5/16	2 9/16	1 10/16
9 8/16	21 4/16	20 13/16	19 8/16	68 4/16	2 1/16	1 1/16	2 6/16	1 6/16	2 11/16	1 11/16
10	22 6/16	21 14/16	20 9/16	71 12/16	2 3/16	1 2/16	2 8/16	1 7/16	2 13/16	1 13/16
10 8/16	23 8/16	23	21 9/16	75 4/16	2 5/16	1 3/16	2 10/16	1 8/16	2 15/16	1 14/16
11	24 10/16	24 1/16	22 10/16	78 12/16	2 7/16	1 4/16	2 12/16	1 10/16	3 2/16	1 15/16
11 8/16	25 12/16	25 3/16	23 10/16	82 4/16	2 8/16	1 5/16	2 14/16	1 11/16	3 4/16	2 1/16
12	26 14/16	26 4/16	24 10/16	85 12/16	2 10/16	1 5/16	3	1 12/16	3 6/16	2 2/16
13	29 2/16	28 8/16	26 11/16	92 12/16	2 14/16	1 7/16	3 4/16	1 14/16	3 11/16	2 5/16
14	31 6/16	30 11/16	28 12/16	99 12/16	3 1/16	1 9/16	3 8/16	2	3 15/16	2 8/16
15	33 10/16	32 14/16	30 13/16	106 12/16	3 5/16	1 11/16	3 12/16	2 3/16	4 4/16	2 11/16
16	35 13/16	35 1/16	32 14/16	113 12/16	3 8/16	1 13/16	4	2 5/16	4 8/16	2 14/16
17	38 1/16	37 4/16	34 15/16	120 12/16	3 12/16	1 14/16	4 4/16	2 7/16	4 13/16	3 1/16
18	40 5/16	39 7/16	37	127 12/16	3 15/16	2	4 8/16	2 10/16	5 1/16	3 3/16
19	42 9/16	41 10/16	39 1/16	134 12/16	4 3/16	2 2/16	4 12/16	2 12/16	5 6/16	3 6/16
20	44 13/16	43 13/16	41 1/16	141 12/16	4 6/16	2 4/16	5	2 14/16	5 10/16	3 9/16
21	47 1/16	46	43 2/16	148 12/16	4 10/16	2 6/16	5 4/16	3 1/16	5 15/16	3 12/16
22	49 4/16	48 3/16	45 3/16	155 12/16	4 13/16	2 7/16	5 8/16	3 3/16	6 3/16	3 15/16
23	51 8/16	50 6/16	47 4/16	162 12/16	5 1/16	2 9/16	5 12/16	3 5/16	6 8/16	4 2/16
24	53 12/16	52 9/16	49 5/16	169 12/16	5 4/16	2 11/16	6	3 8/16	6 12/16	4 4/16
25	56	54 12/16	51 6/16	176 12/16	5 8/16	2 13/16	6 4/16	3 10/16	7 1/16	4 7/16
26	58 4/16	56 15/16	53 7/16	183 12/16	5 11/16	2 15/16	6 8/16	3 12/16	7 5/16	4 10/16
27	60 8/16	59 2/16	55 8/16	190 12/16	5 15/16	3	6 12/16	3 15/16	7 10/16	4 13/16
28	62 12/16	61 5/16	57 8/16	197 12/16	6 2/16	3 2/16	7	4 1/16	7 14/16	5

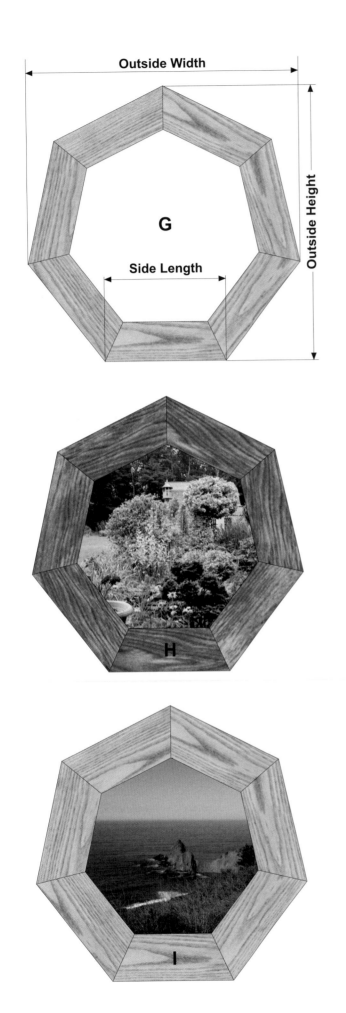
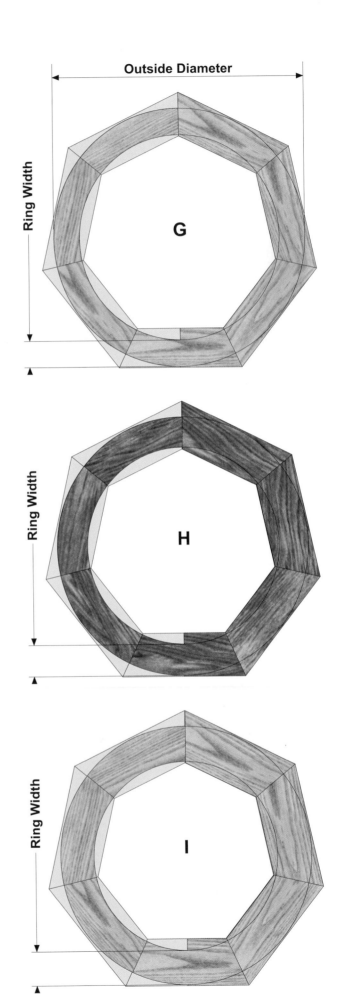

Side Length	Frame Width	Frame Height	Ring Max. OD	Material Req'd.	G Side Width	G Ring Width	H Side Width	H Ring Width	I Side Width	I Ring Width
8/16	1 2/16	1 2/16	1	5 4/16	3/16	2/16	3/16	2/16	3/16	2/16
10/16	1 6/16	1 6/16	1 5/16	6 2/16	3/16	2/16	3/16	2/16	4/16	3/16
12/16	1 11/16	1 10/16	1 9/16	7	4/16	3/16	4/16	3/16	5/16	3/16
14/16	1 15/16	1 15/16	1 13/16	7 14/16	4/16	3/16	5/16	3/16	5/16	4/16
1	2 4/16	2 3/16	2 1/16	8 12/16	5/16	3/16	6/16	4/16	6/16	4/16
1 4/16	2 13/16	2 12/16	2 9/16	10 8/16	6/16	4/16	7/16	5/16	8/16	6/16
1 8/16	3 6/16	3 5/16	3 1/16	12 4/16	8/16	5/16	8/16	6/16	9/16	7/16
1 12/16	3 15/16	3 13/16	3 10/16	14	9/16	6/16	10/16	7/16	11/16	8/16
2	4 8/16	4 6/16	4 2/16	15 12/16	10/16	7/16	11/16	8/16	12/16	9/16
2 4/16	5 1/16	4 15/16	4 10/16	17 8/16	11/16	8/16	12/16	9/16	14/16	10/16
2 8/16	5 10/16	5 8/16	5 2/16	19 4/16	13/16	8/16	14/16	10/16	15/16	11/16
2 12/16	6 3/16	6	5 10/16	21	14/16	9/16	15/16	11/16	1 1/16	12/16
3	6 12/16	6 9/16	6 3/16	22 12/16	15/16	10/16	1 1/16	12/16	1 2/16	13/16
3 4/16	7 4/16	7 2/16	6 11/16	24 8/16	1	11/16	1 2/16	13/16	1 4/16	14/16
3 8/16	7 13/16	7 11/16	7 3/16	26 4/16	1 2/16	12/16	1 3/16	14/16	1 5/16	1
3 12/16	8 6/16	8 3/16	7 11/16	28	1 3/16	13/16	1 5/16	15/16	1 7/16	1 1/16
4	8 15/16	8 12/16	8 3/16	29 12/16	1 4/16	14/16	1 6/16	1	1 8/16	1 2/16
4 4/16	9 8/16	9 5/16	8 12/16	31 8/16	1 5/16	14/16	1 7/16	1 1/16	1 10/16	1 3/16
4 8/16	10 1/16	9 14/16	9 4/16	33 4/16	1 7/16	15/16	1 9/16	1 2/16	1 11/16	1 4/16
4 12/16	10 10/16	10 6/16	9 12/16	35	1 8/16	1	1 10/16	1 3/16	1 13/16	1 5/16
5	11 3/16	10 15/16	10 4/16	36 12/16	1 9/16	1 1/16	1 12/16	1 4/16	1 14/16	1 6/16
5 4/16	11 12/16	11 8/16	10 13/16	38 8/16	1 10/16	1 2/16	1 13/16	1 5/16	2	1 7/16
5 8/16	12 5/16	12 1/16	11 5/16	40 4/16	1 12/16	1 3/16	1 14/16	1 6/16	2 1/16	1 8/16
5 12/16	12 14/16	12 9/16	11 13/16	42	1 13/16	1 3/16	2	1 7/16	2 3/16	1 10/16
6	13 7/16	13 2/16	12 5/16	43 12/16	1 14/16	1 4/16	2 1/16	1 8/16	2 4/16	1 11/16
6 8/16	14 9/16	14 4/16	13 6/16	47 4/16	2 1/16	1 6/16	2 4/16	1 9/16	2 7/16	1 13/16
7	15 11/16	15 5/16	14 6/16	50 12/16	2 3/16	1 8/16	2 7/16	1 11/16	2 10/16	1 15/16
7 8/16	16 13/16	16 7/16	15 7/16	54 4/16	2 6/16	1 9/16	2 9/16	1 13/16	2 13/16	2 1/16
8	17 15/16	17 8/16	16 7/16	57 12/16	2 8/16	1 11/16	2 12/16	1 15/16	3	2 4/16
8 8/16	19 1/16	18 10/16	17 7/16	61 4/16	2 11/16	1 13/16	2 15/16	2 1/16	3 3/16	2 6/16
9	20 3/16	19 11/16	18 8/16	64 12/16	2 13/16	1 14/16	3 2/16	2 3/16	3 6/16	2 8/16
9 8/16	21 4/16	20 13/16	19 8/16	68 4/16	3	2	3 4/16	2 5/16	3 9/16	2 10/16
10	22 6/16	21 14/16	20 9/16	71 12/16	3 2/16	2 2/16	3 7/16	2 7/16	3 12/16	2 13/16
10 8/16	23 8/16	23	21 9/16	75 4/16	3 5/16	2 4/16	3 10/16	2 9/16	3 15/16	2 15/16
11	24 10/16	24 1/16	22 10/16	78 12/16	3 7/16	2 5/16	3 13/16	2 11/16	4 2/16	3 1/16
11 8/16	25 12/16	25 3/16	23 10/16	82 4/16	3 10/16	2 7/16	3 15/16	2 13/16	4 5/16	3 3/16
12	26 14/16	26 4/16	24 10/16	85 12/16	3 12/16	2 9/16	4 2/16	2 15/16	4 8/16	3 5/16
13	29 2/16	28 8/16	26 11/16	92 12/16	4 1/16	2 12/16	4 8/16	3 3/16	4 14/16	3 10/16
14	31 6/16	30 11/16	28 12/16	99 12/16	4 6/16	2 15/16	4 13/16	3 7/16	5 4/16	3 14/16
15	33 10/16	32 14/16	30 13/16	106 12/16	4 11/16	3 3/16	5 3/16	3 11/16	5 10/16	4 3/16
16	35 13/16	35 1/16	32 14/16	113 12/16	5	3 6/16	5 8/16	3 15/16	6	4 7/16
17	38 1/16	37 4/16	34 15/16	120 12/16	5 5/16	3 10/16	5 14/16	4 3/16	6 6/16	4 12/16
18	40 5/16	39 7/16	37	127 12/16	5 10/16	3 13/16	6 3/16	4 7/16	6 12/16	5
19	42 9/16	41 10/16	39 1/16	134 12/16	5 15/16	4	6 9/16	4 10/16	7 2/16	5 5/16
20	44 13/16	43 13/16	41 1/16	141 12/16	6 4/16	4 4/16	6 14/16	4 14/16	7 8/16	5 9/16
21	47 1/16	46	43 2/16	148 12/16	6 9/16	4 7/16	7 4/16	5 2/16	7 14/16	5 14/16
22	49 4/16	48 3/16	45 3/16	155 12/16	6 14/16	4 10/16	7 9/16	5 6/16	8 4/16	6 2/16
23	51 8/16	50 6/16	47 4/16	162 12/16	7 3/16	4 14/16	7 15/16	5 10/16	8 10/16	6 6/16
24	53 12/16	52 9/16	49 5/16	169 12/16	7 8/16	5 1/16	8 4/16	5 14/16	9	6 11/16
25	56	54 12/16	51 6/16	176 12/16	7 13/16	5 5/16	8 10/16	6 2/16	9 6/16	6 15/16
26	58 4/16	56 15/16	53 7/16	183 12/16	8 2/16	5 8/16	8 15/16	6 6/16	9 12/16	7 4/16
27	60 8/16	59 2/16	55 8/16	190 12/16	8 7/16	5 11/16	9 5/16	6 10/16	10 2/16	7 8/16
28	62 12/16	61 5/16	57 8/16	197 12/16	8 12/16	5 15/16	9 10/16	6 14/16	10 8/16	7 13/16

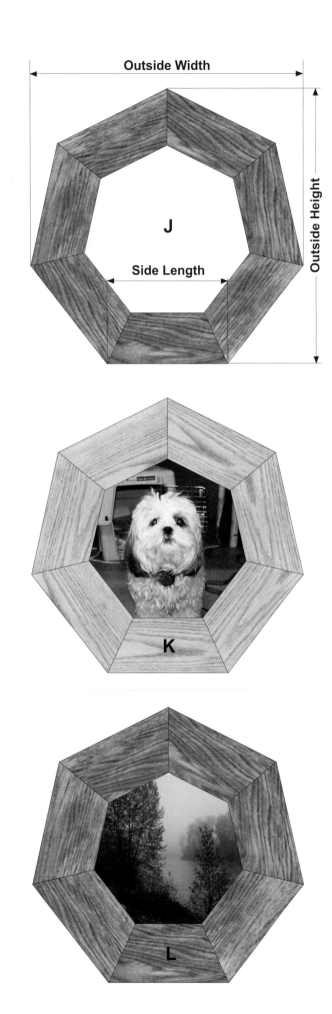

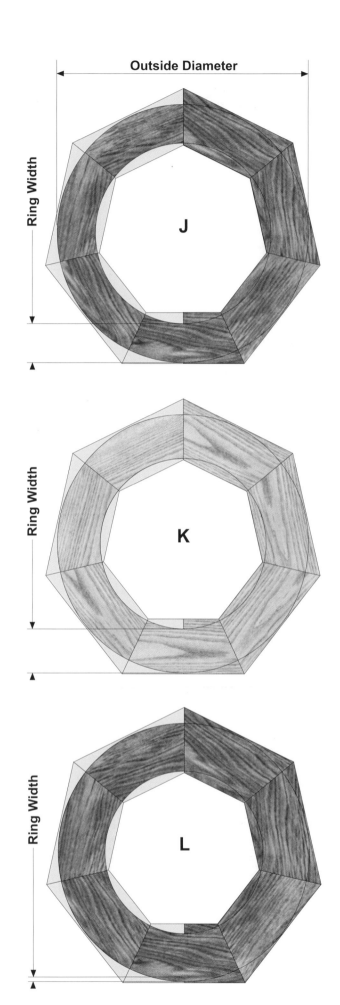

Outside Width

Outside Height

Side Length

Outside Diameter

Ring Width

J

J

K

Ring Width

K

L

Ring Width

L

64

Side Length	Frame Width	Frame Height	Ring Max. OD	Material Req'd.	J Side Width	J Ring Width	K Side Width	K Ring Width	L Side Width	L Ring Width
8/16	1 2/16	1 2/16	1	5 4/16	3/16	2/16	4/16	3/16	4/16	3/16
10/16	1 6/16	1 6/16	1 5/16	6 2/16	4/16	3/16	4/16	3/16	5/16	4/16
12/16	1 11/16	1 10/16	1 9/16	7	5/16	4/16	5/16	4/16	6/16	5/16
14/16	1 15/16	1 15/16	1 13/16	7 14/16	6/16	4/16	6/16	5/16	7/16	5/16
1	2 4/16	2 3/16	2 1/16	8 12/16	7/16	5/16	7/16	6/16	8/16	6/16
1 4/16	2 13/16	2 12/16	2 9/16	10 8/16	8/16	6/16	9/16	7/16	9/16	8/16
1 8/16	3 6/16	3 5/16	3 1/16	12 4/16	10/16	7/16	11/16	8/16	11/16	9/16
1 12/16	3 15/16	3 13/16	3 10/16	14	11/16	9/16	12/16	10/16	13/16	11/16
2	4 8/16	4 6/16	4 2/16	15 12/16	13/16	10/16	14/16	11/16	15/16	12/16
2 4/16	5 1/16	4 15/16	4 10/16	17 8/16	15/16	11/16	1	12/16	1 1/16	14/16
2 8/16	5 10/16	5 8/16	5 2/16	19 4/16	1	12/16	1 2/16	14/16	1 3/16	15/16
2 12/16	6 3/16	6	5 10/16	21	1 2/16	14/16	1 3/16	15/16	1 5/16	1 1/16
3	6 12/16	6 9/16	6 3/16	22 12/16	1 4/16	15/16	1 5/16	1 1/16	1 7/16	1 2/16
3 4/16	7 4/16	7 2/16	6 11/16	24 8/16	1 5/16	1	1 7/16	1 2/16	1 8/16	1 4/16
3 8/16	7 13/16	7 11/16	7 3/16	26 4/16	1 7/16	1 1/16	1 9/16	1 3/16	1 10/16	1 5/16
3 12/16	8 6/16	8 3/16	7 11/16	28	1 8/16	1 3/16	1 10/16	1 5/16	1 12/16	1 7/16
4	8 15/16	8 12/16	8 3/16	29 12/16	1 10/16	1 4/16	1 12/16	1 6/16	1 14/16	1 8/16
4 4/16	9 8/16	9 5/16	8 12/16	31 8/16	1 12/16	1 5/16	1 14/16	1 7/16	2	1 10/16
4 8/16	10 1/16	9 14/16	9 4/16	33 4/16	1 13/16	1 6/16	2	1 9/16	2 2/16	1 11/16
4 12/16	10 10/16	10 6/16	9 12/16	35	1 15/16	1 8/16	2 1/16	1 10/16	2 4/16	1 13/16
5	11 3/16	10 15/16	10 4/16	36 12/16	2 1/16	1 9/16	2 3/16	1 12/16	2 6/16	1 14/16
5 4/16	11 12/16	11 8/16	10 13/16	38 8/16	2 2/16	1 10/16	2 5/16	1 13/16	2 7/16	2
5 8/16	12 5/16	12 1/16	11 5/16	40 4/16	2 4/16	1 11/16	2 7/16	1 14/16	2 9/16	2 1/16
5 12/16	12 14/16	12 9/16	11 13/16	42	2 5/16	1 13/16	2 8/16	2	2 11/16	2 3/16
6	13 7/16	13 2/16	12 5/16	43 12/16	2 7/16	1 14/16	2 10/16	2 1/16	2 13/16	2 4/16
6 8/16	14 9/16	14 4/16	13 6/16	47 4/16	2 10/16	2	2 14/16	2 4/16	3 1/16	2 7/16
7	15 11/16	15 5/16	14 6/16	50 12/16	2 14/16	2 3/16	3 1/16	2 7/16	3 5/16	2 10/16
7 8/16	16 13/16	16 7/16	15 7/16	54 4/16	3 1/16	2 5/16	3 5/16	2 9/16	3 8/16	2 13/16
8	17 15/16	17 8/16	16 7/16	57 12/16	3 4/16	2 8/16	3 8/16	2 12/16	3 12/16	3
8 8/16	19 1/16	18 10/16	17 7/16	61 4/16	3 7/16	2 10/16	3 12/16	2 15/16	4	3 3/16
9	20 3/16	19 11/16	18 8/16	64 12/16	3 11/16	2 13/16	3 15/16	3 2/16	4 4/16	3 6/16
9 8/16	21 4/16	20 13/16	19 8/16	68 4/16	3 14/16	2 15/16	4 3/16	3 4/16	4 7/16	3 9/16
10	22 6/16	21 14/16	20 9/16	71 12/16	4 1/16	3 2/16	4 6/16	3 7/16	4 11/16	3 12/16
10 8/16	23 8/16	23	21 9/16	75 4/16	4 4/16	3 4/16	4 10/16	3 10/16	4 15/16	4
11	24 10/16	24 1/16	22 10/16	78 12/16	4 8/16	3 7/16	4 13/16	3 13/16	5 3/16	4 3/16
11 8/16	25 12/16	25 3/16	23 10/16	82 4/16	4 11/16	3 9/16	5 1/16	3 15/16	5 6/16	4 6/16
12	26 14/16	26 4/16	24 10/16	85 12/16	4 14/16	3 12/16	5 4/16	4 2/16	5 10/16	4 9/16
13	29 2/16	28 8/16	26 11/16	92 12/16	5 5/16	4 1/16	5 11/16	4 8/16	6 2/16	4 15/16
14	31 6/16	30 11/16	28 12/16	99 12/16	5 11/16	4 6/16	6 2/16	4 13/16	6 9/16	5 5/16
15	33 10/16	32 14/16	30 13/16	106 12/16	6 2/16	4 11/16	6 9/16	5 3/16	7 1/16	5 11/16
16	35 13/16	35 1/16	32 14/16	113 12/16	6 8/16	5	7	5 8/16	7 8/16	6 1/16
17	38 1/16	37 4/16	34 15/16	120 12/16	6 15/16	5 5/16	7 7/16	5 14/16	8	6 7/16
18	40 5/16	39 7/16	37	127 12/16	7 5/16	5 10/16	7 14/16	6 3/16	8 7/16	6 13/16
19	42 9/16	41 10/16	39 1/16	134 12/16	7 12/16	5 15/16	8 5/16	6 9/16	8 15/16	7 3/16
20	44 13/16	43 13/16	41 1/16	141 12/16	8 2/16	6 4/16	8 12/16	6 14/16	9 6/16	7 9/16
21	47 1/16	46	43 2/16	148 12/16	8 9/16	6 9/16	9 3/16	7 4/16	9 14/16	7 15/16
22	49 4/16	48 3/16	45 3/16	155 12/16	8 15/16	6 14/16	9 10/16	7 9/16	10 5/16	8 5/16
23	51 8/16	50 6/16	47 4/16	162 12/16	9 6/16	7 3/16	10 1/16	7 15/16	10 13/16	8 11/16
24	53 12/16	52 9/16	49 5/16	169 12/16	9 12/16	7 8/16	10 8/16	8 4/16	11 4/16	9 1/16
25	56	54 12/16	51 6/16	176 12/16	10 3/16	7 13/16	10 15/16	8 10/16	11 12/16	9 7/16
26	58 4/16	56 15/16	53 7/16	183 12/16	10 9/16	8 2/16	11 6/16	8 15/16	12 3/16	9 13/16
27	60 8/16	59 2/16	55 8/16	190 12/16	11	8 7/16	11 13/16	9 5/16	12 11/16	10 3/16
28	62 12/16	61 5/16	57 8/16	197 12/16	11 6/16	8 11/16	12 4/16	9 10/16	13 2/16	10 9/16

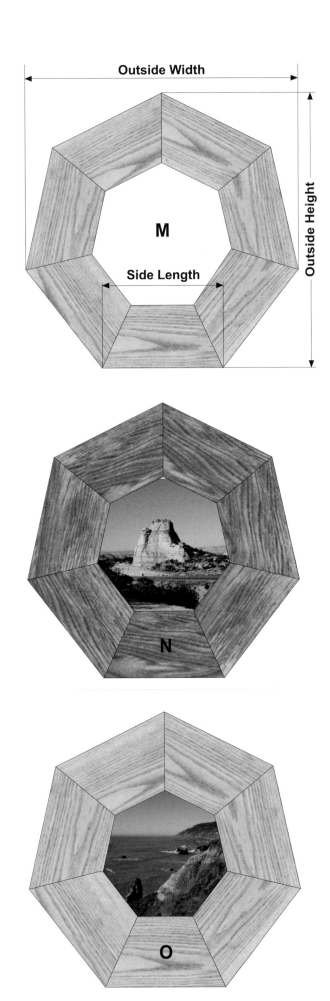

Outside Width

Outside Height

Side Length

M

N

O

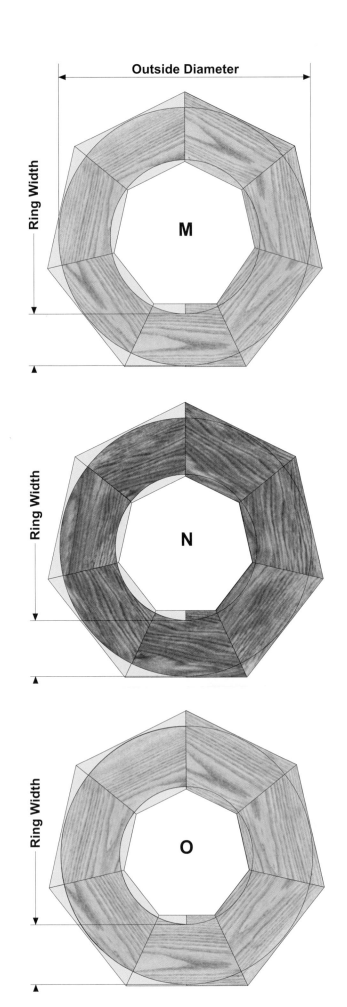

Outside Diameter

Ring Width

Ring Width

Ring Width

M

N

O

Side Length	Frame Width	Frame Height	Ring Max. OD	Material Req'd.	M Side Width	M Ring Width	N Side Width	N Ring Width	O Side Width	O Ring Width
8/16	1 2/16	1 2/16	1	5 4/16	4/16	3/16	4/16	4/16	5/16	4/16
10/16	1 6/16	1 6/16	1 5/16	6 2/16	5/16	4/16	5/16	4/16	6/16	5/16
12/16	1 11/16	1 10/16	1 9/16	7	6/16	5/16	6/16	5/16	7/16	6/16
14/16	1 15/16	1 15/16	1 13/16	7 14/16	7/16	6/16	7/16	6/16	8/16	7/16
1	2 4/16	2 3/16	2 1/16	8 12/16	8/16	7/16	9/16	7/16	9/16	8/16
1 4/16	2 13/16	2 12/16	2 9/16	10 8/16	10/16	8/16	11/16	9/16	11/16	10/16
1 8/16	3 6/16	3 5/16	3 1/16	12 4/16	12/16	10/16	13/16	11/16	14/16	11/16
1 12/16	3 15/16	3 13/16	3 10/16	14	14/16	12/16	15/16	12/16	1	13/16
2	4 8/16	4 6/16	4 2/16	15 12/16	1	13/16	1 1/16	14/16	1 2/16	15/16
2 4/16	5 1/16	4 15/16	4 10/16	17 8/16	1 2/16	15/16	1 3/16	1	1 4/16	1 1/16
2 8/16	5 10/16	5 8/16	5 2/16	19 4/16	1 4/16	1	1 5/16	1 2/16	1 7/16	1 3/16
2 12/16	6 3/16	6	5 10/16	21	1 6/16	1 2/16	1 7/16	1 4/16	1 9/16	1 5/16
3	6 12/16	6 9/16	6 3/16	22 12/16	1 8/16	1 4/16	1 10/16	1 5/16	1 11/16	1 7/16
3 4/16	7 4/16	7 2/16	6 11/16	24 8/16	1 10/16	1 5/16	1 12/16	1 7/16	1 13/16	1 9/16
3 8/16	7 13/16	7 11/16	7 3/16	26 4/16	1 12/16	1 7/16	1 14/16	1 9/16	2	1 11/16
3 12/16	8 6/16	8 3/16	7 11/16	28	1 14/16	1 9/16	2	1 11/16	2 2/16	1 13/16
4	8 15/16	8 12/16	8 3/16	29 12/16	2	1 10/16	2 2/16	1 12/16	2 4/16	1 15/16
4 4/16	9 8/16	9 5/16	8 12/16	31 8/16	2 2/16	1 12/16	2 4/16	1 14/16	2 6/16	2
4 8/16	10 1/16	9 14/16	9 4/16	33 4/16	2 4/16	1 14/16	2 6/16	2	2 9/16	2 2/16
4 12/16	10 10/16	10 6/16	9 12/16	35	2 6/16	1 15/16	2 8/16	2 2/16	2 11/16	2 4/16
5	11 3/16	10 15/16	10 4/16	36 12/16	2 8/16	2 1/16	2 11/16	2 4/16	2 13/16	2 6/16
5 4/16	11 12/16	11 8/16	10 13/16	38 8/16	2 10/16	2 3/16	2 13/16	2 5/16	2 15/16	2 8/16
5 8/16	12 5/16	12 1/16	11 5/16	40 4/16	2 12/16	2 4/16	2 15/16	2 7/16	3 2/16	2 10/16
5 12/16	12 14/16	12 9/16	11 13/16	42	2 14/16	2 6/16	3 1/16	2 9/16	3 4/16	2 12/16
6	13 7/16	13 2/16	12 5/16	43 12/16	3	2 7/16	3 3/16	2 11/16	3 6/16	2 14/16
6 8/16	14 9/16	14 4/16	13 6/16	47 4/16	3 4/16	2 11/16	3 7/16	2 14/16	3 11/16	3 2/16
7	15 11/16	15 5/16	14 6/16	50 12/16	3 8/16	2 14/16	3 12/16	3 2/16	3 15/16	3 5/16
7 8/16	16 13/16	16 7/16	15 7/16	54 4/16	3 12/16	3 1/16	4	3 5/16	4 4/16	3 9/16
8	17 15/16	17 8/16	16 7/16	57 12/16	4	3 5/16	4 4/16	3 9/16	4 8/16	3 13/16
8 8/16	19 1/16	18 10/16	17 7/16	61 4/16	4 4/16	3 8/16	4 8/16	3 12/16	4 13/16	4 1/16
9	20 3/16	19 11/16	18 8/16	64 12/16	4 8/16	3 11/16	4 13/16	4	5 1/16	4 5/16
9 8/16	21 4/16	20 13/16	19 8/16	68 4/16	4 12/16	3 14/16	5 1/16	4 4/16	5 6/16	4 9/16
10	22 6/16	21 14/16	20 9/16	71 12/16	5	4 2/16	5 5/16	4 7/16	5 10/16	4 12/16
10 8/16	23 8/16	23	21 9/16	75 4/16	5 4/16	4 5/16	5 9/16	4 11/16	5 15/16	5
11	24 10/16	24 1/16	22 10/16	78 12/16	5 8/16	4 8/16	5 14/16	4 14/16	6 3/16	5 4/16
11 8/16	25 12/16	25 3/16	23 10/16	82 4/16	5 12/16	4 12/16	6 2/16	5 2/16	6 8/16	5 8/16
12	26 14/16	26 4/16	24 10/16	85 12/16	6	4 15/16	6 6/16	5 5/16	6 12/16	5 12/16
13	29 2/16	28 8/16	26 11/16	92 12/16	6 8/16	5 5/16	6 15/16	5 12/16	7 5/16	6 3/16
14	31 6/16	30 11/16	28 12/16	99 12/16	7	5 12/16	7 7/16	6 4/16	7 14/16	6 11/16
15	33 10/16	32 14/16	30 13/16	106 12/16	7 8/16	6 3/16	8	6 11/16	8 7/16	7 3/16
16	35 13/16	35 1/16	32 14/16	113 12/16	8	6 9/16	8 8/16	7 2/16	9	7 10/16
17	38 1/16	37 4/16	34 15/16	120 12/16	8 8/16	7	9 1/16	7 9/16	9 9/16	8 2/16
18	40 5/16	39 7/16	37	127 12/16	9	7 6/16	9 9/16	8	10 2/16	8 9/16
19	42 9/16	41 10/16	39 1/16	134 12/16	9 8/16	7 13/16	10 2/16	8 7/16	10 11/16	9 1/16
20	44 13/16	43 13/16	41 1/16	141 12/16	10	8 3/16	10 10/16	8 14/16	11 4/16	9 9/16
21	47 1/16	46	43 2/16	148 12/16	10 8/16	8 10/16	11 3/16	9 5/16	11 13/16	10
22	49 4/16	48 3/16	45 3/16	155 12/16	11	9 1/16	11 11/16	9 12/16	12 6/16	10 8/16
23	51 8/16	50 6/16	47 4/16	162 12/16	11 8/16	9 7/16	12 4/16	10 4/16	12 15/16	11
24	53 12/16	52 9/16	49 5/16	169 12/16	12	9 14/16	12 12/16	10 11/16	13 8/16	11 7/16
25	56	54 12/16	51 6/16	176 12/16	12 8/16	10 4/16	13 5/16	11 2/16	14 1/16	11 15/16
26	58 4/16	56 15/16	53 7/16	183 12/16	13	10 11/16	13 13/16	11 9/16	14 10/16	12 7/16
27	60 8/16	59 2/16	55 8/16	190 12/16	13 8/16	11 2/16	14 6/16	12	15 3/16	12 14/16
28	62 12/16	61 5/16	57 8/16	197 12/16	14	11 8/16	14 14/16	12 7/16	15 12/16	13 6/16

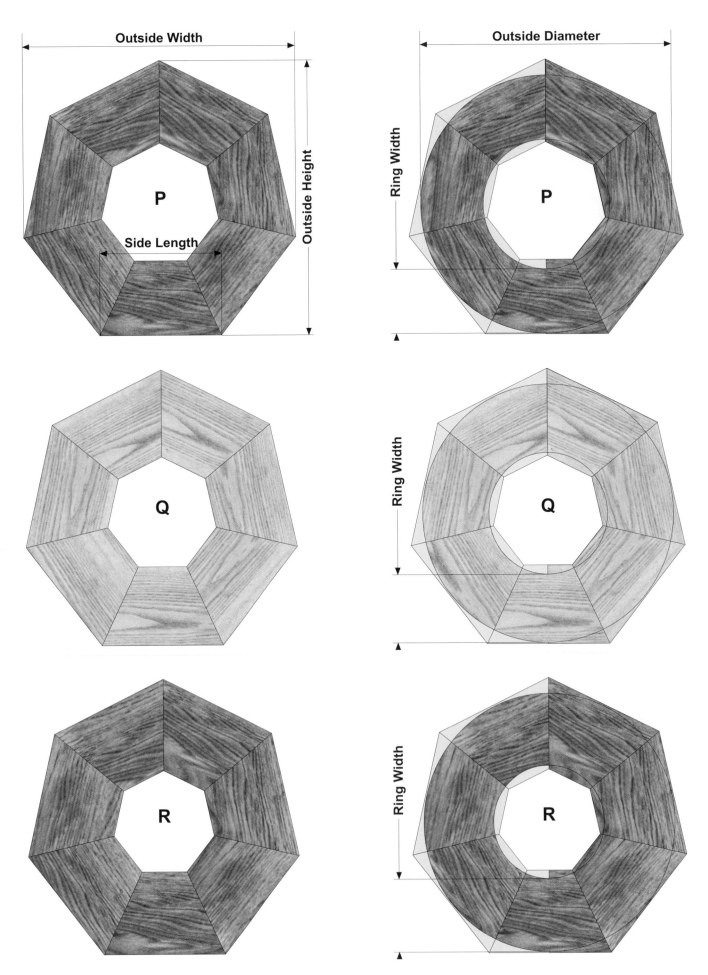

Side Length	Frame Width	Frame Height	Ring Max. OD	Material Req'd.	P Side Width	P Ring Width	Q Side Width	Q Ring Width	R Side Width	R Ring Width
8/16	1 2/16	1 2/16	1	5 4/16	5/16	4/16	5/16	4/16	5/16	5/16
10/16	1 6/16	1 6/16	1 5/16	6 2/16	6/16	5/16	6/16	5/16	7/16	6/16
12/16	1 11/16	1 10/16	1 9/16	7	7/16	6/16	8/16	7/16	8/16	7/16
14/16	1 15/16	1 15/16	1 13/16	7 14/16	8/16	6/16	9/16	8/16	9/16	8/16
1	2 4/16	2 3/16	2 1/16	8 12/16	10/16	7/16	10/16	9/16	11/16	9/16
1 4/16	2 13/16	2 12/16	2 9/16	10 8/16	12/16	8/16	13/16	11/16	13/16	12/16
1 8/16	3 6/16	3 5/16	3 1/16	12 4/16	14/16	10/16	15/16	13/16	1	14/16
1 12/16	3 15/16	3 13/16	3 10/16	14	1 1/16	12/16	1 2/16	15/16	1 2/16	1
2	4 8/16	4 6/16	4 2/16	15 12/16	1 3/16	13/16	1 4/16	1 1/16	1 5/16	1 2/16
2 4/16	5 1/16	4 15/16	4 10/16	17 8/16	1 5/16	15/16	1 7/16	1 4/16	1 8/16	1 5/16
2 8/16	5 10/16	5 8/16	5 2/16	19 4/16	1 8/16	1 1/16	1 9/16	1 6/16	1 10/16	1 7/16
2 12/16	6 3/16	6	5 10/16	21	1 10/16	1 2/16	1 12/16	1 8/16	1 13/16	1 9/16
3	6 12/16	6 9/16	6 3/16	22 12/16	1 13/16	1 4/16	1 14/16	1 10/16	2	1 12/16
3 4/16	7 4/16	7 2/16	6 11/16	24 8/16	1 15/16	1 6/16	2 1/16	1 12/16	2 2/16	1 14/16
3 8/16	7 13/16	7 11/16	7 3/16	26 4/16	2 1/16	1 7/16	2 3/16	1 14/16	2 5/16	2
3 12/16	8 6/16	8 3/16	7 11/16	28	2 4/16	1 9/16	2 6/16	2 1/16	2 7/16	2 3/16
4	8 15/16	8 12/16	8 3/16	29 12/16	2 6/16	1 11/16	2 8/16	2 3/16	2 10/16	2 5/16
4 4/16	9 8/16	9 5/16	8 12/16	31 8/16	2 8/16	1 12/16	2 11/16	2 5/16	2 13/16	2 7/16
4 8/16	10 1/16	9 14/16	9 4/16	33 4/16	2 11/16	1 14/16	2 13/16	2 7/16	2 15/16	2 10/16
4 12/16	10 10/16	10 6/16	9 12/16	35	2 13/16	2	3	2 9/16	3 2/16	2 12/16
5	11 3/16	10 15/16	10 4/16	36 12/16	3	2 1/16	3 2/16	2 12/16	3 5/16	2 14/16
5 4/16	11 12/16	11 8/16	10 13/16	38 8/16	3 2/16	2 3/16	3 5/16	2 14/16	3 7/16	3
5 8/16	12 5/16	12 1/16	11 5/16	40 4/16	3 4/16	2 5/16	3 7/16	3	3 10/16	3 3/16
5 12/16	12 14/16	12 9/16	11 13/16	42	3 7/16	2 6/16	3 10/16	3 2/16	3 12/16	3 5/16
6	13 7/16	13 2/16	12 5/16	43 12/16	3 9/16	2 8/16	3 12/16	3 4/16	3 15/16	3 7/16
6 8/16	14 9/16	14 4/16	13 6/16	47 4/16	3 14/16	2 12/16	4 1/16	3 9/16	4 4/16	3 12/16
7	15 11/16	15 5/16	14 6/16	50 12/16	4 3/16	2 15/16	4 6/16	3 13/16	4 10/16	4 1/16
7 8/16	16 13/16	16 7/16	15 7/16	54 4/16	4 7/16	3 2/16	4 11/16	4 1/16	4 15/16	4 5/16
8	17 15/16	17 8/16	16 7/16	57 12/16	4 12/16	3 6/16	5	4 6/16	5 4/16	4 10/16
8 8/16	19 1/16	18 10/16	17 7/16	61 4/16	5 1/16	3 9/16	5 5/16	4 10/16	5 9/16	4 15/16
9	20 3/16	19 11/16	18 8/16	64 12/16	5 6/16	3 12/16	5 10/16	4 14/16	5 15/16	5 3/16
9 8/16	21 4/16	20 13/16	19 8/16	68 4/16	5 10/16	4	5 15/16	5 3/16	6 4/16	5 8/16
10	22 6/16	21 14/16	20 9/16	71 12/16	5 15/16	4 3/16	6 4/16	5 7/16	6 9/16	5 12/16
10 8/16	23 8/16	23	21 9/16	75 4/16	6 4/16	4 6/16	6 9/16	5 11/16	6 14/16	6 1/16
11	24 10/16	24 1/16	22 10/16	78 12/16	6 9/16	4 10/16	6 14/16	6	7 4/16	6 6/16
11 8/16	25 12/16	25 3/16	23 10/16	82 4/16	6 13/16	4 13/16	7 3/16	6 4/16	7 9/16	6 10/16
12	26 14/16	26 4/16	24 10/16	85 12/16	7 2/16	5	7 8/16	6 8/16	7 14/16	6 15/16
13	29 2/16	28 8/16	26 11/16	92 12/16	7 12/16	5 7/16	8 2/16	7 1/16	8 9/16	7 8/16
14	31 6/16	30 11/16	28 12/16	99 12/16	8 5/16	5 14/16	8 12/16	7 10/16	9 3/16	8 1/16
15	33 10/16	32 14/16	30 13/16	106 12/16	8 15/16	6 4/16	9 6/16	8 3/16	9 14/16	8 11/16
16	35 13/16	35 1/16	32 14/16	113 12/16	9 8/16	6 11/16	10	8 11/16	10 8/16	9 4/16
17	38 1/16	37 4/16	34 15/16	120 12/16	10 2/16	7 2/16	10 10/16	9 4/16	11 3/16	9 13/16
18	40 5/16	39 7/16	37	127 12/16	10 11/16	7 9/16	11 4/16	9 13/16	11 13/16	10 6/16
19	42 9/16	41 10/16	39 1/16	134 12/16	11 5/16	7 15/16	11 14/16	10 5/16	12 8/16	11
20	44 13/16	43 13/16	41 1/16	141 12/16	11 14/16	8 6/16	12 8/16	10 14/16	13 2/16	11 9/16
21	47 1/16	46	43 2/16	148 12/16	12 8/16	8 13/16	13 2/16	11 7/16	13 13/16	12 2/16
22	49 4/16	48 3/16	45 3/16	155 12/16	13 1/16	9 3/16	13 12/16	12	14 7/16	12 11/16
23	51 8/16	50 6/16	47 4/16	162 12/16	13 11/16	9 10/16	14 6/16	12 8/16	15 2/16	13 4/16
24	53 12/16	52 9/16	49 5/16	169 12/16	14 4/16	10 1/16	15	13 1/16	15 12/16	13 14/16
25	56	54 12/16	51 6/16	176 12/16	14 14/16	10 7/16	15 10/16	13 10/16	16 7/16	14 7/16
26	58 4/16	56 15/16	53 7/16	183 12/16	15 7/16	10 14/16	16 4/16	14 2/16	17 1/16	15
27	60 8/16	59 2/16	55 8/16	190 12/16	16 1/16	11 5/16	16 14/16	14 11/16	17 12/16	15 9/16
28	62 12/16	61 5/16	57 8/16	197 12/16	16 10/16	11 11/16	17 8/16	15 4/16	18 6/16	16 3/16

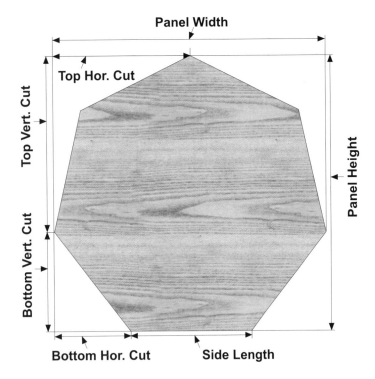

Panel Width

Top Hor. Cut

Top Vert. Cut

Bottom Vert. Cut

Panel Height

Bottom Hor. Cut

Side Length

The Chart below shows the formulas that were used in the process of laying out the 7 sided shapes. These are included to assist you if you are designing a project to a size that is not illustrated in the Dimension Charts provided. We hope you find them helpful as you design your projects.

7 SIDED PANEL FORMULAS		
Panel Width =	Panel Height x	1.025
Panel Height =	Panel Width x	0.976
Side Length =	Panel Height x	0.446
Side Length =	Panel Width x	0.457
Top Hor. Cut =	Panel Width x	0.500
Bott. Hor. Cut =	Panel Width x	0.277
Top Vert. Cut =	Panel Width x	0.623
Bott.Vert. Cut =	Panel Width x	0.352

PANEL WIDTH	PANEL HEIGHT	SIDE LENGTH	TOP HOR. CUT	BOTTOM HOR. CUT	TOP VERT. CUT	BOTTOM VERT. CUT
12/16	12/16	5/16	6/16	3/16	7/16	4/16
1	1	7/16	8/16	4/16	10/16	6/16
1 4/16	1 4/16	9/16	10/16	6/16	12/16	7/16
1 8/16	1 7/16	11/16	12/16	7/16	15/16	8/16
1 12/16	1 11/16	12/16	14/16	8/16	1 1/16	10/16
2	1 15/16	14/16	1	9/16	1 4/16	11/16
2 4/16	2 3/16	1	1 2/16	10/16	1 6/16	13/16
2 8/16	2 7/16	1 2/16	1 4/16	11/16	1 9/16	14/16
2 12/16	2 11/16	1 4/16	1 6/16	12/16	1 11/16	15/16
3	2 15/16	1 5/16	1 8/16	13/16	1 14/16	1 1/16
3 4/16	3 3/16	1 7/16	1 10/16	14/16	2	1 2/16
3 8/16	3 7/16	1 9/16	1 12/16	1	2 3/16	1 4/16
3 12/16	3 11/16	1 11/16	1 14/16	1 1/16	2 5/16	1 5/16
4	3 14/16	1 13/16	2	1 2/16	2 8/16	1 7/16
4 4/16	4 2/16	1 14/16	2 2/16	1 3/16	2 10/16	1 8/16
4 8/16	4 6/16	2	2 4/16	1 4/16	2 13/16	1 9/16
4 12/16	4 10/16	2 2/16	2 6/16	1 5/16	2 15/16	1 11/16
5	4 14/16	2 4/16	2 8/16	1 6/16	3 2/16	1 12/16
5 4/16	5 2/16	2 5/16	2 10/16	1 7/16	3 4/16	1 14/16
5 8/16	5 6/16	2 7/16	2 12/16	1 8/16	3 7/16	1 15/16
5 12/16	5 10/16	2 9/16	2 14/16	1 9/16	3 9/16	2
6	5 14/16	2 11/16	3	1 11/16	3 12/16	2 2/16
6 4/16	6 2/16	2 13/16	3 2/16	1 12/16	3 14/16	2 3/16
6 8/16	6 6/16	2 14/16	3 4/16	1 13/16	4 1/16	2 5/16
6 12/16	6 9/16	3	3 6/16	1 14/16	4 3/16	2 6/16
7	6 13/16	3 2/16	3 8/16	1 15/16	4 6/16	2 7/16
7 4/16	7 1/16	3 4/16	3 10/16	2	4 8/16	2 9/16
7 8/16	7 5/16	3 6/16	3 12/16	2 1/16	4 11/16	2 10/16
7 12/16	7 9/16	3 7/16	3 14/16	2 2/16	4 13/16	2 12/16
8	7 13/16	3 9/16	4	2 3/16	5	2 13/16
8 4/16	8 1/16	3 11/16	4 2/16	2 5/16	5 2/16	2 14/16
8 8/16	8 5/16	3 13/16	4 4/16	2 6/16	5 5/16	3

PANEL WIDTH	PANEL HEIGHT	SIDE LENGTH	TOP HOR. CUT	BOTTOM HOR. CUT	TOP VERT. CUT	BOTTOM VERT. CUT
8 12/16	8 9/16	3 14/16	4 6/16	2 7/16	5 7/16	3 1/16
9	8 13/16	4	4 8/16	2 8/16	5 10/16	3 3/16
9 4/16	9	4 2/16	4 10/16	2 9/16	5 12/16	3 4/16
9 8/16	9 4/16	4 4/16	4 12/16	2 10/16	5 15/16	3 6/16
9 12/16	9 8/16	4 6/16	4 14/16	2 11/16	6 1/16	3 7/16
10	9 12/16	4 7/16	5	2 12/16	6 4/16	3 8/16
10 4/16	10	4 9/16	5 2/16	2 13/16	6 6/16	3 10/16
10 8/16	10 4/16	4 11/16	5 4/16	2 15/16	6 9/16	3 11/16
10 12/16	10 8/16	4 13/16	5 6/16	3	6 11/16	3 13/16
11	10 12/16	4 14/16	5 8/16	3 1/16	6 14/16	3 14/16
11 4/16	11	5	5 10/16	3 2/16	7	3 15/16
11 8/16	11 4/16	5 2/16	5 12/16	3 3/16	7 3/16	4 1/16
12	11 11/16	5 6/16	6	3 5/16	7 8/16	4 4/16
12 4/16	11 15/16	5 7/16	6 2/16	3 6/16	7 10/16	4 5/16
12 8/16	12 3/16	5 9/16	6 4/16	3 7/16	7 13/16	4 6/16
12 12/16	12 7/16	5 11/16	6 6/16	3 9/16	7 15/16	4 8/16
13	12 11/16	5 13/16	6 8/16	3 10/16	8 2/16	4 9/16
13 4/16	12 15/16	5 15/16	6 10/16	3 11/16	8 4/16	4 11/16
13 8/16	13 3/16	6	6 12/16	3 12/16	8 7/16	4 12/16
13 12/16	13 7/16	6 2/16	6 14/16	3 13/16	8 9/16	4 13/16
14	13 11/16	6 4/16	7	3 14/16	8 12/16	4 15/16
14 8/16	14 2/16	6 7/16	7 4/16	4	9 1/16	5 2/16
15	14 10/16	6 11/16	7 8/16	4 2/16	9 6/16	5 4/16
15 8/16	15 2/16	6 15/16	7 12/16	4 5/16	9 11/16	5 7/16
16	15 10/16	7 2/16	8	4 7/16	9 15/16	5 10/16
16 8/16	16 2/16	7 6/16	8 4/16	4 9/16	10 4/16	5 13/16
17	16 9/16	7 9/16	8 8/16	4 11/16	10 9/16	6
17 8/16	17 1/16	7 13/16	8 12/16	4 14/16	10 14/16	6 3/16
18	17 9/16	8	9	5	11 3/16	6 5/16
19	18 9/16	8 8/16	9 8/16	5 4/16	11 13/16	6 11/16
20	19 8/16	8 15/16	10	5 9/16	12 7/16	7 1/16
21	20 8/16	9 6/16	10 8/16	5 13/16	13 1/16	7 6/16
22	21 8/16	9 13/16	11	6 2/16	13 11/16	7 12/16
23	22 7/16	10 4/16	11 8/16	6 6/16	14 5/16	8 2/16
24	23 7/16	10 11/16	12	6 10/16	14 15/16	8 7/16
25	24 6/16	11 2/16	12 8/16	6 15/16	15 9/16	8 13/16
26	25 6/16	11 10/16	13	7 3/16	16 3/16	9 2/16
27	26 6/16	12 1/16	13 8/16	7 8/16	16 13/16	9 8/16
28	27 5/16	12 8/16	14	7 12/16	17 7/16	9 14/16
29	28 5/16	12 15/16	14 8/16	8 1/16	18 1/16	10 3/16
30	29 4/16	13 6/16	15	8 5/16	18 11/16	10 9/16
31	30 4/16	13 13/16	15 8/16	8 9/16	19 5/16	10 15/16
32	31 4/16	14 4/16	16	8 14/16	19 15/16	11 4/16
33	32 3/16	14 11/16	16 8/16	9 2/16	20 9/16	11 10/16
34	33 3/16	15 3/16	17	9 7/16	21 3/16	11 15/16
35	34 3/16	15 10/16	17 8/16	9 11/16	21 13/16	12 5/16
36	35 2/16	16 1/16	18	10	22 7/16	12 11/16
37	36 2/16	16 8/16	18 8/16	10 4/16	23 1/16	13
38	37 1/16	16 15/16	19	10 8/16	23 11/16	13 6/16
39	38 1/16	17 6/16	19 8/16	10 13/16	24 5/16	13 12/16
40	39 1/16	17 13/16	20	11 1/16	24 15/16	14 1/16
41	40	18 5/16	20 8/16	11 6/16	25 9/16	14 7/16
42	41	18 12/16	21	11 10/16	26 3/16	14 13/16

8 SIDED PROJECT INFORMATION

Geometric Name: Octagon
Definition: A Polygon having 8 sides
Miter Angle: 22.5°
Angle Change / Adjoining Sides: 45°

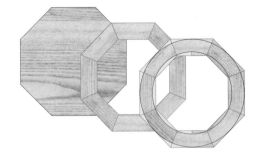

The 8 sided shape (Octagon) is one of the shapes that is very easy to get creative with. It's a fun project to build, and in some cases can be the perfect shape for the item you may wish to frame. The one thing that should be considered when using this shape (with sides of equal length) is that for most standard sizes of pictures, a lot of cropping of the picture will be required. However, the Octagon is very simple to get creative with by simply changing some of the side lengths.

The Illustrations to the right should give you an idea of the amount of cropping that may be required by using an Octagon (with equal length sides) as your choice of shape for a frame.

In the left Illustration, you see a scale (shown in red) 8" x 10" sheet in portrait format. The sheet border is slightly outside the rabbeted area (shown in yellow) of the frame. Note the amount of material that would need to be cropped off the sheet top and/or bottom.

In the right Illustration, you see the same size sheet, but rotated 90° into a landscape format. Note the same amount of material that would need to be cropped off the sheet sides.

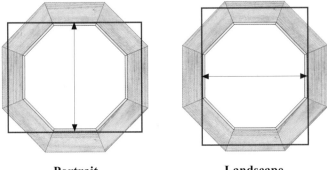

Portrait   **Landscape**

You should note that both of the frames to the right are exactly the same size. This is due to the fact that on an Octagon, each side has a side parallel to it, and the distance between all parallel sides is equal.   In our **8 SIDED FRAME FORMULAS** below, you will be able to see that the dimensions for both formats for the pictures are identical.

If the project you are building is a frame for a specific size object, you should refer to the **8 SIDED FRAME FORMULAS** Chart below as a first step. On an Octagon (with sides of equal length) the height will always be identical to the width, so there is no controlling dimension for the frame. (See all of the formulas in the Chart below**).**

The Octagon is probably the easiest of the Polygons to get creative with, as it has the fewest number of sides (other than a rectangle) where one side of the shape will be parallel to one of the sheet sides of the object that is being framed.

8 SIDED FRAME FORMULAS		
WIDTH	**HEIGHT**	**SIDE LENGTH**
Width = Side Length x 2.42	Height = Side Length x 2.42	Side Length = Width x .413
Width = Height x 1.00	Height = Width x 1.00	Side Length = Height x .413

Though the information above is very helpful, one of the most time consuming (and frustrating) things about building frames is to try to cut to a dimension that is not measured on either the inside or outside edge of the molding. I like to cut miters from the inside to the outside edges of the molding. This not only allows me to eliminate tear out on the inside corners of the frame since I am cutting into the inside edge, I am also cutting with the grain of the molding**.** It also allows me to see the outside edge of the material as I cut it. To help you understand how easy it is to convert a dimension along the rabbeted edge into an outside measurement, I will explain how we can use some basic math to help us determine the outside length of our frame sides. The Illustration below should be helpful in showing you how we designed our **8 SIDED FRAME ADDED WIDTH AND LENGTH CHART** on the next page.

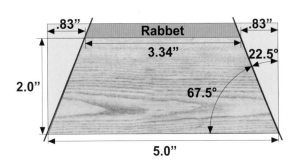

The Illustration to the left represents a piece of wood that is 5" long and 2" wide (to the edge of the rabbet). Note that on the right side that the end of the piece shows the miter angle for an Octagon (22.5°) and the resulting angle of the cut (67.5°).

You should also note that at the rabbet, the 22.5° cuts shorten each end of the piece by .83". Since both ends of the piece are cut, this means that the length at the rabbet is 3.34", which is 1.66" shorter than the outside edge of the molding. What this Illustration tells us is that at a 22.5° cut, we will add 1.66" to the length at a 2" width. This is the basis of our formula.

If we divide the **Added Length** (1.66") by the **Added Width** (2.0") we end up with .83 as our multiplier. In the event that you want to make a frame and need to work in fractions smaller than 1/16 increments, you would multiply the width of the molding outside the rabbet by .83. To determine the decimal equivalent of the fractions you need to use, refer to the **FRACTION TO DECIMAL CONVERSION CHART** provided.

If you are able to use 1/16" increments for the mathematics of your frames, you should use the **8 SIDED FRAME ADDED WIDTH AND LENGTH CHART** below.

Determine how wide you want the material to be (outside the rabbet). Refer to the Chart below to find this dimension in one of the yellow shaded columns. The added length for that width will be shown in the green shaded block to the right of it. Add this dimension to the side length determined in the first step. You should then add whatever waste you want to allow for each side. This total is then multiplied by 8 to determine how much material is needed to build your project.

8 SIDED FRAME ADDED WIDTH AND LENGTH CHART

Added Width	Added Length	Added Width	Added Length	Added Width	Added Length	Added Width	Added Length	Added Width	Added Length
1/16	1/16	1 1/16	14/16	2 1/16	1 11/16	3 1/16	2 9/16	4 1/16	3 6/16
2/16	2/16	1 2/16	15/16	2 2/16	1 12/16	3 2/16	2 10/16	4 2/16	3 7/16
3/16	2/16	1 3/16	1	2 3/16	1 13/16	3 3/16	2 10/16	4 3/16	3 8/16
4/16	3/16	1 4/16	1 1/16	2 4/16	1 14/16	3 4/16	2 11/16	4 4/16	3 8/16
5/16	4/16	1 5/16	1 1/16	2 5/16	1 15/16	3 5/16	2 12/16	4 5/16	3 9/16
6/16	5/16	1 6/16	1 2/16	2 6/16	2	3 6/16	2 13/16	4 6/16	3 10/16
7/16	6/16	1 7/16	1 3/16	2 7/16	2	3 7/16	2 14/16	4 7/16	3 11/16
8/16	7/16	1 8/16	1 4/16	2 8/16	2 1/16	3 8/16	2 14/16	4 8/16	3 12/16
9/16	7/16	1 9/16	1 5/16	2 9/16	2 2/16	3 9/16	2 15/16	4 9/16	3 13/16
10/16	8/16	1 10/16	1 6/16	2 10/16	2 3/16	3 10/16	3	4 10/16	3 13/16
11/16	9/16	1 11/16	1 6/16	2 11/16	2 4/16	3 11/16	3 1/16	4 11/16	3 14/16
12/16	10/16	1 12/16	1 7/16	2 12/16	2 5/16	3 12/16	3 2/16	4 12/16	3 15/16
13/16	11/16	1 13/16	1 8/16	2 13/16	2 5/16	3 13/16	3 3/16	4 13/16	4
14/16	12/16	1 14/16	1 9/16	2 14/16	2 6/16	3 14/16	3 3/16	4 14/16	4 1/16
15/16	12/16	1 15/16	1 10/16	2 15/16	2 7/16	3 15/16	3 4/16	4 15/16	4 2/16
1	13/16	2	1 11/16	3	2 8/16	4	3 5/16	5	4 2/16

The Chart below is provided to enable you to make 8 sided frames using the mathematics of most popular picture sizes. Note that the dimensions are identical in portrait and landscape format. This is because the picture for an Octagon is basically a square with 45° crops on each 90° corner of the picture. In the Charts, the different colored columns represent the following information:

Red: The controlling dimension of the sheet size. (width in portrait, height in landscape)
Gray: The dimension of the sheet size that will need to be cropped.

White: The rabbet length for the frame sides.
Orange: The size of the opening in the direction the picture will need to be cropped.
Blue: The amount of material that will need to be cropped.

RABBET AREA DIMENSIONS FOR 8 SIDED FRAMES

FOR PORTRAIT FORMAT					FOR LANDSCAPE FORMAT				
Object Width	Object Height	Rabbet Length	Opening Height	Vertical Crop	Object Width	Object Height	Rabbet Length	Opening Width	Horizontal Crop
4	5	1 11/16	4 2/16	1	5	4	1 11/16	4 2/16	1
5	7	2 2/16	5 2/16	2	7	5	2 2/16	5 2/16	2
6	8	2 8/16	6 2/16	2	8	6	2 8/16	6 2/16	2
8	10	3 6/16	8 2/16	2	10	8	3 6/16	8 2/16	2
8 1/2	11	3 9/16	8 10/16	2 8/16	11	8 1/2	3 9/16	8 10/16	2 8/16
10	14	4 3/16	10 2/16	4	14	10	4 3/16	10 2/16	4
11	14	4 10/16	11 2/16	3	14	11	4 10/16	11 2/16	3
12	16	5	12 2/16	4	16	12	5	12 2/16	4
16	20	6 11/16	16 2/16	4	20	16	6 11/16	16 2/16	4
18	24	7 8/16	18 2/16	6	24	18	7 8/16	18 2/16	6
20	24	8 5/16	20 2/16	4	24	20	8 5/16	20 2/16	4
24	30	9 15/16	24 2/16	6	30	24	9 15/16	24 2/16	6

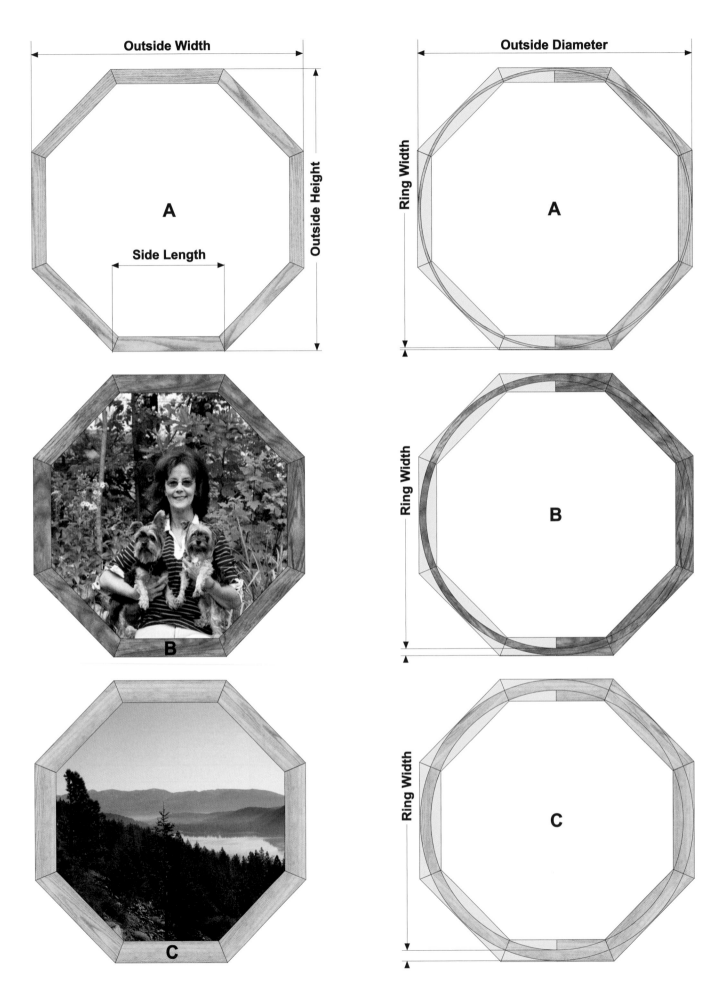

Outside Width

Outside Height

Side Length

A

Outside Diameter

Ring Width

A

B

Ring Width

B

C

Ring Width

C

Side Length	Frame Width	Frame Height	Ring Max. OD	Material Req'd.	A Side Width	A Ring Width	B Side Width	B Ring Width	C Side Width	C Ring Width
8/16	1 3/16	1 3/16	1 3/16	6	1/16	0	1/16	0	2/16	1/16
10/16	1 8/16	1 8/16	1 8/16	7	1/16	0	2/16	1/16	2/16	1/16
12/16	1 13/16	1 13/16	1 13/16	8	2/16	0	2/16	1/16	2/16	1/16
14/16	2 2/16	2 2/16	2 2/16	9	2/16	0	2/16	1/16	3/16	1/16
1	2 7/16	2 7/16	2 7/16	10	2/16	0	3/16	1/16	3/16	1/16
1 4/16	3	3	3	12	3/16	1/16	3/16	1/16	4/16	2/16
1 8/16	3 10/16	3 10/16	3 10/16	14	3/16	1/16	4/16	1/16	5/16	2/16
1 12/16	4 4/16	4 4/16	4 3/16	16	4/16	1/16	4/16	1/16	5/16	2/16
2	4 13/16	4 13/16	4 13/16	18	4/16	1/16	5/16	2/16	6/16	3/16
2 4/16	5 7/16	5 7/16	5 7/16	20	5/16	1/16	6/16	2/16	7/16	3/16
2 8/16	6 1/16	6 1/16	6	22	5/16	1/16	6/16	2/16	8/16	3/16
2 12/16	6 10/16	6 10/16	6 10/16	24	6/16	1/16	7/16	2/16	8/16	4/16
3	7 4/16	7 4/16	7 4/16	26	6/16	1/16	8/16	3/16	9/16	4/16
3 4/16	7 14/16	7 14/16	7 13/16	28	7/16	1/16	8/16	3/16	10/16	5/16
3 8/16	8 8/16	8 8/16	8 7/16	30	7/16	2/16	9/16	3/16	11/16	5/16
3 12/16	9 1/16	9 1/16	9	32	8/16	2/16	9/16	3/16	11/16	5/16
4	9 11/16	9 11/16	9 10/16	34	8/16	2/16	10/16	3/16	12/16	6/16
4 4/16	10 5/16	10 5/16	10 4/16	36	9/16	2/16	11/16	4/16	13/16	6/16
4 8/16	10 14/16	10 14/16	10 13/16	38	9/16	2/16	11/16	4/16	14/16	6/16
4 12/16	11 8/16	11 8/16	11 7/16	40	10/16	2/16	12/16	4/16	14/16	7/16
5	12 2/16	12 2/16	12 1/16	42	10/16	2/16	13/16	4/16	15/16	7/16
5 4/16	12 11/16	12 11/16	12 10/16	44	11/16	2/16	13/16	4/16	1	7/16
5 8/16	13 5/16	13 5/16	13 4/16	46	11/16	2/16	14/16	5/16	1 1/16	8/16
5 12/16	13 15/16	13 15/16	13 13/16	48	12/16	3/16	14/16	5/16	1 1/16	8/16
6	14 8/16	14 8/16	14 7/16	50	12/16	3/16	15/16	5/16	1 2/16	8/16
6 8/16	15 12/16	15 12/16	15 10/16	54	13/16	3/16	1	6/16	1 4/16	9/16
7	16 15/16	16 15/16	16 14/16	58	14/16	3/16	1 2/16	6/16	1 5/16	10/16
7 8/16	18 2/16	18 2/16	18 1/16	62	15/16	3/16	1 3/16	6/16	1 7/16	10/16
8	19 6/16	19 6/16	19 4/16	66	1	4/16	1 4/16	7/16	1 8/16	11/16
8 8/16	20 9/16	20 9/16	20 7/16	70	1 1/16	4/16	1 5/16	7/16	1 10/16	12/16
9	21 12/16	21 12/16	21 11/16	74	1 2/16	4/16	1 7/16	8/16	1 11/16	13/16
9 8/16	23	23	22 14/16	78	1 3/16	4/16	1 8/16	8/16	1 13/16	13/16
10	24 3/16	24 3/16	24 1/16	82	1 4/16	4/16	1 9/16	8/16	1 14/16	14/16
10 8/16	25 7/16	25 7/16	25 4/16	86	1 5/16	5/16	1 10/16	9/16	2	15/16
11	26 10/16	26 10/16	26 8/16	90	1 6/16	5/16	1 12/16	9/16	2 1/16	15/16
11 8/16	27 13/16	27 13/16	27 11/16	94	1 7/16	5/16	1 13/16	10/16	2 3/16	1
12	29 1/16	29 1/16	28 14/16	98	1 8/16	5/16	1 14/16	10/16	2 4/16	1 1/16
13	31 7/16	31 7/16	31 5/16	106	1 10/16	6/16	2 1/16	11/16	2 7/16	1 2/16
14	33 14/16	33 14/16	33 11/16	114	1 12/16	6/16	2 3/16	12/16	2 10/16	1 3/16
15	36 5/16	36 5/16	36 2/16	122	1 14/16	7/16	2 6/16	13/16	2 13/16	1 5/16
16	38 12/16	38 12/16	38 8/16	130	2	7/16	2 8/16	14/16	3	1 6/16
17	41 2/16	41 2/16	40 15/16	138	2 2/16	7/16	2 11/16	14/16	3 3/16	1 8/16
18	43 9/16	43 9/16	43 5/16	146	2 4/16	8/16	2 13/16	15/16	3 6/16	1 9/16
19	46	46	45 12/16	154	2 6/16	8/16	3	1	3 9/16	1 10/16
20	48 6/16	48 6/16	48 2/16	162	2 8/16	9/16	3 2/16	1 1/16	3 12/16	1 12/16
21	50 13/16	50 13/16	50 9/16	170	2 10/16	9/16	3 5/16	1 2/16	3 15/16	1 13/16
22	53 4/16	53 4/16	52 15/16	178	2 12/16	10/16	3 7/16	1 3/16	4 2/16	1 15/16
23	55 11/16	55 11/16	55 6/16	186	2 14/16	10/16	3 10/16	1 4/16	4 5/16	2
24	58 1/16	58 1/16	57 12/16	194	3	11/16	3 12/16	1 4/16	4 8/16	2 1/16
25	60 8/16	60 8/16	60 3/16	202	3 2/16	11/16	3 15/16	1 5/16	4 11/16	2 3/16
26	62 15/16	62 15/16	62 9/16	210	3 4/16	11/16	4 1/16	1 6/16	4 14/16	2 4/16
27	65 5/16	65 5/16	65	218	3 6/16	12/16	4 4/16	1 7/16	5 1/16	2 6/16
28	67 12/16	67 12/16	67 6/16	226	3 8/16	12/16	4 6/16	1 8/16	5 4/16	2 7/16

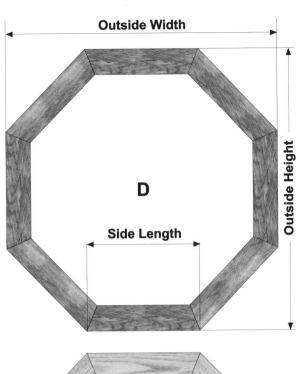

Outside Width

Outside Height

Side Length

D

E

F

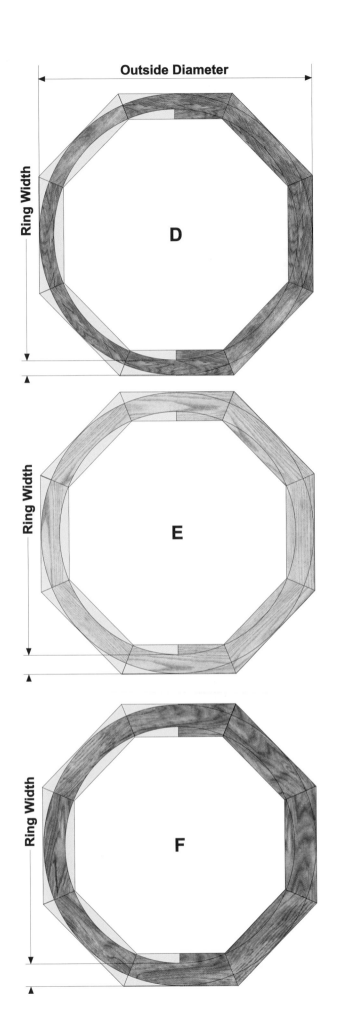

Outside Diameter

Ring Width

D

Ring Width

E

Ring Width

F

Side Length	Frame Width	Frame Height	Ring Max. OD	Material Req'd.	D Side Width	D Ring Width	E Side Width	E Ring Width	F Side Width	F Ring Width
8/16	1 3/16	1 3/16	1 3/16	6	2/16	1/16	2/16	1/16	2/16	2/16
10/16	1 8/16	1 8/16	1 8/16	7	2/16	1/16	3/16	2/16	3/16	2/16
12/16	1 13/16	1 13/16	1 13/16	8	3/16	1/16	3/16	2/16	3/16	2/16
14/16	2 2/16	2 2/16	2 2/16	9	3/16	1/16	4/16	2/16	4/16	3/16
1	2 7/16	2 7/16	2 7/16	10	4/16	2/16	4/16	2/16	5/16	3/16
1 4/16	3	3	3	12	4/16	2/16	5/16	3/16	6/16	4/16
1 8/16	3 10/16	3 10/16	3 10/16	14	5/16	2/16	6/16	4/16	7/16	5/16
1 12/16	4 4/16	4 4/16	4 3/16	16	6/16	3/16	7/16	4/16	8/16	5/16
2	4 13/16	4 13/16	4 13/16	18	7/16	3/16	8/16	5/16	9/16	6/16
2 4/16	5 7/16	5 7/16	5 7/16	20	8/16	4/16	9/16	6/16	10/16	7/16
2 8/16	6 1/16	6 1/16	6	22	9/16	4/16	10/16	6/16	11/16	8/16
2 12/16	6 10/16	6 10/16	6 10/16	24	10/16	5/16	11/16	7/16	12/16	8/16
3	7 4/16	7 4/16	7 4/16	26	11/16	5/16	12/16	7/16	14/16	9/16
3 4/16	7 14/16	7 14/16	7 13/16	28	11/16	6/16	13/16	8/16	15/16	10/16
3 8/16	8 8/16	8 8/16	8 7/16	30	12/16	6/16	14/16	9/16	1	11/16
3 12/16	9 1/16	9 1/16	9	32	13/16	7/16	15/16	9/16	1 1/16	11/16
4	9 11/16	9 11/16	9 10/16	34	14/16	7/16	1	10/16	1 2/16	12/16
4 4/16	10 5/16	10 5/16	10 4/16	36	15/16	8/16	1 1/16	11/16	1 3/16	13/16
4 8/16	10 14/16	10 14/16	10 13/16	38	1	8/16	1 2/16	11/16	1 4/16	14/16
4 12/16	11 8/16	11 8/16	11 7/16	40	1 1/16	9/16	1 3/16	12/16	1 5/16	14/16
5	12 2/16	12 2/16	12 1/16	42	1 2/16	9/16	1 4/16	12/16	1 7/16	15/16
5 4/16	12 11/16	12 11/16	12 10/16	44	1 2/16	10/16	1 5/16	13/16	1 8/16	1
5 8/16	13 5/16	13 5/16	13 4/16	46	1 3/16	10/16	1 6/16	14/16	1 9/16	1 1/16
5 12/16	13 15/16	13 15/16	13 13/16	48	1 4/16	11/16	1 7/16	14/16	1 10/16	1 1/16
6	14 8/16	14 8/16	14 7/16	50	1 5/16	11/16	1 8/16	15/16	1 11/16	1 2/16
6 8/16	15 12/16	15 12/16	15 10/16	54	1 7/16	12/16	1 10/16	1	1 13/16	1 4/16
7	16 15/16	16 15/16	16 14/16	58	1 9/16	13/16	1 12/16	1 1/16	2	1 5/16
7 8/16	18 2/16	18 2/16	18 1/16	62	1 10/16	14/16	1 14/16	1 3/16	2 2/16	1 7/16
8	19 6/16	19 6/16	19 4/16	66	1 12/16	14/16	2	1 4/16	2 4/16	1 8/16
8 8/16	20 9/16	20 9/16	20 7/16	70	1 14/16	15/16	2 2/16	1 5/16	2 6/16	1 10/16
9	21 12/16	21 12/16	21 11/16	74	2	1	2 4/16	1 6/16	2 9/16	1 11/16
9 8/16	23	23	22 14/16	78	2 1/16	1 1/16	2 6/16	1 7/16	2 11/16	1 13/16
10	24 3/16	24 3/16	24 1/16	82	2 3/16	1 2/16	2 8/16	1 9/16	2 13/16	1 14/16
10 8/16	25 7/16	25 7/16	25 4/16	86	2 5/16	1 3/16	2 10/16	1 10/16	2 15/16	2
11	26 10/16	26 10/16	26 8/16	90	2 7/16	1 4/16	2 12/16	1 11/16	3 2/16	2 1/16
11 8/16	27 13/16	27 13/16	27 11/16	94	2 8/16	1 5/16	2 14/16	1 12/16	3 4/16	2 3/16
12	29 1/16	29 1/16	28 14/16	98	2 10/16	1 6/16	3	1 14/16	3 6/16	2 4/16
13	31 7/16	31 7/16	31 5/16	106	2 14/16	1 7/16	3 4/16	2	3 11/16	2 7/16
14	33 14/16	33 14/16	33 11/16	114	3 1/16	1 9/16	3 8/16	2 3/16	3 15/16	2 10/16
15	36 5/16	36 5/16	36 2/16	122	3 5/16	1 11/16	3 12/16	2 5/16	4 4/16	2 13/16
16	38 12/16	38 12/16	38 8/16	130	3 8/16	1 13/16	4	2 8/16	4 8/16	3
17	41 2/16	41 2/16	40 15/16	138	3 12/16	1 15/16	4 4/16	2 10/16	4 13/16	3 3/16
18	43 9/16	43 9/16	43 5/16	146	3 15/16	2 1/16	4 8/16	2 12/16	5 1/16	3 6/16
19	46	46	45 12/16	154	4 3/16	2 3/16	4 12/16	2 15/16	5 6/16	3 9/16
20	48 6/16	48 6/16	48 2/16	162	4 6/16	2 5/16	5	3 1/16	5 10/16	3 12/16
21	50 13/16	50 13/16	50 9/16	170	4 10/16	2 7/16	5 4/16	3 4/16	5 15/16	3 15/16
22	53 4/16	53 4/16	52 15/16	178	4 13/16	2 9/16	5 8/16	3 6/16	6 3/16	4 2/16
23	55 11/16	55 11/16	55 6/16	186	5 1/16	2 10/16	5 12/16	3 9/16	6 8/16	4 5/16
24	58 1/16	58 1/16	57 12/16	194	5 4/16	2 12/16	6	3 11/16	6 12/16	4 8/16
25	60 8/16	60 8/16	60 3/16	202	5 8/16	2 14/16	6 4/16	3 14/16	7 1/16	4 11/16
26	62 15/16	62 15/16	62 9/16	210	5 11/16	3	6 8/16	4	7 5/16	4 14/16
27	65 5/16	65 5/16	65	218	5 15/16	3 2/16	6 12/16	4 3/16	7 10/16	5 1/16
28	67 12/16	67 12/16	67 6/16	226	6 2/16	3 4/16	7	4 5/16	7 14/16	5 4/16

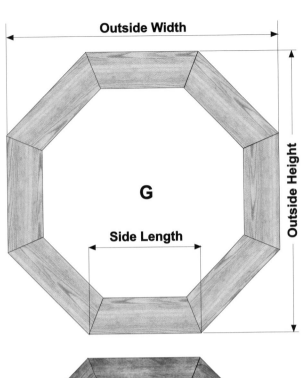

Outside Width

Outside Height

Side Length

G

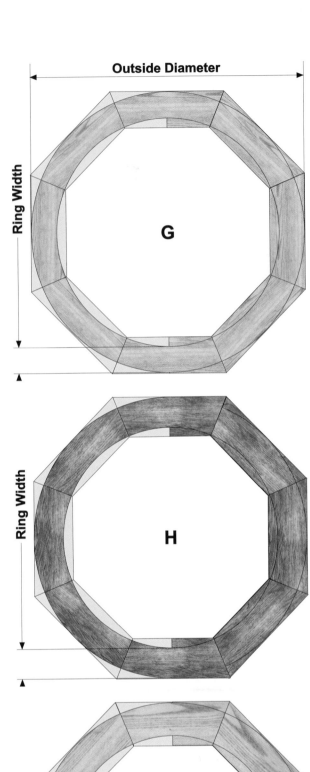

Outside Diameter

Ring Width

G

H

Ring Width

H

I

Ring Width

I

Side Length	Frame Width	Frame Height	Ring Max. OD	Material Req'd.	G Side Width	G Ring Width	H Side Width	H Ring Width	I Side Width	I Ring Width
8/16	1 3/16	1 3/16	1 3/16	6	3/16	2/16	3/16	2/16	3/16	2/16
10/16	1 8/16	1 8/16	1 8/16	7	3/16	2/16	3/16	3/16	4/16	3/16
12/16	1 13/16	1 13/16	1 13/16	8	4/16	3/16	4/16	3/16	5/16	3/16
14/16	2 2/16	2 2/16	2 2/16	9	4/16	3/16	5/16	4/16	5/16	4/16
1	2 7/16	2 7/16	2 7/16	10	5/16	4/16	6/16	4/16	6/16	5/16
1 4/16	3	3	3	12	6/16	4/16	7/16	5/16	8/16	6/16
1 8/16	3 10/16	3 10/16	3 10/16	14	8/16	5/16	8/16	6/16	9/16	7/16
1 12/16	4 4/16	4 4/16	4 3/16	16	9/16	6/16	10/16	7/16	11/16	8/16
2	4 13/16	4 13/16	4 13/16	18	10/16	7/16	11/16	8/16	12/16	9/16
2 4/16	5 7/16	5 7/16	5 7/16	20	11/16	8/16	12/16	9/16	14/16	10/16
2 8/16	6 1/16	6 1/16	6	22	13/16	9/16	14/16	10/16	15/16	12/16
2 12/16	6 10/16	6 10/16	6 10/16	24	14/16	10/16	15/16	11/16	1 1/16	13/16
3	7 4/16	7 4/16	7 4/16	26	15/16	11/16	1 1/16	12/16	1 2/16	14/16
3 4/16	7 14/16	7 14/16	7 13/16	28	1	12/16	1 2/16	13/16	1 4/16	15/16
3 8/16	8 8/16	8 8/16	8 7/16	30	1 2/16	12/16	1 3/16	14/16	1 5/16	1
3 12/16	9 1/16	9 1/16	9	32	1 3/16	13/16	1 5/16	15/16	1 7/16	1 1/16
4	9 11/16	9 11/16	9 10/16	34	1 4/16	14/16	1 6/16	1	1 8/16	1 3/16
4 4/16	10 5/16	10 5/16	10 4/16	36	1 5/16	15/16	1 7/16	1 1/16	1 10/16	1 4/16
4 8/16	10 14/16	10 14/16	10 13/16	38	1 7/16	1	1 9/16	1 2/16	1 11/16	1 5/16
4 12/16	11 8/16	11 8/16	11 7/16	40	1 8/16	1 1/16	1 10/16	1 3/16	1 13/16	1 6/16
5	12 2/16	12 2/16	12 1/16	42	1 9/16	1 2/16	1 12/16	1 4/16	1 14/16	1 7/16
5 4/16	12 11/16	12 11/16	12 10/16	44	1 10/16	1 3/16	1 13/16	1 5/16	2	1 8/16
5 8/16	13 5/16	13 5/16	13 4/16	46	1 12/16	1 4/16	1 14/16	1 7/16	2 1/16	1 9/16
5 12/16	13 15/16	13 15/16	13 13/16	48	1 13/16	1 4/16	2	1 8/16	2 3/16	1 11/16
6	14 8/16	14 8/16	14 7/16	50	1 14/16	1 5/16	2 1/16	1 9/16	2 4/16	1 12/16
6 8/16	15 12/16	15 12/16	15 10/16	54	2 1/16	1 7/16	2 4/16	1 11/16	2 7/16	1 14/16
7	16 15/16	16 15/16	16 14/16	58	2 3/16	1 9/16	2 7/16	1 13/16	2 10/16	2
7 8/16	18 2/16	18 2/16	18 1/16	62	2 6/16	1 11/16	2 9/16	1 15/16	2 13/16	2 3/16
8	19 6/16	19 6/16	19 4/16	66	2 8/16	1 12/16	2 12/16	2 1/16	3	2 5/16
8 8/16	20 9/16	20 9/16	20 7/16	70	2 11/16	1 14/16	2 15/16	2 3/16	3 3/16	2 7/16
9	21 12/16	21 12/16	21 11/16	74	2 13/16	2	3 2/16	2 5/16	3 6/16	2 10/16
9 8/16	23	23	22 14/16	78	3	2 2/16	3 4/16	2 7/16	3 9/16	2 12/16
10	24 3/16	24 3/16	24 1/16	82	3 2/16	2 4/16	3 7/16	2 9/16	3 12/16	2 14/16
10 8/16	25 7/16	25 7/16	25 4/16	86	3 5/16	2 5/16	3 10/16	2 11/16	3 15/16	3 1/16
11	26 10/16	26 10/16	26 8/16	90	3 7/16	2 7/16	3 13/16	2 13/16	4 2/16	3 3/16
11 8/16	27 13/16	27 13/16	27 11/16	94	3 10/16	2 9/16	3 15/16	2 15/16	4 5/16	3 5/16
12	29 1/16	29 1/16	28 14/16	98	3 12/16	2 11/16	4 2/16	3 1/16	4 8/16	3 8/16
13	31 7/16	31 7/16	31 5/16	106	4 1/16	2 14/16	4 8/16	3 5/16	4 14/16	3 12/16
14	33 14/16	33 14/16	33 11/16	114	4 6/16	3 2/16	4 13/16	3 9/16	5 4/16	4 1/16
15	36 5/16	36 5/16	36 2/16	122	4 11/16	3 5/16	5 3/16	3 13/16	5 10/16	4 5/16
16	38 12/16	38 12/16	38 8/16	130	5	3 9/16	5 8/16	4 1/16	6	4 10/16
17	41 2/16	41 2/16	40 15/16	138	5 5/16	3 12/16	5 14/16	4 6/16	6 6/16	4 15/16
18	43 9/16	43 9/16	43 5/16	146	5 10/16	4	6 3/16	4 10/16	6 12/16	5 3/16
19	46	46	45 12/16	154	5 15/16	4 4/16	6 9/16	4 14/16	7 2/16	5 8/16
20	48 6/16	48 6/16	48 2/16	162	6 4/16	4 7/16	6 14/16	5 2/16	7 8/16	5 13/16
21	50 13/16	50 13/16	50 9/16	170	6 9/16	4 11/16	7 4/16	5 6/16	7 14/16	6 1/16
22	53 4/16	53 4/16	52 15/16	178	6 14/16	4 14/16	7 9/16	5 10/16	8 4/16	6 6/16
23	55 11/16	55 11/16	55 6/16	186	7 3/16	5 2/16	7 15/16	5 14/16	8 10/16	6 11/16
24	58 1/16	58 1/16	57 12/16	194	7 8/16	5 5/16	8 4/16	6 2/16	9	6 15/16
25	60 8/16	60 8/16	60 3/16	202	7 13/16	5 9/16	8 10/16	6 6/16	9 6/16	7 4/16
26	62 15/16	62 15/16	62 9/16	210	8 2/16	5 12/16	8 15/16	6 10/16	9 12/16	7 8/16
27	65 5/16	65 5/16	65	218	8 7/16	6	9 5/16	6 14/16	10 2/16	7 13/16
28	67 12/16	67 12/16	67 6/16	226	8 12/16	6 4/16	9 10/16	7 3/16	10 8/16	8 2/16

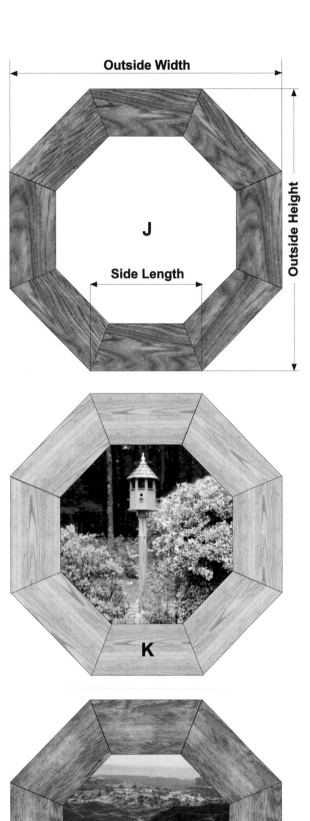

Outside Width

Outside Height

Side Length

J

K

L

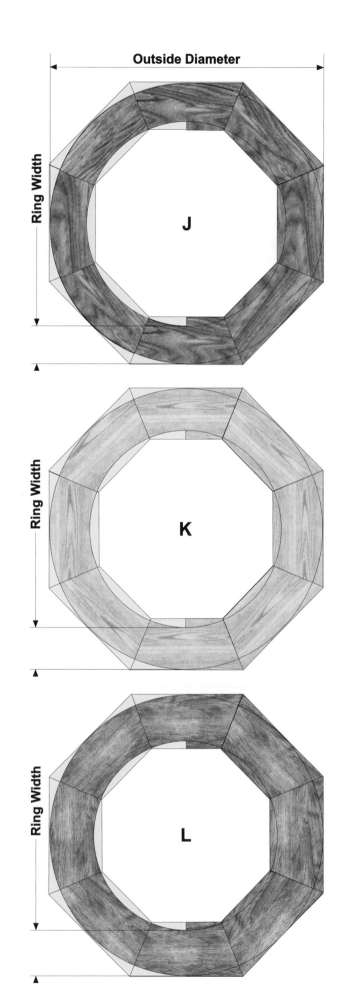

Outside Diameter

Ring Width

J

Ring Width

K

Ring Width

L

Outside Diameter

Side Length	Frame Width	Frame Height	Ring Max. OD	Material Req'd.	J Side Width	J Ring Width	K Side Width	K Ring Width	L Side Width	L Ring Width
8/16	1 3/16	1 3/16	1 3/16	6	3/16	3/16	4/16	3/16	4/16	3/16
10/16	1 8/16	1 8/16	1 8/16	7	4/16	3/16	4/16	4/16	5/16	4/16
12/16	1 13/16	1 13/16	1 13/16	8	5/16	4/16	5/16	4/16	6/16	5/16
14/16	2 2/16	2 2/16	2 2/16	9	6/16	5/16	6/16	5/16	7/16	5/16
1	2 7/16	2 7/16	2 7/16	10	7/16	5/16	7/16	6/16	8/16	6/16
1 4/16	3	3	3	12	8/16	6/16	9/16	7/16	9/16	8/16
1 8/16	3 10/16	3 10/16	3 10/16	14	10/16	8/16	11/16	9/16	11/16	9/16
1 12/16	4 4/16	4 4/16	4 3/16	16	11/16	9/16	12/16	10/16	13/16	11/16
2	4 13/16	4 13/16	4 13/16	18	13/16	10/16	14/16	11/16	15/16	13/16
2 4/16	5 7/16	5 7/16	5 7/16	20	15/16	12/16	1	13/16	1 1/16	14/16
2 8/16	6 1/16	6 1/16	6	22	1	13/16	1 2/16	14/16	1 3/16	1
2 12/16	6 10/16	6 10/16	6 10/16	24	1 2/16	14/16	1 3/16	1	1 5/16	1 1/16
3	7 4/16	7 4/16	7 4/16	26	1 4/16	1	1 5/16	1 1/16	1 7/16	1 3/16
3 4/16	7 14/16	7 14/16	7 13/16	28	1 5/16	1 1/16	1 7/16	1 3/16	1 8/16	1 4/16
3 8/16	8 8/16	8 8/16	8 7/16	30	1 7/16	1 2/16	1 9/16	1 4/16	1 10/16	1 6/16
3 12/16	9 1/16	9 1/16	9	32	1 8/16	1 3/16	1 10/16	1 5/16	1 12/16	1 7/16
4	9 11/16	9 11/16	9 10/16	34	1 10/16	1 5/16	1 12/16	1 7/16	1 14/16	1 9/16
4 4/16	10 5/16	10 5/16	10 4/16	36	1 12/16	1 6/16	1 14/16	1 8/16	2	1 11/16
4 8/16	10 14/16	10 14/16	10 13/16	38	1 13/16	1 7/16	2	1 10/16	2 2/16	1 12/16
4 12/16	11 8/16	11 8/16	11 7/16	40	1 15/16	1 9/16	2 1/16	1 11/16	2 4/16	1 14/16
5	12 2/16	12 2/16	12 1/16	42	2 1/16	1 10/16	2 3/16	1 13/16	2 6/16	1 15/16
5 4/16	12 11/16	12 11/16	12 10/16	44	2 2/16	1 11/16	2 5/16	1 14/16	2 7/16	2 1/16
5 8/16	13 5/16	13 5/16	13 4/16	46	2 4/16	1 12/16	2 7/16	1 15/16	2 9/16	2 2/16
5 12/16	13 15/16	13 15/16	13 13/16	48	2 5/16	1 14/16	2 8/16	2 1/16	2 11/16	2 4/16
6	14 8/16	14 8/16	14 7/16	50	2 7/16	1 15/16	2 10/16	2 2/16	2 13/16	2 6/16
6 8/16	15 12/16	15 12/16	15 10/16	54	2 10/16	2 2/16	2 14/16	2 5/16	3 1/16	2 9/16
7	16 15/16	16 15/16	16 14/16	58	2 14/16	2 4/16	3 1/16	2 8/16	3 5/16	2 12/16
7 8/16	18 2/16	18 2/16	18 1/16	62	3 1/16	2 7/16	3 5/16	2 11/16	3 8/16	2 15/16
8	19 6/16	19 6/16	19 4/16	66	3 4/16	2 9/16	3 8/16	2 14/16	3 12/16	3 2/16
8 8/16	20 9/16	20 9/16	20 7/16	70	3 7/16	2 12/16	3 12/16	3 1/16	4	3 5/16
9	21 12/16	21 12/16	21 11/16	74	3 11/16	2 15/16	3 15/16	3 3/16	4 4/16	3 8/16
9 8/16	23	23	22 14/16	78	3 14/16	3 1/16	4 3/16	3 6/16	4 7/16	3 11/16
10	24 3/16	24 3/16	24 1/16	82	4 1/16	3 4/16	4 6/16	3 9/16	4 11/16	3 15/16
10 8/16	25 7/16	25 7/16	25 4/16	86	4 4/16	3 6/16	4 10/16	3 12/16	4 15/16	4 2/16
11	26 10/16	26 10/16	26 8/16	90	4 8/16	3 9/16	4 13/16	3 15/16	5 3/16	4 5/16
11 8/16	27 13/16	27 13/16	27 11/16	94	4 11/16	3 12/16	5 1/16	4 2/16	5 6/16	4 8/16
12	29 1/16	29 1/16	28 14/16	98	4 14/16	3 14/16	5 4/16	4 5/16	5 10/16	4 11/16
13	31 7/16	31 7/16	31 5/16	106	5 5/16	4 3/16	5 11/16	4 10/16	6 2/16	5 1/16
14	33 14/16	33 14/16	33 11/16	114	5 11/16	4 8/16	6 2/16	5	6 9/16	5 8/16
15	36 5/16	36 5/16	36 2/16	122	6 2/16	4 14/16	6 9/16	5 6/16	7 1/16	5 14/16
16	38 12/16	38 12/16	38 8/16	130	6 8/16	5 3/16	7	5 11/16	7 8/16	6 4/16
17	41 2/16	41 2/16	40 15/16	138	6 15/16	5 8/16	7 7/16	6 1/16	8	6 10/16
18	43 9/16	43 9/16	43 5/16	146	7 5/16	5 13/16	7 14/16	6 7/16	8 7/16	7 1/16
19	46	46	45 12/16	154	7 12/16	6 2/16	8 5/16	6 13/16	8 15/16	7 7/16
20	48 6/16	48 6/16	48 2/16	162	8 2/16	6 7/16	8 12/16	7 2/16	9 6/16	7 13/16
21	50 13/16	50 13/16	50 9/16	170	8 9/16	6 13/16	9 3/16	7 8/16	9 14/16	8 3/16
22	53 4/16	53 4/16	52 15/16	178	8 15/16	7 2/16	9 10/16	7 14/16	10 5/16	8 10/16
23	55 11/16	55 11/16	55 6/16	186	9 6/16	7 7/16	10 1/16	8 3/16	10 13/16	9
24	58 1/16	58 1/16	57 12/16	194	9 12/16	7 12/16	10 8/16	8 9/16	11 4/16	9 6/16
25	60 8/16	60 8/16	60 3/16	202	10 3/16	8 1/16	10 15/16	8 15/16	11 12/16	9 12/16
26	62 15/16	62 15/16	62 9/16	210	10 9/16	8 7/16	11 6/16	9 5/16	12 3/16	10 3/16
27	65 5/16	65 5/16	65	218	11	8 12/16	11 13/16	9 10/16	12 11/16	10 9/16
28	67 12/16	67 12/16	67 6/16	226	11 6/16	9 1/16	12 4/16	10	13 2/16	10 15/16

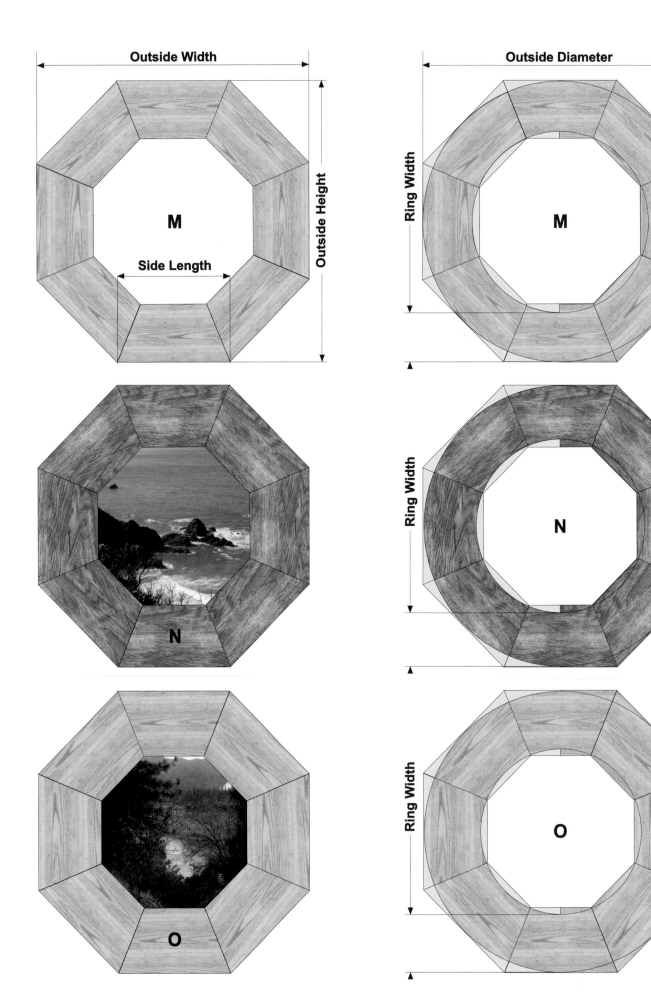

Side Length	Frame Width	Frame Height	Ring Max. OD	Material Req'd.	M Side Width	M Ring Width	N Side Width	N Ring Width	O Side Width	O Ring Width
8/16	1 3/16	1 3/16	1 3/16	6	4/16	3/16	4/16	4/16	5/16	4/16
10/16	1 8/16	1 8/16	1 8/16	7	5/16	4/16	5/16	5/16	6/16	5/16
12/16	1 13/16	1 13/16	1 13/16	8	6/16	5/16	6/16	6/16	7/16	6/16
14/16	2 2/16	2 2/16	2 2/16	9	7/16	6/16	7/16	6/16	8/16	7/16
1	2 7/16	2 7/16	2 7/16	10	8/16	7/16	9/16	7/16	9/16	8/16
1 4/16	3	3	3	12	10/16	8/16	11/16	9/16	11/16	10/16
1 8/16	3 10/16	3 10/16	3 10/16	14	12/16	10/16	13/16	11/16	14/16	12/16
1 12/16	4 4/16	4 4/16	4 3/16	16	14/16	12/16	15/16	13/16	1	14/16
2	4 13/16	4 13/16	4 13/16	18	1	14/16	1 1/16	15/16	1 2/16	1
2 4/16	5 7/16	5 7/16	5 7/16	20	1 2/16	15/16	1 3/16	1 1/16	1 4/16	1 2/16
2 8/16	6 1/16	6 1/16	6	22	1 4/16	1 1/16	1 5/16	1 2/16	1 7/16	1 4/16
2 12/16	6 10/16	6 10/16	6 10/16	24	1 6/16	1 3/16	1 7/16	1 4/16	1 9/16	1 6/16
3	7 4/16	7 4/16	7 4/16	26	1 8/16	1 4/16	1 10/16	1 6/16	1 11/16	1 8/16
3 4/16	7 14/16	7 14/16	7 13/16	28	1 10/16	1 6/16	1 12/16	1 8/16	1 13/16	1 10/16
3 8/16	8 8/16	8 8/16	8 7/16	30	1 12/16	1 8/16	1 14/16	1 10/16	2	1 12/16
3 12/16	9 1/16	9 1/16	9	32	1 14/16	1 9/16	2	1 12/16	2 2/16	1 14/16
4	9 11/16	9 11/16	9 10/16	34	2	1 11/16	2 2/16	1 13/16	2 4/16	2
4 4/16	10 5/16	10 5/16	10 4/16	36	2 2/16	1 13/16	2 4/16	1 15/16	2 6/16	2 1/16
4 8/16	10 14/16	10 14/16	10 13/16	38	2 4/16	1 15/16	2 6/16	2 1/16	2 9/16	2 3/16
4 12/16	11 8/16	11 8/16	11 7/16	40	2 6/16	2	2 8/16	2 3/16	2 11/16	2 5/16
5	12 2/16	12 2/16	12 1/16	42	2 8/16	2 2/16	2 11/16	2 5/16	2 13/16	2 7/16
5 4/16	12 11/16	12 11/16	12 10/16	44	2 10/16	2 4/16	2 13/16	2 7/16	2 15/16	2 9/16
5 8/16	13 5/16	13 5/16	13 4/16	46	2 12/16	2 5/16	2 15/16	2 8/16	3 2/16	2 11/16
5 12/16	13 15/16	13 15/16	13 13/16	48	2 14/16	2 7/16	3 1/16	2 10/16	3 4/16	2 13/16
6	14 8/16	14 8/16	14 7/16	50	3	2 9/16	3 3/16	2 12/16	3 6/16	2 15/16
6 8/16	15 12/16	15 12/16	15 10/16	54	3 4/16	2 12/16	3 7/16	3	3 11/16	3 3/16
7	16 15/16	16 15/16	16 14/16	58	3 8/16	3	3 12/16	3 3/16	3 15/16	3 7/16
7 8/16	18 2/16	18 2/16	18 1/16	62	3 12/16	3 3/16	4	3 7/16	4 4/16	3 11/16
8	19 6/16	19 6/16	19 4/16	66	4	3 6/16	4 4/16	3 11/16	4 8/16	3 15/16
8 8/16	20 9/16	20 9/16	20 7/16	70	4 4/16	3 10/16	4 8/16	3 14/16	4 13/16	4 3/16
9	21 12/16	21 12/16	21 11/16	74	4 8/16	3 13/16	4 13/16	4 2/16	5 1/16	4 7/16
9 8/16	23	23	22 14/16	78	4 12/16	4 1/16	5 1/16	4 6/16	5 6/16	4 11/16
10	24 3/16	24 3/16	24 1/16	82	5	4 4/16	5 5/16	4 9/16	5 10/16	4 15/16
10 8/16	25 7/16	25 7/16	25 4/16	86	5 4/16	4 7/16	5 9/16	4 13/16	5 15/16	5 3/16
11	26 10/16	26 10/16	26 8/16	90	5 8/16	4 11/16	5 14/16	5 1/16	6 3/16	5 7/16
11 8/16	27 13/16	27 13/16	27 11/16	94	5 12/16	4 14/16	6 2/16	5 4/16	6 8/16	5 11/16
12	29 1/16	29 1/16	28 14/16	98	6	5 2/16	6 6/16	5 8/16	6 12/16	5 15/16
13	31 7/16	31 7/16	31 5/16	106	6 8/16	5 8/16	6 15/16	5 15/16	7 5/16	6 6/16
14	33 14/16	33 14/16	33 11/16	114	7	5 15/16	7 7/16	6 7/16	7 14/16	6 14/16
15	36 5/16	36 5/16	36 2/16	122	7 8/16	6 6/16	8	6 14/16	8 7/16	7 6/16
16	38 12/16	38 12/16	38 8/16	130	8	6 13/16	8 8/16	7 5/16	9	7 14/16
17	41 2/16	41 2/16	40 15/16	138	8 8/16	7 3/16	9 1/16	7 13/16	9 9/16	8 6/16
18	43 9/16	43 9/16	43 5/16	146	9	7 10/16	9 9/16	8 4/16	10 2/16	8 14/16
19	46	46	45 12/16	154	9 8/16	8 1/16	10 2/16	8 11/16	10 11/16	9 6/16
20	48 6/16	48 6/16	48 2/16	162	10	8 8/16	10 10/16	9 3/16	11 4/16	9 14/16
21	50 13/16	50 13/16	50 9/16	170	10 8/16	8 15/16	11 3/16	9 10/16	11 13/16	10 5/16
22	53 4/16	53 4/16	52 15/16	178	11	9 5/16	11 11/16	10 1/16	12 6/16	10 13/16
23	55 11/16	55 11/16	55 6/16	186	11 8/16	9 12/16	12 4/16	10 9/16	12 15/16	11 5/16
24	58 1/16	58 1/16	57 12/16	194	12	10 3/16	12 12/16	11	13 8/16	11 13/16
25	60 8/16	60 8/16	60 3/16	202	12 8/16	10 10/16	13 5/16	11 7/16	14 1/16	12 5/16
26	62 15/16	62 15/16	62 9/16	210	13	11 1/16	13 13/16	11 15/16	14 10/16	12 13/16
27	65 5/16	65 5/16	65	218	13 8/16	11 7/16	14 6/16	12 6/16	15 3/16	13 5/16
28	67 12/16	67 12/16	67 6/16	226	14	11 14/16	14 14/16	12 13/16	15 12/16	13 13/16

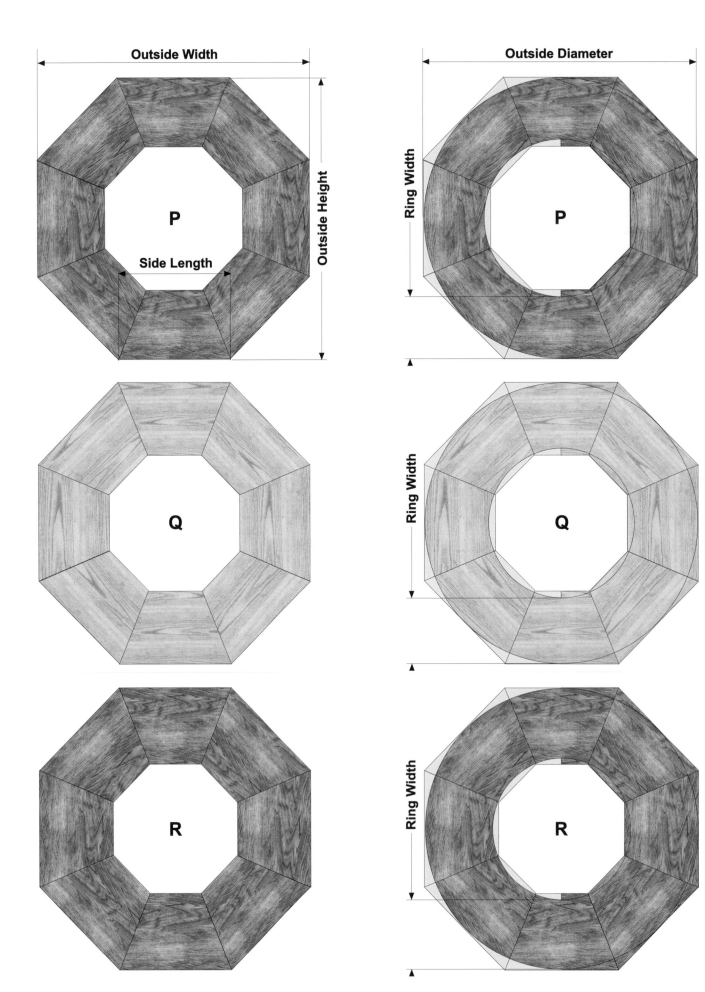

Side Length	Frame Width	Frame Height	Ring Max. OD	Material Req'd.	P Side Width	P Ring Width	Q Side Width	Q Ring Width	R Side Width	R Ring Width
8/16	1 3/16	1 3/16	1 3/16	6	5/16	4/16	5/16	4/16	5/16	5/16
10/16	1 8/16	1 8/16	1 8/16	7	6/16	5/16	6/16	6/16	7/16	6/16
12/16	1 13/16	1 13/16	1 13/16	8	7/16	6/16	8/16	7/16	8/16	7/16
14/16	2 2/16	2 2/16	2 2/16	9	8/16	7/16	9/16	8/16	9/16	8/16
1	2 7/16	2 7/16	2 7/16	10	10/16	8/16	10/16	9/16	11/16	9/16
1 4/16	3	3	3	12	12/16	11/16	13/16	11/16	13/16	12/16
1 8/16	3 10/16	3 10/16	3 10/16	14	14/16	13/16	15/16	13/16	1	14/16
1 12/16	4 4/16	4 4/16	4 3/16	16	1 1/16	15/16	1 2/16	1	1 2/16	1 1/16
2	4 13/16	4 13/16	4 13/16	18	1 3/16	1 1/16	1 4/16	1 2/16	1 5/16	1 3/16
2 4/16	5 7/16	5 7/16	5 7/16	20	1 5/16	1 3/16	1 7/16	1 4/16	1 8/16	1 5/16
2 8/16	6 1/16	6 1/16	6	22	1 8/16	1 5/16	1 9/16	1 6/16	1 10/16	1 8/16
2 12/16	6 10/16	6 10/16	6 10/16	24	1 10/16	1 7/16	1 12/16	1 9/16	1 13/16	1 10/16
3	7 4/16	7 4/16	7 4/16	26	1 13/16	1 9/16	1 14/16	1 11/16	2	1 12/16
3 4/16	7 14/16	7 14/16	7 13/16	28	1 15/16	1 11/16	2 1/16	1 13/16	2 2/16	1 15/16
3 8/16	8 8/16	8 8/16	8 7/16	30	2 1/16	1 13/16	2 3/16	1 15/16	2 5/16	2 1/16
3 12/16	9 1/16	9 1/16	9	32	2 4/16	2	2 6/16	2 2/16	2 7/16	2 4/16
4	9 11/16	9 11/16	9 10/16	34	2 6/16	2 2/16	2 8/16	2 4/16	2 10/16	2 6/16
4 4/16	10 5/16	10 5/16	10 4/16	36	2 8/16	2 4/16	2 11/16	2 6/16	2 13/16	2 8/16
4 8/16	10 14/16	10 14/16	10 13/16	38	2 11/16	2 6/16	2 13/16	2 8/16	2 15/16	2 11/16
4 12/16	11 8/16	11 8/16	11 7/16	40	2 13/16	2 8/16	3	2 11/16	3 2/16	2 13/16
5	12 2/16	12 2/16	12 1/16	42	3	2 10/16	3 2/16	2 13/16	3 5/16	2 15/16
5 4/16	12 11/16	12 11/16	12 10/16	44	3 2/16	2 12/16	3 5/16	2 15/16	3 7/16	3 2/16
5 8/16	13 5/16	13 5/16	13 4/16	46	3 4/16	2 14/16	3 7/16	3 1/16	3 10/16	3 4/16
5 12/16	13 15/16	13 15/16	13 13/16	48	3 7/16	3	3 10/16	3 3/16	3 12/16	3 7/16
6	14 8/16	14 8/16	14 7/16	50	3 9/16	3 2/16	3 12/16	3 6/16	3 15/16	3 9/16
6 8/16	15 12/16	15 12/16	15 10/16	54	3 14/16	3 7/16	4 1/16	3 10/16	4 4/16	3 14/16
7	16 15/16	16 15/16	16 14/16	58	4 3/16	3 11/16	4 6/16	3 15/16	4 10/16	4 2/16
7 8/16	18 2/16	18 2/16	18 1/16	62	4 7/16	3 15/16	4 11/16	4 3/16	4 15/16	4 7/16
8	19 6/16	19 6/16	19 4/16	66	4 12/16	4 3/16	5	4 8/16	5 4/16	4 12/16
8 8/16	20 9/16	20 9/16	20 7/16	70	5 1/16	4 8/16	5 5/16	4 12/16	5 9/16	5 1/16
9	21 12/16	21 12/16	21 11/16	74	5 6/16	4 12/16	5 10/16	5 1/16	5 15/16	5 5/16
9 8/16	23	23	22 14/16	78	5 10/16	5	5 15/16	5 5/16	6 4/16	5 10/16
10	24 3/16	24 3/16	24 1/16	82	5 15/16	5 4/16	6 4/16	5 10/16	6 9/16	5 15/16
10 8/16	25 7/16	25 7/16	25 4/16	86	6 4/16	5 8/16	6 9/16	5 14/16	6 14/16	6 4/16
11	26 10/16	26 10/16	26 8/16	90	6 9/16	5 13/16	6 14/16	6 3/16	7 4/16	6 8/16
11 8/16	27 13/16	27 13/16	27 11/16	94	6 13/16	6 1/16	7 3/16	6 7/16	7 9/16	6 13/16
12	29 1/16	29 1/16	28 14/16	98	7 2/16	6 5/16	7 8/16	6 11/16	7 14/16	7 2/16
13	31 7/16	31 7/16	31 5/16	106	7 12/16	6 13/16	8 2/16	7 4/16	8 9/16	7 11/16
14	33 14/16	33 14/16	33 11/16	114	8 5/16	7 6/16	8 12/16	7 13/16	9 3/16	8 5/16
15	36 5/16	36 5/16	36 2/16	122	8 15/16	7 14/16	9 6/16	8 6/16	9 14/16	8 14/16
16	38 12/16	38 12/16	38 8/16	130	9 8/16	8 7/16	10	8 15/16	10 8/16	9 8/16
17	41 2/16	41 2/16	40 15/16	138	10 2/16	8 15/16	10 10/16	9 8/16	11 3/16	10 1/16
18	43 9/16	43 9/16	43 5/16	146	10 11/16	9 7/16	11 4/16	10 1/16	11 13/16	10 11/16
19	46	46	45 12/16	154	11 5/16	10	11 14/16	10 10/16	12 8/16	11 4/16
20	48 6/16	48 6/16	48 2/16	162	11 14/16	10 8/16	12 8/16	11 3/16	13 2/16	11 14/16
21	50 13/16	50 13/16	50 9/16	170	12 8/16	11 1/16	13 2/16	11 12/16	13 13/16	12 7/16
22	53 4/16	53 4/16	52 15/16	178	13 1/16	11 9/16	13 12/16	12 5/16	14 7/16	13 1/16
23	55 11/16	55 11/16	55 6/16	186	13 11/16	12 2/16	14 6/16	12 14/16	15 2/16	13 10/16
24	58 1/16	58 1/16	57 12/16	194	14 4/16	12 10/16	15	13 7/16	15 12/16	14 4/16
25	60 8/16	60 8/16	60 3/16	202	14 14/16	13 2/16	15 10/16	14	16 7/16	14 13/16
26	62 15/16	62 15/16	62 9/16	210	15 7/16	13 11/16	16 4/16	14 9/16	17 1/16	15 7/16
27	65 5/16	65 5/16	65	218	16 1/16	14 3/16	16 14/16	15 2/16	17 12/16	16
28	67 12/16	67 12/16	67 6/16	226	16 10/16	14 12/16	17 8/16	15 11/16	18 6/16	16 10/16

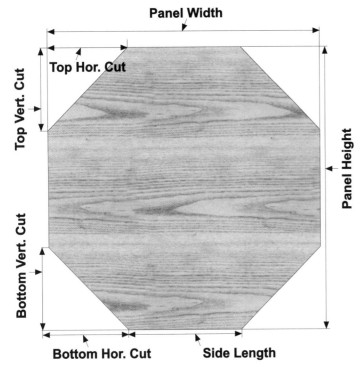

Panel Width (top label)

Top Hor. Cut

Top Vert. Cut

Bottom Vert. Cut

Bottom Hor. Cut

Side Length

Panel Height

The Chart below shows the formulas that were used in the process of laying out the 8 sided shapes. These are included to assist you if you are designing a project to a size that is not illustrated in the Dimension Charts provided. We hope you find them helpful as you design your projects.

8 SIDED PANEL FORMULAS		
Panel Width =	Panel Height x	1.000
Panel Height =	Panel Width x	1.000
Side Length =	Panel Height x	0.414
Side Length =	Panel Width x	0.414
Top Hor. Cut =	Panel Width x	0.291
Bott. Hor. Cut =	Panel Width x	0.291
Top Vert. Cut =	Panel Width x	0.291
Bott.Vert. Cut =	Panel Width x	0.291

PANEL WIDTH	PANEL HEIGHT	SIDE LENGTH	TOP HOR. CUT	BOTTOM HOR. CUT	TOP VERT. CUT	BOTTOM VERT. CUT
12/16	12/16	5/16	3/16	3/16	3/16	3/16
1	1	7/16	5/16	5/16	5/16	5/16
1 4/16	1 4/16	8/16	6/16	6/16	6/16	6/16
1 8/16	1 8/16	10/16	7/16	7/16	7/16	7/16
1 12/16	1 12/16	12/16	8/16	8/16	8/16	8/16
2	2	13/16	9/16	9/16	9/16	9/16
2 4/16	2 4/16	15/16	10/16	10/16	10/16	10/16
2 8/16	2 8/16	1 1/16	12/16	12/16	12/16	12/16
2 12/16	2 12/16	1 2/16	13/16	13/16	13/16	13/16
3	3	1 4/16	14/16	14/16	14/16	14/16
3 4/16	3 4/16	1 6/16	15/16	15/16	15/16	15/16
3 8/16	3 8/16	1 7/16	1	1	1	1
3 12/16	3 12/16	1 9/16	1 1/16	1 1/16	1 1/16	1 1/16
4	4	1 10/16	1 3/16	1 3/16	1 3/16	1 3/16
4 4/16	4 4/16	1 12/16	1 4/16	1 4/16	1 4/16	1 4/16
4 8/16	4 8/16	1 14/16	1 5/16	1 5/16	1 5/16	1 5/16
4 12/16	4 12/16	1 15/16	1 6/16	1 6/16	1 6/16	1 6/16
5	5	2 1/16	1 7/16	1 7/16	1 7/16	1 7/16
5 4/16	5 4/16	2 3/16	1 8/16	1 8/16	1 8/16	1 8/16
5 8/16	5 8/16	2 4/16	1 10/16	1 10/16	1 10/16	1 10/16
5 12/16	5 12/16	2 6/16	1 11/16	1 11/16	1 11/16	1 11/16
6	6	2 8/16	1 12/16	1 12/16	1 12/16	1 12/16
6 4/16	6 4/16	2 9/16	1 13/16	1 13/16	1 13/16	1 13/16
6 8/16	6 8/16	2 11/16	1 14/16	1 14/16	1 14/16	1 14/16
6 12/16	6 12/16	2 13/16	1 15/16	1 15/16	1 15/16	1 15/16
7	7	2 14/16	2 1/16	2 1/16	2 1/16	2 1/16
7 4/16	7 4/16	3	2 2/16	2 2/16	2 2/16	2 2/16
7 8/16	7 8/16	3 2/16	2 3/16	2 3/16	2 3/16	2 3/16
7 12/16	7 12/16	3 3/16	2 4/16	2 4/16	2 4/16	2 4/16
8	8	3 5/16	2 5/16	2 5/16	2 5/16	2 5/16
8 4/16	8 4/16	3 7/16	2 6/16	2 6/16	2 6/16	2 6/16
8 8/16	8 8/16	3 8/16	2 8/16	2 8/16	2 8/16	2 8/16

PANEL WIDTH	PANEL HEIGHT	SIDE LENGTH	TOP HOR. CUT	BOTTOM HOR. CUT	TOP VERT. CUT	BOTTOM VERT. CUT
8 12/16	8 12/16	3 10/16	2 9/16	2 9/16	2 9/16	2 9/16
9	9	3 12/16	2 10/16	2 10/16	2 10/16	2 10/16
9 4/16	9 4/16	3 13/16	2 11/16	2 11/16	2 11/16	2 11/16
9 8/16	9 8/16	3 15/16	2 12/16	2 12/16	2 12/16	2 12/16
9 12/16	9 12/16	4 1/16	2 13/16	2 13/16	2 13/16	2 13/16
10	10	4 2/16	2 15/16	2 15/16	2 15/16	2 15/16
10 4/16	10 4/16	4 4/16	3	3	3	3
10 8/16	10 8/16	4 6/16	3 1/16	3 1/16	3 1/16	3 1/16
10 12/16	10 12/16	4 7/16	3 2/16	3 2/16	3 2/16	3 2/16
11	11	4 9/16	3 3/16	3 3/16	3 3/16	3 3/16
11 4/16	11 4/16	4 11/16	3 4/16	3 4/16	3 4/16	3 4/16
11 8/16	11 8/16	4 12/16	3 6/16	3 6/16	3 6/16	3 6/16
12	12	4 15/16	3 8/16	3 8/16	3 8/16	3 8/16
12 4/16	12 4/16	5 1/16	3 9/16	3 9/16	3 9/16	3 9/16
12 8/16	12 8/16	5 3/16	3 10/16	3 10/16	3 10/16	3 10/16
12 12/16	12 12/16	5 4/16	3 11/16	3 11/16	3 11/16	3 11/16
13	13	5 6/16	3 13/16	3 13/16	3 13/16	3 13/16
13 4/16	13 4/16	5 8/16	3 14/16	3 14/16	3 14/16	3 14/16
13 8/16	13 8/16	5 9/16	3 15/16	3 15/16	3 15/16	3 15/16
13 12/16	13 12/16	5 11/16	4	4	4	4
14	14	5 13/16	4 1/16	4 1/16	4 1/16	4 1/16
14 8/16	14 8/16	6	4 4/16	4 4/16	4 4/16	4 4/16
15	15	6 3/16	4 6/16	4 6/16	4 6/16	4 6/16
15 8/16	15 8/16	6 7/16	4 8/16	4 8/16	4 8/16	4 8/16
16	16	6 10/16	4 10/16	4 10/16	4 10/16	4 10/16
16 8/16	16 8/16	6 13/16	4 13/16	4 13/16	4 13/16	4 13/16
17	17	7 1/16	4 15/16	4 15/16	4 15/16	4 15/16
17 8/16	17 8/16	7 4/16	5 1/16	5 1/16	5 1/16	5 1/16
18	18	7 7/16	5 4/16	5 4/16	5 4/16	5 4/16
19	19	7 14/16	5 8/16	5 8/16	5 8/16	5 8/16
20	20	8 4/16	5 13/16	5 13/16	5 13/16	5 13/16
21	21	8 11/16	6 2/16	6 2/16	6 2/16	6 2/16
22	22	9 2/16	6 6/16	6 6/16	6 6/16	6 6/16
23	23	9 8/16	6 11/16	6 11/16	6 11/16	6 11/16
24	24	9 15/16	7	7	7	7
25	25	10 6/16	7 4/16	7 4/16	7 4/16	7 4/16
26	26	10 12/16	7 9/16	7 9/16	7 9/16	7 9/16
27	27	11 3/16	7 14/16	7 14/16	7 14/16	7 14/16
28	28	11 9/16	8 2/16	8 2/16	8 2/16	8 2/16
29	29	12	8 7/16	8 7/16	8 7/16	8 7/16
30	30	12 7/16	8 12/16	8 12/16	8 12/16	8 12/16
31	31	12 13/16	9	9	9	9
32	32	13 4/16	9 5/16	9 5/16	9 5/16	9 5/16
33	33	13 11/16	9 10/16	9 10/16	9 10/16	9 10/16
34	34	14 1/16	9 14/16	9 14/16	9 14/16	9 14/16
35	35	14 8/16	10 3/16	10 3/16	10 3/16	10 3/16
36	36	14 14/16	10 8/16	10 8/16	10 8/16	10 8/16
37	37	15 5/16	10 12/16	10 12/16	10 12/16	10 12/16
38	38	15 12/16	11 1/16	11 1/16	11 1/16	11 1/16
39	39	16 2/16	11 6/16	11 6/16	11 6/16	11 6/16
40	40	16 9/16	11 10/16	11 10/16	11 10/16	11 10/16
41	41	17	11 15/16	11 15/16	11 15/16	11 15/16
42	42	17 6/16	12 4/16	12 4/16	12 4/16	12 4/16

9 SIDED PROJECT INFORMATION

Geometric Name: Nonagon
Definition: A Polygon having 9 sides
Miter Angle: 20°
Angle Change / Adjoining Sides: 40°

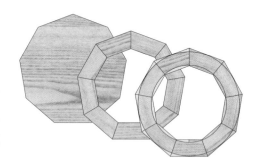

As another one of the "odd numbered" shape Illustrated in this book, the 9 sided shape (Nonagon) is one of the shapes that is pretty difficult to get creative with. With that said, it's still a fun project to build, and in some cases can be the perfect shape for the item you may wish to frame. The one thing that should be considered when using this shape is that for most standard sizes of pictures, a lot of cropping of the picture will be required.

The Illustrations to the right should give you an idea of the amount of cropping that may be required by using a Nonagon as your choice of shape for a frame.

In the left Illustration, you see a scale (shown in red) 8" x 10" sheet in portrait format. The sheet border is slightly outside the rabbeted area (shown in yellow) of the frame. Note the amount of material that would need to be cropped off the sheet top and/or bottom.

In the right Illustration, you see the same size sheet, but rotated 90° into a landscape format. Note the amount of material that would need to be cropped off the sheet sides.

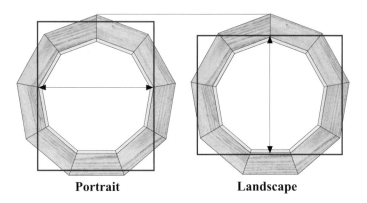

Portrait   **Landscape**

Note that the frame for the sheet shown in portrait format is very slightly smaller than the frame for the sheet shown in landscape format. This is due to the fact that on a Nonagon, the dimension "point-to-point" is slightly larger than the dimension "point-to-flat." In our **9 SIDED FRAME FORMULAS** below, you will be able to see exactly what the changes between these dimensions will be.

If the project you are building is a frame for a specific size object, you should refer to the **9 SIDED FRAME FORMULAS** Chart below as a first step. On a Nonagon, the height is shorter than the width, and is the controlling dimension for the frame for a picture in landscape format. In landscape format, the picture height would be multiplied by .352 to determine the length of the sides at the rabbeted edge. (See the bottom formula under **SIDE LENGTH** in the Chart below). In a portrait format, the width is the controlling dimension. In portrait format, the picture width should be multiplied by .347 to determine the lengths of the sides of the rabbeted edge. (See the top formula under **SIDE LENGTH** in the Chart below).

9 SIDED FRAME FORMULAS		
WIDTH	**HEIGHT**	**SIDE LENGTH**
Width = Side Length x 2.88	Height = Side Length x 2.84	Side Length = Width x .347
Width = Height x 1.014	Height = Width x .986	Side Length = Height x .352

Though the information above is very helpful, one of the most time consuming (and frustrating) things about building frames is to try to cut to a dimension that is not measured on either the inside or outside edge of the molding. I like to cut miters from the inside to the outside edges of the molding. This not only allows me to eliminate tear out on the inside corners of the frame since I am cutting into the inside edge, I am also cutting with the grain of the molding. It also allows me to see the outside edge of the material as I cut it. To help you understand how easy it is to convert a dimension along the rabbeted edge into an outside measurement, I will explain how we can use some basic math to help us determine the outside length of our frame sides. The Illustration below should be helpful in showing you how we designed our **9 SIDED FRAME ADDED WIDTH AND LENGTH CHART** on the next page.

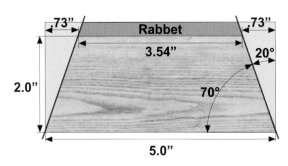

The Illustration to the left represents a piece of wood that is 5" long and 2" wide (to the edge of the rabbet). Note that on the right side that the end of the piece shows the miter angle for a Nonagon (20°) and the resulting angle of the cut (70°).

You should also note that at the rabbet, the 20° cuts shorten each end of the piece by .73". Since both ends of the piece are cut, this means that the length at the rabbet is 3.54", which is 1.46" shorter than the outside edge of the molding. This Illustration tells us is that at a 20° cut, we will add 1.46" to the length at a 2" width. This is the basis of our formula.

If we divide the **Added Length** (1.46") by the **Added Width** (2.0") we end up with .73 as our multiplier. In the event that you want to make a frame and need to work in fractions smaller than 1/16 increments, you would multiply the width of the molding outside the rabbet by .73. To determine the decimal equivalent of the fractions you will need to use, refer to the **FRACTION TO DECIMAL CONVERSION CHART** provided.

If you are able to use 1/16" increments for the mathematics of your frames, you should use the **9 SIDED FRAME ADDED WIDTH AND LENGTH CHART** below.

Determine how wide you want the material to be (outside the rabbet). Refer to the Chart below to find this dimension in one of the yellow shaded columns. The added length for that width will be shown in the green shaded block to the right of it. Add this dimension to the side length determined in the first step. You should then add whatever waste you want to allow for each side. This total is then multiplied by 9 to determine how much material is needed to build your project.

9 SIDED FRAME ADDED WIDTH AND LENGTH CHART									
Added Width	Added Length	Added Width	Added Length	Added Width	Added Length	Added Width	Added Length	Added Width	Added Length
1/16	1/16	1 1/16	12/16	2 1/16	1 8/16	3 1/16	2 4/16	4 1/16	2 15/16
2/16	1/16	1 2/16	13/16	2 2/16	1 9/16	3 2/16	2 5/16	4 2/16	3
3/16	2/16	1 3/16	14/16	2 3/16	1 10/16	3 3/16	2 5/16	4 3/16	3 1/16
4/16	3/16	1 4/16	15/16	2 4/16	1 10/16	3 4/16	2 6/16	4 4/16	3 2/16
5/16	4/16	1 5/16	15/16	2 5/16	1 11/16	3 5/16	2 7/16	4 5/16	3 2/16
6/16	4/16	1 6/16	1	2 6/16	1 12/16	3 6/16	2 7/16	4 6/16	3 3/16
7/16	5/16	1 7/16	1 1/16	2 7/16	1 12/16	3 7/16	2 8/16	4 7/16	3 4/16
8/16	6/16	1 8/16	1 2/16	2 8/16	1 13/16	3 8/16	2 9/16	4 8/16	3 5/16
9/16	7/16	1 9/16	1 2/16	2 9/16	1 14/16	3 9/16	2 10/16	4 9/16	3 5/16
10/16	7/16	1 10/16	1 3/16	2 10/16	1 15/16	3 10/16	2 10/16	4 10/16	3 6/16
11/16	8/16	1 11/16	1 4/16	2 11/16	1 15/16	3 11/16	2 11/16	4 11/16	3 7/16
12/16	9/16	1 12/16	1 4/16	2 12/16	2	3 12/16	2 12/16	4 12/16	3 7/16
13/16	9/16	1 13/16	1 5/16	2 13/16	2 1/16	3 13/16	2 13/16	4 13/16	3 8/16
14/16	10/16	1 14/16	1 6/16	2 14/16	2 2/16	3 14/16	2 13/16	4 14/16	3 9/16
15/16	11/16	1 15/16	1 7/16	2 15/16	2 2/16	3 15/16	2 14/16	4 15/16	3 10/16
1	12/16	2	1 7/16	3	2 3/16	4	2 15/16	5	3 10/16

The Chart below is provided to enable you to make 9 sided frames using the mathematics of most popular picture sizes. The Chart is divided into 2 parts; the left section, which shows the sheet sizes in portrait format, and the right section, which shows the sheet sizes in landscape format. In the Charts, the different colored columns represent the following information:

Red: The controlling dimension of the sheet size. (width in portrait, height in landscape)
Gray: The dimension of the sheet size that will need to be cropped.

White: The rabbet length for the frame sides.
Orange: The size of the opening in the direction the picture will need to be cropped.
Blue: The amount of material that will need to be cropped.

RABBET AREA DIMENSIONS FOR 9 SIDED FRAMES										
FOR PORTRAIT FORMAT					FOR LANDSCAPE FORMAT					
Object Width	Object Height	Rabbet Length	Opening Height	Vertical Crop	Object Width	Object Height	Rabbet Length	Opening Width	Horizontal Crop	
4	5	1 7/16	4 1/16	15/16	5	4	1 7/16	4 3/16	13/16	
5	7	1 12/16	5 1/16	1 15/16	7	5	1 13/16	5 3/16	1 13/16	
6	8	2 2/16	6 1/16	1 15/16	8	6	2 2/16	6 3/16	1 13/16	
8	10	2 13/16	8	2	10	8	2 14/16	8 4/16	1 12/16	
8 1/2	11	3	8 8/16	2 8/16	11	8 1/2	3 1/16	8 12/16	2 4/16	
10	14	3 8/16	10	4	14	10	3 9/16	10 4/16	3 12/16	
11	14	3 14/16	11	3	14	11	3 15/16	11 4/16	2 12/16	
12	16	4 3/16	11 15/16	4 1/16	16	12	4 4/16	12 5/16	3 11/16	
16	20	5 10/16	15 14/16	4 2/16	20	16	5 11/16	16 6/16	3 10/16	
18	24	6 5/16	17 14/16	6 2/16	24	18	6 6/16	18 6/16	5 10/16	
20	24	7	19 13/16	4 3/16	24	20	7 1/16	20 7/16	3 9/16	
24	30	8 6/16	23 13/16	6 3/16	30	24	8 8/16	24 7/16	5 9/16	

Outside Width

Outside Height

Side Length

A

B

C

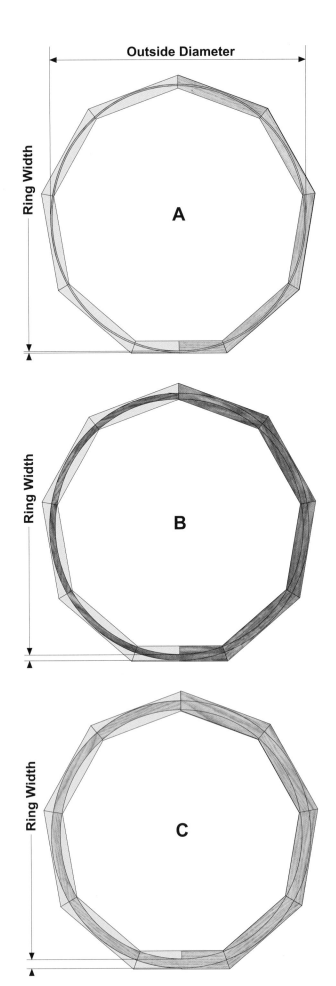

Outside Diameter

Ring Width

A

Ring Width

B

Ring Width

C

90

Side Length	Frame Width	Frame Height	Ring Max. OD	Material Req'd.	A Side Width	A Ring Width	B Side Width	B Ring Width	C Side Width	C Ring Width
8/16	1 7/16	1 7/16	1 6/16	6 12/16	1/16		1/16		2/16	1/16
10/16	1 13/16	1 12/16	1 11/16	7 14/16	1/16		2/16	1/16	2/16	1/16
12/16	2 3/16	2 2/16	2 1/16	9	2/16		2/16	1/16	2/16	1/16
14/16	2 8/16	2 8/16	2 6/16	10 2/16	2/16		2/16	1/16	3/16	1/16
1	2 14/16	2 13/16	2 12/16	11 4/16	2/16		3/16	1/16	3/16	1/16
1 4/16	3 10/16	3 9/16	3 7/16	13 8/16	3/16	1/16	3/16	1/16	4/16	2/16
1 8/16	4 5/16	4 4/16	4 1/16	15 12/16	3/16	1/16	4/16	1/16	5/16	2/16
1 12/16	5 1/16	5	4 12/16	18	4/16	1/16	4/16	2/16	5/16	3/16
2	5 12/16	5 11/16	5 7/16	20 4/16	4/16	1/16	5/16	2/16	6/16	3/16
2 4/16	6 8/16	6 6/16	6 2/16	22 8/16	5/16	1/16	6/16	2/16	7/16	3/16
2 8/16	7 3/16	7 2/16	6 13/16	24 12/16	5/16	1/16	6/16	2/16	8/16	4/16
2 12/16	7 15/16	7 13/16	7 8/16	27	6/16	1/16	7/16	3/16	8/16	4/16
3	8 10/16	8 8/16	8 3/16	29 4/16	6/16	1/16	8/16	3/16	9/16	4/16
3 4/16	9 6/16	9 4/16	8 14/16	31 8/16	7/16	1/16	8/16	3/16	10/16	5/16
3 8/16	10 1/16	9 15/16	9 9/16	33 12/16	7/16	2/16	9/16	3/16	11/16	5/16
3 12/16	10 13/16	10 10/16	10 4/16	36	8/16	2/16	9/16	4/16	11/16	6/16
4	11 8/16	11 6/16	10 15/16	38 4/16	8/16	2/16	10/16	4/16	12/16	6/16
4 4/16	12 4/16	12 1/16	11 10/16	40 8/16	9/16	2/16	11/16	4/16	13/16	6/16
4 8/16	12 15/16	12 12/16	12 4/16	42 12/16	9/16	2/16	11/16	4/16	14/16	7/16
4 12/16	13 11/16	13 8/16	12 15/16	45	10/16	2/16	12/16	5/16	14/16	7/16
5	14 6/16	14 3/16	13 10/16	47 4/16	10/16	2/16	13/16	5/16	15/16	7/16
5 4/16	15 2/16	14 15/16	14 5/16	49 8/16	11/16	2/16	13/16	5/16	1	8/16
5 8/16	15 13/16	15 10/16	15	51 12/16	11/16	2/16	14/16	5/16	1 1/16	8/16
5 12/16	16 9/16	16 5/16	15 11/16	54	12/16	3/16	14/16	6/16	1 1/16	9/16
6	17 4/16	17 1/16	16 6/16	56 4/16	12/16	3/16	15/16	6/16	1 2/16	9/16
6 8/16	18 12/16	18 7/16	17 12/16	60 12/16	13/16	3/16	1	6/16	1 4/16	10/16
7	20 3/16	19 14/16	19 2/16	65 4/16	14/16	3/16	1 2/16	7/16	1 5/16	10/16
7 8/16	21 10/16	21 5/16	20 7/16	69 12/16	15/16	3/16	1 3/16	7/16	1 7/16	11/16
8	23 1/16	22 12/16	21 13/16	74 4/16	1	4/16	1 4/16	8/16	1 8/16	12/16
8 8/16	24 8/16	24 2/16	23 3/16	78 12/16	1 1/16	4/16	1 5/16	8/16	1 10/16	13/16
9	25 15/16	25 9/16	24 9/16	83 4/16	1 2/16	4/16	1 7/16	9/16	1 11/16	13/16
9 8/16	27 6/16	27	25 15/16	87 12/16	1 3/16	4/16	1 8/16	9/16	1 13/16	14/16
10	28 13/16	28 6/16	27 5/16	92 4/16	1 4/16	4/16	1 9/16	10/16	1 14/16	15/16
10 8/16	30 4/16	29 13/16	28 10/16	96 12/16	1 5/16	5/16	1 10/16	10/16	2	1
11	31 11/16	31 4/16	30	101 4/16	1 6/16	5/16	1 12/16	11/16	2 1/16	1
11 8/16	33 2/16	32 11/16	31 6/16	105 12/16	1 7/16	5/16	1 13/16	11/16	2 3/16	1 1/16
12	34 9/16	34 1/16	32 12/16	110 4/16	1 8/16	5/16	1 14/16	12/16	2 4/16	1 2/16
13	37 7/16	36 15/16	35 8/16	119 4/16	1 10/16	6/16	2 1/16	13/16	2 7/16	1 3/16
14	40 5/16	39 12/16	38 3/16	128 4/16	1 12/16	6/16	2 3/16	14/16	2 10/16	1 5/16
15	43 3/16	42 10/16	40 15/16	137 4/16	1 14/16	7/16	2 6/16	15/16	2 13/16	1 6/16
16	46 1/16	45 7/16	43 11/16	146 4/16	2	7/16	2 8/16	15/16	3	1 8/16
17	48 15/16	48 4/16	46 6/16	155 4/16	2 2/16	8/16	2 11/16	1	3 3/16	1 9/16
18	51 13/16	51 2/16	49 2/16	164 4/16	2 4/16	8/16	2 13/16	1 1/16	3 6/16	1 11/16
19	54 12/16	53 15/16	51 14/16	173 4/16	2 6/16	8/16	3	1 2/16	3 9/16	1 12/16
20	57 10/16	56 13/16	54 9/16	182 4/16	2 8/16	9/16	3 2/16	1 3/16	3 12/16	1 14/16
21	60 8/16	59 10/16	57 5/16	191 4/16	2 10/16	9/16	3 5/16	1 4/16	3 15/16	1 15/16
22	63 6/16	62 8/16	60 1/16	200 4/16	2 12/16	10/16	3 7/16	1 5/16	4 2/16	2 1/16
23	66 4/16	65 5/16	62 12/16	209 4/16	2 14/16	10/16	3 10/16	1 6/16	4 5/16	2 2/16
24	69 2/16	68 3/16	65 8/16	218 4/16	3	11/16	3 12/16	1 7/16	4 8/16	2 4/16
25	72	71	68 4/16	227 4/16	3 2/16	11/16	3 15/16	1 8/16	4 11/16	2 5/16
26	74 14/16	73 13/16	70 15/16	236 4/16	3 4/16	12/16	4 1/16	1 9/16	4 14/16	2 7/16
27	77 12/16	76 11/16	73 11/16	245 4/16	3 6/16	12/16	4 4/16	1 10/16	5 1/16	2 8/16
28	80 10/16	79 8/16	76 7/16	254 4/16	3 8/16	12/16	4 6/16	1 11/16	5 4/16	2 10/16

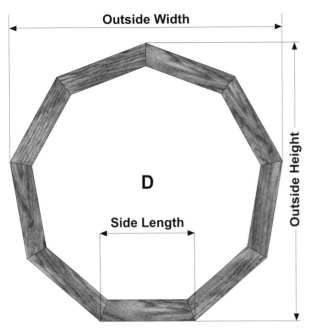

Outside Width

Outside Height

Side Length

D

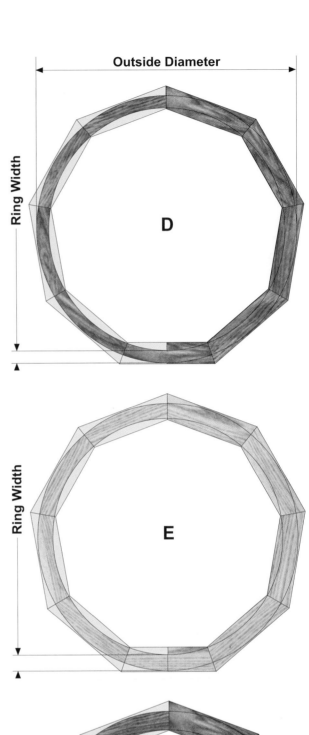

Outside Diameter

Ring Width

D

I ♥ MY DUBBY

E

Ring Width

E

F

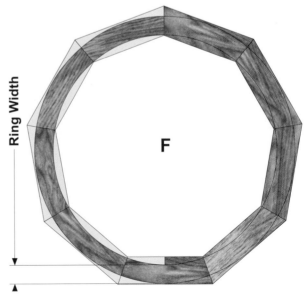

Ring Width

F

Side Length	Frame Width	Frame Height	Ring Max. OD	Material Req'd.	D Side Width	D Ring Width	E Side Width	E Ring Width	F Side Width	F Ring Width
8/16	1 7/16	1 7/16	1 6/16	6 12/16	2/16	1/16	2/16	1/16	2/16	2/16
10/16	1 13/16	1 12/16	1 11/16	7 14/16	2/16	1/16	3/16	2/16	3/16	2/16
12/16	2 3/16	2 2/16	2 1/16	9	3/16	2/16	3/16	2/16	3/16	2/16
14/16	2 8/16	2 8/16	2 6/16	10 2/16	3/16	2/16	4/16	2/16	4/16	3/16
1	2 14/16	2 13/16	2 12/16	11 4/16	4/16	2/16	4/16	3/16	5/16	3/16
1 4/16	3 10/16	3 9/16	3 7/16	13 8/16	4/16	3/16	5/16	3/16	6/16	4/16
1 8/16	4 5/16	4 4/16	4 1/16	15 12/16	5/16	3/16	6/16	4/16	7/16	5/16
1 12/16	5 1/16	5	4 12/16	18	6/16	4/16	7/16	4/16	8/16	5/16
2	5 12/16	5 11/16	5 7/16	20 4/16	7/16	4/16	8/16	5/16	9/16	6/16
2 4/16	6 8/16	6 6/16	6 2/16	22 8/16	8/16	5/16	9/16	6/16	10/16	7/16
2 8/16	7 3/16	7 2/16	6 13/16	24 12/16	9/16	5/16	10/16	6/16	11/16	8/16
2 12/16	7 15/16	7 13/16	7 8/16	27	10/16	6/16	11/16	7/16	12/16	8/16
3	8 10/16	8 8/16	8 3/16	29 4/16	11/16	6/16	12/16	8/16	14/16	9/16
3 4/16	9 6/16	9 4/16	8 14/16	31 8/16	11/16	7/16	13/16	8/16	15/16	10/16
3 8/16	10 1/16	9 15/16	9 9/16	33 12/16	12/16	7/16	14/16	9/16	1	11/16
3 12/16	10 13/16	10 10/16	10 4/16	36	13/16	8/16	15/16	9/16	1 1/16	11/16
4	11 8/16	11 6/16	10 15/16	38 4/16	14/16	8/16	1	10/16	1 2/16	12/16
4 4/16	12 4/16	12 1/16	11 10/16	40 8/16	15/16	9/16	1 1/16	11/16	1 3/16	13/16
4 8/16	12 15/16	12 12/16	12 4/16	42 12/16	1	9/16	1 2/16	11/16	1 4/16	14/16
4 12/16	13 11/16	13 8/16	12 15/16	45	1 1/16	10/16	1 3/16	12/16	1 5/16	15/16
5	14 6/16	14 3/16	13 10/16	47 4/16	1 2/16	10/16	1 4/16	13/16	1 7/16	15/16
5 4/16	15 2/16	14 15/16	14 5/16	49 8/16	1 2/16	11/16	1 5/16	13/16	1 8/16	1
5 8/16	15 13/16	15 10/16	15	51 12/16	1 3/16	11/16	1 6/16	14/16	1 9/16	1 1/16
5 12/16	16 9/16	16 5/16	15 11/16	54	1 4/16	12/16	1 7/16	15/16	1 10/16	1 2/16
6	17 4/16	17 1/16	16 6/16	56 4/16	1 5/16	12/16	1 8/16	15/16	1 11/16	1 2/16
6 8/16	18 12/16	18 7/16	17 12/16	60 12/16	1 7/16	13/16	1 10/16	1	1 13/16	1 4/16
7	20 3/16	19 14/16	19 2/16	65 4/16	1 9/16	14/16	1 12/16	1 2/16	2	1 5/16
7 8/16	21 10/16	21 5/16	20 7/16	69 12/16	1 10/16	15/16	1 14/16	1 3/16	2 2/16	1 7/16
8	23 1/16	22 12/16	21 13/16	74 4/16	1 12/16	1	2	1 4/16	2 4/16	1 8/16
8 8/16	24 8/16	24 2/16	23 3/16	78 12/16	1 14/16	1 1/16	2 2/16	1 6/16	2 6/16	1 10/16
9	25 15/16	25 9/16	24 9/16	83 4/16	2	1 2/16	2 4/16	1 7/16	2 9/16	1 12/16
9 8/16	27 6/16	27	25 15/16	87 12/16	2 1/16	1 3/16	2 6/16	1 8/16	2 11/16	1 13/16
10	28 13/16	28 6/16	27 5/16	92 4/16	2 3/16	1 4/16	2 8/16	1 9/16	2 13/16	1 15/16
10 8/16	30 4/16	29 13/16	28 10/16	96 12/16	2 5/16	1 5/16	2 10/16	1 11/16	2 15/16	2
11	31 11/16	31 4/16	30	101 4/16	2 7/16	1 6/16	2 12/16	1 12/16	3 2/16	2 2/16
11 8/16	33 2/16	32 11/16	31 6/16	105 12/16	2 8/16	1 7/16	2 14/16	1 13/16	3 4/16	2 3/16
12	34 9/16	34 1/16	32 12/16	110 4/16	2 10/16	1 8/16	3	1 14/16	3 6/16	2 5/16
13	37 7/16	36 15/16	35 8/16	119 4/16	2 14/16	1 10/16	3 4/16	2 1/16	3 11/16	2 8/16
14	40 5/16	39 12/16	38 3/16	128 4/16	3 1/16	1 12/16	3 8/16	2 3/16	3 15/16	2 11/16
15	43 3/16	42 10/16	40 15/16	137 4/16	3 5/16	1 14/16	3 12/16	2 6/16	4 4/16	2 14/16
16	46 1/16	45 7/16	43 11/16	146 4/16	3 8/16	2	4	2 9/16	4 8/16	3 1/16
17	48 15/16	48 4/16	46 6/16	155 4/16	3 12/16	2 2/16	4 4/16	2 11/16	4 13/16	3 4/16
18	51 13/16	51 2/16	49 2/16	164 4/16	3 15/16	2 4/16	4 8/16	2 14/16	5 1/16	3 7/16
19	54 12/16	53 15/16	51 14/16	173 4/16	4 3/16	2 6/16	4 12/16	3	5 6/16	3 10/16
20	57 10/16	56 13/16	54 9/16	182 4/16	4 6/16	2 8/16	5	3 3/16	5 10/16	3 13/16
21	60 8/16	59 10/16	57 5/16	191 4/16	4 10/16	2 10/16	5 4/16	3 5/16	5 15/16	4
22	63 6/16	62 8/16	60 1/16	200 4/16	4 13/16	2 12/16	5 8/16	3 8/16	6 3/16	4 3/16
23	66 4/16	65 5/16	62 12/16	209 4/16	5 1/16	2 14/16	5 12/16	3 10/16	6 8/16	4 6/16
24	69 2/16	68 3/16	65 8/16	218 4/16	5 4/16	3	6	3 13/16	6 12/16	4 9/16
25	72	71	68 4/16	227 4/16	5 8/16	3 2/16	6 4/16	3 15/16	7 1/16	4 12/16
26	74 14/16	73 13/16	70 15/16	236 4/16	5 11/16	3 4/16	6 8/16	4 2/16	7 5/16	4 15/16
27	77 12/16	76 11/16	73 11/16	245 4/16	5 15/16	3 6/16	6 12/16	4 4/16	7 10/16	5 3/16
28	80 10/16	79 8/16	76 7/16	254 4/16	6 2/16	3 8/16	7	4 7/16	7 14/16	5 6/16

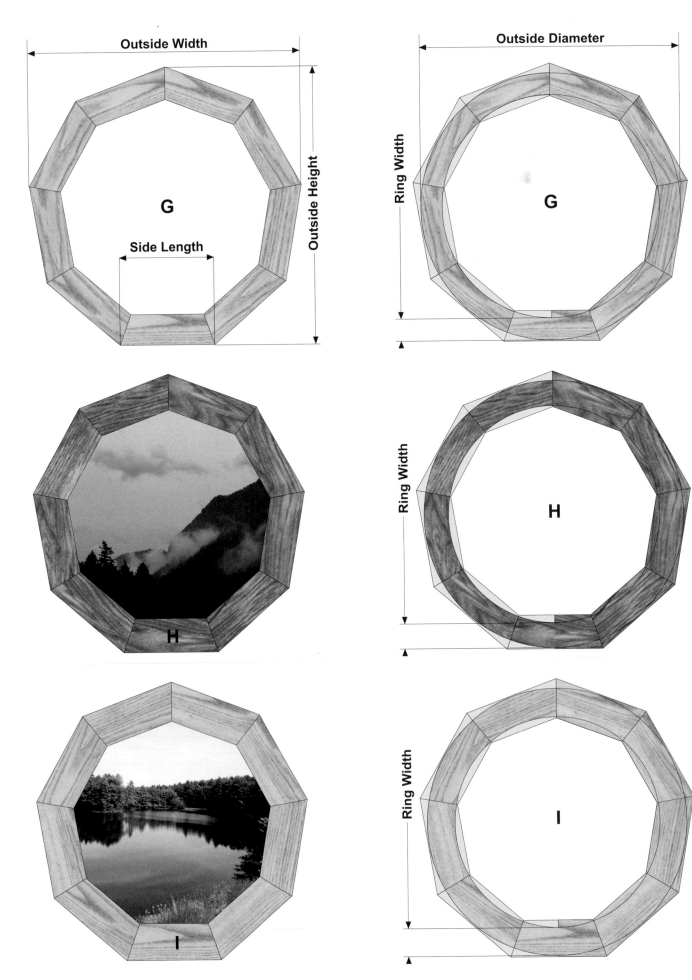

Side Length	Frame Width	Frame Height	Ring Max. OD	Material Req'd.	G Side Width	G Ring Width	H Side Width	H Ring Width	I Side Width	I Ring Width
8/16	1 7/16	1 7/16	1 6/16	6 12/16	3/16	2/16	3/16	2/16	3/16	2/16
10/16	1 13/16	1 12/16	1 11/16	7 14/16	3/16	2/16	3/16	3/16	4/16	3/16
12/16	2 3/16	2 2/16	2 1/16	9	4/16	3/16	4/16	3/16	5/16	3/16
14/16	2 8/16	2 8/16	2 6/16	10 2/16	4/16	3/16	5/16	4/16	5/16	4/16
1	2 14/16	2 13/16	2 12/16	11 4/16	5/16	4/16	6/16	4/16	6/16	5/16
1 4/16	3 10/16	3 9/16	3 7/16	13 8/16	6/16	4/16	7/16	5/16	8/16	6/16
1 8/16	4 5/16	4 4/16	4 1/16	15 12/16	8/16	5/16	8/16	6/16	9/16	7/16
1 12/16	5 1/16	5	4 12/16	18	9/16	6/16	10/16	7/16	11/16	8/16
2	5 12/16	5 11/16	5 7/16	20 4/16	10/16	7/16	11/16	8/16	12/16	9/16
2 4/16	6 8/16	6 6/16	6 2/16	22 8/16	11/16	8/16	12/16	9/16	14/16	10/16
2 8/16	7 3/16	7 2/16	6 13/16	24 12/16	13/16	9/16	14/16	10/16	15/16	12/16
2 12/16	7 15/16	7 13/16	7 8/16	27	14/16	10/16	15/16	11/16	1 1/16	13/16
3	8 10/16	8 8/16	8 3/16	29 4/16	15/16	11/16	1 1/16	12/16	1 2/16	14/16
3 4/16	9 6/16	9 4/16	8 14/16	31 8/16	1	12/16	1 2/16	13/16	1 4/16	15/16
3 8/16	10 1/16	9 15/16	9 9/16	33 12/16	1 2/16	13/16	1 3/16	14/16	1 5/16	1
3 12/16	10 13/16	10 10/16	10 4/16	36	1 3/16	13/16	1 5/16	15/16	1 7/16	1 1/16
4	11 8/16	11 6/16	10 15/16	38 4/16	1 4/16	14/16	1 6/16	1	1 8/16	1 2/16
4 4/16	12 4/16	12 1/16	11 10/16	40 8/16	1 5/16	15/16	1 7/16	1 1/16	1 10/16	1 4/16
4 8/16	12 15/16	12 12/16	12 4/16	42 12/16	1 7/16	1	1 9/16	1 2/16	1 11/16	1 5/16
4 12/16	13 11/16	13 8/16	12 15/16	45	1 8/16	1 1/16	1 10/16	1 3/16	1 13/16	1 6/16
5	14 6/16	14 3/16	13 10/16	47 4/16	1 9/16	1 2/16	1 12/16	1 4/16	1 14/16	1 7/16
5 4/16	15 2/16	14 15/16	14 5/16	49 8/16	1 10/16	1 3/16	1 13/16	1 6/16	2	1 8/16
5 8/16	15 13/16	15 10/16	15	51 12/16	1 12/16	1 4/16	1 14/16	1 7/16	2 1/16	1 9/16
5 12/16	16 9/16	16 5/16	15 11/16	54	1 13/16	1 5/16	2	1 8/16	2 3/16	1 11/16
6	17 4/16	17 1/16	16 6/16	56 4/16	1 14/16	1 5/16	2 1/16	1 9/16	2 4/16	1 12/16
6 8/16	18 12/16	18 7/16	17 12/16	60 12/16	2 1/16	1 7/16	2 4/16	1 11/16	2 7/16	1 14/16
7	20 3/16	19 14/16	19 2/16	65 4/16	2 3/16	1 9/16	2 7/16	1 13/16	2 10/16	2
7 8/16	21 10/16	21 5/16	20 7/16	69 12/16	2 6/16	1 11/16	2 9/16	1 15/16	2 13/16	2 3/16
8	23 1/16	22 12/16	21 13/16	74 4/16	2 8/16	1 13/16	2 12/16	2 1/16	3	2 5/16
8 8/16	24 8/16	24 2/16	23 3/16	78 12/16	2 11/16	1 14/16	2 15/16	2 3/16	3 3/16	2 7/16
9	25 15/16	25 9/16	24 9/16	83 4/16	2 13/16	2	3 2/16	2 5/16	3 6/16	2 10/16
9 8/16	27 6/16	27	25 15/16	87 12/16	3	2 2/16	3 4/16	2 7/16	3 9/16	2 12/16
10	28 13/16	28 6/16	27 5/16	92 4/16	3 2/16	2 4/16	3 7/16	2 9/16	3 12/16	2 14/16
10 8/16	30 4/16	29 13/16	28 10/16	96 12/16	3 5/16	2 6/16	3 10/16	2 11/16	3 15/16	3 1/16
11	31 11/16	31 4/16	30	101 4/16	3 7/16	2 7/16	3 13/16	2 13/16	4 2/16	3 3/16
11 8/16	33 2/16	32 11/16	31 6/16	105 12/16	3 10/16	2 9/16	3 15/16	2 15/16	4 5/16	3 5/16
12	34 9/16	34 1/16	32 12/16	110 4/16	3 12/16	2 11/16	4 2/16	3 1/16	4 8/16	3 7/16
13	37 7/16	36 15/16	35 8/16	119 4/16	4 1/16	2 15/16	4 8/16	3 5/16	4 14/16	3 12/16
14	40 5/16	39 12/16	38 3/16	128 4/16	4 6/16	3 2/16	4 13/16	3 9/16	5 4/16	4 1/16
15	43 3/16	42 10/16	40 15/16	137 4/16	4 11/16	3 6/16	5 3/16	3 13/16	5 10/16	4 5/16
16	46 1/16	45 7/16	43 11/16	146 4/16	5	3 9/16	5 8/16	4 2/16	6	4 10/16
17	48 15/16	48 4/16	46 6/16	155 4/16	5 5/16	3 13/16	5 14/16	4 6/16	6 6/16	4 15/16
18	51 13/16	51 2/16	49 2/16	164 4/16	5 10/16	4	6 3/16	4 10/16	6 12/16	5 3/16
19	54 12/16	53 15/16	51 14/16	173 4/16	5 15/16	4 4/16	6 9/16	4 14/16	7 2/16	5 8/16
20	57 10/16	56 13/16	54 9/16	182 4/16	6 4/16	4 8/16	6 14/16	5 2/16	7 8/16	5 12/16
21	60 8/16	59 10/16	57 5/16	191 4/16	6 9/16	4 11/16	7 4/16	5 6/16	7 14/16	6 1/16
22	63 6/16	62 8/16	60 1/16	200 4/16	6 14/16	4 15/16	7 9/16	5 10/16	8 4/16	6 6/16
23	66 4/16	65 5/16	62 12/16	209 4/16	7 3/16	5 2/16	7 15/16	5 14/16	8 10/16	6 10/16
24	69 2/16	68 3/16	65 8/16	218 4/16	7 8/16	5 6/16	8 4/16	6 2/16	9	6 15/16
25	72	71	68 4/16	227 4/16	7 13/16	5 9/16	8 10/16	6 6/16	9 6/16	7 4/16
26	74 14/16	73 13/16	70 15/16	236 4/16	8 2/16	5 13/16	8 15/16	6 11/16	9 12/16	7 8/16
27	77 12/16	76 11/16	73 11/16	245 4/16	8 7/16	6 1/16	9 5/16	6 15/16	10 2/16	7 13/16
28	80 10/16	79 8/16	76 7/16	254 4/16	8 12/16	6 4/16	9 10/16	7 3/16	10 8/16	8 1/16

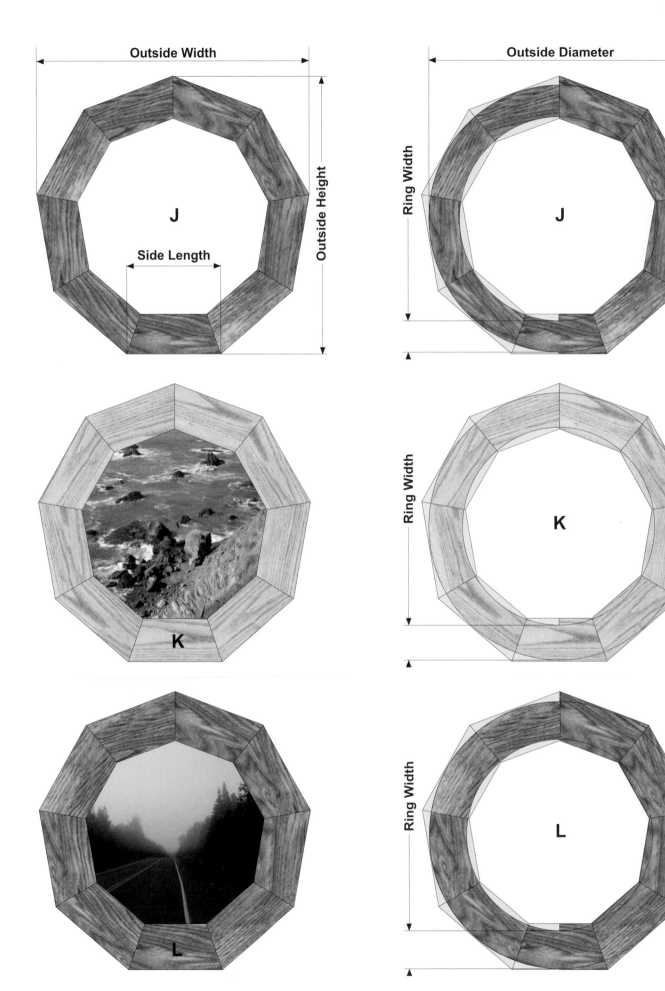

Outside Width

Outside Height

Side Length

Outside Diameter

Ring Width

Ring Width

Ring Width

J

J

K

K

L

L

Side Length	Frame Width	Frame Height	Ring Max. OD	Material Req'd.	J Side Width	J Ring Width	K Side Width	K Ring Width	L Side Width	L Ring Width
8/16	1 7/16	1 7/16	1 6/16	6 12/16	3/16	3/16	4/16	3/16	4/16	3/16
10/16	1 13/16	1 12/16	1 11/16	7 14/16	4/16	3/16	4/16	4/16	5/16	4/16
12/16	2 3/16	2 2/16	2 1/16	9	5/16	4/16	5/16	4/16	6/16	5/16
14/16	2 8/16	2 8/16	2 6/16	10 2/16	6/16	5/16	6/16	5/16	7/16	5/16
1	2 14/16	2 13/16	2 12/16	11 4/16	7/16	5/16	7/16	6/16	8/16	6/16
1 4/16	3 10/16	3 9/16	3 7/16	13 8/16	8/16	6/16	9/16	7/16	9/16	8/16
1 8/16	4 5/16	4 4/16	4 1/16	15 12/16	10/16	8/16	11/16	9/16	11/16	9/16
1 12/16	5 1/16	5	4 12/16	18	11/16	9/16	12/16	10/16	13/16	11/16
2	5 12/16	5 11/16	5 7/16	20 4/16	13/16	10/16	14/16	11/16	15/16	12/16
2 4/16	6 8/16	6 6/16	6 2/16	22 8/16	15/16	12/16	1	13/16	1 1/16	14/16
2 8/16	7 3/16	7 2/16	6 13/16	24 12/16	1	13/16	1 2/16	14/16	1 3/16	15/16
2 12/16	7 15/16	7 13/16	7 8/16	27	1 2/16	14/16	1 3/16	1	1 5/16	1 1/16
3	8 10/16	8 8/16	8 3/16	29 4/16	1 4/16	15/16	1 5/16	1 1/16	1 7/16	1 3/16
3 4/16	9 6/16	9 4/16	8 14/16	31 8/16	1 5/16	1 1/16	1 7/16	1 2/16	1 8/16	1 4/16
3 8/16	10 1/16	9 15/16	9 9/16	33 12/16	1 7/16	1 2/16	1 9/16	1 4/16	1 10/16	1 6/16
3 12/16	10 13/16	10 10/16	10 4/16	36	1 8/16	1 3/16	1 10/16	1 5/16	1 12/16	1 7/16
4	11 8/16	11 6/16	10 15/16	38 4/16	1 10/16	1 5/16	1 12/16	1 7/16	1 14/16	1 9/16
4 4/16	12 4/16	12 1/16	11 10/16	40 8/16	1 12/16	1 6/16	1 14/16	1 8/16	2	1 10/16
4 8/16	12 15/16	12 12/16	12 4/16	42 12/16	1 13/16	1 7/16	2	1 10/16	2 2/16	1 12/16
4 12/16	13 11/16	13 8/16	12 15/16	45	1 15/16	1 8/16	2 1/16	1 11/16	2 4/16	1 13/16
5	14 6/16	14 3/16	13 10/16	47 4/16	2 1/16	1 10/16	2 3/16	1 12/16	2 6/16	1 15/16
5 4/16	15 2/16	14 15/16	14 5/16	49 8/16	2 2/16	1 11/16	2 5/16	1 14/16	2 7/16	2
5 8/16	15 13/16	15 10/16	15	51 12/16	2 4/16	1 12/16	2 7/16	1 15/16	2 9/16	2 2/16
5 12/16	16 9/16	16 5/16	15 11/16	54	2 5/16	1 14/16	2 8/16	2 1/16	2 11/16	2 4/16
6	17 4/16	17 1/16	16 6/16	56 4/16	2 7/16	1 15/16	2 10/16	2 2/16	2 13/16	2 5/16
6 8/16	18 12/16	18 7/16	17 12/16	60 12/16	2 10/16	2 1/16	2 14/16	2 5/16	3 1/16	2 8/16
7	20 3/16	19 14/16	19 2/16	65 4/16	2 14/16	2 4/16	3 1/16	2 8/16	3 5/16	2 11/16
7 8/16	21 10/16	21 5/16	20 7/16	69 12/16	3 1/16	2 7/16	3 5/16	2 11/16	3 8/16	2 14/16
8	23 1/16	22 12/16	21 13/16	74 4/16	3 4/16	2 9/16	3 8/16	2 13/16	3 12/16	3 2/16
8 8/16	24 8/16	24 2/16	23 3/16	78 12/16	3 7/16	2 12/16	3 12/16	3	4	3 5/16
9	25 15/16	25 9/16	24 9/16	83 4/16	3 11/16	2 14/16	3 15/16	3 3/16	4 4/16	3 8/16
9 8/16	27 6/16	27	25 15/16	87 12/16	3 14/16	3 1/16	4 3/16	3 6/16	4 7/16	3 11/16
10	28 13/16	28 6/16	27 5/16	92 4/16	4 1/16	3 3/16	4 6/16	3 9/16	4 11/16	3 14/16
10 8/16	30 4/16	29 13/16	28 10/16	96 12/16	4 4/16	3 6/16	4 10/16	3 12/16	4 15/16	4 1/16
11	31 11/16	31 4/16	30	101 4/16	4 8/16	3 9/16	4 13/16	3 14/16	5 3/16	4 4/16
11 8/16	33 2/16	32 11/16	31 6/16	105 12/16	4 11/16	3 11/16	5 1/16	4 1/16	5 6/16	4 7/16
12	34 9/16	34 1/16	32 12/16	110 4/16	4 14/16	3 14/16	5 4/16	4 4/16	5 10/16	4 10/16
13	37 7/16	36 15/16	35 8/16	119 4/16	5 5/16	4 3/16	5 11/16	4 10/16	6 2/16	5
14	40 5/16	39 12/16	38 3/16	128 4/16	5 11/16	4 8/16	6 2/16	4 15/16	6 9/16	5 7/16
15	43 3/16	42 10/16	40 15/16	137 4/16	6 2/16	4 13/16	6 9/16	5 5/16	7 1/16	5 13/16
16	46 1/16	45 7/16	43 11/16	146 4/16	6 8/16	5 2/16	7	5 11/16	7 8/16	6 3/16
17	48 15/16	48 4/16	46 6/16	155 4/16	6 15/16	5 7/16	7 7/16	6	8	6 9/16
18	51 13/16	51 2/16	49 2/16	164 4/16	7 5/16	5 13/16	7 14/16	6 6/16	8 7/16	6 15/16
19	54 12/16	53 15/16	51 14/16	173 4/16	7 12/16	6 2/16	8 5/16	6 12/16	8 15/16	7 6/16
20	57 10/16	56 13/16	54 9/16	182 4/16	8 2/16	6 7/16	8 12/16	7 1/16	9 6/16	7 12/16
21	60 8/16	59 10/16	57 5/16	191 4/16	8 9/16	6 12/16	9 3/16	7 7/16	9 14/16	8 2/16
22	63 6/16	62 8/16	60 1/16	200 4/16	8 15/16	7 1/16	9 10/16	7 13/16	10 5/16	8 8/16
23	66 4/16	65 5/16	62 12/16	209 4/16	9 6/16	7 6/16	10 1/16	8 2/16	10 13/16	8 14/16
24	69 2/16	68 3/16	65 8/16	218 4/16	9 12/16	7 11/16	10 8/16	8 8/16	11 4/16	9 5/16
25	72	71	68 4/16	227 4/16	10 3/16	8 1/16	10 15/16	8 14/16	11 12/16	9 11/16
26	74 14/16	73 13/16	70 15/16	236 4/16	10 9/16	8 6/16	11 6/16	9 3/16	12 3/16	10 1/16
27	77 12/16	76 11/16	73 11/16	245 4/16	11	8 11/16	11 13/16	9 9/16	12 11/16	10 7/16
28	80 10/16	79 8/16	76 7/16	254 4/16	11 6/16	9	12 4/16	9 15/16	13 2/16	10 13/16

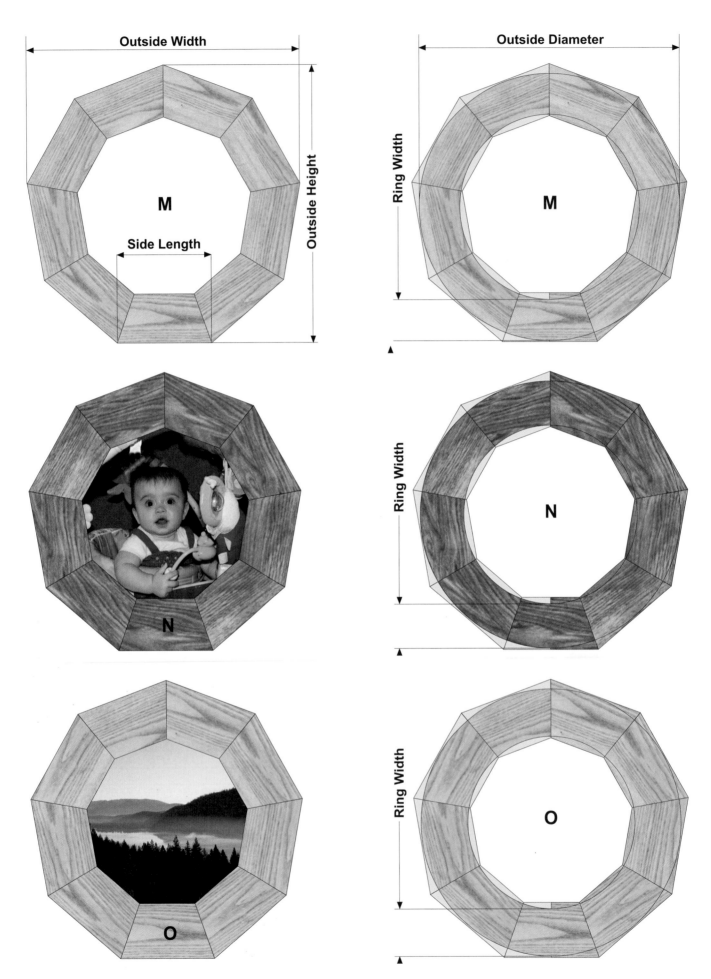

Side Length	Frame Width	Frame Height	Ring Max. OD	Material Req'd.	M Side Width	M Ring Width	N Side Width	N Ring Width	O Side Width	O Ring Width
8/16	1 7/16	1 7/16	1 6/16	6 12/16	4/16	3/16	4/16	4/16	5/16	4/16
10/16	1 13/16	1 12/16	1 11/16	7 14/16	5/16	4/16	5/16	5/16	6/16	5/16
12/16	2 3/16	2 2/16	2 1/16	9	6/16	5/16	6/16	5/16	7/16	6/16
14/16	2 8/16	2 8/16	2 6/16	10 2/16	7/16	6/16	7/16	6/16	8/16	7/16
1	2 14/16	2 13/16	2 12/16	11 4/16	8/16	7/16	9/16	7/16	9/16	8/16
1 4/16	3 10/16	3 9/16	3 7/16	13 8/16	10/16	8/16	11/16	9/16	11/16	10/16
1 8/16	4 5/16	4 4/16	4 1/16	15 12/16	12/16	10/16	13/16	11/16	14/16	12/16
1 12/16	5 1/16	5	4 12/16	18	14/16	12/16	15/16	13/16	1	14/16
2	5 12/16	5 11/16	5 7/16	20 4/16	1	13/16	1 1/16	14/16	1 2/16	1
2 4/16	6 8/16	6 6/16	6 2/16	22 8/16	1 2/16	15/16	1 3/16	1	1 4/16	1 1/16
2 8/16	7 3/16	7 2/16	6 13/16	24 12/16	1 4/16	1 1/16	1 5/16	1 2/16	1 7/16	1 3/16
2 12/16	7 15/16	7 13/16	7 8/16	27	1 6/16	1 2/16	1 7/16	1 4/16	1 9/16	1 5/16
3	8 10/16	8 8/16	8 3/16	29 4/16	1 8/16	1 4/16	1 10/16	1 6/16	1 11/16	1 7/16
3 4/16	9 6/16	9 4/16	8 14/16	31 8/16	1 10/16	1 6/16	1 12/16	1 8/16	1 13/16	1 9/16
3 8/16	10 1/16	9 15/16	9 9/16	33 12/16	1 12/16	1 7/16	1 14/16	1 9/16	2	1 11/16
3 12/16	10 13/16	10 10/16	10 4/16	36	1 14/16	1 9/16	2	1 11/16	2 2/16	1 13/16
4	11 8/16	11 6/16	10 15/16	38 4/16	2	1 11/16	2 2/16	1 13/16	2 4/16	1 15/16
4 4/16	12 4/16	12 1/16	11 10/16	40 8/16	2 2/16	1 13/16	2 4/16	1 15/16	2 6/16	2 1/16
4 8/16	12 15/16	12 12/16	12 4/16	42 12/16	2 4/16	1 14/16	2 6/16	2 1/16	2 9/16	2 3/16
4 12/16	13 11/16	13 8/16	12 15/16	45	2 6/16	2	2 8/16	2 2/16	2 11/16	2 5/16
5	14 6/16	14 3/16	13 10/16	47 4/16	2 8/16	2 2/16	2 11/16	2 4/16	2 13/16	2 7/16
5 4/16	15 2/16	14 15/16	14 5/16	49 8/16	2 10/16	2 3/16	2 13/16	2 6/16	2 15/16	2 9/16
5 8/16	15 13/16	15 10/16	15	51 12/16	2 12/16	2 5/16	2 15/16	2 8/16	3 2/16	2 11/16
5 12/16	16 9/16	16 5/16	15 11/16	54	2 14/16	2 7/16	3 1/16	2 10/16	3 4/16	2 13/16
6	17 4/16	17 1/16	16 6/16	56 4/16	3	2 8/16	3 3/16	2 11/16	3 6/16	2 15/16
6 8/16	18 12/16	18 7/16	17 12/16	60 12/16	3 4/16	2 12/16	3 7/16	2 15/16	3 11/16	3 2/16
7	20 3/16	19 14/16	19 2/16	65 4/16	3 8/16	2 15/16	3 12/16	3 3/16	3 15/16	3 6/16
7 8/16	21 10/16	21 5/16	20 7/16	69 12/16	3 12/16	3 2/16	4	3 6/16	4 4/16	3 10/16
8	23 1/16	22 12/16	21 13/16	74 4/16	4	3 6/16	4 4/16	3 10/16	4 8/16	3 14/16
8 8/16	24 8/16	24 2/16	23 3/16	78 12/16	4 4/16	3 9/16	4 8/16	3 13/16	4 13/16	4 2/16
9	25 15/16	25 9/16	24 9/16	83 4/16	4 8/16	3 12/16	4 13/16	4 1/16	5 1/16	4 6/16
9 8/16	27 6/16	27	25 15/16	87 12/16	4 12/16	4	5 1/16	4 5/16	5 6/16	4 10/16
10	28 13/16	28 6/16	27 5/16	92 4/16	5	4 3/16	5 5/16	4 8/16	5 10/16	4 14/16
10 8/16	30 4/16	29 13/16	28 10/16	96 12/16	5 4/16	4 6/16	5 9/16	4 12/16	5 15/16	5 1/16
11	31 11/16	31 4/16	30	101 4/16	5 8/16	4 10/16	5 14/16	5	6 3/16	5 5/16
11 8/16	33 2/16	32 11/16	31 6/16	105 12/16	5 12/16	4 13/16	6 2/16	5 3/16	6 8/16	5 9/16
12	34 9/16	34 1/16	32 12/16	110 4/16	6	5 1/16	6 6/16	5 7/16	6 12/16	5 13/16
13	37 7/16	36 15/16	35 8/16	119 4/16	6 8/16	5 7/16	6 15/16	5 14/16	7 5/16	6 5/16
14	40 5/16	39 12/16	38 3/16	128 4/16	7	5 14/16	7 7/16	6 5/16	7 14/16	6 13/16
15	43 3/16	42 10/16	40 15/16	137 4/16	7 8/16	6 5/16	8	6 13/16	8 7/16	7 4/16
16	46 1/16	45 7/16	43 11/16	146 4/16	8	6 11/16	8 8/16	7 4/16	9	7 12/16
17	48 15/16	48 4/16	46 6/16	155 4/16	8 8/16	7 2/16	9 1/16	7 11/16	9 9/16	8 4/16
18	51 13/16	51 2/16	49 2/16	164 4/16	9	7 9/16	9 9/16	8 2/16	10 2/16	8 12/16
19	54 12/16	53 15/16	51 14/16	173 4/16	9 8/16	8	10 2/16	8 9/16	10 11/16	9 3/16
20	57 10/16	56 13/16	54 9/16	182 4/16	10	8 6/16	10 10/16	9 1/16	11 4/16	9 11/16
21	60 8/16	59 10/16	57 5/16	191 4/16	10 8/16	8 13/16	11 3/16	9 8/16	11 13/16	10 3/16
22	63 6/16	62 8/16	60 1/16	200 4/16	11	9 4/16	11 11/16	9 15/16	12 6/16	10 11/16
23	66 4/16	65 5/16	62 12/16	209 4/16	11 8/16	9 10/16	12 4/16	10 6/16	12 15/16	11 2/16
24	69 2/16	68 3/16	65 8/16	218 4/16	12	10 1/16	12 12/16	10 14/16	13 8/16	11 10/16
25	72	71	68 4/16	227 4/16	12 8/16	10 8/16	13 5/16	11 5/16	14 1/16	12 2/16
26	74 14/16	73 13/16	70 15/16	236 4/16	13	10 14/16	13 13/16	11 12/16	14 10/16	12 10/16
27	77 12/16	76 11/16	73 11/16	245 4/16	13 8/16	11 5/16	14 6/16	12 3/16	15 3/16	13 1/16
28	80 10/16	79 8/16	76 7/16	254 4/16	14	11 12/16	14 14/16	12 11/16	15 12/16	13 9/16

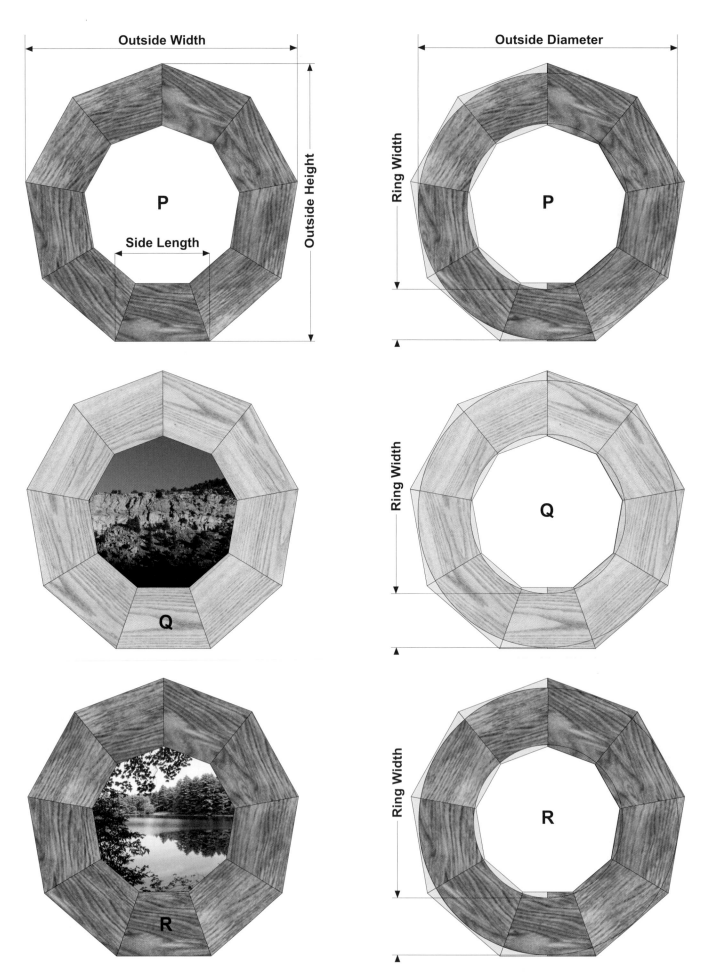

Side Length	Frame Width	Frame Height	Ring Max. OD	Material Req'd.	P Side Width	P Ring Width	Q Side Width	Q Ring Width	R Side Width	R Ring Width
8/16	1 7/16	1 7/16	1 6/16	6 12/16	5/16	4/16	5/16	4/16	5/16	5/16
10/16	1 13/16	1 12/16	1 11/16	7 14/16	6/16	5/16	6/16	6/16	7/16	6/16
12/16	2 3/16	2 2/16	2 1/16	9	7/16	6/16	8/16	7/16	8/16	7/16
14/16	2 8/16	2 8/16	2 6/16	10 2/16	8/16	7/16	9/16	8/16	9/16	8/16
1	2 14/16	2 13/16	2 12/16	11 4/16	10/16	8/16	10/16	9/16	11/16	9/16
1 4/16	3 10/16	3 9/16	3 7/16	13 8/16	12/16	10/16	13/16	11/16	13/16	12/16
1 8/16	4 5/16	4 4/16	4 1/16	15 12/16	14/16	12/16	15/16	13/16	1	14/16
1 12/16	5 1/16	5	4 12/16	18	1 1/16	14/16	1 2/16	15/16	1 2/16	1
2	5 12/16	5 11/16	5 7/16	20 4/16	1 3/16	1 1/16	1 4/16	1 2/16	1 5/16	1 3/16
2 4/16	6 8/16	6 6/16	6 2/16	22 8/16	1 5/16	1 3/16	1 7/16	1 4/16	1 8/16	1 5/16
2 8/16	7 3/16	7 2/16	6 13/16	24 12/16	1 8/16	1 5/16	1 9/16	1 6/16	1 10/16	1 7/16
2 12/16	7 15/16	7 13/16	7 8/16	27	1 10/16	1 7/16	1 12/16	1 8/16	1 13/16	1 10/16
3	8 10/16	8 8/16	8 3/16	29 4/16	1 13/16	1 9/16	1 14/16	1 10/16	2	1 12/16
3 4/16	9 6/16	9 4/16	8 14/16	31 8/16	1 15/16	1 11/16	2 1/16	1 13/16	2 2/16	1 14/16
3 8/16	10 1/16	9 15/16	9 9/16	33 12/16	2 1/16	1 13/16	2 3/16	1 15/16	2 5/16	2 1/16
3 12/16	10 13/16	10 10/16	10 4/16	36	2 4/16	1 15/16	2 6/16	2 1/16	2 7/16	2 3/16
4	11 8/16	11 6/16	10 15/16	38 4/16	2 6/16	2 1/16	2 8/16	2 3/16	2 10/16	2 5/16
4 4/16	12 4/16	12 1/16	11 10/16	40 8/16	2 8/16	2 3/16	2 11/16	2 5/16	2 13/16	2 8/16
4 8/16	12 15/16	12 12/16	12 4/16	42 12/16	2 11/16	2 5/16	2 13/16	2 8/16	2 15/16	2 10/16
4 12/16	13 11/16	13 8/16	12 15/16	45	2 13/16	2 7/16	3	2 10/16	3 2/16	2 12/16
5	14 6/16	14 3/16	13 10/16	47 4/16	3	2 9/16	3 2/16	2 12/16	3 5/16	2 15/16
5 4/16	15 2/16	14 15/16	14 5/16	49 8/16	3 2/16	2 11/16	3 5/16	2 14/16	3 7/16	3 1/16
5 8/16	15 13/16	15 10/16	15	51 12/16	3 4/16	2 14/16	3 7/16	3	3 10/16	3 3/16
5 12/16	16 9/16	16 5/16	15 11/16	54	3 7/16	3	3 10/16	3 3/16	3 12/16	3 6/16
6	17 4/16	17 1/16	16 6/16	56 4/16	3 9/16	3 2/16	3 12/16	3 5/16	3 15/16	3 8/16
6 8/16	18 12/16	18 7/16	17 12/16	60 12/16	3 14/16	3 6/16	4 1/16	3 9/16	4 4/16	3 13/16
7	20 3/16	19 14/16	19 2/16	65 4/16	4 3/16	3 10/16	4 6/16	3 14/16	4 10/16	4 1/16
7 8/16	21 10/16	21 5/16	20 7/16	69 12/16	4 7/16	3 14/16	4 11/16	4 2/16	4 15/16	4 6/16
8	23 1/16	22 12/16	21 13/16	74 4/16	4 12/16	4 2/16	5	4 6/16	5 4/16	4 11/16
8 8/16	24 8/16	24 2/16	23 3/16	78 12/16	5 1/16	4 6/16	5 5/16	4 11/16	5 9/16	4 15/16
9	25 15/16	25 9/16	24 9/16	83 4/16	5 6/16	4 10/16	5 10/16	4 15/16	5 15/16	5 4/16
9 8/16	27 6/16	27	25 15/16	87 12/16	5 10/16	4 15/16	5 15/16	5 4/16	6 4/16	5 9/16
10	28 13/16	28 6/16	27 5/16	92 4/16	5 15/16	5 3/16	6 4/16	5 8/16	6 9/16	5 13/16
10 8/16	30 4/16	29 13/16	28 10/16	96 12/16	6 4/16	5 7/16	6 9/16	5 12/16	6 14/16	6 2/16
11	31 11/16	31 4/16	30	101 4/16	6 9/16	5 11/16	6 14/16	6 1/16	7 4/16	6 7/16
11 8/16	33 2/16	32 11/16	31 6/16	105 12/16	6 13/16	5 15/16	7 3/16	6 5/16	7 9/16	6 11/16
12	34 9/16	34 1/16	32 12/16	110 4/16	7 2/16	6 3/16	7 8/16	6 10/16	7 14/16	7
13	37 7/16	36 15/16	35 8/16	119 4/16	7 12/16	6 12/16	8 2/16	7 2/16	8 9/16	7 9/16
14	40 5/16	39 12/16	38 3/16	128 4/16	8 5/16	7 4/16	8 12/16	7 11/16	9 3/16	8 3/16
15	43 3/16	42 10/16	40 15/16	137 4/16	8 15/16	7 12/16	9 6/16	8 4/16	9 14/16	8 12/16
16	46 1/16	45 7/16	43 11/16	146 4/16	9 8/16	8 4/16	10	8 13/16	10 8/16	9 5/16
17	48 15/16	48 4/16	46 6/16	155 4/16	10 2/16	8 13/16	10 10/16	9 6/16	11 3/16	9 15/16
18	51 13/16	51 2/16	49 2/16	164 4/16	10 11/16	9 5/16	11 4/16	9 14/16	11 13/16	10 8/16
19	54 12/16	53 15/16	51 14/16	173 4/16	11 5/16	9 13/16	11 14/16	10 7/16	12 8/16	11 1/16
20	57 10/16	56 13/16	54 9/16	182 4/16	11 14/16	10 6/16	12 8/16	11	13 2/16	11 10/16
21	60 8/16	59 10/16	57 5/16	191 4/16	12 8/16	10 14/16	13 2/16	11 9/16	13 13/16	12 4/16
22	63 6/16	62 8/16	60 1/16	200 4/16	13 1/16	11 6/16	13 12/16	12 2/16	14 7/16	12 13/16
23	66 4/16	65 5/16	62 12/16	209 4/16	13 11/16	11 14/16	14 6/16	12 10/16	15 2/16	13 6/16
24	69 2/16	68 3/16	65 8/16	218 4/16	14 4/16	12 7/16	15	13 3/16	15 12/16	14
25	72	71	68 4/16	227 4/16	14 14/16	12 15/16	15 10/16	13 12/16	16 7/16	14 9/16
26	74 14/16	73 13/16	70 15/16	236 4/16	15 7/16	13 7/16	16 4/16	14 5/16	17 1/16	15 2/16
27	77 12/16	76 11/16	73 11/16	245 4/16	16 1/16	13 15/16	16 14/16	14 14/16	17 12/16	15 12/16
28	80 10/16	79 8/16	76 7/16	254 4/16	16 10/16	14 8/16	17 8/16	15 6/16	18 6/16	16 5/16

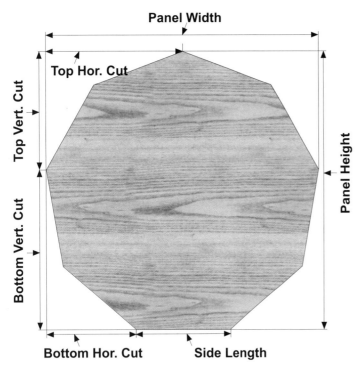

Panel Width

Top Hor. Cut

Top Vert. Cut

Bottom Vert. Cut

Panel Height

Bottom Hor. Cut

Side Length

The Chart below shows the formulas that were used in the process of laying out the 9 sided shapes. These are included to assist you if you are designing a project to a size that is not illustrated in the Dimension Charts provided. We hope you find them helpful as you design your projects.

9 SIDED PANEL FORMULAS		
Panel Width =	Panel Height x	1.015
Panel Height =	Panel Width x	0.985
Side Length =	Panel Height x	0.347
Side Length =	Panel Width x	0.352
Top Hor. Cut =	Panel Width x	0.500
Bott. Hor. Cut =	Panel Width x	0.325
Top Vert. Cut =	Panel Width x	0.420
Bott.Vert. Cut =	Panel Width x	0.564

PANEL WIDTH	PANEL HEIGHT	SIDE LENGTH	TOP HOR. CUT	BOTTOM HOR. CUT	TOP VERT. CUT	BOTTOM VERT. CUT
12/16	12/16	4/16	6/16	4/16	5/16	7/16
1	1	6/16	8/16	5/16	7/16	9/16
1 4/16	1 4/16	7/16	10/16	7/16	8/16	11/16
1 8/16	1 8/16	8/16	12/16	8/16	10/16	14/16
1 12/16	1 12/16	10/16	14/16	9/16	12/16	1
2	2	11/16	1	10/16	13/16	1 2/16
2 4/16	2 3/16	12/16	1 2/16	12/16	15/16	1 4/16
2 8/16	2 7/16	14/16	1 4/16	13/16	1 1/16	1 7/16
2 12/16	2 11/16	15/16	1 6/16	14/16	1 2/16	1 9/16
3	2 15/16	1 1/16	1 8/16	1	1 4/16	1 11/16
3 4/16	3 3/16	1 2/16	1 10/16	1 1/16	1 6/16	1 13/16
3 8/16	3 7/16	1 3/16	1 12/16	1 2/16	1 8/16	2
3 12/16	3 11/16	1 5/16	1 14/16	1 4/16	1 9/16	2 2/16
4	3 15/16	1 6/16	2	1 5/16	1 11/16	2 4/16
4 4/16	4 3/16	1 8/16	2 2/16	1 6/16	1 13/16	2 6/16
4 8/16	4 7/16	1 9/16	2 4/16	1 7/16	1 14/16	2 9/16
4 12/16	4 11/16	1 10/16	2 6/16	1 9/16	2	2 11/16
5	4 15/16	1 12/16	2 8/16	1 10/16	2 2/16	2 13/16
5 4/16	5 3/16	1 13/16	2 10/16	1 11/16	2 3/16	2 15/16
5 8/16	5 7/16	1 15/16	2 12/16	1 13/16	2 5/16	3 2/16
5 12/16	5 11/16	2	2 14/16	1 14/16	2 7/16	3 4/16
6	5 15/16	2 1/16	3	1 15/16	2 8/16	3 6/16
6 4/16	6 3/16	2 3/16	3 2/16	2 1/16	2 10/16	3 8/16
6 8/16	6 6/16	2 4/16	3 4/16	2 2/16	2 12/16	3 11/16
6 12/16	6 10/16	2 5/16	3 6/16	2 3/16	2 13/16	3 13/16
7	6 14/16	2 7/16	3 8/16	2 4/16	2 15/16	3 15/16
7 4/16	7 2/16	2 8/16	3 10/16	2 6/16	3 1/16	4 1/16
7 8/16	7 6/16	2 10/16	3 12/16	2 7/16	3 2/16	4 4/16
7 12/16	7 10/16	2 11/16	3 14/16	2 8/16	3 4/16	4 6/16
8	7 14/16	2 12/16	4	2 10/16	3 6/16	4 8/16
8 4/16	8 2/16	2 14/16	4 2/16	2 11/16	3 7/16	4 10/16
8 8/16	8 6/16	2 15/16	4 4/16	2 12/16	3 9/16	4 13/16

PANEL WIDTH	PANEL HEIGHT	SIDE LENGTH	TOP HOR. CUT	BOTTOM HOR. CUT	TOP VERT. CUT	BOTTOM VERT. CUT
8 12/16	8 10/16	3 1/16	4 6/16	2 14/16	3 11/16	4 15/16
9	8 14/16	3 2/16	4 8/16	2 15/16	3 12/16	5 1/16
9 4/16	9 2/16	3 3/16	4 10/16	3	3 14/16	5 3/16
9 8/16	9 6/16	3 5/16	4 12/16	3 1/16	4	5 6/16
9 12/16	9 10/16	3 6/16	4 14/16	3 3/16	4 2/16	5 8/16
10	9 14/16	3 8/16	5	3 4/16	4 3/16	5 10/16
10 4/16	10 2/16	3 9/16	5 2/16	3 5/16	4 5/16	5 12/16
10 8/16	10 5/16	3 10/16	5 4/16	3 7/16	4 7/16	5 15/16
10 12/16	10 9/16	3 12/16	5 6/16	3 8/16	4 8/16	6 1/16
11	10 13/16	3 13/16	5 8/16	3 9/16	4 10/16	6 3/16
11 4/16	11 1/16	3 14/16	5 10/16	3 11/16	4 12/16	6 6/16
11 8/16	11 5/16	4	5 12/16	3 12/16	4 13/16	6 8/16
12	11 13/16	4 3/16	6	3 14/16	5 1/16	6 12/16
12 4/16	12 1/16	4 4/16	6 2/16	4	5 2/16	6 15/16
12 8/16	12 5/16	4 5/16	6 4/16	4 1/16	5 4/16	7 1/16
12 12/16	12 9/16	4 7/16	6 6/16	4 2/16	5 6/16	7 3/16
13	12 13/16	4 8/16	6 8/16	4 4/16	5 7/16	7 5/16
13 4/16	13 1/16	4 10/16	6 10/16	4 5/16	5 9/16	7 8/16
13 8/16	13 5/16	4 11/16	6 12/16	4 6/16	5 11/16	7 10/16
13 12/16	13 9/16	4 12/16	6 14/16	4 8/16	5 12/16	7 12/16
14	13 13/16	4 14/16	7	4 9/16	5 14/16	7 14/16
14 8/16	14 5/16	5 1/16	7 4/16	4 11/16	6 1/16	8 3/16
15	14 12/16	5 3/16	7 8/16	4 14/16	6 5/16	8 7/16
15 8/16	15 4/16	5 6/16	7 12/16	5 1/16	6 8/16	8 12/16
16	15 12/16	5 9/16	8	5 3/16	6 12/16	9
16 8/16	16 4/16	5 12/16	8 4/16	5 6/16	6 15/16	9 5/16
17	16 12/16	5 14/16	8 8/16	5 8/16	7 2/16	9 9/16
17 8/16	17 4/16	6 1/16	8 12/16	5 11/16	7 6/16	9 14/16
18	17 12/16	6 4/16	9	5 14/16	7 9/16	10 2/16
19	18 11/16	6 9/16	9 8/16	6 3/16	8	10 11/16
20	19 11/16	6 15/16	10	6 8/16	8 6/16	11 4/16
21	20 11/16	7 5/16	10 8/16	6 13/16	8 13/16	11 14/16
22	21 11/16	7 10/16	11	7 2/16	9 4/16	12 7/16
23	22 10/16	8	11 8/16	7 8/16	9 11/16	13
24	23 10/16	8 5/16	12	7 13/16	10 1/16	13 9/16
25	24 10/16	8 11/16	12 8/16	8 2/16	10 8/16	14 2/16
26	25 10/16	9	13	8 7/16	10 15/16	14 11/16
27	26 10/16	9 6/16	13 8/16	8 12/16	11 5/16	15 4/16
28	27 9/16	9 11/16	14	9 2/16	11 12/16	15 13/16
29	28 9/16	10 1/16	14 8/16	9 7/16	12 3/16	16 6/16
30	29 9/16	10 7/16	15	9 12/16	12 10/16	16 15/16
31	30 9/16	10 12/16	15 8/16	10 1/16	13	17 8/16
32	31 8/16	11 2/16	16	10 6/16	13 7/16	18 1/16
33	32 8/16	11 7/16	16 8/16	10 12/16	13 14/16	18 10/16
34	33 8/16	11 13/16	17	11 1/16	14 4/16	19 3/16
35	34 8/16	12 2/16	17 8/16	11 6/16	14 11/16	19 12/16
36	35 7/16	12 8/16	18	11 11/16	15 2/16	20 5/16
37	36 7/16	12 13/16	18 8/16	12	15 9/16	20 14/16
38	37 7/16	13 3/16	19	12 6/16	15 15/16	21 7/16
39	38 7/16	13 9/16	19 8/16	12 11/16	16 6/16	22
40	39 6/16	13 14/16	20	13	16 13/16	22 9/16
41	40 6/16	14 4/16	20 8/16	13 5/16	17 4/16	23 2/16
42	41 6/16	14 9/16	21	13 10/16	17 10/16	23 11/16

10 SIDED PROJECT INFORMATION

Geometric Name: Decagon
Definition: A Polygon having 10 sides
Miter Angle: 18°
Angle Change / Adjoining Sides: 36°

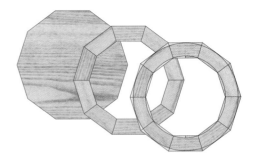

The 10 sided shape (Decagon) is one of the "even numbered" shapes that's not very easy to get creative with, because a pair of points on the frame will point toward a pair of parallel sides on a picture. The one thing that should be considered when using this shape (with sides of equal length) is that for most standard sizes of pictures, a lot of cropping of the picture will be required. However, the Decagon is a fun frame to build using sides of equal length for your frame.

The Illustrations to the right should give you an idea of the amount of cropping that may be required by using a Decagon (with equal length sides) as your choice of shape for a frame.

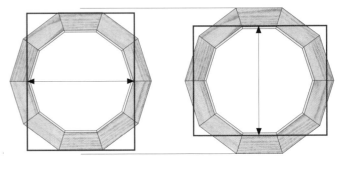

Portrait   **Landscape**

In the left Illustration, you see a scale (shown in red) 8" x 10" sheet in portrait format. The sheet border is slightly outside the rabbeted area (shown in yellow) of the frame. Note the amount of material that would need to be cropped off the sheet top and/or bottom.

In the right Illustration, you see the same size sheet, but rotated 90° into a landscape format. Note a different amount of material would need to be cropped off the sheet sides.

You should note that the frames to the right are not the same size. This is due to the fact that on a Decagon, two sides are parallel to the picture edges, and two points meet at the other two sides of the picture. In our **10 SIDED FRAME FORMULAS** below, you will be able to see that the dimensions for both formats for the pictures are not identical.

If the project you are building is a frame for a specific size object, you should refer to the **10 SIDED FRAME FORMULAS** Chart below as a first step. On a Decagon (with sides of equal length) the height will not be identical to the width. The picture width is the controlling dimension in a portrait format, and the height is the controlling dimension in a landscape format.

Though the Decagon is one of the hardest of the Polygons to get creative with, you can build a very pretty frame if you have the patience and time to make test cuts (to length) to make a specific size frame for your picture(s).

10 SIDED FRAME FORMULAS		
WIDTH	**HEIGHT**	**SIDE LENGTH**
Width = Side Length x 3.23	Height = Side Length x 3.075	Side Length = Width x .310
Width = Height x 1.05	Height = Width x .952	Side Length = Height x .325

Though the information above is very helpful, one of the most time consuming (and frustrating) things about building frames is to try to cut to a dimension that is not measured on either the inside or outside edge of the molding. I like to cut miters from the inside to the outside edges of the molding. This not only allows me to eliminate tear out on the inside corners of the frame since I am cutting into the inside edge, I am also cutting with the grain of the molding. It also allows me to see the outside edge of the material as I cut it. To help you understand how easy it is to convert a dimension along the rabbeted edge into an outside measurement, I will explain how we can use some basic math to help us determine the outside length of our frame sides. The Illustration below should be helpful in showing you how we designed our **10 SIDED FRAME ADDED WIDTH AND LENGTH CHART** on the next page.

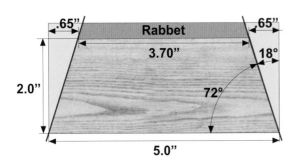

The Illustration to the left represents a piece of wood that is 5" long and 2" wide (to the edge of the rabbet). Note that on the right side that the end of the piece shows the miter angle for an Decagon (18°) and the resulting angle of the cut (72°).

You should also note that at the rabbet, the 18° cuts shorten each end of the piece by .65". Since both ends of the piece are cut, this means that the length at the rabbet is 3.70", which is 1.30" shorter than the outside edge of the molding. What this Illustration tells us is that at an 18°cut, we will add 1.30" to the length at a 2" width. This is the basis of our formula.

If we divide the **Added Length** (1.30") by the **Added Width** (2.0") we end up with .65 as our multiplier. In the event that you want to make a frame and need to work in fractions smaller than 1/16 increments, you would multiply the width of the molding outside the rabbet by .65. To determine the decimal equivalent of the fractions you need to use, refer to the **FRACTION TO DECIMAL CONVERSION CHART** provided.

If you are able to use 1/16" increments for the mathematics of your frames, you should use the **10 SIDED FRAME ADDED WIDTH AND LENGTH CHART** below.

Determine how wide you want the material to be (outside the rabbet). Refer to the Chart below to find this dimension in one of the yellow shaded columns. The added length for that width will be shown in the green shaded block to the right of it. Add this dimension to the side length determined in the first step. You should then add whatever waste you want to allow for each side. This total is then multiplied by 10 to determine how much material is needed to build your project.

10 SIDED FRAME ADDED WIDTH AND LENGTH CHART

Added Width	Added Length	Added Width	Added Length	Added Width	Added Length	Added Width	Added Length	Added Width	Added Length
1/16	1/16	1 1/16	11/16	2 1/16	1 5/16	3 1/16	2	4 1/16	2 10/16
2/16	1/16	1 2/16	12/16	2 2/16	1 6/16	3 2/16	2 1/16	4 2/16	2 11/16
3/16	2/16	1 3/16	12/16	2 3/16	1 7/16	3 3/16	2 1/16	4 3/16	2 12/16
4/16	3/16	1 4/16	13/16	2 4/16	1 7/16	3 4/16	2 2/16	4 4/16	2 12/16
5/16	3/16	1 5/16	14/16	2 5/16	1 8/16	3 5/16	2 2/16	4 5/16	2 13/16
6/16	4/16	1 6/16	14/16	2 6/16	1 9/16	3 6/16	2 3/16	4 6/16	2 14/16
7/16	5/16	1 7/16	15/16	2 7/16	1 9/16	3 7/16	2 4/16	4 7/16	2 14/16
8/16	5/16	1 8/16	1	2 8/16	1 10/16	3 8/16	2 4/16	4 8/16	2 15/16
9/16	6/16	1 9/16	1	2 9/16	1 11/16	3 9/16	2 5/16	4 9/16	2 15/16
10/16	7/16	1 10/16	1 1/16	2 10/16	1 11/16	3 10/16	2 6/16	4 10/16	3
11/16	7/16	1 11/16	1 2/16	2 11/16	1 12/16	3 11/16	2 6/16	4 11/16	3 1/16
12/16	8/16	1 12/16	1 2/16	2 12/16	1 13/16	3 12/16	2 7/16	4 12/16	3 1/16
13/16	8/16	1 13/16	1 3/16	2 13/16	1 13/16	3 13/16	2 8/16	4 13/16	3 2/16
14/16	9/16	1 14/16	1 4/16	2 14/16	1 14/16	3 14/16	2 8/16	4 14/16	3 3/16
15/16	10/16	1 15/16	1 4/16	2 15/16	1 15/16	3 15/16	2 9/16	4 15/16	3 3/16
1	10/16	2	1 5/16	3	1 15/16	4	2 10/16	5	3 4/16

The Chart below is provided to enable you to make 10 sided frames using the mathematics of most popular picture sizes. Note that the dimensions are not the same in portrait and landscape format. This is because the point-to-point dimension of the frame is larger than the side-to-side dimension. In the Charts, the different colored columns represent the following information:

Red: The controlling dimension of the sheet size. (width in portrait, height in landscape)
Gray: The dimension of the sheet size that will need to be cropped.

White: The rabbet length for the frame sides.
Orange: The size of the opening in the direction the picture will need to be cropped.
Blue: The amount of material that will need to be cropped.

RABBET AREA DIMENSIONS FOR 10 SIDED FRAMES

FOR PORTRAIT FORMAT					FOR LANDSCAPE FORMAT				
Object Width	Object Height	Rabbet Length	Opening Height	Vertical Crop	Object Width	Object Height	Rabbet Length	Opening Width	Horizontal Crop
4	5	1 4/16	4 2/16	1	5	4	1 5/16	4 2/16	1
5	7	1 9/16	5 2/16	2	7	5	1 11/16	5 2/16	2
6	8	1 14/16	6 2/16	2	8	6	2	6 2/16	2
8	10	2 8/16	8 2/16	2	10	8	2 10/16	8 2/16	2
8 1/2	11	2 11/16	8 10/16	2 8/16	11	8 1/2	2 13/16	8 10/16	2 8/16
10	14	3 2/16	10 2/16	4	14	10	3 5/16	10 2/16	4
11	14	3 7/16	11 2/16	3	14	11	3 10/16	11 2/16	3
12	16	3 12/16	12 2/16	4	16	12	3 15/16	12 2/16	4
16	20	5	16 2/16	4	20	16	5 4/16	16 2/16	4
18	24	5 10/16	18 2/16	6	24	18	5 14/16	18 2/16	6
20	24	6 4/16	20 2/16	4	24	20	6 9/16	20 2/16	4
24	30	7 8/16	24 2/16	6	30	24	7 13/16	24 2/16	6

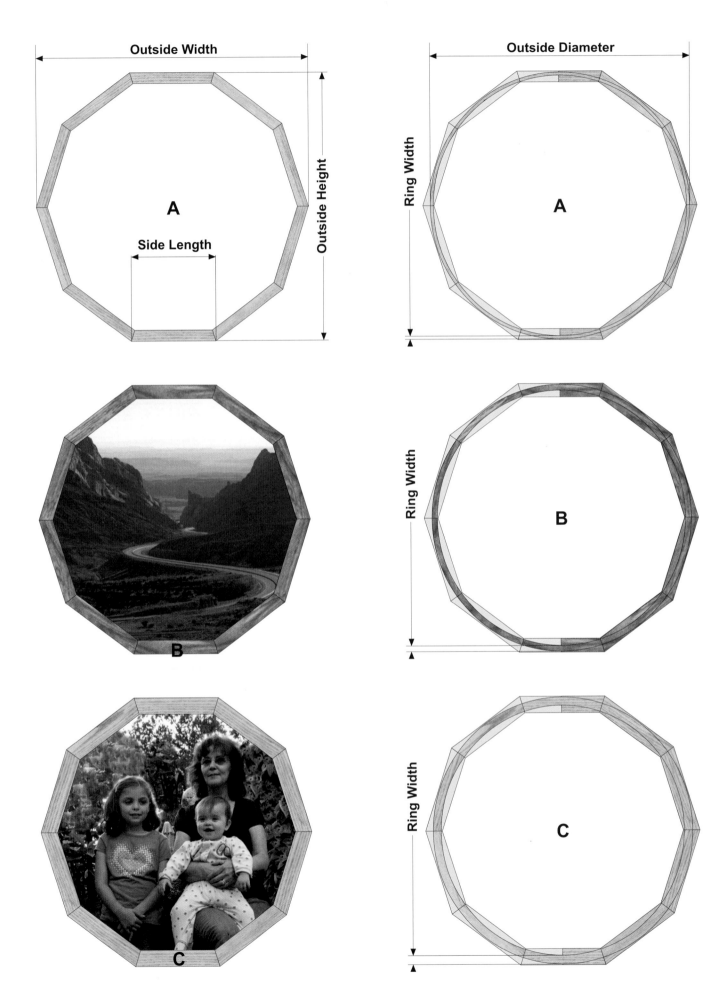

Side Length	Frame Width	Frame Height	Ring Max. OD	Material Req'd.	A Side Width	A Ring Width	B Side Width	B Ring Width	C Side Width	C Ring Width
8/16	1 10/16	1 9/16	1 8/16	7 8/16	1/16		1/16	1/16	2/16	1/16
10/16	2	1 15/16	1 14/16	8 12/16	1/16		2/16	1/16	2/16	1/16
12/16	2 7/16	2 5/16	2 5/16	10	2/16		2/16	1/16	2/16	1/16
14/16	2 13/16	2 11/16	2 11/16	11 4/16	2/16		2/16	1/16	3/16	1/16
1	3 4/16	3 1/16	3 1/16	12 8/16	2/16	1/16	3/16	1/16	3/16	2/16
1 4/16	4 1/16	3 13/16	3 13/16	15	3/16	1/16	3/16	1/16	4/16	2/16
1 8/16	4 14/16	4 10/16	4 9/16	17 8/16	3/16	1/16	4/16	2/16	5/16	2/16
1 12/16	5 10/16	5 6/16	5 5/16	20	4/16	1/16	4/16	2/16	5/16	3/16
2	6 7/16	6 2/16	6 2/16	22 8/16	4/16	1/16	5/16	2/16	6/16	3/16
2 4/16	7 4/16	6 15/16	6 14/16	25	5/16	1/16	6/16	2/16	7/16	4/16
2 8/16	8 1/16	7 11/16	7 10/16	27 8/16	5/16	1/16	6/16	3/16	8/16	4/16
2 12/16	8 14/16	8 7/16	8 6/16	30	6/16	2/16	7/16	3/16	8/16	4/16
3	9 11/16	9 3/16	9 2/16	32 8/16	6/16	2/16	8/16	3/16	9/16	5/16
3 4/16	10 8/16	10	9 14/16	35	7/16	2/16	8/16	4/16	10/16	5/16
3 8/16	11 5/16	10 12/16	10 11/16	37 8/16	7/16	2/16	9/16	4/16	11/16	6/16
3 12/16	12 2/16	11 8/16	11 7/16	40	8/16	2/16	9/16	4/16	11/16	6/16
4	12 15/16	12 4/16	12 3/16	42 8/16	8/16	2/16	10/16	4/16	12/16	6/16
4 4/16	13 12/16	13 1/16	12 15/16	45	9/16	2/16	11/16	5/16	13/16	7/16
4 8/16	14 9/16	13 13/16	13 11/16	47 8/16	9/16	3/16	11/16	5/16	14/16	7/16
4 12/16	15 5/16	14 9/16	14 8/16	50	10/16	3/16	12/16	5/16	14/16	8/16
5	16 2/16	15 6/16	15 4/16	52 8/16	10/16	3/16	13/16	5/16	15/16	8/16
5 4/16	16 15/16	16 2/16	16	55	11/16	3/16	13/16	6/16	1	8/16
5 8/16	17 12/16	16 14/16	16 12/16	57 8/16	11/16	3/16	14/16	6/16	1 1/16	9/16
5 12/16	18 9/16	17 10/16	17 8/16	60	12/16	3/16	14/16	6/16	1 1/16	9/16
6	19 6/16	18 7/16	18 5/16	62 8/16	12/16	3/16	15/16	7/16	1 2/16	10/16
6 8/16	21	19 15/16	19 13/16	67 8/16	13/16	4/16	1	7/16	1 4/16	11/16
7	22 10/16	21 8/16	21 5/16	72 8/16	14/16	4/16	1 2/16	8/16	1 5/16	11/16
7 8/16	24 4/16	23	22 14/16	77 8/16	15/16	4/16	1 3/16	8/16	1 7/16	12/16
8	25 13/16	24 9/16	24 6/16	82 8/16	1	5/16	1 4/16	9/16	1 8/16	13/16
8 8/16	27 7/16	26 2/16	25 15/16	87 8/16	1 1/16	5/16	1 5/16	9/16	1 10/16	14/16
9	29 1/16	27 10/16	27 7/16	92 8/16	1 2/16	5/16	1 7/16	10/16	1 11/16	15/16
9 8/16	30 11/16	29 3/16	28 15/16	97 8/16	1 3/16	5/16	1 8/16	10/16	1 13/16	15/16
10	32 5/16	30 11/16	30 8/16	102 8/16	1 4/16	6/16	1 9/16	11/16	1 14/16	1
10 8/16	33 15/16	32 4/16	32	107 8/16	1 5/16	6/16	1 10/16	11/16	2	1 1/16
11	35 8/16	33 12/16	33 8/16	112 8/16	1 6/16	6/16	1 12/16	12/16	2 1/16	1 2/16
11 8/16	37 2/16	35 5/16	35 1/16	117 8/16	1 7/16	7/16	1 13/16	13/16	2 3/16	1 3/16
12	38 12/16	36 13/16	36 9/16	122 8/16	1 8/16	7/16	1 14/16	13/16	2 4/16	1 3/16
13	42	39 15/16	39 10/16	132 8/16	1 10/16	7/16	2 1/16	14/16	2 7/16	1 5/16
14	45 4/16	43	42 11/16	142 8/16	1 12/16	8/16	2 3/16	15/16	2 10/16	1 7/16
15	48 7/16	46 1/16	45 11/16	152 8/16	1 14/16	9/16	2 6/16	1	2 13/16	1 8/16
16	51 11/16	49 2/16	48 12/16	162 8/16	2	9/16	2 8/16	1 2/16	3	1 10/16
17	54 15/16	52 3/16	51 13/16	172 8/16	2 2/16	10/16	2 11/16	1 3/16	3 3/16	1 11/16
18	58 2/16	55 4/16	54 14/16	182 8/16	2 4/16	10/16	2 13/16	1 4/16	3 6/16	1 13/16
19	61 6/16	58 5/16	57 15/16	192 8/16	2 6/16	11/16	3	1 5/16	3 9/16	1 15/16
20	64 10/16	61 6/16	60 15/16	202 8/16	2 8/16	11/16	3 2/16	1 6/16	3 12/16	2
21	67 13/16	64 8/16	64	212 8/16	2 10/16	12/16	3 5/16	1 7/16	3 15/16	2 2/16
22	71 1/16	67 9/16	67 1/16	222 8/16	2 12/16	13/16	3 7/16	1 8/16	4 2/16	2 4/16
23	74 5/16	70 10/16	70 2/16	232 8/16	2 14/16	13/16	3 10/16	1 9/16	4 5/16	2 5/16
24	77 8/16	73 11/16	73 2/16	242 8/16	3	14/16	3 12/16	1 10/16	4 8/16	2 7/16
25	80 12/16	76 12/16	76 3/16	252 8/16	3 2/16	14/16	3 15/16	1 11/16	4 11/16	2 8/16
26	84	79 13/16	79 4/16	262 8/16	3 4/16	15/16	4 1/16	1 12/16	4 14/16	2 10/16
27	87 3/16	82 14/16	82 5/16	272 8/16	3 6/16	15/16	4 4/16	1 14/16	5 1/16	2 12/16
28	90 7/16	85 15/16	85 5/16	282 8/16	3 8/16	1	4 6/16	1 15/16	5 4/16	2 13/16

Outside Width

D

Side Length

Outside Height

E

F

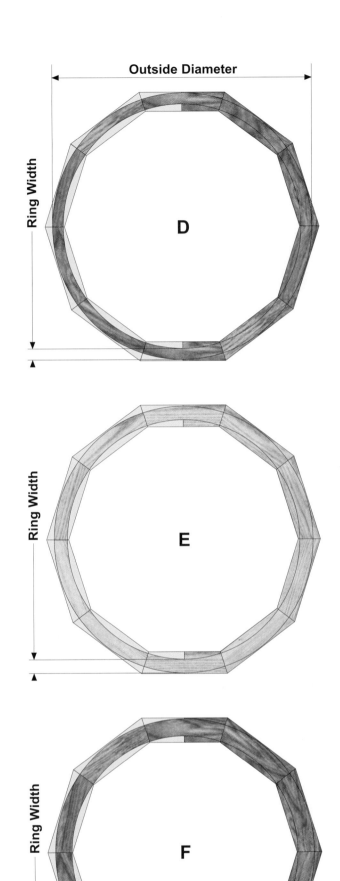

Outside Diameter

Ring Width

D

Ring Width

E

Ring Width

F

Side Length	Frame Width	Frame Height	Ring Max. OD	Material Req'd.	D Side Width	D Ring Width	E Side Width	E Ring Width	F Side Width	F Ring Width
8/16	1 10/16	1 9/16	1 8/16	7 8/16	2/16	1/16	2/16	1/16	2/16	2/16
10/16	2	1 15/16	1 14/16	8 12/16	2/16	1/16	3/16	2/16	3/16	2/16
12/16	2 7/16	2 5/16	2 5/16	10	3/16	2/16	3/16	2/16	3/16	2/16
14/16	2 13/16	2 11/16	2 11/16	11 4/16	3/16	2/16	4/16	2/16	4/16	3/16
1	3 4/16	3 1/16	3 1/16	12 8/16	4/16	2/16	4/16	3/16	5/16	3/16
1 4/16	4 1/16	3 13/16	3 13/16	15	4/16	3/16	5/16	3/16	6/16	4/16
1 8/16	4 14/16	4 10/16	4 9/16	17 8/16	5/16	3/16	6/16	4/16	7/16	5/16
1 12/16	5 10/16	5 6/16	5 5/16	20	6/16	4/16	7/16	5/16	8/16	6/16
2	6 7/16	6 2/16	6 2/16	22 8/16	7/16	4/16	8/16	5/16	9/16	6/16
2 4/16	7 4/16	6 15/16	6 14/16	25	8/16	5/16	9/16	6/16	10/16	7/16
2 8/16	8 1/16	7 11/16	7 10/16	27 8/16	9/16	5/16	10/16	7/16	11/16	8/16
2 12/16	8 14/16	8 7/16	8 6/16	30	10/16	6/16	11/16	7/16	12/16	9/16
3	9 11/16	9 3/16	9 2/16	32 8/16	11/16	6/16	12/16	8/16	14/16	10/16
3 4/16	10 8/16	10	9 14/16	35	11/16	7/16	13/16	9/16	15/16	10/16
3 8/16	11 5/16	10 12/16	10 11/16	37 8/16	12/16	7/16	14/16	9/16	1	11/16
3 12/16	12 2/16	11 8/16	11 7/16	40	13/16	8/16	15/16	10/16	1 1/16	12/16
4	12 15/16	12 4/16	12 3/16	42 8/16	14/16	9/16	1	11/16	1 2/16	13/16
4 4/16	13 12/16	13 1/16	12 15/16	45	15/16	9/16	1 1/16	11/16	1 3/16	14/16
4 8/16	14 9/16	13 13/16	13 11/16	47 8/16	1	10/16	1 2/16	12/16	1 4/16	14/16
4 12/16	15 5/16	14 9/16	14 8/16	50	1 1/16	10/16	1 3/16	13/16	1 5/16	15/16
5	16 2/16	15 6/16	15 4/16	52 8/16	1 2/16	11/16	1 4/16	13/16	1 7/16	1
5 4/16	16 15/16	16 2/16	16	55	1 2/16	11/16	1 5/16	14/16	1 8/16	1 1/16
5 8/16	17 12/16	16 14/16	16 12/16	57 8/16	1 3/16	12/16	1 6/16	15/16	1 9/16	1 2/16
5 12/16	18 9/16	17 10/16	17 8/16	60	1 4/16	12/16	1 7/16	15/16	1 10/16	1 2/16
6	19 6/16	18 7/16	18 5/16	62 8/16	1 5/16	13/16	1 8/16	1	1 11/16	1 3/16
6 8/16	21	19 15/16	19 13/16	67 8/16	1 7/16	14/16	1 10/16	1 1/16	1 13/16	1 5/16
7	22 10/16	21 8/16	21 5/16	72 8/16	1 9/16	15/16	1 12/16	1 3/16	2	1 6/16
7 8/16	24 4/16	23	22 14/16	77 8/16	1 10/16	1	1 14/16	1 4/16	2 2/16	1 8/16
8	25 13/16	24 9/16	24 6/16	82 8/16	1 12/16	1 1/16	2	1 5/16	2 4/16	1 9/16
8 8/16	27 7/16	26 2/16	25 15/16	87 8/16	1 14/16	1 2/16	2 2/16	1 7/16	2 6/16	1 11/16
9	29 1/16	27 10/16	27 7/16	92 8/16	2	1 3/16	2 4/16	1 8/16	2 9/16	1 13/16
9 8/16	30 11/16	29 3/16	28 15/16	97 8/16	2 1/16	1 4/16	2 6/16	1 9/16	2 11/16	1 14/16
10	32 5/16	30 11/16	30 8/16	102 8/16	2 3/16	1 5/16	2 8/16	1 11/16	2 13/16	2
10 8/16	33 15/16	32 4/16	32	107 8/16	2 5/16	1 6/16	2 10/16	1 12/16	2 15/16	2 1/16
11	35 8/16	33 12/16	33 8/16	112 8/16	2 7/16	1 8/16	2 12/16	1 13/16	3 2/16	2 3/16
11 8/16	37 2/16	35 5/16	35 1/16	117 8/16	2 8/16	1 9/16	2 14/16	1 15/16	3 4/16	2 5/16
12	38 12/16	36 13/16	36 9/16	122 8/16	2 10/16	1 10/16	3	2	3 6/16	2 6/16
13	42	39 15/16	39 10/16	132 8/16	2 14/16	1 12/16	3 4/16	2 3/16	3 11/16	2 9/16
14	45 4/16	43	42 11/16	142 8/16	3 1/16	1 14/16	3 8/16	2 5/16	3 15/16	2 13/16
15	48 7/16	46 1/16	45 11/16	152 8/16	3 5/16	2	3 12/16	2 8/16	4 4/16	3
16	51 11/16	49 2/16	48 12/16	162 8/16	3 8/16	2 2/16	4	2 11/16	4 8/16	3 3/16
17	54 15/16	52 3/16	51 13/16	172 8/16	3 12/16	2 4/16	4 4/16	2 13/16	4 13/16	3 6/16
18	58 2/16	55 4/16	54 14/16	182 8/16	3 15/16	2 6/16	4 8/16	3	5 1/16	3 9/16
19	61 6/16	58 5/16	57 15/16	192 8/16	4 3/16	2 9/16	4 12/16	3 3/16	5 6/16	3 13/16
20	64 10/16	61 6/16	60 15/16	202 8/16	4 6/16	2 11/16	5	3 5/16	5 10/16	4
21	67 13/16	64 8/16	64	212	4 10/16	2 13/16	5 4/16	3 8/16	5 15/16	4 3/16
22	71 1/16	67 9/16	67 1/16	222 8/16	4 13/16	2 15/16	5 8/16	3 11/16	6 3/16	4 6/16
23	74 5/16	70 10/16	70 2/16	232 8/16	5 1/16	3 1/16	5 12/16	3 13/16	6 8/16	4 9/16
24	77 8/16	73 11/16	73 2/16	242 8/16	5 4/16	3 3/16	6	4	6 12/16	4 12/16
25	80 12/16	76 12/16	76 3/16	252 8/16	5 8/16	3 5/16	6 4/16	4 3/16	7 1/16	5
26	84	79 13/16	79 4/16	262 8/16	5 11/16	3 8/16	6 8/16	4 5/16	7 5/16	5 3/16
27	87 3/16	82 14/16	82 5/16	272 8/16	5 15/16	3 10/16	6 12/16	4 8/16	7 10/16	5 6/16
28	90 7/16	85 15/16	85 5/16	282 8/16	6 2/16	3 12/16	7	4 11/16	7 14/16	5 9/16

Outside Width

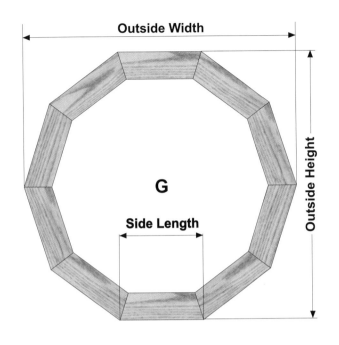

Outside Height

Side Length

G

Outside Diameter

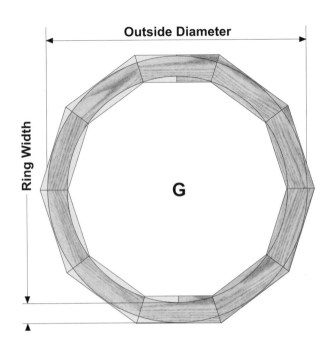

Ring Width

G

H

Ring Width

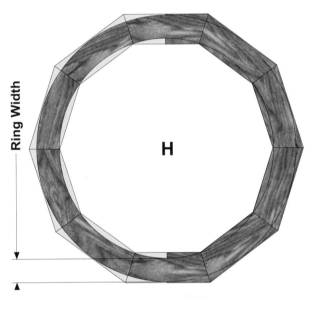

H

I

Ring Width

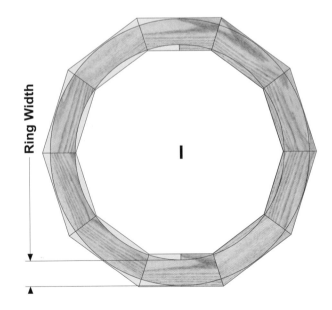

I

Outside Diameter

Side Length	Frame Width	Frame Height	Ring Max. OD	Material Req'd.	G Side Width	G Ring Width	H Side Width	H Ring Width	I Side Width	I Ring Width
8/16	1 10/16	1 9/16	1 8/16	7 8/16	3/16	2/16	3/16	2/16	3/16	2/16
10/16	2	1 15/16	1 14/16	8 12/16	3/16	2/16	3/16	3/16	4/16	3/16
12/16	2 7/16	2 5/16	2 5/16	10	4/16	3/16	4/16	3/16	5/16	4/16
14/16	2 13/16	2 11/16	2 11/16	11 4/16	4/16	3/16	5/16	4/16	5/16	4/16
1	3 4/16	3 1/16	3 1/16	12 8/16	5/16	4/16	6/16	4/16	6/16	5/16
1 4/16	4 1/16	3 13/16	3 13/16	15	6/16	5/16	7/16	5/16	8/16	6/16
1 8/16	4 14/16	4 10/16	4 9/16	17 8/16	8/16	6/16	8/16	6/16	9/16	7/16
1 12/16	5 10/16	5 6/16	5 5/16	20	9/16	6/16	10/16	7/16	11/16	8/16
2	6 7/16	6 2/16	6 2/16	22 8/16	10/16	7/16	11/16	8/16	12/16	10/16
2 4/16	7 4/16	6 15/16	6 14/16	25	11/16	8/16	12/16	10/16	14/16	11/16
2 8/16	8 1/16	7 11/16	7 10/16	27 8/16	13/16	9/16	14/16	11/16	15/16	12/16
2 12/16	8 14/16	8 7/16	8 6/16	30	14/16	10/16	15/16	12/16	1 1/16	13/16
3	9 11/16	9 3/16	9 2/16	32 8/16	15/16	11/16	1 1/16	13/16	1 2/16	14/16
3 4/16	10 8/16	10	9 14/16	35	1	12/16	1 2/16	14/16	1 4/16	15/16
3 8/16	11 5/16	10 12/16	10 11/16	37 8/16	1 2/16	13/16	1 3/16	15/16	1 5/16	1 1/16
3 12/16	12 2/16	11 8/16	11 7/16	40	1 3/16	14/16	1 5/16	1	1 7/16	1 2/16
4	12 15/16	12 4/16	12 3/16	42 8/16	1 4/16	15/16	1 6/16	1 1/16	1 8/16	1 3/16
4 4/16	13 12/16	13 1/16	12 15/16	45	1 5/16	1	1 7/16	1 2/16	1 10/16	1 4/16
4 8/16	14 9/16	13 13/16	13 11/16	47 8/16	1 7/16	1 1/16	1 9/16	1 3/16	1 11/16	1 5/16
4 12/16	15 5/16	14 9/16	14 8/16	50	1 8/16	1 2/16	1 10/16	1 4/16	1 13/16	1 7/16
5	16 2/16	15 6/16	15 4/16	52 8/16	1 9/16	1 3/16	1 12/16	1 5/16	1 14/16	1 8/16
5 4/16	16 15/16	16 2/16	16	55	1 10/16	1 3/16	1 13/16	1 6/16	2	1 9/16
5 8/16	17 12/16	16 14/16	16 12/16	57 8/16	1 12/16	1 4/16	1 14/16	1 7/16	2 1/16	1 10/16
5 12/16	18 9/16	17 10/16	17 8/16	60	1 13/16	1 5/16	2	1 8/16	2 3/16	1 11/16
6	19 6/16	18 7/16	18 5/16	62 8/16	1 14/16	1 6/16	2 1/16	1 9/16	2 4/16	1 13/16
6 8/16	21	19 15/16	19 13/16	67 8/16	2 1/16	1 8/16	2 4/16	1 11/16	2 7/16	1 15/16
7	22 10/16	21 8/16	21 5/16	72 8/16	2 3/16	1 10/16	2 7/16	1 14/16	2 10/16	2 1/16
7 8/16	24 4/16	23	22 14/16	77 8/16	2 6/16	1 12/16	2 9/16	2	2 13/16	2 4/16
8	25 13/16	24 9/16	24 6/16	82 8/16	2 8/16	1 14/16	2 12/16	2 2/16	3	2 6/16
8 8/16	27 7/16	26 2/16	25 15/16	87 8/16	2 11/16	2	2 15/16	2 4/16	3 3/16	2 8/16
9	29 1/16	27 10/16	27 7/16	92 8/16	2 13/16	2 1/16	3 2/16	2 6/16	3 6/16	2 11/16
9 8/16	30 11/16	29 3/16	28 15/16	97 8/16	3	2 3/16	3 4/16	2 8/16	3 9/16	2 13/16
10	32 5/16	30 11/16	30 8/16	102 8/16	3 2/16	2 5/16	3 7/16	2 10/16	3 12/16	3
10 8/16	33 15/16	32 4/16	32	107 8/16	3 5/16	2 7/16	3 10/16	2 12/16	3 15/16	3 2/16
11	35 8/16	33 12/16	33 8/16	112 8/16	3 7/16	2 9/16	3 13/16	2 15/16	4 2/16	3 4/16
11 8/16	37 2/16	35 5/16	35 1/16	117 8/16	3 10/16	2 11/16	3 15/16	3 1/16	4 5/16	3 7/16
12	38 12/16	36 13/16	36 9/16	122 8/16	3 12/16	2 13/16	4 2/16	3 3/16	4 8/16	3 9/16
13	42	39 15/16	39 10/16	132 8/16	4 1/16	3	4 8/16	3 7/16	4 14/16	3 14/16
14	45 4/16	43	42 11/16	142 8/16	4 6/16	3 4/16	4 13/16	3 11/16	5 4/16	4 3/16
15	48 7/16	46 1/16	45 11/16	152 8/16	4 11/16	3 8/16	5 3/16	3 15/16	5 10/16	4 7/16
16	51 11/16	49 2/16	48 12/16	162 8/16	5	3 11/16	5 8/16	4 4/16	6	4 12/16
17	54 15/16	52 3/16	51 13/16	172 8/16	5 5/16	3 15/16	5 14/16	4 8/16	6 6/16	5 1/16
18	58 2/16	55 4/16	54 14/16	182 8/16	5 10/16	4 3/16	6 3/16	4 12/16	6 12/16	5 6/16
19	61 6/16	58 5/16	57 15/16	192 8/16	5 15/16	4 6/16	6 9/16	5	7 2/16	5 10/16
20	64 10/16	61 6/16	60 15/16	202 8/16	6 4/16	4 10/16	6 14/16	5 5/16	7 8/16	5 15/16
21	67 13/16	64 8/16	64	212 8/16	6 9/16	4 14/16	7 4/16	5 9/16	7 14/16	6 4/16
22	71 1/16	67 9/16	67 1/16	222 8/16	6 14/16	5 2/16	7 9/16	5 13/16	8 4/16	6 9/16
23	74 5/16	70 10/16	70 2/16	232 8/16	7 3/16	5 5/16	7 15/16	6 1/16	8 10/16	6 13/16
24	77 8/16	73 11/16	73 2/16	242 8/16	7 8/16	5 9/16	8 4/16	6 6/16	9	7 2/16
25	80 12/16	76 12/16	76 3/16	252 8/16	7 13/16	5 13/16	8 10/16	6 10/16	9 6/16	7 7/16
26	84	79 13/16	79 4/16	262 8/16	8 2/16	6	8 15/16	6 14/16	9 12/16	7 12/16
27	87 3/16	82 14/16	82 5/16	272 8/16	8 7/16	6 4/16	9 5/16	7 2/16	10 2/16	8
28	90 7/16	85 15/16	85 5/16	282 8/16	8 12/16	6 8/16	9 10/16	7 6/16	10 8/16	8 5/16

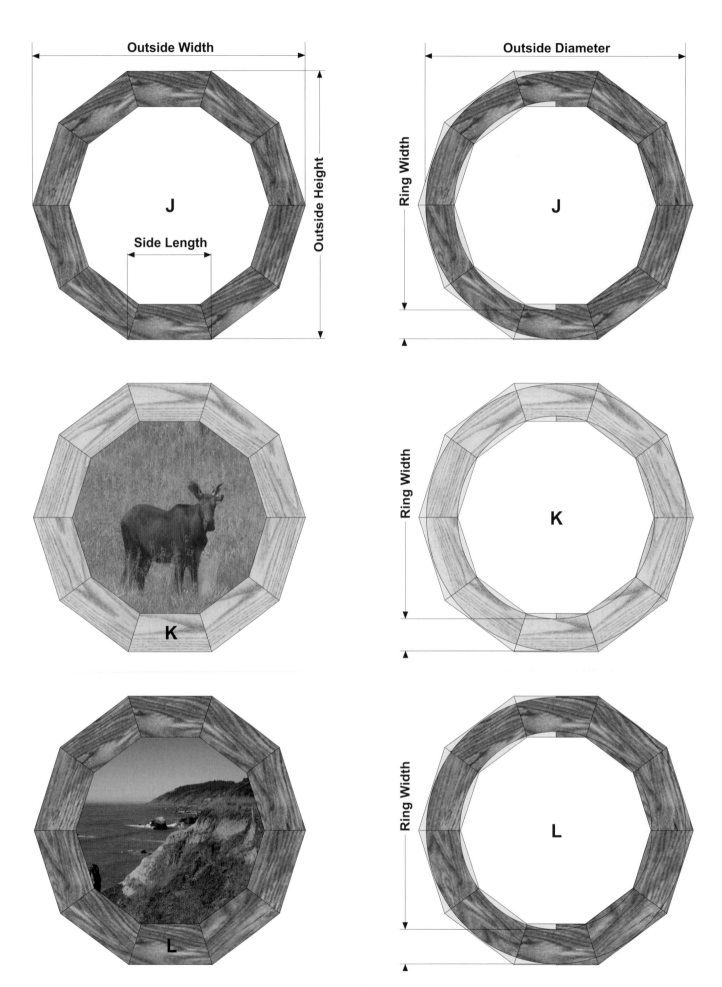

Outside Width

Outside Diameter

Outside Height

Side Length

Ring Width

J

J

K

K

L

L

Side Length	Frame Width	Frame Height	Ring Max. OD	Material Req'd.	J Side Width	J Ring Width	K Side Width	K Ring Width	L Side Width	L Ring Width
8/16	1 10/16	1 9/16	1 8/16	7 8/16	3/16	3/16	4/16	3/16	4/16	3/16
10/16	2	1 15/16	1 14/16	8 12/16	4/16	3/16	4/16	4/16	5/16	4/16
12/16	2 7/16	2 5/16	2 5/16	10	5/16	4/16	5/16	4/16	6/16	5/16
14/16	2 13/16	2 11/16	2 11/16	11 4/16	6/16	5/16	6/16	5/16	7/16	6/16
1	3 4/16	3 1/16	3 1/16	12 8/16	7/16	5/16	7/16	6/16	8/16	6/16
1 4/16	4 1/16	3 13/16	3 13/16	15	8/16	7/16	9/16	7/16	9/16	8/16
1 8/16	4 14/16	4 10/16	4 9/16	17 8/16	10/16	8/16	11/16	9/16	11/16	9/16
1 12/16	5 10/16	5 6/16	5 5/16	20	11/16	9/16	12/16	10/16	13/16	11/16
2	6 7/16	6 2/16	6 2/16	22 8/16	13/16	11/16	14/16	12/16	15/16	13/16
2 4/16	7 4/16	6 15/16	6 14/16	25	15/16	12/16	1	13/16	1 1/16	14/16
2 8/16	8 1/16	7 11/16	7 10/16	27 8/16	1	13/16	1 2/16	14/16	1 3/16	1
2 12/16	8 14/16	8 7/16	8 6/16	30	1 2/16	15/16	1 3/16	1	1 5/16	1 1/16
3	9 11/16	9 3/16	9 2/16	32 8/16	1 4/16	1	1 5/16	1 1/16	1 7/16	1 3/16
3 4/16	10 8/16	10	9 14/16	35	1 5/16	1 1/16	1 7/16	1 3/16	1 8/16	1 5/16
3 8/16	11 5/16	10 12/16	10 11/16	37 8/16	1 7/16	1 2/16	1 9/16	1 4/16	1 10/16	1 6/16
3 12/16	12 2/16	11 8/16	11 7/16	40	1 8/16	1 4/16	1 10/16	1 6/16	1 12/16	1 8/16
4	12 15/16	12 4/16	12 3/16	42 8/16	1 10/16	1 5/16	1 12/16	1 7/16	1 14/16	1 9/16
4 4/16	13 12/16	13 1/16	12 15/16	45	1 12/16	1 6/16	1 14/16	1 9/16	2	1 11/16
4 8/16	14 9/16	13 13/16	13 11/16	47 8/16	1 13/16	1 8/16	2	1 10/16	2 2/16	1 12/16
4 12/16	15 5/16	14 9/16	14 8/16	50	1 15/16	1 9/16	2 1/16	1 12/16	2 4/16	1 14/16
5	16 2/16	15 6/16	15 4/16	52 8/16	2 1/16	1 10/16	2 3/16	1 13/16	2 6/16	2
5 4/16	16 15/16	16 2/16	16	55	2 2/16	1 12/16	2 5/16	1 14/16	2 7/16	2 1/16
5 8/16	17 12/16	16 14/16	16 12/16	57 8/16	2 4/16	1 13/16	2 7/16	2	2 9/16	2 3/16
5 12/16	18 9/16	17 10/16	17 8/16	60	2 5/16	1 14/16	2 8/16	2 1/16	2 11/16	2 4/16
6	19 6/16	18 7/16	18 5/16	62 8/16	2 7/16	2	2 10/16	2 3/16	2 13/16	2 6/16
6 8/16	21	19 15/16	19 13/16	67 8/16	2 10/16	2 2/16	2 14/16	2 6/16	3 1/16	2 9/16
7	22 10/16	21 8/16	21 5/16	72 8/16	2 14/16	2 5/16	3 1/16	2 9/16	3 5/16	2 12/16
7 8/16	24 4/16	23	22 14/16	77 8/16	3 1/16	2 8/16	3 5/16	2 11/16	3 8/16	2 15/16
8	25 13/16	24 9/16	24 6/16	82 8/16	3 4/16	2 10/16	3 8/16	2 14/16	3 12/16	3 3/16
8 8/16	27 7/16	26 2/16	25 15/16	87 8/16	3 7/16	2 13/16	3 12/16	3 1/16	4	3 6/16
9	29 1/16	27 10/16	27 7/16	92 8/16	3 11/16	2 15/16	3 15/16	3 4/16	4 4/16	3 9/16
9 8/16	30 11/16	29 3/16	28 15/16	97 8/16	3 14/16	3 2/16	4 3/16	3 7/16	4 7/16	3 12/16
10	32 5/16	30 11/16	30 8/16	102 8/16	4 1/16	3 5/16	4 6/16	3 10/16	4 11/16	3 15/16
10 8/16	33 15/16	32 4/16	32	107 8/16	4 4/16	3 7/16	4 10/16	3 13/16	4 15/16	4 2/16
11	35 8/16	33 12/16	33 8/16	112 8/16	4 8/16	3 10/16	4 13/16	4	5 3/16	4 6/16
11 8/16	37 2/16	35 5/16	35 1/16	117 8/16	4 11/16	3 13/16	5 1/16	4 3/16	5 6/16	4 9/16
12	38 12/16	36 13/16	36 9/16	122 8/16	4 14/16	3 15/16	5 4/16	4 6/16	5 10/16	4 12/16
13	42	39 15/16	39 10/16	132 8/16	5 5/16	4 5/16	5 11/16	4 11/16	6 2/16	5 2/16
14	45 4/16	43	42 11/16	142 8/16	5 11/16	4 10/16	6 2/16	5 1/16	6 9/16	5 9/16
15	48 7/16	46 1/16	45 11/16	152 8/16	6 2/16	4 15/16	6 9/16	5 7/16	7 1/16	5 15/16
16	51 11/16	49 2/16	48 12/16	162 8/16	6 8/16	5 4/16	7	5 13/16	7 8/16	6 5/16
17	54 15/16	52 3/16	51 13/16	172 8/16	6 15/16	5 10/16	7 7/16	6 3/16	8	6 11/16
18	58 2/16	55 4/16	54 14/16	182 8/16	7 5/16	5 15/16	7 14/16	6 8/16	8 7/16	7 2/16
19	61 6/16	58 5/16	57 15/16	192 8/16	7 12/16	6 4/16	8 5/16	6 14/16	8 15/16	7 8/16
20	64 10/16	61 6/16	60 15/16	202 8/16	8 2/16	6 10/16	8 12/16	7 4/16	9 6/16	7 14/16
21	67 13/16	64 8/16	64	212 8/16	8 9/16	6 15/16	9 3/16	7 10/16	9 14/16	8 5/16
22	71 1/16	67 9/16	67 1/16	222 8/16	8 15/16	7 4/16	9 10/16	8	10 5/16	8 11/16
23	74 5/16	70 10/16	70 2/16	232 8/16	9 6/16	7 9/16	10 1/16	8 5/16	10 13/16	9 1/16
24	77 8/16	73 11/16	73 2/16	242 8/16	9 12/16	7 15/16	10 8/16	8 11/16	11 4/16	9 8/16
25	80 12/16	76 12/16	76 3/16	252 8/16	10 3/16	8 4/16	10 15/16	9 1/16	11 12/16	9 14/16
26	84	79 13/16	79 4/16	262 8/16	10 9/16	8 9/16	11 6/16	9 7/16	12 3/16	10 4/16
27	87 3/16	82 14/16	82 5/16	272 8/16	11	8 14/16	11 13/16	9 13/16	12 11/16	10 11/16
28	90 7/16	85 15/16	85 5/16	282 8/16	11 6/16	9 4/16	12 4/16	10 2/16	13 2/16	11 1/16

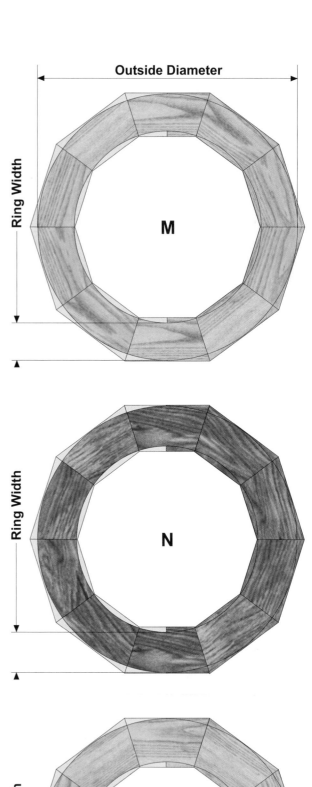

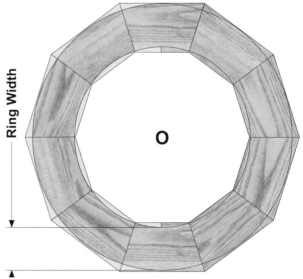

Side Length	Frame Width	Frame Height	Ring Max. OD	Material Req'd.	M Side Width	M Ring Width	N Side Width	N Ring Width	O Side Width	O Ring Width
8/16	1 10/16	1 9/16	1 8/16	7 8/16	4/16	3/16	4/16	4/16	5/16	4/16
10/16	2	1 15/16	1 14/16	8 12/16	5/16	4/16	5/16	5/16	6/16	5/16
12/16	2 7/16	2 5/16	2 5/16	10	6/16	5/16	6/16	6/16	7/16	6/16
14/16	2 13/16	2 11/16	2 11/16	11 4/16	7/16	6/16	7/16	6/16	8/16	7/16
1	3 4/16	3 1/16	3 1/16	12 8/16	8/16	7/16	9/16	7/16	9/16	8/16
1 4/16	4 1/16	3 13/16	3 13/16	15	10/16	9/16	11/16	9/16	11/16	10/16
1 8/16	4 14/16	4 10/16	4 9/16	17 8/16	12/16	10/16	13/16	11/16	14/16	12/16
1 12/16	5 10/16	5 6/16	5 5/16	20	14/16	12/16	15/16	13/16	1	14/16
2	6 7/16	6 2/16	6 2/16	22 8/16	1	14/16	1 1/16	15/16	1 2/16	1
2 4/16	7 4/16	6 15/16	6 14/16	25	1 2/16	15/16	1 3/16	1 1/16	1 4/16	1 2/16
2 8/16	8 1/16	7 11/16	7 10/16	27 8/16	1 4/16	1 1/16	1 5/16	1 2/16	1 7/16	1 4/16
2 12/16	8 14/16	8 7/16	8 6/16	30	1 6/16	1 3/16	1 7/16	1 4/16	1 9/16	1 6/16
3	9 11/16	9 3/16	9 2/16	32 8/16	1 8/16	1 5/16	1 10/16	1 6/16	1 11/16	1 8/16
3 4/16	10 8/16	10	9 14/16	35	1 10/16	1 6/16	1 12/16	1 8/16	1 13/16	1 10/16
3 8/16	11 5/16	10 12/16	10 11/16	37 8/16	1 12/16	1 8/16	1 14/16	1 10/16	2	1 12/16
3 12/16	12 2/16	11 8/16	11 7/16	40	1 14/16	1 10/16	2	1 12/16	2 2/16	1 14/16
4	12 15/16	12 4/16	12 3/16	42 8/16	2	1 11/16	2 2/16	1 13/16	2 4/16	2
4 4/16	13 12/16	13 1/16	12 15/16	45	2 2/16	1 13/16	2 4/16	1 15/16	2 6/16	2 2/16
4 8/16	14 9/16	13 13/16	13 11/16	47 8/16	2 4/16	1 15/16	2 6/16	2 1/16	2 9/16	2 4/16
4 12/16	15 5/16	14 9/16	14 8/16	50	2 6/16	2 1/16	2 8/16	2 3/16	2 11/16	2 5/16
5	16 2/16	15 6/16	15 4/16	52 8/16	2 8/16	2 2/16	2 11/16	2 5/16	2 13/16	2 7/16
5 4/16	16 15/16	16 2/16	16	55	2 10/16	2 4/16	2 13/16	2 7/16	2 15/16	2 9/16
5 8/16	17 12/16	16 14/16	16 12/16	57 8/16	2 12/16	2 6/16	2 15/16	2 9/16	3 2/16	2 11/16
5 12/16	18 9/16	17 10/16	17 8/16	60	2 14/16	2 7/16	3 1/16	2 10/16	3 4/16	2 13/16
6	19 6/16	18 7/16	18 5/16	62 8/16	3	2 9/16	3 3/16	2 12/16	3 6/16	2 15/16
6 8/16	21	19 15/16	19 13/16	67 8/16	3 4/16	2 12/16	3 7/16	3	3 11/16	3 3/16
7	22 10/16	21 8/16	21 5/16	72 8/16	3 8/16	3	3 12/16	3 4/16	3 15/16	3 7/16
7 8/16	24 4/16	23	22 14/16	77 8/16	3 12/16	3 3/16	4	3 7/16	4 4/16	3 11/16
8	25 13/16	24 9/16	24 6/16	82 8/16	4	3 7/16	4 4/16	3 11/16	4 8/16	3 15/16
8 8/16	27 7/16	26 2/16	25 15/16	87 8/16	4 4/16	3 10/16	4 8/16	3 15/16	4 13/16	4 3/16
9	29 1/16	27 10/16	27 7/16	92 8/16	4 8/16	3 14/16	4 13/16	4 2/16	5 1/16	4 7/16
9 8/16	30 11/16	29 3/16	28 15/16	97 8/16	4 12/16	4 1/16	5 1/16	4 6/16	5 6/16	4 11/16
10	32 5/16	30 11/16	30 8/16	102 8/16	5	4 4/16	5 5/16	4 10/16	5 10/16	4 15/16
10 8/16	33 15/16	32 4/16	32	107 8/16	5 4/16	4 8/16	5 9/16	4 13/16	5 15/16	5 3/16
11	35 8/16	33 12/16	33 8/16	112 8/16	5 8/16	4 11/16	5 14/16	5 1/16	6 3/16	5 7/16
11 8/16	37 2/16	35 5/16	35 1/16	117 8/16	5 12/16	4 15/16	6 2/16	5 5/16	6 8/16	5 11/16
12	38 12/16	36 13/16	36 9/16	122 8/16	6	5 2/16	6 6/16	5 8/16	6 12/16	5 15/16
13	42	39 15/16	39 10/16	132 8/16	6 8/16	5 9/16	6 15/16	6	7 5/16	6 7/16
14	45 4/16	43	42 11/16	142 8/16	7	6	7 7/16	6 7/16	7 14/16	6 14/16
15	48 7/16	46 1/16	45 11/16	152 8/16	7 8/16	6 7/16	8	6 15/16	8 7/16	7 6/16
16	51 11/16	49 2/16	48 12/16	162 8/16	8	6 14/16	8 8/16	7 6/16	9	7 14/16
17	54 15/16	52 3/16	51 13/16	172 8/16	8 8/16	7 4/16	9 1/16	7 13/16	9 9/16	8 6/16
18	58 2/16	55 4/16	54 14/16	182 8/16	9	7 11/16	9 9/16	8 5/16	10 2/16	8 14/16
19	61 6/16	58 5/16	57 15/16	192 8/16	9 8/16	8 2/16	10 2/16	8 12/16	10 11/16	9 6/16
20	64 10/16	61 6/16	60 15/16	202 8/16	10	8 9/16	10 10/16	9 3/16	11 4/16	9 14/16
21	67 13/16	64 8/16	64	212 8/16	10 8/16	9	11 3/16	9 11/16	11 13/16	10 6/16
22	71 1/16	67 9/16	67 1/16	222 8/16	11	9 7/16	11 11/16	10 2/16	12 6/16	10 14/16
23	74 5/16	70 10/16	70 2/16	232 8/16	11 8/16	9 13/16	12 4/16	10 9/16	12 15/16	11 5/16
24	77 8/16	73 11/16	73 2/16	242 8/16	12	10 4/16	12 12/16	11 1/16	13 8/16	11 13/16
25	80 12/16	76 12/16	76 3/16	252 8/16	12 8/16	10 11/16	13 5/16	11 8/16	14 1/16	12 5/16
26	84	79 13/16	79 4/16	262 8/16	13	11 2/16	13 13/16	12	14 10/16	12 13/16
27	87 3/16	82 14/16	82 5/16	272 8/16	13 8/16	11 9/16	14 6/16	12 7/16	15 3/16	13 5/16
28	90 7/16	85 15/16	85 5/16	282 8/16	14	12	14 14/16	12 14/16	15 12/16	13 13/16

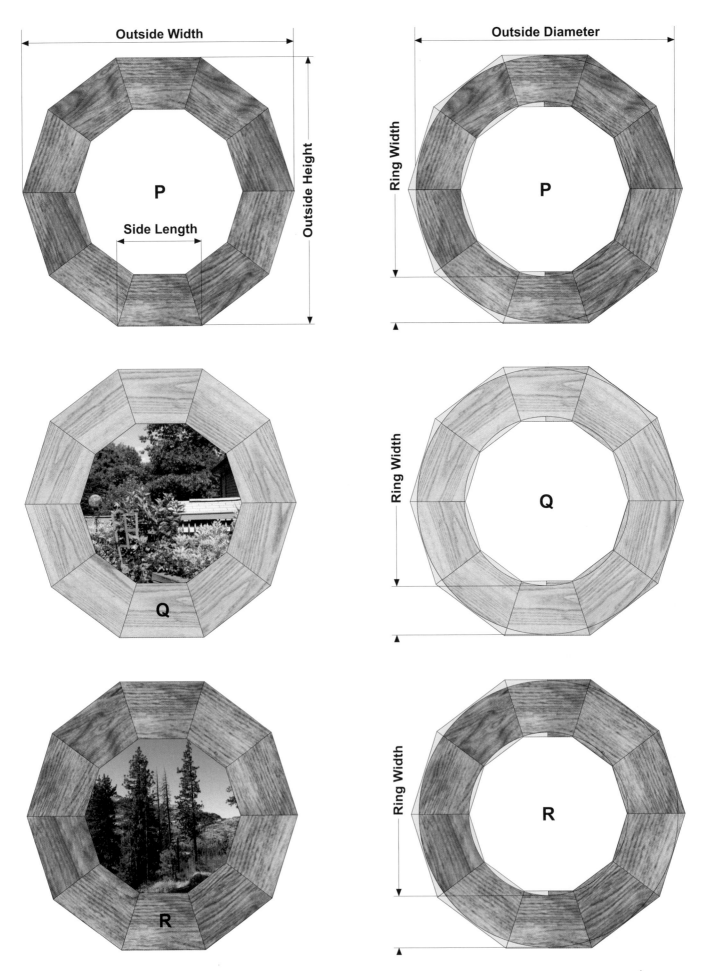

Side Length	Frame Width	Frame Height	Ring Max. OD	Material Req'd.	P Side Width	P Ring Width	Q Side Width	Q Ring Width	R Side Width	R Ring Width
8/16	1 10/16	1 9/16	1 8/16	7 8/16	5/16	4/16	5/16	4/16	5/16	5/16
10/16	2	1 15/16	1 14/16	8 12/16	6/16	5/16	6/16	6/16	7/16	6/16
12/16	2 7/16	2 5/16	2 5/16	10	7/16	6/16	8/16	7/16	8/16	7/16
14/16	2 13/16	2 11/16	2 11/16	11 4/16	8/16	7/16	9/16	8/16	9/16	8/16
1	3 4/16	3 1/16	3 1/16	12 8/16	10/16	8/16	10/16	9/16	11/16	9/16
1 4/16	4 1/16	3 13/16	3 13/16	15	12/16	11/16	13/16	11/16	13/16	12/16
1 8/16	4 14/16	4 10/16	4 9/16	17 8/16	14/16	13/16	15/16	13/16	1	14/16
1 12/16	5 10/16	5 6/16	5 5/16	20	1 1/16	15/16	1 2/16	1	1 2/16	1 1/16
2	6 7/16	6 2/16	6 2/16	22 8/16	1 3/16	1 1/16	1 4/16	1 2/16	1 5/16	1 3/16
2 4/16	7 4/16	6 15/16	6 14/16	25	1 5/16	1 3/16	1 7/16	1 4/16	1 8/16	1 5/16
2 8/16	8 1/16	7 11/16	7 10/16	27 8/16	1 8/16	1 5/16	1 9/16	1 6/16	1 10/16	1 8/16
2 12/16	8 14/16	8 7/16	8 6/16	30	1 10/16	1 7/16	1 12/16	1 8/16	1 13/16	1 10/16
3	9 11/16	9 3/16	9 2/16	32 8/16	1 13/16	1 9/16	1 14/16	1 11/16	2	1 12/16
3 4/16	10 8/16	10	9 14/16	35	1 15/16	1 11/16	2 1/16	1 13/16	2 2/16	1 15/16
3 8/16	11 5/16	10 12/16	10 11/16	37 8/16	2 1/16	1 13/16	2 3/16	1 15/16	2 5/16	2 1/16
3 12/16	12 2/16	11 8/16	11 7/16	40	2 4/16	2	2 6/16	2 1/16	2 7/16	2 3/16
4	12 15/16	12 4/16	12 3/16	42 8/16	2 6/16	2 2/16	2 8/16	2 4/16	2 10/16	2 6/16
4 4/16	13 12/16	13 1/16	12 15/16	45	2 8/16	2 4/16	2 11/16	2 6/16	2 13/16	2 8/16
4 8/16	14 9/16	13 13/16	13 11/16	47 8/16	2 11/16	2 6/16	2 13/16	2 8/16	2 15/16	2 11/16
4 12/16	15 5/16	14 9/16	14 8/16	50	2 13/16	2 8/16	3	2 10/16	3 2/16	2 13/16
5	16 2/16	15 6/16	15 4/16	52 8/16	3	2 10/16	3 2/16	2 12/16	3 5/16	2 15/16
5 4/16	16 15/16	16 2/16	16	55	3 2/16	2 12/16	3 5/16	2 15/16	3 7/16	3 2/16
5 8/16	17 12/16	16 14/16	16 12/16	57 8/16	3 4/16	2 14/16	3 7/16	3 1/16	3 10/16	3 4/16
5 12/16	18 9/16	17 10/16	17 8/16	60	3 7/16	3	3 10/16	3 3/16	3 12/16	3 6/16
6	19 6/16	18 7/16	18 5/16	62 8/16	3 9/16	3 2/16	3 12/16	3 5/16	3 15/16	3 9/16
6 8/16	21	19 15/16	19 13/16	67 8/16	3 14/16	3 7/16	4 1/16	3 10/16	4 4/16	3 13/16
7	22 10/16	21 8/16	21 5/16	72 8/16	4 3/16	3 11/16	4 6/16	3 14/16	4 10/16	4 2/16
7 8/16	24 4/16	23	22 14/16	77 8/16	4 7/16	3 15/16	4 11/16	4 3/16	4 15/16	4 7/16
8	25 13/16	24 9/16	24 6/16	82 8/16	4 12/16	4 3/16	5	4 7/16	5 4/16	4 12/16
8 8/16	27 7/16	26 2/16	25 15/16	87 8/16	5 1/16	4 8/16	5 5/16	4 12/16	5 9/16	5
9	29 1/16	27 10/16	27 7/16	92 8/16	5 6/16	4 12/16	5 10/16	5	5 15/16	5 5/16
9 8/16	30 11/16	29 3/16	28 15/16	97 8/16	5 10/16	5	5 15/16	5 4/16	6 4/16	5 10/16
10	32 5/16	30 11/16	30 8/16	102 8/16	5 15/16	5 4/16	6 4/16	5 9/16	6 9/16	5 15/16
10 8/16	33 15/16	32 4/16	32	107 8/16	6 4/16	5 8/16	6 9/16	5 13/16	6 14/16	6 3/16
11	35 8/16	33 12/16	33 8/16	112 8/16	6 9/16	5 13/16	6 14/16	6 2/16	7 4/16	6 8/16
11 8/16	37 2/16	35 5/16	35 1/16	117 8/16	6 13/16	6 1/16	7 3/16	6 6/16	7 9/16	6 13/16
12	38 12/16	36 13/16	36 9/16	122 8/16	7 2/16	6 5/16	7 8/16	6 11/16	7 14/16	7 1/16
13	42	39 15/16	39 10/16	132 8/16	7 12/16	6 13/16	8 2/16	7 4/16	8 9/16	7 11/16
14	45 4/16	43	42 11/16	142 8/16	8 5/16	7 6/16	8 12/16	7 12/16	9 3/16	8 4/16
15	48 7/16	46 1/16	45 11/16	152 8/16	8 15/16	7 14/16	9 6/16	8 5/16	9 14/16	8 14/16
16	51 11/16	49 2/16	48 12/16	162 8/16	9 8/16	8 7/16	10	8 14/16	10 8/16	9 7/16
17	54 15/16	52 3/16	51 13/16	172 8/16	10 2/16	8 15/16	10 10/16	9 7/16	11 3/16	10 1/16
18	58 2/16	55 4/16	54 14/16	182 8/16	10 11/16	9 7/16	11 4/16	10	11 13/16	10 10/16
19	61 6/16	58 5/16	57 15/16	192 8/16	11 5/16	10	11 14/16	10 9/16	12 8/16	11 4/16
20	64 10/16	61 6/16	60 15/16	202 8/16	11 14/16	10 8/16	12 8/16	11 2/16	13 2/16	11 13/16
21	67 13/16	64 8/16	64	212 8/16	12 8/16	11 1/16	13 2/16	11 11/16	13 13/16	12 7/16
22	71 1/16	67 9/16	67 1/16	222 8/16	13 1/16	11 9/16	13 12/16	12 4/16	14 7/16	13
23	74 5/16	70 10/16	70 2/16	232 8/16	13 11/16	12 1/16	14 6/16	12 12/16	15 2/16	13 10/16
24	77 8/16	73 11/16	73 2/16	242 8/16	14 4/16	12 10/16	15	13 5/16	15 12/16	14 3/16
25	80 12/16	76 12/16	76 3/16	252 8/16	14 14/16	13 2/16	15 10/16	13 14/16	16 7/16	14 12/16
26	84	79 13/16	79 4/16	262 8/16	15 7/16	13 11/16	16 4/16	14 7/16	17 1/16	15 6/16
27	87 3/16	82 14/16	82 5/16	272 8/16	16 1/16	14 3/16	16 14/16	15	17 12/16	15 15/16
28	90 7/16	85 15/16	85 5/16	282 8/16	16 10/16	14 12/16	17 8/16	15 9/16	18 6/16	16 9/16

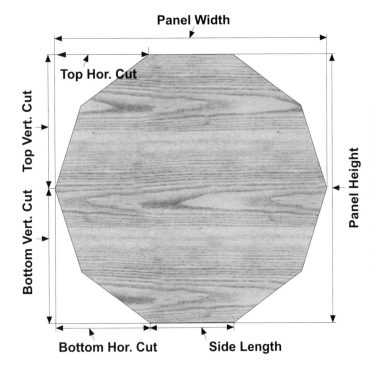

Panel Width

Top Hor. Cut

Top Vert. Cut

Bottom Vert. Cut

Panel Height

Bottom Hor. Cut

Side Length

The Chart below shows the formulas that were used in the process of laying out the 10 sided shapes. These are included to assist you if you are designing a project to a size that is not illustrated in the Dimension Charts provided. We hope you find them helpful as you design your projects.

10 SIDED PANEL FORMULAS		
Panel Width =	Panel Height x	1.052
Panel Height =	Panel Width x	0.951
Side Length =	Panel Height x	0.309
Side Length =	Panel Width x	0.325
Top Hor. Cut =	Panel Width x	0.345
Bott. Hor. Cut =	Panel Width x	0.345
Top Vert. Cut =	Panel Width x	0.474
Bott.Vert. Cut =	Panel Width x	0.474

PANEL WIDTH	PANEL HEIGHT	SIDE LENGTH	TOP HOR. CUT	BOTTOM HOR. CUT	TOP VERT. CUT	BOTTOM VERT. CUT
12/16	11/16	4/16	4/16	4/16	6/16	6/16
1	15/16	5/16	6/16	6/16	8/16	8/16
1 4/16	1 3/16	6/16	7/16	7/16	9/16	9/16
1 8/16	1 7/16	7/16	8/16	8/16	11/16	11/16
1 12/16	1 11/16	9/16	10/16	10/16	13/16	13/16
2	1 14/16	10/16	11/16	11/16	15/16	15/16
2 4/16	2 2/16	11/16	12/16	12/16	1 1/16	1 1/16
2 8/16	2 6/16	12/16	14/16	14/16	1 3/16	1 3/16
2 12/16	2 10/16	14/16	15/16	15/16	1 5/16	1 5/16
3	2 14/16	15/16	1 1/16	1 1/16	1 7/16	1 7/16
3 4/16	3 1/16	1	1 2/16	1 2/16	1 9/16	1 9/16
3 8/16	3 5/16	1 1/16	1 3/16	1 3/16	1 11/16	1 11/16
3 12/16	3 9/16	1 3/16	1 5/16	1 5/16	1 12/16	1 12/16
4	3 13/16	1 4/16	1 6/16	1 6/16	1 14/16	1 14/16
4 4/16	4 1/16	1 5/16	1 7/16	1 7/16	2	2
4 8/16	4 4/16	1 6/16	1 9/16	1 9/16	2 2/16	2 2/16
4 12/16	4 8/16	1 7/16	1 10/16	1 10/16	2 4/16	2 4/16
5	4 12/16	1 9/16	1 12/16	1 12/16	2 6/16	2 6/16
5 4/16	5	1 10/16	1 13/16	1 13/16	2 8/16	2 8/16
5 8/16	5 4/16	1 11/16	1 14/16	1 14/16	2 10/16	2 10/16
5 12/16	5 7/16	1 12/16	2	2	2 12/16	2 12/16
6	5 11/16	1 14/16	2 1/16	2 1/16	2 14/16	2 14/16
6 4/16	5 15/16	1 15/16	2 3/16	2 3/16	2 15/16	2 15/16
6 8/16	6 3/16	2	2 4/16	2 4/16	3 1/16	3 1/16
6 12/16	6 7/16	2 1/16	2 5/16	2 5/16	3 3/16	3 3/16
7	6 11/16	2 3/16	2 7/16	2 7/16	3 5/16	3 5/16
7 4/16	6 14/16	2 4/16	2 8/16	2 8/16	3 7/16	3 7/16
7 8/16	7 2/16	2 5/16	2 9/16	2 9/16	3 9/16	3 9/16
7 12/16	7 6/16	2 6/16	2 11/16	2 11/16	3 11/16	3 11/16
8	7 10/16	2 8/16	2 12/16	2 12/16	3 13/16	3 13/16
8 4/16	7 14/16	2 9/16	2 14/16	2 14/16	3 15/16	3 15/16
8 8/16	8 1/16	2 10/16	2 15/16	2 15/16	4	4

PANEL WIDTH	PANEL HEIGHT	SIDE LENGTH	TOP HOR. CUT	BOTTOM HOR. CUT	TOP VERT. CUT	BOTTOM VERT. CUT
8 12/16	8 5/16	2 11/16	3	3	4 2/16	4 2/16
9	8 9/16	2 12/16	3 2/16	3 2/16	4 4/16	4 4/16
9 4/16	8 13/16	2 14/16	3 3/16	3 3/16	4 6/16	4 6/16
9 8/16	9 1/16	2 15/16	3 4/16	3 4/16	4 8/16	4 8/16
9 12/16	9 4/16	3	3 6/16	3 6/16	4 10/16	4 10/16
10	9 8/16	3 1/16	3 7/16	3 7/16	4 12/16	4 12/16
10 4/16	9 12/16	3 3/16	3 9/16	3 9/16	4 14/16	4 14/16
10 8/16	10	3 4/16	3 10/16	3 10/16	5	5
10 12/16	10 4/16	3 5/16	3 11/16	3 11/16	5 2/16	5 2/16
11	10 7/16	3 6/16	3 13/16	3 13/16	5 3/16	5 3/16
11 4/16	10 11/16	3 8/16	3 14/16	3 14/16	5 5/16	5 5/16
11 8/16	10 15/16	3 9/16	3 15/16	3 15/16	5 7/16	5 7/16
12	11 7/16	3 11/16	4 2/16	4 2/16	5 11/16	5 11/16
12 4/16	11 10/16	3 13/16	4 4/16	4 4/16	5 13/16	5 13/16
12 8/16	11 14/16	3 14/16	4 5/16	4 5/16	5 15/16	5 15/16
12 12/16	12 2/16	3 15/16	4 6/16	4 6/16	6 1/16	6 1/16
13	12 6/16	4	4 8/16	4 8/16	6 3/16	6 3/16
13 4/16	12 10/16	4 2/16	4 9/16	4 9/16	6 4/16	6 4/16
13 8/16	12 13/16	4 3/16	4 11/16	4 11/16	6 6/16	6 6/16
13 12/16	13 1/16	4 4/16	4 12/16	4 12/16	6 8/16	6 8/16
14	13 5/16	4 5/16	4 13/16	4 13/16	6 10/16	6 10/16
14 8/16	13 13/16	4 8/16	5	5	6 14/16	6 14/16
15	14 4/16	4 10/16	5 3/16	5 3/16	7 2/16	7 2/16
15 8/16	14 12/16	4 13/16	5 6/16	5 6/16	7 6/16	7 6/16
16	15 3/16	4 15/16	5 8/16	5 8/16	7 9/16	7 9/16
16 8/16	15 11/16	5 2/16	5 11/16	5 11/16	7 13/16	7 13/16
17	16 3/16	5 4/16	5 14/16	5 14/16	8 1/16	8 1/16
17 8/16	16 10/16	5 7/16	6 1/16	6 1/16	8 5/16	8 5/16
18	17 2/16	5 9/16	6 3/16	6 3/16	8 9/16	8 9/16
19	18 1/16	5 14/16	6 9/16	6 9/16	9	9
20	19	6 3/16	6 14/16	6 14/16	9 8/16	9 8/16
21	20	6 8/16	7 4/16	7 4/16	9 15/16	9 15/16
22	20 15/16	6 13/16	7 9/16	7 9/16	10 7/16	10 7/16
23	21 14/16	7 2/16	7 15/16	7 15/16	10 14/16	10 14/16
24	22 13/16	7 7/16	8 4/16	8 4/16	11 6/16	11 6/16
25	23 12/16	7 12/16	8 10/16	8 10/16	11 14/16	11 14/16
26	24 12/16	8 1/16	9	9	12 5/16	12 5/16
27	25 11/16	8 5/16	9 5/16	9 5/16	12 13/16	12 13/16
28	26 10/16	8 10/16	9 11/16	9 11/16	13 4/16	13 4/16
29	27 9/16	8 15/16	10	10	13 12/16	13 12/16
30	28 8/16	9 4/16	10 6/16	10 6/16	14 4/16	14 4/16
31	29 8/16	9 9/16	10 11/16	10 11/16	14 11/16	14 11/16
32	30 7/16	9 14/16	11 1/16	11 1/16	15 3/16	15 3/16
33	31 6/16	10 3/16	11 6/16	11 6/16	15 10/16	15 10/16
34	32 5/16	10 8/16	11 12/16	11 12/16	16 2/16	16 2/16
35	33 5/16	10 13/16	12 1/16	12 1/16	16 9/16	16 9/16
36	34 4/16	11 2/16	12 7/16	12 7/16	17 1/16	17 1/16
37	35 3/16	11 7/16	12 12/16	12 12/16	17 9/16	17 9/16
38	36 2/16	11 12/16	13 2/16	13 2/16	18	18
39	37 1/16	12 1/16	13 7/16	13 7/16	18 8/16	18 8/16
40	38 1/16	12 6/16	13 13/16	13 13/16	18 15/16	18 15/16
41	39	12 11/16	14 2/16	14 2/16	19 7/16	19 7/16
42	39 15/16	13	14 8/16	14 8/16	19 15/16	19 15/16

12 SIDED PROJECT INFORMATION

Geometric Name: Dodecagon
Definition: A Polygon having 12 sides
Miter Angle: 15°
Angle Change / Adjoining Sides: 30°

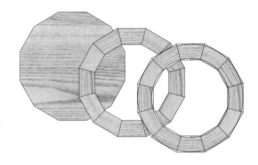

The 12 sided shape (Dodecagon) is one of the "even numbered" shapes that's fairly easy to get creative with, because two pairs of parallel sides on the frame will be parallel to the 4 sides on a picture. The one thing that should be considered when using this shape (with sides of equal length) is that for most standard sizes of pictures, a lot of cropping of the picture will be required. However, the Dodecagon is a fun frame to build using sides of different lengths for your frame.

The Illustrations to the right should give you an idea of the amount of cropping required by using a Dodecagon (with equal length sides) as your choice of shape for a frame.

In the left Illustration, you see a scale (shown in red) 8" x 10" sheet in portrait format. The sheet border is slightly outside the rabbeted area (shown in yellow) of the frame. Note the amount of material that would need to be cropped off the sheet top and/or bottom.

In the right Illustration, you see the same size sheet, but rotated 90° into a landscape format. The same amount of material would need to be cropped off the sheet sides.

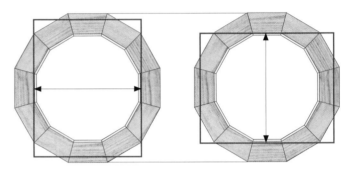

Portrait　　　　　**Landscape**

You should note that the frames are the same size. On a Dodecagon, (with sides of equal length) the dimension between opposing sides is equal. Like the Octagon, pictures for these frames will start as squares, and are cropped at angles to fit the frame. In our **12 SIDED FRAME FORMULAS** below, you will be able to see that the dimensions for both formats for the pictures are identical.

If the project you are building is a frame for a specific size object, you should refer to the **12 SIDED FRAME FORMULAS** Chart below as a first step. On a Dodecagon (with sides of equal length) the height will be identical to the width, so there is no controlling dimension for this shape of frame.

The Dodecagon is one of the "medium difficulty" Polygons to get creative with. You can get creative and build a very pretty frame by using as few as 2 different lengths of sides for the frame for your picture.

12 SIDED FRAME FORMULAS		
WIDTH	**HEIGHT**	**SIDE LENGTH**
Width = Side Length x 3.75	Height = Side Length x 3.75	Side Length = Width x .267
Width = Height x 1.00	Height = Width x 1.00	Side Length = Height x .267

Though the information above is very helpful, one of the most time consuming (and frustrating) things about building frames is to try to cut to a dimension that is not measured on either the inside or outside edge of the molding. I like to cut miters from the inside to the outside edges of the molding. This not only allows me to eliminate tear out on the inside corners of the frame since I am cutting into the inside edge, I am also cutting with the grain of the molding. It also allows me to see the outside edge of the material as I cut it. To help you understand how easy it is to convert a dimension along the rabbeted edge into an outside measurement, I will explain how we can use some basic math to help us determine the outside length of our frame sides. The Illustration below should be helpful in showing you how we designed our **12 SIDED FRAME ADDED WIDTH AND LENGTH CHART** on the next page.

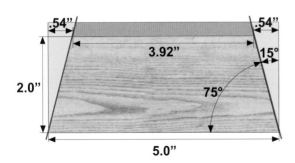

The Illustration to the left represents a piece of wood that is 5" long and 2" wide (to the edge of the rabbet). Note that on the right side that the end of the piece shows the miter angle for an Dodecagon (15°) and the resulting angle of the cut (75°).

You should also note that at the rabbet, the 15° cuts shorten each end of the piece by .54". Since both ends of the piece are cut, this means that the length at the rabbet is 3.92", which is 1.08" shorter than the outside edge of the molding. What this Illustration tells us is that at an 15° cut, we will add 1.08" to the length at a 2" width. This is the basis of our formula.

If we divide the **Added Length** (1.08") by the **Added Width** (2.0") we end up with .54 as our multiplier. In the event that you want to make a frame and need to work in fractions smaller than 1/16 increments, you would multiply the width of the molding outside the rabbet by .54. To determine the decimal equivalent of the fractions you need to use, refer to the **FRACTION TO DECIMAL CONVERSION CHART** provided.

If you are able to use 1/16" increments for the mathematics of your frames, you should use the **12 SIDED FRAME ADDED WIDTH AND LENGTH CHART** below.

Determine how wide you want the material to be (outside the rabbet). Refer to the Chart below to find this dimension in one of the yellow shaded columns. The added length for that width will be shown in the green shaded block to the right of it. Add this dimension to the side length determined in the first step. You should then add whatever waste you want to allow for each side. This total is then multiplied by 12 to determine how much material is needed to build your project.

12 SIDED FRAME ADDED WIDTH AND LENGTH CHART

Added Width	Added Length	Added Width	Added Length	Added Width	Added Length	Added Width	Added Length	Added Width	Added Length	Added Width	Added Length
1/16	1/16	1 1/16	9/16	2 1/16	1 2/16	3 1/16	1 10/16	4 1/16	2 3/16
2/16	1/16	1 2/16	10/16	2 2/16	1 2/16	3 2/16	1 11/16	4 2/16	2 4/16
3/16	2/16	1 3/16	10/16	2 3/16	1 3/16	3 3/16	1 12/16	4 3/16	2 4/16
4/16	2/16	1 4/16	11/16	2 4/16	1 3/16	3 4/16	1 12/16	4 4/16	2 5/16
5/16	3/16	1 5/16	11/16	2 5/16	1 4/16	3 5/16	1 13/16	4 5/16	2 5/16
6/16	3/16	1 6/16	12/16	2 6/16	1 5/16	3 6/16	1 13/16	4 6/16	2 6/16
7/16	4/16	1 7/16	12/16	2 7/16	1 5/16	3 7/16	1 14/16	4 7/16	2 6/16
8/16	4/16	1 8/16	13/16	2 8/16	1 6/16	3 8/16	1 14/16	4 8/16	2 7/16
9/16	5/16	1 9/16	14/16	2 9/16	1 6/16	3 9/16	1 15/16	4 9/16	2 7/16
10/16	5/16	1 10/16	14/16	2 10/16	1 7/16	3 10/16	1 15/16	4 10/16	2 8/16
11/16	6/16	1 11/16	15/16	2 11/16	1 7/16	3 11/16	2	4 11/16	2 9/16
12/16	6/16	1 12/16	15/16	2 12/16	1 8/16	3 12/16	2	4 12/16	2 9/16
13/16	7/16	1 13/16	1	2 13/16	1 8/16	3 13/16	2 1/16	4 13/16	2 10/16
14/16	8/16	1 14/16	1	2 14/16	1 9/16	3 14/16	2 1/16	4 14/16	2 10/16
15/16	8/16	1 15/16	1 1/16	2 15/16	1 9/16	3 15/16	2 2/16	4 15/16	2 11/16
1	9/16	2	1 1/16	3	1 10/16	4	2 3/16	5	2 11/16

The Chart below is provided to enable you to make 12 sided frames using the mathematics of most popular picture sizes. Note that the dimensions are identical in portrait and landscape format. This is because the picture for a Dodecagon is basically square with 2 (30°) crops on each 90° corner of the picture. In the Charts, the different colored columns represent the following information:

Red: The controlling dimension of the sheet size. (width in portrait, height in landscape)
Gray: The dimension of the sheet size that will need to be cropped.

White: The rabbet length for the frame sides.
Orange: The size of the opening in the direction the picture will need to be cropped.
Blue: The amount of material that will need to be cropped.

RABBET AREA DIMENSIONS FOR 12 SIDED FRAMES

FOR PORTRAIT FORMAT					FOR LANDSCAPE FORMAT				
Object Width	Object Height	Rabbet Length	Opening Height	Vertical Crop	Object Width	Object Height	Rabbet Length	Opening Width	Horizontal Crop
4	5	1 2/16	4 2/16	1	5	4	1 2/16	4 2/16	1
5	7	1 6/16	5 2/16	2	7	5	1 6/16	5 2/16	2
6	8	1 10/16	6 2/16	2	8	6	1 10/16	6 2/16	2
8	10	2 3/16	8 2/16	2	10	8	2 3/16	8 2/16	2
8 1/2	11	2 5/16	8 10/16	2 8/16	11	8 1/2	2 5/16	8 10/16	2 8/16
10	14	2 11/16	10 2/16	4	14	10	2 11/16	10 2/16	4
11	14	3	11 2/16	3	14	11	3	11 2/16	3
12	16	3 4/16	12 2/16	4	16	12	3 4/16	12 2/16	4
16	20	4 5/16	16 2/16	4	20	16	4 5/16	16 2/16	4
18	24	4 13/16	18 2/16	6	24	18	4 13/16	18 2/16	6
20	24	5 6/16	20 2/16	4	24	20	5 6/16	20 2/16	4
24	30	6 7/16	24 2/16	6	30	24	6 7/16	24 2/16	6

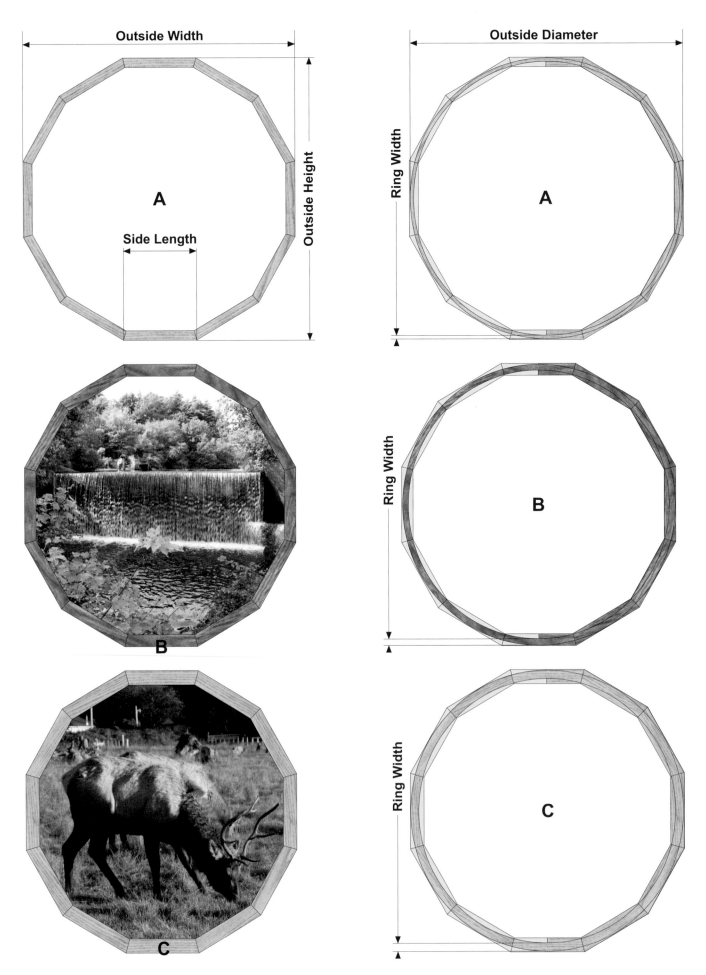

Outside Width

Outside Height

Side Length

A

Outside Diameter

Ring Width

A

Ring Width

B

Ring Width

C

B

C

122

Side Length	Frame Width	Frame Height	Ring Max. OD	Material Req'd.	A Side Width	A Ring Width	B Side Width	B Ring Width	C Side Width	C Ring Width
8/16	1 14/16	1 14/16	1 14/16	9	1/16		1/16	1/16	2/16	1/16
10/16	2 6/16	2 6/16	2 5/16	10 8/16	1/16		2/16	1/16	2/16	1/16
12/16	2 13/16	2 13/16	2 13/16	12	2/16	1/16	2/16	1/16	2/16	1/16
14/16	3 5/16	3 5/16	3 4/16	13 8/16	2/16	1/16	2/16	1/16	3/16	1/16
1	3 12/16	3 12/16	3 12/16	15	2/16	1/16	3/16	1/16	3/16	2/16
1 4/16	4 11/16	4 11/16	4 11/16	18	3/16	1/16	3/16	2/16	4/16	2/16
1 8/16	5 10/16	5 10/16	5 10/16	21	3/16	1/16	4/16	2/16	5/16	3/16
1 12/16	6 9/16	6 9/16	6 8/16	24	4/16	1/16	4/16	2/16	5/16	3/16
2	7 8/16	7 8/16	7 7/16	27	4/16	1/16	5/16	2/16	6/16	3/16
2 4/16	8 7/16	8 7/16	8 6/16	30	5/16	2/16	6/16	3/16	7/16	4/16
2 8/16	9 6/16	9 6/16	9 5/16	33	5/16	2/16	6/16	3/16	8/16	4/16
2 12/16	10 5/16	10 5/16	10 4/16	36	6/16	2/16	7/16	3/16	8/16	5/16
3	11 4/16	11 4/16	11 3/16	39	6/16	2/16	8/16	4/16	9/16	5/16
3 4/16	12 3/16	12 3/16	12 2/16	42	7/16	2/16	8/16	4/16	10/16	5/16
3 8/16	13 2/16	13 2/16	13 1/16	45	7/16	3/16	9/16	4/16	11/16	6/16
3 12/16	14 1/16	14 1/16	14	48	8/16	3/16	9/16	5/16	11/16	6/16
4	15	15	14 15/16	51	8/16	3/16	10/16	5/16	12/16	7/16
4 4/16	15 15/16	15 15/16	15 14/16	54	9/16	3/16	11/16	5/16	13/16	7/16
4 8/16	16 14/16	16 14/16	16 13/16	57	9/16	3/16	11/16	6/16	14/16	8/16
4 12/16	17 13/16	17 13/16	17 11/16	60	10/16	3/16	12/16	6/16	14/16	8/16
5	18 12/16	18 12/16	18 10/16	63	10/16	4/16	13/16	6/16	15/16	8/16
5 4/16	19 11/16	19 11/16	19 9/16	66	11/16	4/16	13/16	7/16	1	9/16
5 8/16	20 10/16	20 10/16	20 8/16	69	11/16	4/16	14/16	7/16	1 1/16	9/16
5 12/16	21 9/16	21 9/16	21 7/16	72	12/16	4/16	14/16	7/16	1 1/16	10/16
6	22 8/16	22 8/16	22 6/16	75	12/16	4/16	15/16	7/16	1 2/16	10/16
6 8/16	24 6/16	24 6/16	24 4/16	81	13/16	5/16	1	8/16	1 4/16	11/16
7	26 4/16	26 4/16	26 2/16	87	14/16	5/16	1 2/16	9/16	1 5/16	12/16
7 8/16	28 2/16	28 2/16	28	93	15/16	6/16	1 3/16	9/16	1 7/16	13/16
8	30	30	29 13/16	99	1	6/16	1 4/16	10/16	1 8/16	13/16
8 8/16	31 14/16	31 14/16	31 11/16	105	1 1/16	6/16	1 5/16	11/16	1 10/16	14/16
9	33 12/16	33 12/16	33 9/16	111	1 2/16	7/16	1 7/16	11/16	1 11/16	15/16
9 8/16	35 10/16	35 10/16	35 7/16	117	1 3/16	7/16	1 8/16	12/16	1 13/16	1
10	37 8/16	37 8/16	37 5/16	123	1 4/16	7/16	1 9/16	12/16	1 14/16	1 1/16
10 8/16	39 6/16	39 6/16	39 3/16	129	1 5/16	8/16	1 10/16	13/16	2	1 2/16
11	41 4/16	41 4/16	41 1/16	135	1 6/16	8/16	1 12/16	14/16	2 1/16	1 2/16
11 8/16	43 2/16	43 2/16	42 14/16	141	1 7/16	8/16	1 13/16	14/16	2 3/16	1 3/16
12	45	45	44 12/16	147	1 8/16	9/16	1 14/16	15/16	2 4/16	1 4/16
13	48 12/16	48 12/16	48 8/16	159	1 10/16	10/16	2 1/16	1	2 7/16	1 6/16
14	52 8/16	52 8/16	52 4/16	171	1 12/16	10/16	2 3/16	1 1/16	2 10/16	1 7/16
15	56 4/16	56 4/16	55 15/16	183	1 14/16	11/16	2 6/16	1 3/16	2 13/16	1 9/16
16	60	60	59 11/16	195	2	12/16	2 8/16	1 4/16	3	1 11/16
17	63 12/16	63 12/16	63 7/16	207	2 2/16	12/16	2 11/16	1 5/16	3 3/16	1 12/16
18	67 8/16	67 8/16	67 2/16	219	2 4/16	13/16	2 13/16	1 6/16	3 6/16	1 14/16
19	71 4/16	71 4/16	70 14/16	231	2 6/16	14/16	3	1 8/16	3 9/16	2
20	75	75	74 10/16	243	2 8/16	15/16	3 2/16	1 9/16	3 12/16	2 1/16
21	78 12/16	78 12/16	78 5/16	255	2 10/16	15/16	3 5/16	1 10/16	3 15/16	2 3/16
22	82 8/16	82 8/16	82 1/16	267	2 12/16	1	3 7/16	1 11/16	4 2/16	2 5/16
23	86 4/16	86 4/16	85 13/16	279	2 14/16	1 1/16	3 10/16	1 13/16	4 5/16	2 6/16
24	90	90	89 8/16	291	3	1 2/16	3 12/16	1 14/16	4 8/16	2 8/16
25	93 12/16	93 12/16	93 4/16	303	3 2/16	1 2/16	3 15/16	1 15/16	4 11/16	2 10/16
26	97 8/16	97 8/16	97	315	3 4/16	1 3/16	4 1/16	2	4 14/16	2 11/16
27	101 4/16	101 4/16	100 11/16	327	3 6/16	1 4/16	4 4/16	2 2/16	5 1/16	2 13/16
28	105	105	104 7/16	339	3 8/16	1 5/16	4 6/16	2 3/16	5 4/16	2 15/16

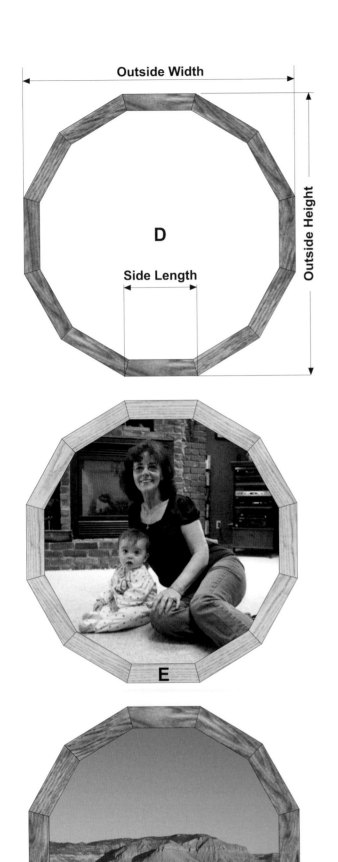

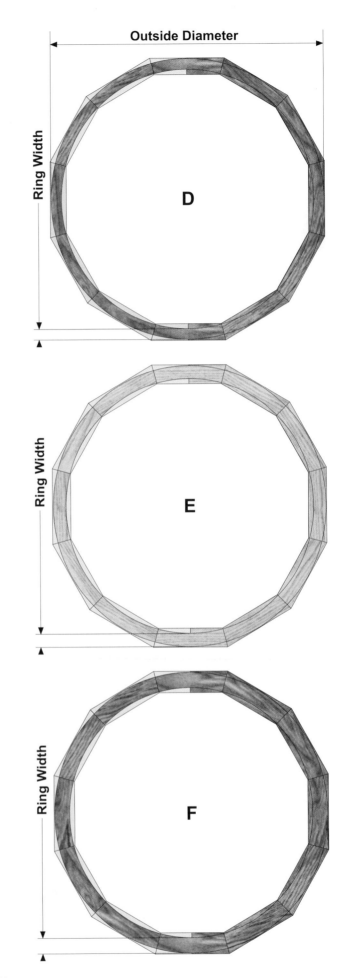

Outside Width

Outside Height

Side Length

D

Outside Diameter

Ring Width

D

Ring Width

E

Ring Width

F

Side Length	Frame Width	Frame Height	Ring Max. OD	Material Req'd.	D Side Width	D Ring Width	E Side Width	E Ring Width	F Side Width	F Ring Width
8/16	1 14/16	1 14/16	1 14/16	9	2/16	1/16	2/16	1/16	2/16	2/16
10/16	2 6/16	2 6/16	2 5/16	10 8/16	2/16	1/16	3/16	2/16	3/16	2/16
12/16	2 13/16	2 13/16	2 13/16	12	3/16	2/16	3/16	2/16	3/16	2/16
14/16	3 5/16	3 5/16	3 4/16	13 8/16	3/16	2/16	4/16	2/16	4/16	3/16
1	3 12/16	3 12/16	3 12/16	15	4/16	2/16	4/16	3/16	5/16	3/16
1 4/16	4 11/16	4 11/16	4 11/16	18	4/16	3/16	5/16	3/16	6/16	4/16
1 8/16	5 10/16	5 10/16	5 10/16	21	5/16	3/16	6/16	4/16	7/16	5/16
1 12/16	6 9/16	6 9/16	6 8/16	24	6/16	4/16	7/16	5/16	8/16	6/16
2	7 8/16	7 8/16	7 7/16	27	7/16	5/16	8/16	6/16	9/16	7/16
2 4/16	8 7/16	8 7/16	8 6/16	30	8/16	5/16	9/16	6/16	10/16	7/16
2 8/16	9 6/16	9 6/16	9 5/16	33	9/16	6/16	10/16	7/16	11/16	8/16
2 12/16	10 5/16	10 5/16	10 4/16	36	10/16	6/16	11/16	8/16	12/16	9/16
3	11 4/16	11 4/16	11 3/16	39	11/16	7/16	12/16	8/16	14/16	10/16
3 4/16	12 3/16	12 3/16	12 2/16	42	11/16	7/16	13/16	9/16	15/16	11/16
3 8/16	13 2/16	13 2/16	13 1/16	45	12/16	8/16	14/16	10/16	1	12/16
3 12/16	14 1/16	14 1/16	14	48	13/16	9/16	15/16	10/16	1 1/16	12/16
4	15	15	14 15/16	51	14/16	9/16	1	11/16	1 2/16	13/16
4 4/16	15 15/16	15 15/16	15 14/16	54	15/16	10/16	1 1/16	12/16	1 3/16	14/16
4 8/16	16 14/16	16 14/16	16 13/16	57	1	10/16	1 2/16	13/16	1 4/16	15/16
4 12/16	17 13/16	17 13/16	17 11/16	60	1 1/16	11/16	1 3/16	13/16	1 5/16	1
5	18 12/16	18 12/16	18 10/16	63	1 2/16	11/16	1 4/16	14/16	1 7/16	1
5 4/16	19 11/16	19 11/16	19 9/16	66	1 2/16	12/16	1 5/16	15/16	1 8/16	1 1/16
5 8/16	20 10/16	20 10/16	20 8/16	69	1 3/16	12/16	1 6/16	15/16	1 9/16	1 2/16
5 12/16	21 9/16	21 9/16	21 7/16	72	1 4/16	13/16	1 7/16	1	1 10/16	1 3/16
6	22 8/16	22 8/16	22 6/16	75	1 5/16	14/16	1 8/16	1 1/16	1 11/16	1 4/16
6 8/16	24 6/16	24 6/16	24 4/16	81	1 7/16	15/16	1 10/16	1 2/16	1 13/16	1 5/16
7	26 4/16	26 4/16	26 2/16	87	1 9/16	1	1 12/16	1 3/16	2	1 7/16
7 8/16	28 2/16	28 2/16	28	93	1 10/16	1 1/16	1 14/16	1 5/16	2 2/16	1 9/16
8	30	30	29 13/16	99	1 12/16	1 2/16	2	1 6/16	2 4/16	1 10/16
8 8/16	31 14/16	31 14/16	31 11/16	105	1 14/16	1 3/16	2 2/16	1 8/16	2 6/16	1 12/16
9	33 12/16	33 12/16	33 9/16	111	2	1 4/16	2 4/16	1 9/16	2 9/16	1 14/16
9 8/16	35 10/16	35 10/16	35 7/16	117	2 1/16	1 6/16	2 6/16	1 10/16	2 11/16	1 15/16
10	37 8/16	37 8/16	37 5/16	123	2 3/16	1 7/16	2 8/16	1 12/16	2 13/16	2 1/16
10 8/16	39 6/16	39 6/16	39 3/16	129	2 5/16	1 8/16	2 10/16	1 13/16	2 15/16	2 3/16
11	41 4/16	41 4/16	41 1/16	135	2 7/16	1 9/16	2 12/16	1 15/16	3 2/16	2 4/16
11 8/16	43 2/16	43 2/16	42 14/16	141	2 8/16	1 10/16	2 14/16	2	3 4/16	2 6/16
12	45	45	44 12/16	147	2 10/16	1 11/16	3	2 1/16	3 6/16	2 7/16
13	48 12/16	48 12/16	48 8/16	159	2 14/16	1 13/16	3 4/16	2 4/16	3 11/16	2 11/16
14	52 8/16	52 8/16	52 4/16	171	3 1/16	2	3 8/16	2 7/16	3 15/16	2 14/16
15	56 4/16	56 4/16	55 15/16	183	3 5/16	2 2/16	3 12/16	2 10/16	4 4/16	3 1/16
16	60	60	59 11/16	195	3 8/16	2 4/16	4	2 12/16	4 8/16	3 5/16
17	63 12/16	63 12/16	63 7/16	207	3 12/16	2 7/16	4 4/16	2 15/16	4 13/16	3 8/16
18	67 8/16	67 8/16	67 2/16	219	3 15/16	2 9/16	4 8/16	3 2/16	5 1/16	3 11/16
19	71 4/16	71 4/16	70 14/16	231	4 3/16	2 11/16	4 12/16	3 5/16	5 6/16	3 14/16
20	75	75	74 10/16	243	4 6/16	2 13/16	5	3 8/16	5 10/16	4 2/16
21	78 12/16	78 12/16	78 5/16	255	4 10/16	3	5 4/16	3 10/16	5 15/16	4 5/16
22	82 8/16	82 8/16	82 1/16	267	4 13/16	3 2/16	5 8/16	3 13/16	6 3/16	4 8/16
23	86 4/16	86 4/16	85 13/16	279	5 1/16	3 4/16	5 12/16	4	6 8/16	4 12/16
24	90	90	89 8/16	291	5 4/16	3 6/16	6	4 3/16	6 12/16	4 15/16
25	93 12/16	93 12/16	93 4/16	303	5 8/16	3 9/16	6 4/16	4 5/16	7 1/16	5 2/16
26	97 8/16	97 8/16	97	315	5 11/16	3 11/16	6 8/16	4 8/16	7 5/16	5 6/16
27	101 4/16	101 4/16	100 11/16	327	5 15/16	3 13/16	6 12/16	4 11/16	7 10/16	5 9/16
28	105	105	104 7/16	339	6 2/16	4	7	4 14/16	7 14/16	5 12/16

Outside Width

Outside Height

Side Length

G

H

I

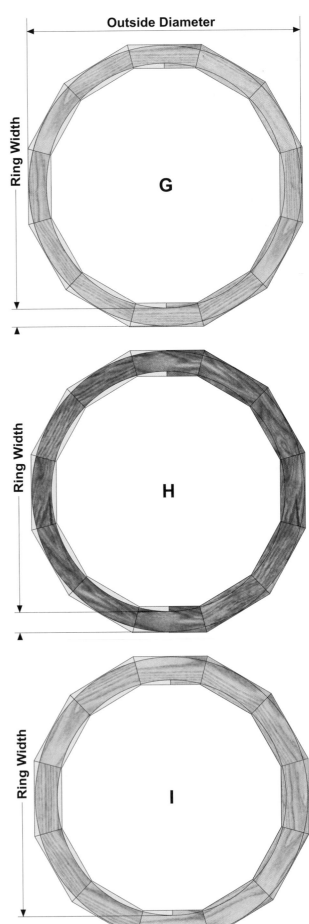

Outside Diameter

Ring Width

G

Ring Width

H

Ring Width

I

126

Side Length	Frame Width	Frame Height	Ring Max. OD	Material Req'd.	G Side Width	G Ring Width	H Side Width	H Ring Width	I Side Width	I Ring Width
8/16	1 14/16	1 14/16	1 14/16	9	3/16	2/16	3/16	2/16	3/16	2/16
10/16	2 6/16	2 6/16	2 5/16	10 8/16	3/16	2/16	3/16	3/16	4/16	3/16
12/16	2 13/16	2 13/16	2 13/16	12	4/16	3/16	4/16	3/16	5/16	4/16
14/16	3 5/16	3 5/16	3 4/16	13 8/16	4/16	3/16	5/16	4/16	5/16	4/16
1	3 12/16	3 12/16	3 12/16	15	5/16	4/16	6/16	4/16	6/16	5/16
1 4/16	4 11/16	4 11/16	4 11/16	18	6/16	5/16	7/16	5/16	8/16	6/16
1 8/16	5 10/16	5 10/16	5 10/16	21	8/16	6/16	8/16	6/16	9/16	7/16
1 12/16	6 9/16	6 9/16	6 8/16	24	9/16	7/16	10/16	8/16	11/16	8/16
2	7 8/16	7 8/16	7 7/16	27	10/16	8/16	11/16	9/16	12/16	10/16
2 4/16	8 7/16	8 7/16	8 6/16	30	11/16	9/16	12/16	10/16	14/16	11/16
2 8/16	9 6/16	9 6/16	9 5/16	33	13/16	9/16	14/16	11/16	15/16	12/16
2 12/16	10 5/16	10 5/16	10 4/16	36	14/16	10/16	15/16	12/16	1 1/16	13/16
3	11 4/16	11 4/16	11 3/16	39	15/16	11/16	1 1/16	13/16	1 2/16	14/16
3 4/16	12 3/16	12 3/16	12 2/16	42	1	12/16	1 2/16	14/16	1 4/16	1
3 8/16	13 2/16	13 2/16	13 1/16	45	1 2/16	13/16	1 3/16	15/16	1 5/16	1 1/16
3 12/16	14 1/16	14 1/16	14	48	1 3/16	14/16	1 5/16	1	1 7/16	1 2/16
4	15	15	14 15/16	51	1 4/16	15/16	1 6/16	1 1/16	1 8/16	1 3/16
4 4/16	15 15/16	15 15/16	15 14/16	54	1 5/16	1	1 7/16	1 2/16	1 10/16	1 4/16
4 8/16	16 14/16	16 14/16	16 13/16	57	1 7/16	1 1/16	1 9/16	1 3/16	1 11/16	1 6/16
4 12/16	17 13/16	17 13/16	17 11/16	60	1 8/16	1 2/16	1 10/16	1 4/16	1 13/16	1 7/16
5	18 12/16	18 12/16	18 10/16	63	1 9/16	1 3/16	1 12/16	1 6/16	1 14/16	1 8/16
5 4/16	19 11/16	19 11/16	19 9/16	66	1 10/16	1 4/16	1 13/16	1 7/16	2	1 9/16
5 8/16	20 10/16	20 10/16	20 8/16	69	1 12/16	1 5/16	1 14/16	1 8/16	2 1/16	1 11/16
5 12/16	21 9/16	21 9/16	21 7/16	72	1 13/16	1 6/16	2	1 9/16	2 3/16	1 12/16
6	22 8/16	22 8/16	22 6/16	75	1 14/16	1 7/16	2 1/16	1 10/16	2 4/16	1 13/16
6 8/16	24 6/16	24 6/16	24 4/16	81	2 1/16	1 9/16	2 4/16	1 12/16	2 7/16	1 15/16
7	26 4/16	26 4/16	26 2/16	87	2 3/16	1 11/16	2 7/16	1 14/16	2 10/16	2 2/16
7 8/16	28 2/16	28 2/16	28	93	2 6/16	1 12/16	2 9/16	2	2 13/16	2 4/16
8	30	30	29 13/16	99	2 8/16	1 14/16	2 12/16	2 2/16	3	2 7/16
8 8/16	31 14/16	31 14/16	31 11/16	105	2 11/16	2	2 15/16	2 5/16	3 3/16	2 9/16
9	33 12/16	33 12/16	33 9/16	111	2 13/16	2 2/16	3 2/16	2 7/16	3 6/16	2 11/16
9 8/16	35 10/16	35 10/16	35 7/16	117	3	2 4/16	3 4/16	2 9/16	3 9/16	2 14/16
10	37 8/16	37 8/16	37 5/16	123	3 2/16	2 6/16	3 7/16	2 11/16	3 12/16	3
10 8/16	39 6/16	39 6/16	39 3/16	129	3 5/16	2 8/16	3 10/16	2 13/16	3 15/16	3 3/16
11	41 4/16	41 4/16	41 1/16	135	3 7/16	2 10/16	3 13/16	2 15/16	4 2/16	3 5/16
11 8/16	43 2/16	43 2/16	42 14/16	141	3 10/16	2 12/16	3 15/16	3 2/16	4 5/16	3 7/16
12	45	45	44 12/16	147	3 12/16	2 14/16	4 2/16	3 4/16	4 8/16	3 10/16
13	48 12/16	48 12/16	48 8/16	159	4 1/16	3 1/16	4 8/16	3 8/16	4 14/16	3 15/16
14	52 8/16	52 8/16	52 4/16	171	4 6/16	3 5/16	4 13/16	3 12/16	5 4/16	4 3/16
15	56 4/16	56 4/16	55 15/16	183	4 11/16	3 9/16	5 3/16	4 1/16	5 10/16	4 8/16
16	60	60	59 11/16	195	5	3 13/16	5 8/16	4 5/16	6	4 13/16
17	63 12/16	63 12/16	63 7/16	207	5 5/16	4 1/16	5 14/16	4 9/16	6 6/16	5 2/16
18	67 8/16	67 8/16	67 2/16	219	5 10/16	4 4/16	6 3/16	4 14/16	6 12/16	5 7/16
19	71 4/16	71 4/16	70 14/16	231	5 15/16	4 8/16	6 9/16	5 2/16	7 2/16	5 12/16
20	75	75	74 10/16	243	6 4/16	4 12/16	6 14/16	5 6/16	7 8/16	6
21	78 12/16	78 12/16	78 5/16	255	6 9/16	5	7 4/16	5 10/16	7 14/16	6 5/16
22	82 8/16	82 8/16	82 1/16	267	6 14/16	5 4/16	7 9/16	5 15/16	8 4/16	6 10/16
23	86 4/16	86 4/16	85 13/16	279	7 3/16	5 7/16	7 15/16	6 3/16	8 10/16	6 15/16
24	90	90	89 8/16	291	7 8/16	5 11/16	8 4/16	6 7/16	9	7 4/16
25	93 12/16	93 12/16	93 4/16	303	7 13/16	5 15/16	8 10/16	6 12/16	9 6/16	7 8/16
26	97 8/16	97 8/16	97	315	8 2/16	6 3/16	8 15/16	7	9 12/16	7 13/16
27	101 4/16	101 4/16	100 11/16	327	8 7/16	6 7/16	9 5/16	7 4/16	10 2/16	8 2/16
28	105	105	104 7/16	339	8 12/16	6 10/16	9 10/16	7 9/16	10 8/16	8 7/16

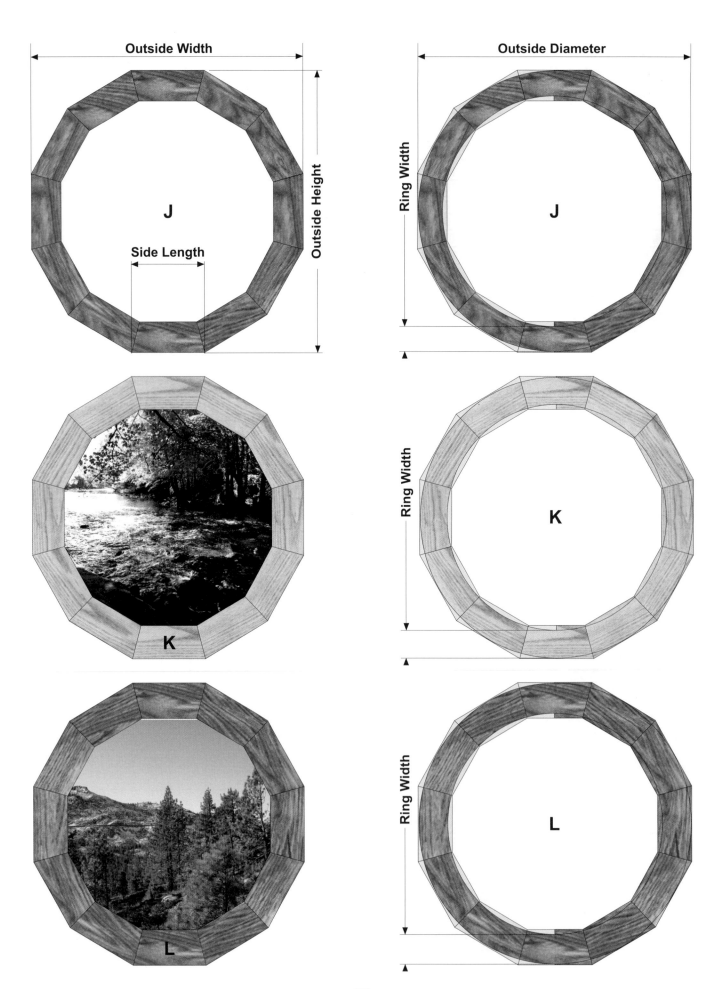

Outside Width

Outside Height

Side Length

J

Outside Diameter

Ring Width

J

K

Ring Width

K

L

Ring Width

L

Side Length	Frame Width	Frame Height	Ring Max. OD	Material Req'd.	J Side Width	J Ring Width	K Side Width	K Ring Width	L Side Width	L Ring Width
8/16	1 14/16	1 14/16	1 14/16	9	3/16	3/16	4/16	3/16	4/16	3/16
10/16	2 6/16	2 6/16	2 5/16	10 8/16	4/16	3/16	4/16	4/16	5/16	4/16
12/16	2 13/16	2 13/16	2 13/16	12	5/16	4/16	5/16	4/16	6/16	5/16
14/16	3 5/16	3 5/16	3 4/16	13 8/16	6/16	5/16	6/16	5/16	7/16	6/16
1	3 12/16	3 12/16	3 12/16	15	7/16	5/16	7/16	6/16	8/16	6/16
1 4/16	4 11/16	4 11/16	4 11/16	18	8/16	7/16	9/16	7/16	9/16	8/16
1 8/16	5 10/16	5 10/16	5 10/16	21	10/16	8/16	11/16	9/16	11/16	10/16
1 12/16	6 9/16	6 9/16	6 8/16	24	11/16	9/16	12/16	10/16	13/16	11/16
2	7 8/16	7 8/16	7 7/16	27	13/16	11/16	14/16	12/16	15/16	13/16
2 4/16	8 7/16	8 7/16	8 6/16	30	15/16	12/16	1	13/16	1 1/16	14/16
2 8/16	9 6/16	9 6/16	9 5/16	33	1	13/16	1 2/16	15/16	1 3/16	1
2 12/16	10 5/16	10 5/16	10 4/16	36	1 2/16	15/16	1 3/16	1	1 5/16	1 1/16
3	11 4/16	11 4/16	11 3/16	39	1 4/16	1	1 5/16	1 2/16	1 7/16	1 3/16
3 4/16	12 3/16	12 3/16	12 2/16	42	1 5/16	1 1/16	1 7/16	1 3/16	1 8/16	1 5/16
3 8/16	13 2/16	13 2/16	13 1/16	45	1 7/16	1 3/16	1 9/16	1 4/16	1 10/16	1 6/16
3 12/16	14 1/16	14 1/16	14	48	1 8/16	1 4/16	1 10/16	1 6/16	1 12/16	1 8/16
4	15	15	14 15/16	51	1 10/16	1 5/16	1 12/16	1 7/16	1 14/16	1 9/16
4 4/16	15 15/16	15 15/16	15 14/16	54	1 12/16	1 7/16	1 14/16	1 9/16	2	1 11/16
4 8/16	16 14/16	16 14/16	16 13/16	57	1 13/16	1 8/16	2	1 10/16	2 2/16	1 13/16
4 12/16	17 13/16	17 13/16	17 11/16	60	1 15/16	1 9/16	2 1/16	1 12/16	2 4/16	1 14/16
5	18 12/16	18 12/16	18 10/16	63	2 1/16	1 11/16	2 3/16	1 13/16	2 6/16	2
5 4/16	19 11/16	19 11/16	19 9/16	66	2 2/16	1 12/16	2 5/16	1 15/16	2 7/16	2 1/16
5 8/16	20 10/16	20 10/16	20 8/16	69	2 4/16	1 13/16	2 7/16	2	2 9/16	2 3/16
5 12/16	21 9/16	21 9/16	21 7/16	72	2 5/16	1 15/16	2 8/16	2 2/16	2 11/16	2 5/16
6	22 8/16	22 8/16	22 6/16	75	2 7/16	2	2 10/16	2 3/16	2 13/16	2 6/16
6 8/16	24 6/16	24 6/16	24 4/16	81	2 10/16	2 3/16	2 14/16	2 6/16	3 1/16	2 9/16
7	26 4/16	26 4/16	26 2/16	87	2 14/16	2 5/16	3 1/16	2 9/16	3 5/16	2 12/16
7 8/16	28 2/16	28 2/16	28	93	3 1/16	2 8/16	3 5/16	2 12/16	3 8/16	3
8	30	30	29 13/16	99	3 4/16	2 11/16	3 8/16	2 15/16	3 12/16	3 3/16
8 8/16	31 14/16	31 14/16	31 11/16	105	3 7/16	2 13/16	3 12/16	3 2/16	4	3 6/16
9	33 12/16	33 12/16	33 9/16	111	3 11/16	3	3 15/16	3 5/16	4 4/16	3 9/16
9 8/16	35 10/16	35 10/16	35 7/16	117	3 14/16	3 3/16	4 3/16	3 8/16	4 7/16	3 12/16
10	37 8/16	37 8/16	37 5/16	123	4 1/16	3 5/16	4 6/16	3 10/16	4 11/16	4
10 8/16	39 6/16	39 6/16	39 3/16	129	4 4/16	3 8/16	4 10/16	3 13/16	4 15/16	4 3/16
11	41 4/16	41 4/16	41 1/16	135	4 8/16	3 11/16	4 13/16	4	5 3/16	4 6/16
11 8/16	43 2/16	43 2/16	42 14/16	141	4 11/16	3 13/16	5 1/16	4 3/16	5 6/16	4 9/16
12	45	45	44 12/16	147	4 14/16	4	5 4/16	4 6/16	5 10/16	4 12/16
13	48 12/16	48 12/16	48 8/16	159	5 5/16	4 5/16	5 11/16	4 12/16	6 2/16	5 3/16
14	52 8/16	52 8/16	52 4/16	171	5 11/16	4 11/16	6 2/16	5 2/16	6 9/16	5 9/16
15	56 4/16	56 4/16	55 15/16	183	6 2/16	5	6 9/16	5 8/16	7 1/16	5 15/16
16	60	60	59 11/16	195	6 8/16	5 5/16	7	5 13/16	7 8/16	6 6/16
17	63 12/16	63 12/16	63 7/16	207	6 15/16	5 11/16	7 7/16	6 3/16	8	6 12/16
18	67 8/16	67 8/16	67 2/16	219	7 5/16	6	7 14/16	6 9/16	8 7/16	7 2/16
19	71 4/16	71 4/16	70 14/16	231	7 12/16	6 5/16	8 5/16	6 15/16	8 15/16	7 9/16
20	75	75	74 10/16	243	8 2/16	6 11/16	8 12/16	7 5/16	9 6/16	7 15/16
21	78 12/16	78 12/16	78 5/16	255	8 9/16	7	9 3/16	7 11/16	9 14/16	8 5/16
22	82 8/16	82 8/16	82 1/16	267	8 15/16	7 5/16	9 10/16	8 1/16	10 5/16	8 12/16
23	86 4/16	86 4/16	85 13/16	279	9 6/16	7 11/16	10 1/16	8 6/16	10 13/16	9 2/16
24	90	90	89 8/16	291	9 12/16	8	10 8/16	8 12/16	11 4/16	9 8/16
25	93 12/16	93 12/16	93 4/16	303	10 3/16	8 5/16	10 15/16	9 2/16	11 12/16	9 15/16
26	97 8/16	97 8/16	97	315	10 9/16	8 11/16	11 6/16	9 8/16	12 3/16	10 5/16
27	101 4/16	101 4/16	100 11/16	327	11	9	11 13/16	9 14/16	12 11/16	10 12/16
28	105	105	104 7/16	339	11 6/16	9 5/16	12 4/16	10 4/16	13 2/16	11 2/16

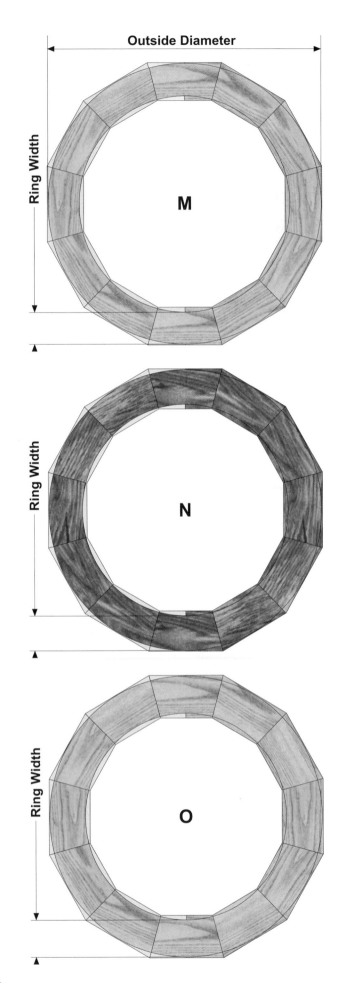

Side Length	Frame Width	Frame Height	Ring Max. OD	Material Req'd.	M Side Width	M Ring Width	N Side Width	N Ring Width	O Side Width	O Ring Width
8/16	1 14/16	1 14/16	1 14/16	9	4/16	3/16	4/16	4/16	5/16	4/16
10/16	2 6/16	2 6/16	2 5/16	10 8/16	5/16	4/16	5/16	5/16	6/16	5/16
12/16	2 13/16	2 13/16	2 13/16	12	6/16	5/16	6/16	6/16	7/16	6/16
14/16	3 5/16	3 5/16	3 4/16	13 8/16	7/16	6/16	7/16	6/16	8/16	7/16
1	3 12/16	3 12/16	3 12/16	15	8/16	7/16	9/16	7/16	9/16	8/16
1 4/16	4 11/16	4 11/16	4 11/16	18	10/16	9/16	11/16	9/16	11/16	10/16
1 8/16	5 10/16	5 10/16	5 10/16	21	12/16	10/16	13/16	11/16	14/16	12/16
1 12/16	6 9/16	6 9/16	6 8/16	24	14/16	12/16	15/16	13/16	1	14/16
2	7 8/16	7 8/16	7 7/16	27	1	14/16	1 1/16	15/16	1 2/16	1
2 4/16	8 7/16	8 7/16	8 6/16	30	1 2/16	15/16	1 3/16	1 1/16	1 4/16	1 2/16
2 8/16	9 6/16	9 6/16	9 5/16	33	1 4/16	1 1/16	1 5/16	1 2/16	1 7/16	1 4/16
2 12/16	10 5/16	10 5/16	10 4/16	36	1 6/16	1 3/16	1 7/16	1 4/16	1 9/16	1 6/16
3	11 4/16	11 4/16	11 3/16	39	1 8/16	1 5/16	1 10/16	1 6/16	1 11/16	1 8/16
3 4/16	12 3/16	12 3/16	12 2/16	42	1 10/16	1 6/16	1 12/16	1 8/16	1 13/16	1 10/16
3 8/16	13 2/16	13 2/16	13 1/16	45	1 12/16	1 8/16	1 14/16	1 10/16	2	1 12/16
3 12/16	14 1/16	14 1/16	14	48	1 14/16	1 10/16	2	1 12/16	2 2/16	1 14/16
4	15	15	14 15/16	51	2	1 11/16	2 2/16	1 13/16	2 4/16	2
4 4/16	15 15/16	15 15/16	15 14/16	54	2 2/16	1 13/16	2 4/16	1 15/16	2 6/16	2 2/16
4 8/16	16 14/16	16 14/16	16 13/16	57	2 4/16	1 15/16	2 6/16	2 1/16	2 9/16	2 3/16
4 12/16	17 13/16	17 13/16	17 11/16	60	2 6/16	2 1/16	2 8/16	2 3/16	2 11/16	2 5/16
5	18 12/16	18 12/16	18 10/16	63	2 8/16	2 2/16	2 11/16	2 5/16	2 13/16	2 7/16
5 4/16	19 11/16	19 11/16	19 9/16	66	2 10/16	2 4/16	2 13/16	2 7/16	2 15/16	2 9/16
5 8/16	20 10/16	20 10/16	20 8/16	69	2 12/16	2 6/16	2 15/16	2 9/16	3 2/16	2 11/16
5 12/16	21 9/16	21 9/16	21 7/16	72	2 14/16	2 7/16	3 1/16	2 10/16	3 4/16	2 13/16
6	22 8/16	22 8/16	22 6/16	75	3	2 9/16	3 3/16	2 12/16	3 6/16	2 15/16
6 8/16	24 6/16	24 6/16	24 4/16	81	3 4/16	2 13/16	3 7/16	3	3 11/16	3 3/16
7	26 4/16	26 4/16	26 2/16	87	3 8/16	3	3 12/16	3 4/16	3 15/16	3 7/16
7 8/16	28 2/16	28 2/16	28	93	3 12/16	3 3/16	4	3 7/16	4 4/16	3 11/16
8	30	30	29 13/16	99	4	3 7/16	4 4/16	3 11/16	4 8/16	3 15/16
8 8/16	31 14/16	31 14/16	31 11/16	105	4 4/16	3 10/16	4 8/16	3 15/16	4 13/16	4 3/16
9	33 12/16	33 12/16	33 9/16	111	4 8/16	3 14/16	4 13/16	4 2/16	5 1/16	4 7/16
9 8/16	35 10/16	35 10/16	35 7/16	117	4 12/16	4 1/16	5 1/16	4 6/16	5 6/16	4 11/16
10	37 8/16	37 8/16	37 5/16	123	5	4 5/16	5 5/16	4 10/16	5 10/16	4 15/16
10 8/16	39 6/16	39 6/16	39 3/16	129	5 4/16	4 8/16	5 9/16	4 13/16	5 15/16	5 3/16
11	41 4/16	41 4/16	41 1/16	135	5 8/16	4 11/16	5 14/16	5 1/16	6 3/16	5 7/16
11 8/16	43 2/16	43 2/16	42 14/16	141	5 12/16	4 15/16	6 2/16	5 5/16	6 8/16	5 11/16
12	45	45	44 12/16	147	6	5 2/16	6 6/16	5 8/16	6 12/16	5 15/16
13	48 12/16	48 12/16	48 8/16	159	6 8/16	5 9/16	6 15/16	6	7 5/16	6 6/16
14	52 8/16	52 8/16	52 4/16	171	7	6	7 7/16	6 7/16	7 14/16	6 14/16
15	56 4/16	56 4/16	55 15/16	183	7 8/16	6 7/16	8	6 15/16	8 7/16	7 6/16
16	60	60	59 11/16	195	8	6 14/16	8 8/16	7 6/16	9	7 14/16
17	63 12/16	63 12/16	63 7/16	207	8 8/16	7 5/16	9 1/16	7 13/16	9 9/16	8 6/16
18	67 8/16	67 8/16	67 2/16	219	9	7 12/16	9 9/16	8 5/16	10 2/16	8 14/16
19	71 4/16	71 4/16	70 14/16	231	9 8/16	8 2/16	10 2/16	8 12/16	10 11/16	9 6/16
20	75	75	74 10/16	243	10	8 9/16	10 10/16	9 3/16	11 4/16	9 14/16
21	78 12/16	78 12/16	78 5/16	255	10 8/16	9	11 3/16	9 11/16	11 13/16	10 6/16
22	82 8/16	82 8/16	82 1/16	267	11	9 7/16	11 11/16	10 2/16	12 6/16	10 13/16
23	86 4/16	86 4/16	85 13/16	279	11 8/16	9 14/16	12 4/16	10 10/16	12 15/16	11 5/16
24	90	90	89 8/16	291	12	10 5/16	12 12/16	11 1/16	13 8/16	11 13/16
25	93 12/16	93 12/16	93 4/16	303	12 8/16	10 12/16	13 5/16	11 8/16	14 1/16	12 5/16
26	97 8/16	97 8/16	97	315	13	11 2/16	13 13/16	12	14 10/16	12 13/16
27	101 4/16	101 4/16	100 11/16	327	13 8/16	11 9/16	14 6/16	12 7/16	15 3/16	13 5/16
28	105	105	104 7/16	339	14	12	14 14/16	12 14/16	15 12/16	13 13/16

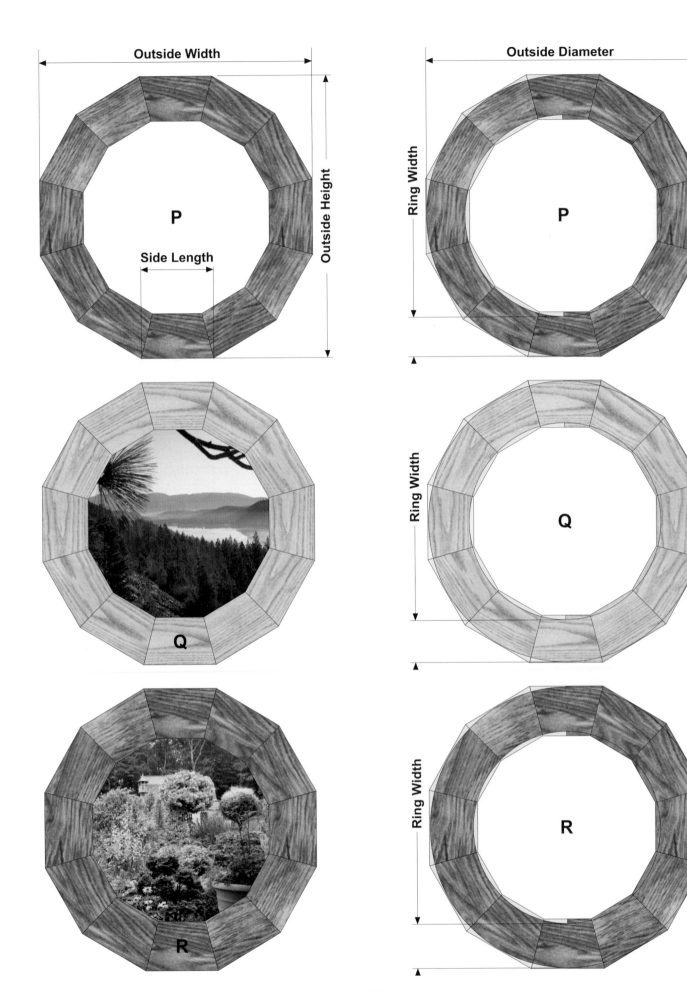

Side Length	Frame Width	Frame Height	Ring Max. OD	Material Req'd.	P Side Width	P Ring Width	Q Side Width	Q Ring Width	R Side Width	R Ring Width
8/16	1 14/16	1 14/16	1 14/16	9	5/16	4/16	5/16	4/16	5/16	5/16
10/16	2 6/16	2 6/16	2 5/16	10 8/16	6/16	5/16	6/16	6/16	7/16	6/16
12/16	2 13/16	2 13/16	2 13/16	12	7/16	6/16	8/16	7/16	8/16	7/16
14/16	3 5/16	3 5/16	3 4/16	13 8/16	8/16	7/16	9/16	8/16	9/16	8/16
1	3 12/16	3 12/16	3 12/16	15	10/16	8/16	10/16	9/16	11/16	9/16
1 4/16	4 11/16	4 11/16	4 11/16	18	12/16	10/16	13/16	11/16	13/16	12/16
1 8/16	5 10/16	5 10/16	5 10/16	21	14/16	13/16	15/16	13/16	1	14/16
1 12/16	6 9/16	6 9/16	6 8/16	24	1 1/16	15/16	1 2/16	1	1 2/16	1
2	7 8/16	7 8/16	7 7/16	27	1 3/16	1 1/16	1 4/16	1 2/16	1 5/16	1 3/16
2 4/16	8 7/16	8 7/16	8 6/16	30	1 5/16	1 3/16	1 7/16	1 4/16	1 8/16	1 5/16
2 8/16	9 6/16	9 6/16	9 5/16	33	1 8/16	1 5/16	1 9/16	1 6/16	1 10/16	1 8/16
2 12/16	10 5/16	10 5/16	10 4/16	36	1 10/16	1 7/16	1 12/16	1 8/16	1 13/16	1 10/16
3	11 4/16	11 4/16	11 3/16	39	1 13/16	1 9/16	1 14/16	1 11/16	2	1 12/16
3 4/16	12 3/16	12 3/16	12 2/16	42	1 15/16	1 11/16	2 1/16	1 13/16	2 2/16	1 15/16
3 8/16	13 2/16	13 2/16	13 1/16	45	2 1/16	1 13/16	2 3/16	1 15/16	2 5/16	2 1/16
3 12/16	14 1/16	14 1/16	14	48	2 4/16	1 15/16	2 6/16	2 1/16	2 7/16	2 3/16
4	15	15	14 15/16	51	2 6/16	2 2/16	2 8/16	2 4/16	2 10/16	2 6/16
4 4/16	15 15/16	15 15/16	15 14/16	54	2 8/16	2 4/16	2 11/16	2 6/16	2 13/16	2 8/16
4 8/16	16 14/16	16 14/16	16 13/16	57	2 11/16	2 6/16	2 13/16	2 8/16	2 15/16	2 10/16
4 12/16	17 13/16	17 13/16	17 11/16	60	2 13/16	2 8/16	3	2 10/16	3 2/16	2 13/16
5	18 12/16	18 12/16	18 10/16	63	3	2 10/16	3 2/16	2 13/16	3 5/16	2 15/16
5 4/16	19 11/16	19 11/16	19 9/16	66	3 2/16	2 12/16	3 5/16	2 15/16	3 7/16	3 1/16
5 8/16	20 10/16	20 10/16	20 8/16	69	3 4/16	2 14/16	3 7/16	3 1/16	3 10/16	3 4/16
5 12/16	21 9/16	21 9/16	21 7/16	72	3 7/16	3	3 10/16	3 3/16	3 12/16	3 6/16
6	22 8/16	22 8/16	22 6/16	75	3 9/16	3 2/16	3 12/16	3 5/16	3 15/16	3 8/16
6 8/16	24 6/16	24 6/16	24 4/16	81	3 14/16	3 7/16	4 1/16	3 10/16	4 4/16	3 13/16
7	26 4/16	26 4/16	26 2/16	87	4 3/16	3 11/16	4 6/16	3 14/16	4 10/16	4 2/16
7 8/16	28 2/16	28 2/16	28	93	4 7/16	3 15/16	4 11/16	4 3/16	4 15/16	4 7/16
8	30	30	29 13/16	99	4 12/16	4 3/16	5	4 7/16	5 4/16	4 11/16
8 8/16	31 14/16	31 14/16	31 11/16	105	5 1/16	4 7/16	5 5/16	4 12/16	5 9/16	5
9	33 12/16	33 12/16	33 9/16	111	5 6/16	4 12/16	5 10/16	5	5 15/16	5 5/16
9 8/16	35 10/16	35 10/16	35 7/16	117	5 10/16	5	5 15/16	5 5/16	6 4/16	5 9/16
10	37 8/16	37 8/16	37 5/16	123	5 15/16	5 4/16	6 4/16	5 9/16	6 9/16	5 14/16
10 8/16	39 6/16	39 6/16	39 3/16	129	6 4/16	5 8/16	6 9/16	5 13/16	6 14/16	6 3/16
11	41 4/16	41 4/16	41 1/16	135	6 9/16	5 12/16	6 14/16	6 2/16	7 4/16	6 8/16
11 8/16	43 2/16	43 2/16	42 14/16	141	6 13/16	6 1/16	7 3/16	6 6/16	7 9/16	6 12/16
12	45	45	44 12/16	147	7 2/16	6 5/16	7 8/16	6 11/16	7 14/16	7 1/16
13	48 12/16	48 12/16	48 8/16	159	7 12/16	6 13/16	8 2/16	7 4/16	8 9/16	7 10/16
14	52 8/16	52 8/16	52 4/16	171	8 5/16	7 6/16	8 12/16	7 13/16	9 3/16	8 4/16
15	56 4/16	56 4/16	55 15/16	183	8 15/16	7 14/16	9 6/16	8 6/16	9 14/16	8 13/16
16	60	60	59 11/16	195	9 8/16	8 6/16	10	8 14/16	10 8/16	9 7/16
17	63 12/16	63 12/16	63 7/16	207	10 2/16	8 15/16	10 10/16	9 7/16	11 3/16	10
18	67 8/16	67 8/16	67 2/16	219	10 11/16	9 7/16	11 4/16	10	11 13/16	10 9/16
19	71 4/16	71 4/16	70 14/16	231	11 5/16	9 15/16	11 14/16	10 9/16	12 8/16	11 3/16
20	75	75	74 10/16	243	11 14/16	10 8/16	12 8/16	11 2/16	13 2/16	11 12/16
21	78 12/16	78 12/16	78 5/16	255	12 8/16	11	13 2/16	11 11/16	13 13/16	12 6/16
22	82 8/16	82 8/16	82 1/16	267	13 1/16	11 9/16	13 12/16	12 4/16	14 7/16	12 15/16
23	86 4/16	86 4/16	85 13/16	279	13 11/16	12 1/16	14 6/16	12 13/16	15 2/16	13 9/16
24	90	90	89 8/16	291	14 4/16	12 9/16	15	13 6/16	15 12/16	14 2/16
25	93 12/16	93 12/16	93 4/16	303	14 14/16	13 2/16	15 10/16	13 15/16	16 7/16	14 11/16
26	97 8/16	97 8/16	97	315	15 7/16	13 10/16	16 4/16	14 8/16	17 1/16	15 5/16
27	101 4/16	101 4/16	100 11/16	327	16 1/16	14 3/16	16 14/16	15	17 12/16	15 14/16
28	105	105	104 7/16	339	16 10/16	14 11/16	17 8/16	15 9/16	18 6/16	16 8/16

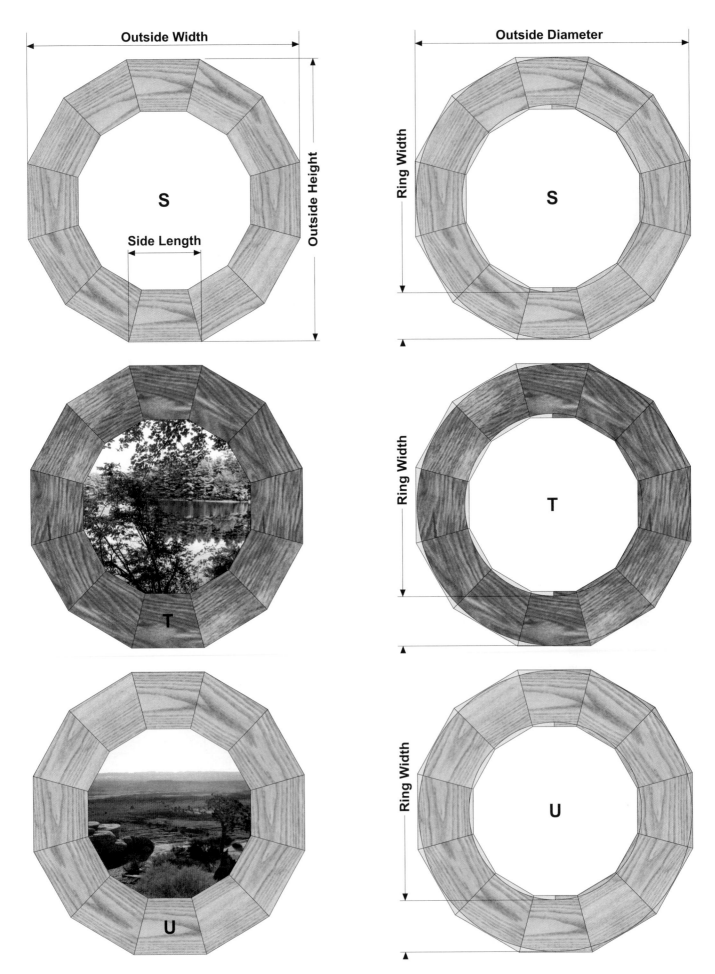

Outside Width

Outside Height

Side Length

S

Outside Diameter

Ring Width

S

T

Ring Width

T

U

Ring Width

U

Outside Diameter

Side Length	Frame Width	Frame Height	Ring Max. OD	Material Req'd.	S Side Width	S Ring Width	T Side Width	T Ring Width	U Side Width	U Ring Width
8/16	1 14/16	1 14/16	1 14/16	9	6/16	5/16	6/16	5/16	6/16	5/16
10/16	2 6/16	2 6/16	2 5/16	10 8/16	7/16	6/16	7/16	7/16	8/16	7/16
12/16	2 13/16	2 13/16	2 13/16	12	8/16	7/16	9/16	8/16	9/16	8/16
14/16	3 5/16	3 5/16	3 4/16	13 8/16	10/16	9/16	10/16	9/16	11/16	10/16
1	3 12/16	3 12/16	3 12/16	15	11/16	10/16	12/16	10/16	12/16	11/16
1 4/16	4 11/16	4 11/16	4 11/16	18	14/16	12/16	14/16	13/16	15/16	14/16
1 8/16	5 10/16	5 10/16	5 10/16	21	1 1/16	15/16	1 1/16	1	1 2/16	1
1 12/16	6 9/16	6 9/16	6 8/16	24	1 3/16	1 1/16	1 4/16	1 2/16	1 5/16	1 3/16
2	7 8/16	7 8/16	7 7/16	27	1 6/16	1 4/16	1 7/16	1 5/16	1 8/16	1 6/16
2 4/16	8 7/16	8 7/16	8 6/16	30	1 9/16	1 6/16	1 10/16	1 7/16	1 11/16	1 9/16
2 8/16	9 6/16	9 6/16	9 5/16	33	1 12/16	1 9/16	1 13/16	1 10/16	1 14/16	1 11/16
2 12/16	10 5/16	10 5/16	10 4/16	36	1 14/16	1 11/16	2	1 13/16	2 1/16	1 14/16
3	11 4/16	11 4/16	11 3/16	39	2 1/16	1 14/16	2 3/16	1 15/16	2 4/16	2 1/16
3 4/16	12 3/16	12 3/16	12 2/16	42	2 4/16	2	2 5/16	2 2/16	2 7/16	2 4/16
3 8/16	13 2/16	13 2/16	13 1/16	45	2 7/16	2 3/16	2 8/16	2 5/16	2 10/16	2 6/16
3 12/16	14 1/16	14 1/16	14	48	2 9/16	2 5/16	2 11/16	2 7/16	2 13/16	2 9/16
4	15	15	14 15/16	51	2 12/16	2 8/16	2 14/16	2 10/16	3	2 12/16
4 4/16	15 15/16	15 15/16	15 14/16	54	2 15/16	2 10/16	3 1/16	2 12/16	3 3/16	2 15/16
4 8/16	16 14/16	16 14/16	16 13/16	57	3 2/16	2 13/16	3 4/16	2 15/16	3 6/16	3 1/16
4 12/16	17 13/16	17 13/16	17 11/16	60	3 4/16	2 15/16	3 7/16	3 2/16	3 9/16	3 4/16
5	18 12/16	18 12/16	18 10/16	63	3 7/16	3 2/16	3 10/16	3 4/16	3 12/16	3 7/16
5 4/16	19 11/16	19 11/16	19 9/16	66	3 10/16	3 4/16	3 12/16	3 7/16	3 15/16	3 9/16
5 8/16	20 10/16	20 10/16	20 8/16	69	3 13/16	3 7/16	3 15/16	3 9/16	4 2/16	3 12/16
5 12/16	21 9/16	21 9/16	21 7/16	72	3 15/16	3 9/16	4 2/16	3 12/16	4 5/16	3 15/16
6	22 8/16	22 8/16	22 6/16	75	4 2/16	3 12/16	4 5/16	3 15/16	4 8/16	4 2/16
6 8/16	24 6/16	24 6/16	24 4/16	81	4 8/16	4 1/16	4 11/16	4 4/16	4 14/16	4 7/16
7	26 4/16	26 4/16	26 2/16	87	4 13/16	4 5/16	5 1/16	4 9/16	5 4/16	4 13/16
7 8/16	28 2/16	28 2/16	28	93	5 3/16	4 10/16	5 6/16	4 14/16	5 10/16	5 2/16
8	30	30	29 13/16	99	5 8/16	4 15/16	5 12/16	5 4/16	6	5 8/16
8 8/16	31 14/16	31 14/16	31 11/16	105	5 14/16	5 4/16	6 2/16	5 9/16	6 6/16	5 13/16
9	33 12/16	33 12/16	33 9/16	111	6 3/16	5 9/16	6 8/16	5 14/16	6 12/16	6 3/16
9 8/16	35 10/16	35 10/16	35 7/16	117	6 9/16	5 14/16	6 13/16	6 3/16	7 2/16	6 8/16
10	37 8/16	37 8/16	37 5/16	123	6 14/16	6 3/16	7 3/16	6 8/16	7 8/16	6 13/16
10 8/16	39 6/16	39 6/16	39 3/16	129	7 4/16	6 8/16	7 9/16	6 14/16	7 14/16	7 3/16
11	41 4/16	41 4/16	41 1/16	135	7 9/16	6 13/16	7 15/16	7 3/16	8 4/16	7 8/16
11 8/16	43 2/16	43 2/16	42 14/16	141	7 15/16	7 2/16	8 4/16	7 8/16	8 10/16	7 14/16
12	45	45	44 12/16	147	8 4/16	7 7/16	8 10/16	7 13/16	9	8 3/16
13	48 12/16	48 12/16	48 8/16	159	8 15/16	8 1/16	9 6/16	8 8/16	9 12/16	8 14/16
14	52 8/16	52 8/16	52 4/16	171	9 10/16	8 11/16	10 1/16	9 2/16	10 8/16	9 9/16
15	56 4/16	56 4/16	55 15/16	183	10 5/16	9 5/16	10 13/16	9 13/16	11 4/16	10 4/16
16	60	60	59 11/16	195	11	9 15/16	11 8/16	10 7/16	12	10 15/16
17	63 12/16	63 12/16	63 7/16	207	11 11/16	10 9/16	12 4/16	11 1/16	12 12/16	11 10/16
18	67 8/16	67 8/16	67 2/16	219	12 6/16	11 3/16	12 15/16	11 12/16	13 8/16	12 5/16
19	71 4/16	71 4/16	70 14/16	231	13 1/16	11 13/16	13 11/16	12 6/16	14 4/16	13
20	75	75	74 10/16	243	13 12/16	12 7/16	14 6/16	13 1/16	15	13 11/16
21	78 12/16	78 12/16	78 5/16	255	14 7/16	13	15 2/16	13 11/16	15 12/16	14 6/16
22	82 8/16	82 8/16	82 1/16	267	15 2/16	13 10/16	15 13/16	14 6/16	16 8/16	15 1/16
23	86 4/16	86 4/16	85 13/16	279	15 13/16	14 4/16	16 9/16	15	17 4/16	15 12/16
24	90	90	89 8/16	291	16 8/16	14 14/16	17 4/16	15 11/16	18	16 7/16
25	93 12/16	93 12/16	93 4/16	303	17 3/16	15 8/16	18	16 5/16	18 12/16	17 2/16
26	97 8/16	97 8/16	97	315	17 14/16	16 2/16	18 11/16	16 15/16	19 8/16	17 13/16
27	101 4/16	101 4/16	100 11/16	327	18 9/16	16 12/16	19 7/16	17 10/16	20 4/16	18 8/16
28	105	105	104 7/16	339	19 4/16	17 6/16	20 2/16	18 4/16	21	19 3/16

Panel Width

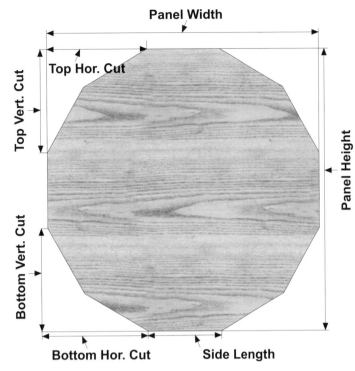

Top Hor. Cut

Top Vert. Cut

Panel Height

Bottom Vert. Cut

Bottom Hor. Cut   **Side Length**

The Chart below shows the formulas that were used in the process of laying out the 12 sided shapes. These are included to assist you if you are designing a project to a size that is not illustrated in the Dimension Charts provided. We hope you find them helpful as you design your projects.

12 SIDED PANEL FORMULAS		
Panel Width =	Panel Height x	1.000
Panel Height =	Panel Width x	1.000
Side Length =	Panel Height x	0.268
Side Length =	Panel Width x	0.268
Top Hor. Cut =	Panel Width x	0.366
Bott. Hor. Cut =	Panel Width x	0.366
Top Vert. Cut =	Panel Width x	0.366
Bott.Vert. Cut =	Panel Width x	0.366

PANEL WIDTH	PANEL HEIGHT	SIDE LENGTH	TOP HOR. CUT	BOTTOM HOR. CUT	TOP VERT. CUT	BOTTOM VERT. CUT
12/16	12/16	3/16	4/16	4/16	4/16	4/16
1	1	4/16	6/16	6/16	6/16	6/16
1 4/16	1 4/16	5/16	7/16	7/16	7/16	7/16
1 8/16	1 8/16	6/16	9/16	9/16	9/16	9/16
1 12/16	1 12/16	8/16	10/16	10/16	10/16	10/16
2	2	9/16	12/16	12/16	12/16	12/16
2 4/16	2 4/16	10/16	13/16	13/16	13/16	13/16
2 8/16	2 8/16	11/16	15/16	15/16	15/16	15/16
2 12/16	2 12/16	12/16	1	1	1	1
3	3	13/16	1 2/16	1 2/16	1 2/16	1 2/16
3 4/16	3 4/16	14/16	1 3/16	1 3/16	1 3/16	1 3/16
3 8/16	3 8/16	15/16	1 4/16	1 4/16	1 4/16	1 4/16
3 12/16	3 12/16	1	1 6/16	1 6/16	1 6/16	1 6/16
4	4	1 1/16	1 7/16	1 7/16	1 7/16	1 7/16
4 4/16	4 4/16	1 2/16	1 9/16	1 9/16	1 9/16	1 9/16
4 8/16	4 8/16	1 3/16	1 10/16	1 10/16	1 10/16	1 10/16
4 12/16	4 12/16	1 4/16	1 12/16	1 12/16	1 12/16	1 12/16
5	5	1 5/16	1 13/16	1 13/16	1 13/16	1 13/16
5 4/16	5 4/16	1 7/16	1 15/16	1 15/16	1 15/16	1 15/16
5 8/16	5 8/16	1 8/16	2	2	2	2
5 12/16	5 12/16	1 9/16	2 2/16	2 2/16	2 2/16	2 2/16
6	6	1 10/16	2 3/16	2 3/16	2 3/16	2 3/16
6 4/16	6 4/16	1 11/16	2 5/16	2 5/16	2 5/16	2 5/16
6 8/16	6 8/16	1 12/16	2 6/16	2 6/16	2 6/16	2 6/16
6 12/16	6 12/16	1 13/16	2 8/16	2 8/16	2 8/16	2 8/16
7	7	1 14/16	2 9/16	2 9/16	2 9/16	2 9/16
7 4/16	7 4/16	1 15/16	2 10/16	2 10/16	2 10/16	2 10/16
7 8/16	7 8/16	2	2 12/16	2 12/16	2 12/16	2 12/16
7 12/16	7 12/16	2 1/16	2 13/16	2 13/16	2 13/16	2 13/16
8	8	2 2/16	2 15/16	2 15/16	2 15/16	2 15/16
8 4/16	8 4/16	2 3/16	3	3	3	3
8 8/16	8 8/16	2 4/16	3 2/16	3 2/16	3 2/16	3 2/16

PANEL WIDTH	PANEL HEIGHT	SIDE LENGTH	TOP HOR. CUT	BOTTOM HOR. CUT	TOP VERT. CUT	BOTTOM VERT. CUT
8 12/16	8 12/16	2 6/16	3 3/16	3 3/16	3 3/16	3 3/16
9	9	2 7/16	3 5/16	3 5/16	3 5/16	3 5/16
9 4/16	9 4/16	2 8/16	3 6/16	3 6/16	3 6/16	3 6/16
9 8/16	9 8/16	2 9/16	3 8/16	3 8/16	3 8/16	3 8/16
9 12/16	9 12/16	2 10/16	3 9/16	3 9/16	3 9/16	3 9/16
10	10	2 11/16	3 11/16	3 11/16	3 11/16	3 11/16
10 4/16	10 4/16	2 12/16	3 12/16	3 12/16	3 12/16	3 12/16
10 8/16	10 8/16	2 13/16	3 13/16	3 13/16	3 13/16	3 13/16
10 12/16	10 12/16	2 14/16	3 15/16	3 15/16	3 15/16	3 15/16
11	11	2 15/16	4	4	4	4
11 4/16	11 4/16	3	4 2/16	4 2/16	4 2/16	4 2/16
11 8/16	11 8/16	3 1/16	4 3/16	4 3/16	4 3/16	4 3/16
12	12	3 3/16	4 6/16	4 6/16	4 6/16	4 6/16
12 4/16	12 4/16	3 5/16	4 8/16	4 8/16	4 8/16	4 8/16
12 8/16	12 8/16	3 6/16	4 9/16	4 9/16	4 9/16	4 9/16
12 12/16	12 12/16	3 7/16	4 11/16	4 11/16	4 11/16	4 11/16
13	13	3 8/16	4 12/16	4 12/16	4 12/16	4 12/16
13 4/16	13 4/16	3 9/16	4 14/16	4 14/16	4 14/16	4 14/16
13 8/16	13 8/16	3 10/16	4 15/16	4 15/16	4 15/16	4 15/16
13 12/16	13 12/16	3 11/16	5 1/16	5 1/16	5 1/16	5 1/16
14	14	3 12/16	5 2/16	5 2/16	5 2/16	5 2/16
14 8/16	14 8/16	3 14/16	5 5/16	5 5/16	5 5/16	5 5/16
15	15	4	5 8/16	5 8/16	5 8/16	5 8/16
15 8/16	15 8/16	4 2/16	5 11/16	5 11/16	5 11/16	5 11/16
16	16	4 5/16	5 14/16	5 14/16	5 14/16	5 14/16
16 8/16	16 8/16	4 7/16	6 1/16	6 1/16	6 1/16	6 1/16
17	17	4 9/16	6 4/16	6 4/16	6 4/16	6 4/16
17 8/16	17 8/16	4 11/16	6 6/16	6 6/16	6 6/16	6 6/16
18	18	4 13/16	6 9/16	6 9/16	6 9/16	6 9/16
19	19	5 1/16	6 15/16	6 15/16	6 15/16	6 15/16
20	20	5 6/16	7 5/16	7 5/16	7 5/16	7 5/16
21	21	5 10/16	7 11/16	7 11/16	7 11/16	7 11/16
22	22	5 14/16	8 1/16	8 1/16	8 1/16	8 1/16
23	23	6 3/16	8 7/16	8 7/16	8 7/16	8 7/16
24	24	6 7/16	8 13/16	8 13/16	8 13/16	8 13/16
25	25	6 11/16	9 2/16	9 2/16	9 2/16	9 2/16
26	26	6 15/16	9 8/16	9 8/16	9 8/16	9 8/16
27	27	7 4/16	9 14/16	9 14/16	9 14/16	9 14/16
28	28	7 8/16	10 4/16	10 4/16	10 4/16	10 4/16
29	29	7 12/16	10 10/16	10 10/16	10 10/16	10 10/16
30	30	8 1/16	11	11	11	11
31	31	8 5/16	11 6/16	11 6/16	11 6/16	11 6/16
32	32	8 9/16	11 11/16	11 11/16	11 11/16	11 11/16
33	33	8 14/16	12 1/16	12 1/16	12 1/16	12 1/16
34	34	9 2/16	12 7/16	12 7/16	12 7/16	12 7/16
35	35	9 6/16	12 13/16	12 13/16	12 13/16	12 13/16
36	36	9 10/16	13 3/16	13 3/16	13 3/16	13 3/16
37	37	9 15/16	13 9/16	13 9/16	13 9/16	13 9/16
38	38	10 3/16	13 15/16	13 15/16	13 15/16	13 15/16
39	39	10 7/16	14 4/16	14 4/16	14 4/16	14 4/16
40	40	10 12/16	14 10/16	14 10/16	14 10/16	14 10/16
41	41	11	15	15	15	15
42	42	11 4/16	15 6/16	15 6/16	15 6/16	15 6/16

14 SIDED PROJECT INFORMATION

Geometric Name: Tetradecagon
Definition: A Polygon having 14 sides
Miter Angle: 12.857°
Angle Change / Adjoining Sides: 25.714°

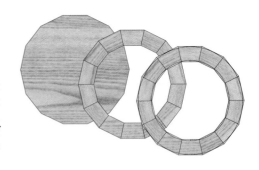

The 14 sided shape (Tetradecagon) is one of the "even numbered" shapes that's not very easy to get creative with, because a pair of points on the frame will point toward a pair of parallel sides on a picture. The one thing that should be considered when using this shape (with sides of equal length) is that for most standard sizes of pictures, a lot of cropping of the picture corners will be required. However, the Tetradecagon is a fun frame to build using sides of equal length for your frame.

The Illustrations to the right should give you an idea of the amount of cropping required using a Tetradecagon (with equal length sides) as your choice of shape for a frame.

In the left Illustration, you see a scale (shown in red) 8" x 10" sheet in portrait format. The sheet border is slightly outside the rabbeted area (shown in yellow) of the frame. Note the amount of material that would need to be cropped off the sheet top and/or bottom.

In the right Illustration, you see the same size sheet, but rotated 90° into a landscape format. Note a different amount of material would need to be cropped off the sheet sides.

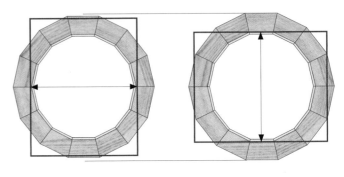

Portrait   **Landscape**

You should note that the frames to the right are not the same size. This is due to the fact that on a Tetradecagon, two sides are parallel to the picture edges, and two points meet at the other two sides of the picture. In our **14 SIDED FRAME FORMULAS** below, you will be able to see that the dimensions for both formats for the pictures are not identical.

If the project you are building is a frame for a specific size object, you should refer to the **14 SIDED FRAME FORMULAS** Chart below as a first step. On a Tetradecagon (with sides of equal length) the height will not be identical to the width. The picture width is the controlling dimension in a portrait format, and the height is the controlling dimension in a landscape format.

Though the Tetradecagon is one of the hardest of the Polygons to get creative with, you can build a very pretty frame if you use just two different side lengths to make a specific size frame for your picture(s).

14 SIDED FRAME FORMULAS		
WIDTH	**HEIGHT**	**SIDE LENGTH**
Width = Side Length x 4.49	Height = Side Length x 4.37	Side Length = Width x .223
Width = Height x 1.031	Height = Width x .970	Side Length = Height x .229

Though the information above is very helpful, one of the most time consuming (and frustrating) things about building frames is to try to cut to a dimension that is not measured on either the inside or outside edge of the molding. I like to cut miters from the inside to the outside edges of the molding. This not only allows me to eliminate tear out on the inside corners of the frame since I am cutting into the inside edge, I am also cutting with the grain of the molding. It also allows me to see the outside edge of the material as I cut it. To help you understand how easy it is to convert a dimension along the rabbeted edge into an outside measurement, I will explain how we can use some basic math to help us determine the outside length of our frame sides. The Illustration below should be helpful in showing you how we designed our **14 SIDED FRAME ADDED WIDTH AND LENGTH CHART** on the next page.

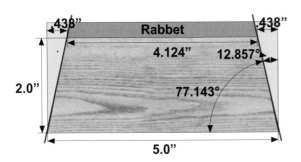

The Illustration to the left represents a piece of wood that is 5" long and 2" wide (to the edge of the rabbet). Note that on the right side that the end of the piece shows the miter angle for a Tetradecagon (12.857°) and the resulting angle of the cut (77.143°).

You should also note that at the rabbet, the cuts shorten each end of the piece by .438". Since both ends of the piece are cut, this means that the length at the rabbet is 4.124", which is .876" shorter than the outside edge of the molding. What this Illustration tells us is at a 12.857° cut, we will add .876" to the length at a 2" width. This is the basis of our formula.

If we divide the **Added Length** (.876") by the **Added Width** (2.0") we end up with .438 as our multiplier. In the event that you want to make a frame and need to work in fractions smaller than 1/16 increments, you would multiply the width of the molding outside the rabbet by .438. To determine the decimal equivalent of the fractions you need to use, refer to the **FRACTION TO DECIMAL CONVERSION CHART** provided.

If you are able to use 1/16" increments for the mathematics of your frames, you should use the **14 SIDED FRAME ADDED WIDTH AND LENGTH CHART** below.

Determine how wide you want the material to be (outside the rabbet). Refer to the Chart below to find this dimension in one of the yellow shaded columns. The added length for that width will be shown in the green shaded block to the right of it. Add this dimension to the side length determined in the first step. You should then add whatever waste you want to allow for each side. This total is then multiplied by14 to determine how much material is needed to build your project.

14 SIDED FRAME ADDED WIDTH AND LENGTH CHART

Added Width	Added Length	Added Width	Added Length	Added Width	Added Length	Added Width	Added Length	Added Width	Added Length
1/16	0	1 1/16	7/16	2 1/16	14/16	3 1/16	1 5/16	4 1/16	1 12/16
2/16	1/16	1 2/16	8/16	2 2/16	15/16	3 2/16	1 6/16	4 2/16	1 13/16
3/16	1/16	1 3/16	8/16	2 3/16	15/16	3 3/16	1 6/16	4 3/16	1 13/16
4/16	2/16	1 4/16	9/16	2 4/16	1	3 4/16	1 7/16	4 4/16	1 14/16
5/16	2/16	1 5/16	9/16	2 5/16	1	3 5/16	1 7/16	4 5/16	1 14/16
6/16	3/16	1 6/16	10/16	2 6/16	1 1/16	3 6/16	1 8/16	4 6/16	1 15/16
7/16	3/16	1 7/16	10/16	2 7/16	1 1/16	3 7/16	1 8/16	4 7/16	1 15/16
8/16	4/16	1 8/16	11/16	2 8/16	1 2/16	3 8/16	1 9/16	4 8/16	2
9/16	4/16	1 9/16	11/16	2 9/16	1 2/16	3 9/16	1 9/16	4 9/16	2
10/16	4/16	1 10/16	11/16	2 10/16	1 2/16	3 10/16	1 9/16	4 10/16	2
11/16	5/16	1 11/16	12/16	2 11/16	1 3/16	3 11/16	1 10/16	4 11/16	2 1/16
12/16	5/16	1 12/16	12/16	2 12/16	1 3/16	3 12/16	1 10/16	4 12/16	2 1/16
13/16	6/16	1 13/16	13/16	2 13/16	1 4/16	3 13/16	1 11/16	4 13/16	2 2/16
14/16	6/16	1 14/16	13/16	2 14/16	1 4/16	3 14/16	1 11/16	4 14/16	2 2/16
15/16	7/16	1 15/16	14/16	2 15/16	1 5/16	3 15/16	1 12/16	4 15/16	2 3/16
1	7/16	2	14/16	3	1 5/16	4	1 12/16	5	2 3/16

The Chart below is provided to enable you to make 14 sided frames using the mathematics of most popular picture sizes. Note that the dimensions are not the same in portrait and landscape format. This is because the point-to-point dimension of the frame is larger than the side-to-side dimension. In the Charts, the different colored columns represent the following information:

Red: The controlling dimension of the sheet size. (width in portrait, height in landscape)
Gray: The dimension of the sheet size that will need to be cropped.

White: The rabbet length for the frame sides.
Orange: The size of the opening in the direction the picture will need to be cropped.
Blue: The amount of material that will need to be cropped.

RABBET AREA DIMENSIONS FOR 14 SIDED FRAMES

FOR PORTRAIT FORMAT					FOR LANDSCAPE FORMAT				
Object Width	Object Height	Rabbet Length	Opening Height	Vertical Crop	Object Width	Object Height	Rabbet Length	Opening Width	Horizontal Crop
4	5	15/16	4 2/16	1	5	4	15/16	4 2/16	1
5	7	1 2/16	5 2/16	2	7	5	1 3/16	5 2/16	2
6	8	1 6/16	6 2/16	2	8	6	1 6/16	6 2/16	2
8	10	1 13/16	8 2/16	2	10	8	1 14/16	8 2/16	2
8 1/2	11	1 15/16	8 10/16	2 8/16	11	8 1/2	2	8 10/16	2 8/16
10	14	2 4/16	10 2/16	4	14	10	2 5/16	10 2/16	4
11	14	2 8/16	11 2/16	3	14	11	2 9/16	11 2/16	3
12	16	2 11/16	12 2/16	4	16	12	2 12/16	12 2/16	4
16	20	3 10/16	16 2/16	4	20	16	3 11/16	16 2/16	4
18	24	4 1/16	18 2/16	6	24	18	4 2/16	18 2/16	6
20	24	4 8/16	20 2/16	4	24	20	4 10/16	20 2/16	4
24	30	5 6/16	24 2/16	6	30	24	5 8/16	24 2/16	6

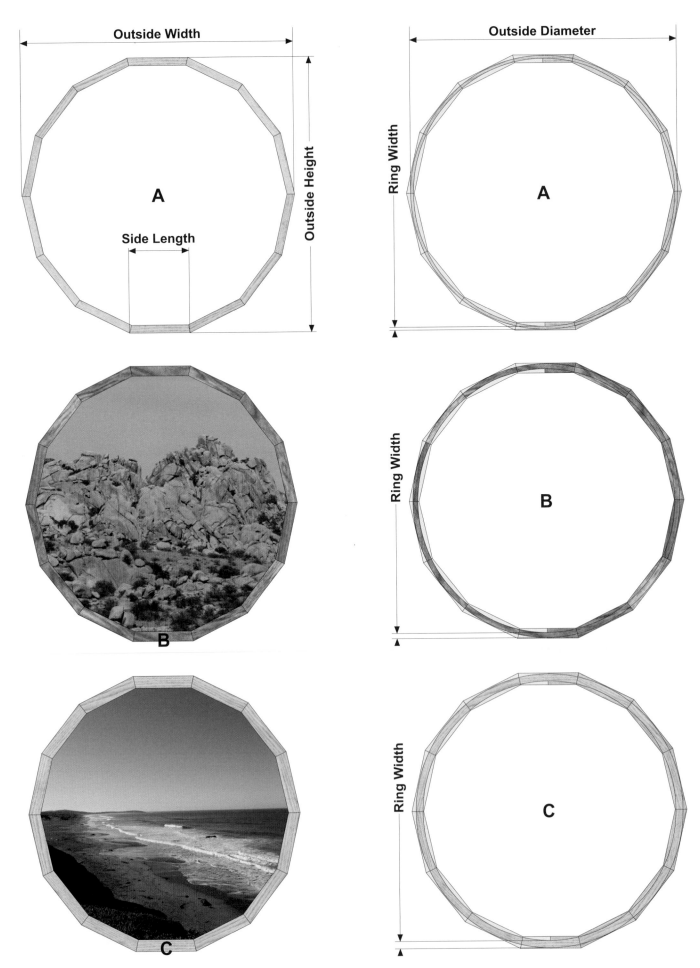

Side Length	Frame Width	Frame Height	Ring Max. OD	Material Req'd.	A Side Width	A Ring Width	B Side Width	B Ring Width	C Side Width	C Ring Width
8/16	2 4/16	2 3/16	2 3/16	10 8/16	1/16		1/16	1/16	2/16	1/16
10/16	2 13/16	2 12/16	2 11/16	12 4/16	1/16		2/16	1/16	2/16	1/16
12/16	3 6/16	3 4/16	3 4/16	14	2/16		2/16	1/16	2/16	1/16
14/16	3 15/16	3 13/16	3 13/16	15 12/16	2/16	1/16	2/16	1/16	3/16	2/16
1	4 8/16	4 6/16	4 6/16	17 8/16	2/16	1/16	3/16	1/16	3/16	2/16
1 4/16	5 10/16	5 7/16	5 7/16	21	3/16	1/16	3/16	2/16	4/16	2/16
1 8/16	6 12/16	6 9/16	6 8/16	24 8/16	3/16	1/16	4/16	2/16	5/16	3/16
1 12/16	7 14/16	7 10/16	7 10/16	28	4/16	1/16	4/16	2/16	5/16	3/16
2	9	8 12/16	8 11/16	31 8/16	4/16	1/16	5/16	2/16	6/16	3/16
2 4/16	10 2/16	9 13/16	9 12/16	35	5/16	2/16	6/16	3/16	7/16	4/16
2 8/16	11 4/16	10 15/16	10 14/16	38 8/16	5/16	2/16	6/16	3/16	8/16	4/16
2 12/16	12 6/16	12	11 15/16	42	6/16	2/16	7/16	3/16	8/16	5/16
3	13 8/16	13 2/16	13 1/16	45 8/16	6/16	2/16	8/16	4/16	9/16	5/16
3 4/16	14 9/16	14 3/16	14 2/16	49	7/16	2/16	8/16	4/16	10/16	6/16
3 8/16	15 11/16	15 5/16	15 3/16	52 8/16	7/16	3/16	9/16	4/16	11/16	6/16
3 12/16	16 13/16	16 6/16	16 5/16	56	8/16	3/16	9/16	5/16	11/16	7/16
4	17 15/16	17 8/16	17 6/16	59 8/16	8/16	3/16	10/16	5/16	12/16	7/16
4 4/16	19 1/16	18 9/16	18 7/16	63	9/16	3/16	11/16	5/16	13/16	7/16
4 8/16	20 3/16	19 11/16	19 9/16	66 8/16	9/16	3/16	11/16	6/16	14/16	8/16
4 12/16	21 5/16	20 12/16	20 10/16	70	10/16	3/16	12/16	6/16	14/16	8/16
5	22 7/16	21 14/16	21 12/16	73 8/16	10/16	4/16	13/16	6/16	15/16	9/16
5 4/16	23 9/16	22 15/16	22 13/16	77	11/16	4/16	13/16	6/16	1	9/16
5 8/16	24 11/16	24 1/16	23 14/16	80 8/16	11/16	4/16	14/16	7/16	1 1/16	10/16
5 12/16	25 13/16	25 2/16	25	84	12/16	4/16	14/16	7/16	1 1/16	10/16
6	26 15/16	26 4/16	26 1/16	87 8/16	12/16	4/16	15/16	7/16	1 2/16	10/16
6 8/16	29 3/16	28 6/16	28 4/16	94 8/16	13/16	5/16	1	8/16	1 4/16	11/16
7	31 7/16	30 9/16	30 7/16	101 8/16	14/16	5/16	1 2/16	9/16	1 5/16	12/16
7 8/16	33 11/16	32 12/16	32 9/16	108 8/16	15/16	6/16	1 3/16	9/16	1 7/16	13/16
8	35 15/16	34 15/16	34 12/16	115 8/16	1	6/16	1 4/16	10/16	1 8/16	14/16
8 8/16	38 3/16	37 2/16	36 15/16	122 8/16	1 1/16	6/16	1 5/16	11/16	1 10/16	15/16
9	40 7/16	39 5/16	39 2/16	129 8/16	1 2/16	7/16	1 7/16	11/16	1 11/16	1
9 8/16	42 10/16	41 8/16	41 4/16	136 8/16	1 3/16	7/16	1 8/16	12/16	1 13/16	1 1/16
10	44 14/16	43 11/16	43 7/16	143 8/16	1 4/16	7/16	1 9/16	12/16	1 14/16	1 1/16
10 8/16	47 2/16	45 14/16	45 10/16	150 8/16	1 5/16	8/16	1 10/16	13/16	2	1 2/16
11	49 6/16	48 1/16	47 13/16	157 8/16	1 6/16	8/16	1 12/16	14/16	2 1/16	1 3/16
11 8/16	51 10/16	50 4/16	49 15/16	164 8/16	1 7/16	8/16	1 13/16	14/16	2 3/16	1 4/16
12	53 14/16	52 7/16	52 2/16	171 8/16	1 8/16	9/16	1 14/16	15/16	2 4/16	1 5/16
13	58 6/16	56 13/16	56 8/16	185 8/16	1 10/16	10/16	2 1/16	1	2 7/16	1 7/16
14	62 14/16	61 3/16	60 13/16	199 8/16	1 12/16	10/16	2 3/16	1 1/16	2 10/16	1 8/16
15	67 6/16	65 9/16	65 3/16	213 8/16	1 14/16	11/16	2 6/16	1 3/16	2 13/16	1 10/16
16	71 13/16	69 15/16	69 8/16	227 8/16	2	12/16	2 8/16	1 4/16	3	1 12/16
17	76 5/16	74 5/16	73 14/16	241 8/16	2 2/16	12/16	2 11/16	1 5/16	3 3/16	1 14/16
18	80 13/16	78 11/16	78 3/16	255 8/16	2 4/16	13/16	2 13/16	1 6/16	3 6/16	1 15/16
19	85 5/16	83	82 9/16	269 8/16	2 6/16	14/16	3	1 8/16	3 9/16	2 1/16
20	89 13/16	87 6/16	86 14/16	283 8/16	2 8/16	15/16	3 2/16	1 9/16	3 12/16	2 3/16
21	94 5/16	91 12/16	91 4/16	297 8/16	2 10/16	15/16	3 5/16	1 10/16	3 15/16	2 5/16
22	98 12/16	96 2/16	95 9/16	311 8/16	2 12/16	1	3 7/16	1 11/16	4 2/16	2 6/16
23	103 4/16	100 8/16	99 15/16	325 8/16	2 14/16	1 1/16	3 10/16	1 12/16	4 5/16	2 8/16
24	107 12/16	104 14/16	104 4/16	339 8/16	3	1 2/16	3 12/16	1 14/16	4 8/16	2 10/16
25	112 4/16	109 4/16	108 10/16	353 8/16	3 2/16	1 2/16	3 15/16	1 15/16	4 11/16	2 12/16
26	116 12/16	113 10/16	112 15/16	367 8/16	3 4/16	1 3/16	4 1/16	2	4 14/16	2 13/16
27	121 4/16	118	117 5/16	381 8/16	3 6/16	1 4/16	4 4/16	2 1/16	5 1/16	2 15/16
28	125 12/16	122 6/16	121 10/16	395 8/16	3 8/16	1 5/16	4 6/16	2 3/16	5 4/16	3 1/16

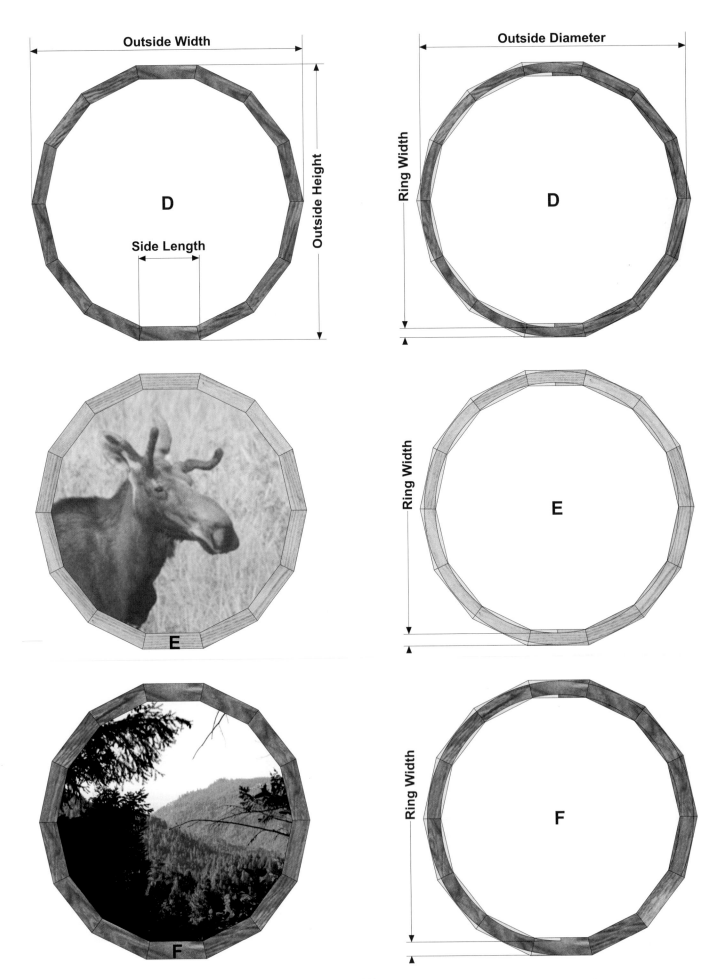

142

Side Length	Frame Width	Frame Height	Ring Max. OD	Material Req'd.	D Side Width	D Ring Width	E Side Width	E Ring Width	F Side Width	F Ring Width
8/16	2 4/16	2 3/16	2 3/16	10 8/16	2/16	1/16	2/16	1/16	2/16	2/16
10/16	2 13/16	2 12/16	2 11/16	12 4/16	2/16	1/16	3/16	2/16	3/16	2/16
12/16	3 6/16	3 4/16	3 4/16	14	3/16	2/16	3/16	2/16	3/16	2/16
14/16	3 15/16	3 13/16	3 13/16	15 12/16	3/16	2/16	4/16	2/16	4/16	3/16
1	4 8/16	4 6/16	4 6/16	17 8/16	4/16	2/16	4/16	3/16	5/16	3/16
1 4/16	5 10/16	5 7/16	5 7/16	21	4/16	3/16	5/16	3/16	6/16	4/16
1 8/16	6 12/16	6 9/16	6 8/16	24 8/16	5/16	3/16	6/16	4/16	7/16	5/16
1 12/16	7 14/16	7 10/16	7 10/16	28	6/16	4/16	7/16	5/16	8/16	6/16
2	9	8 12/16	8 11/16	31 8/16	7/16	4/16	8/16	6/16	9/16	7/16
2 4/16	10 2/16	9 13/16	9 12/16	35	8/16	5/16	9/16	6/16	10/16	7/16
2 8/16	11 4/16	10 15/16	10 14/16	38 8/16	9/16	6/16	10/16	7/16	11/16	8/16
2 12/16	12 6/16	12	11 15/16	42	10/16	6/16	11/16	8/16	12/16	9/16
3	13 8/16	13 2/16	13 1/16	45 8/16	11/16	7/16	12/16	8/16	14/16	10/16
3 4/16	14 9/16	14 3/16	14 2/16	49	11/16	7/16	13/16	9/16	15/16	11/16
3 8/16	15 11/16	15 5/16	15 3/16	52 8/16	12/16	8/16	14/16	10/16	1	11/16
3 12/16	16 13/16	16 6/16	16 5/16	56	13/16	8/16	15/16	10/16	1 1/16	12/16
4	17 15/16	17 8/16	17 6/16	59 8/16	14/16	9/16	1	11/16	1 2/16	13/16
4 4/16	19 1/16	18 9/16	18 7/16	63	15/16	10/16	1 1/16	12/16	1 3/16	14/16
4 8/16	20 3/16	19 11/16	19 9/16	66 8/16	1	10/16	1 2/16	12/16	1 4/16	15/16
4 12/16	21 5/16	20 12/16	20 10/16	70	1 1/16	11/16	1 3/16	13/16	1 5/16	1
5	22 7/16	21 14/16	21 12/16	73 8/16	1 2/16	11/16	1 4/16	14/16	1 7/16	1
5 4/16	23 9/16	22 15/16	22 13/16	77	1 2/16	12/16	1 5/16	14/16	1 8/16	1 1/16
5 8/16	24 11/16	24 1/16	23 14/16	80 8/16	1 3/16	12/16	1 6/16	15/16	1 9/16	1 2/16
5 12/16	25 13/16	25 2/16	25	84	1 4/16	13/16	1 7/16	1	1 10/16	1 3/16
6	26 15/16	26 4/16	26 1/16	87 8/16	1 5/16	13/16	1 8/16	1 1/16	1 11/16	1 4/16
6 8/16	29 3/16	28 6/16	28 4/16	94 8/16	1 7/16	15/16	1 10/16	1 2/16	1 13/16	1 5/16
7	31 7/16	30 9/16	30 7/16	101 8/16	1 9/16	1	1 12/16	1 3/16	2	1 7/16
7 8/16	33 11/16	32 12/16	32 9/16	108 8/16	1 10/16	1 1/16	1 14/16	1 5/16	2 2/16	1 8/16
8	35 15/16	34 15/16	34 12/16	115 8/16	1 12/16	1 2/16	2	1 6/16	2 4/16	1 10/16
8 8/16	38 3/16	37 2/16	36 15/16	122 8/16	1 14/16	1 3/16	2 2/16	1 7/16	2 6/16	1 12/16
9	40 7/16	39 5/16	39 2/16	129 8/16	2	1 4/16	2 4/16	1 9/16	2 9/16	1 13/16
9 8/16	42 10/16	41 8/16	41 4/16	136 8/16	2 1/16	1 5/16	2 6/16	1 10/16	2 11/16	1 15/16
10	44 14/16	43 11/16	43 7/16	143 8/16	2 3/16	1 6/16	2 8/16	1 12/16	2 13/16	2 1/16
10 8/16	47 2/16	45 14/16	45 10/16	150 8/16	2 5/16	1 8/16	2 10/16	1 13/16	2 15/16	2 2/16
11	49 6/16	48 1/16	47 13/16	157 8/16	2 7/16	1 9/16	2 12/16	1 14/16	3 2/16	2 4/16
11 8/16	51 10/16	50 4/16	49 15/16	164 8/16	2 8/16	1 10/16	2 14/16	2	3 4/16	2 6/16
12	53 14/16	52 7/16	52 2/16	171 8/16	2 10/16	1 11/16	3	2 1/16	3 6/16	2 7/16
13	58 6/16	56 13/16	56 8/16	185 8/16	2 14/16	1 13/16	3 4/16	2 4/16	3 11/16	2 10/16
14	62 14/16	61 3/16	60 13/16	199 8/16	3 1/16	1 15/16	3 8/16	2 7/16	3 15/16	2 14/16
15	67 6/16	65 9/16	65 3/16	213 8/16	3 5/16	2 2/16	3 12/16	2 9/16	4 4/16	3 1/16
16	71 13/16	69 15/16	69 8/16	227 8/16	3 8/16	2 4/16	4	2 12/16	4 8/16	3 4/16
17	76 5/16	74 5/16	73 14/16	241 8/16	3 12/16	2 6/16	4 4/16	2 15/16	4 13/16	3 7/16
18	80 13/16	78 11/16	78 3/16	255 8/16	3 15/16	2 8/16	4 8/16	3 2/16	5 1/16	3 11/16
19	85 5/16	83	82 9/16	269 8/16	4 3/16	2 11/16	4 12/16	3 4/16	5 6/16	3 14/16
20	89 13/16	87 6/16	86 14/16	283 8/16	4 6/16	2 13/16	5	3 7/16	5 10/16	4 1/16
21	94 5/16	91 12/16	91 4/16	297 8/16	4 10/16	2 15/16	5 4/16	3 10/16	5 15/16	4 5/16
22	98 12/16	96 2/16	95 9/16	311 8/16	4 13/16	3 1/16	5 8/16	3 13/16	6 3/16	4 8/16
23	103 4/16	100 8/16	99 15/16	325 8/16	5 1/16	3 4/16	5 12/16	3 15/16	6 8/16	4 11/16
24	107 12/16	104 14/16	104 4/16	339 8/16	5 4/16	3 6/16	6	4 2/16	6 12/16	4 14/16
25	112 4/16	109 4/16	108 10/16	353 8/16	5 8/16	3 8/16	6 4/16	4 5/16	7 1/16	5 2/16
26	116 12/16	113 10/16	112 15/16	367 8/16	5 11/16	3 10/16	6 8/16	4 8/16	7 5/16	5 5/16
27	121 4/16	118	117 5/16	381 8/16	5 15/16	3 13/16	6 12/16	4 10/16	7 10/16	5 8/16
28	125 12/16	122 6/16	121 10/16	395 8/16	6 2/16	3 15/16	7	4 13/16	7 14/16	5 11/16

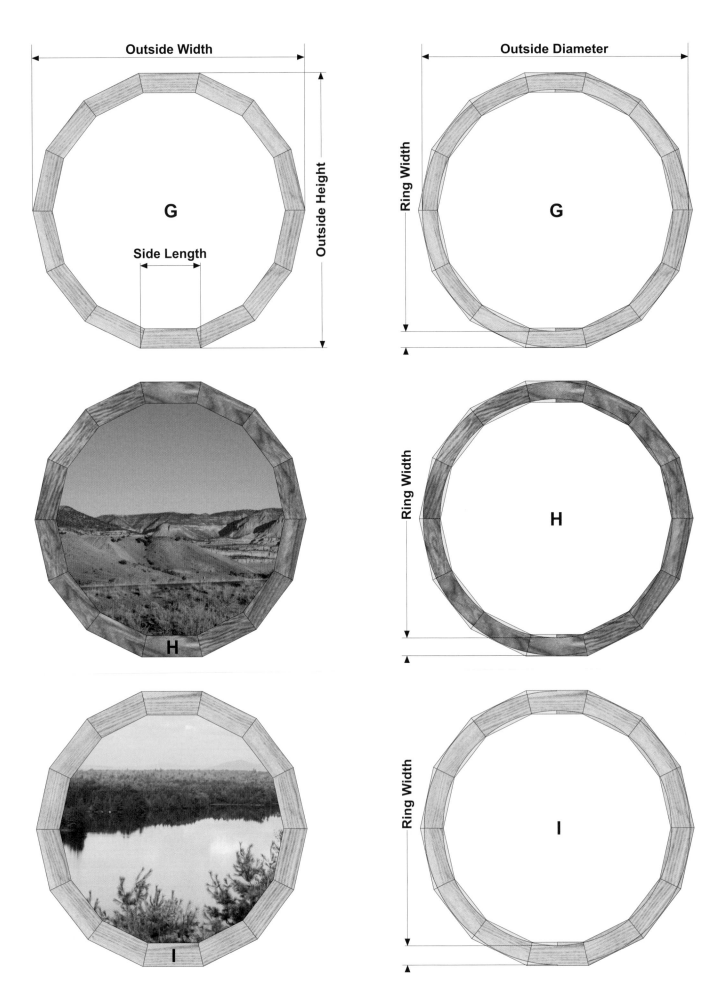

Side Length	Frame Width	Frame Height	Ring Max. OD	Material Req'd.	G Side Width	G Ring Width	H Side Width	H Ring Width	I Side Width	I Ring Width
8/16	2 4/16	2 3/16	2 3/16	10 8/16	3/16	2/16	3/16	2/16	3/16	2/16
10/16	2 13/16	2 12/16	2 11/16	12 4/16	3/16	2/16	3/16	3/16	4/16	3/16
12/16	3 6/16	3 4/16	3 4/16	14	4/16	3/16	4/16	3/16	5/16	4/16
14/16	3 15/16	3 13/16	3 13/16	15 12/16	4/16	3/16	5/16	4/16	5/16	4/16
1	4 8/16	4 6/16	4 6/16	17 8/16	5/16	4/16	6/16	4/16	6/16	5/16
1 4/16	5 10/16	5 7/16	5 7/16	21	6/16	5/16	7/16	5/16	8/16	6/16
1 8/16	6 12/16	6 9/16	6 8/16	24 8/16	8/16	6/16	8/16	6/16	9/16	7/16
1 12/16	7 14/16	7 10/16	7 10/16	28	9/16	7/16	10/16	7/16	11/16	8/16
2	9	8 12/16	8 11/16	31 8/16	10/16	8/16	11/16	9/16	12/16	10/16
2 4/16	10 2/16	9 13/16	9 12/16	35	11/16	8/16	12/16	10/16	14/16	11/16
2 8/16	11 4/16	10 15/16	10 14/16	38 8/16	13/16	9/16	14/16	11/16	15/16	12/16
2 12/16	12 6/16	12	11 15/16	42	14/16	10/16	15/16	12/16	1 1/16	13/16
3	13 8/16	13 2/16	13 1/16	45 8/16	15/16	11/16	1 1/16	13/16	1 2/16	14/16
3 4/16	14 9/16	14 3/16	14 2/16	49	1	12/16	1 2/16	14/16	1 4/16	1
3 8/16	15 11/16	15 5/16	15 3/16	52 8/16	1 2/16	13/16	1 3/16	15/16	1 5/16	1 1/16
3 12/16	16 13/16	16 6/16	16 5/16	56	1 3/16	14/16	1 5/16	1	1 7/16	1 2/16
4	17 15/16	17 8/16	17 6/16	59 8/16	1 4/16	15/16	1 6/16	1 1/16	1 8/16	1 3/16
4 4/16	19 1/16	18 9/16	18 7/16	63	1 5/16	1	1 7/16	1 2/16	1 10/16	1 4/16
4 8/16	20 3/16	19 11/16	19 9/16	66 8/16	1 7/16	1 1/16	1 9/16	1 3/16	1 11/16	1 6/16
4 12/16	21 5/16	20 12/16	20 10/16	70	1 8/16	1 2/16	1 10/16	1 4/16	1 13/16	1 7/16
5	22 7/16	21 14/16	21 12/16	73 8/16	1 9/16	1 3/16	1 12/16	1 5/16	1 14/16	1 8/16
5 4/16	23 9/16	22 15/16	22 13/16	77	1 10/16	1 4/16	1 13/16	1 6/16	2	1 9/16
5 8/16	24 11/16	24 1/16	23 14/16	80 8/16	1 12/16	1 5/16	1 14/16	1 8/16	2 1/16	1 10/16
5 12/16	25 13/16	25 2/16	25	84	1 13/16	1 6/16	2	1 9/16	2 3/16	1 11/16
6	26 15/16	26 4/16	26 1/16	87 8/16	1 14/16	1 7/16	2 1/16	1 10/16	2 4/16	1 13/16
6 8/16	29 3/16	28 6/16	28 4/16	94 8/16	2 1/16	1 8/16	2 4/16	1 12/16	2 7/16	1 15/16
7	31 7/16	30 9/16	30 7/16	101 8/16	2 3/16	1 10/16	2 7/16	1 14/16	2 10/16	2 1/16
7 8/16	33 11/16	32 12/16	32 9/16	108 8/16	2 6/16	1 12/16	2 9/16	2	2 13/16	2 4/16
8	35 15/16	34 15/16	34 12/16	115 8/16	2 8/16	1 14/16	2 12/16	2 2/16	3	2 6/16
8 8/16	38 3/16	37 2/16	36 15/16	122 8/16	2 11/16	2	2 15/16	2 4/16	3 3/16	2 9/16
9	40 7/16	39 5/16	39 2/16	129 8/16	2 13/16	2 2/16	3 2/16	2 6/16	3 6/16	2 11/16
9 8/16	42 10/16	41 8/16	41 4/16	136 8/16	3	2 4/16	3 4/16	2 9/16	3 9/16	2 13/16
10	44 14/16	43 11/16	43 7/16	143 8/16	3 2/16	2 6/16	3 7/16	2 11/16	3 12/16	3
10 8/16	47 2/16	45 14/16	45 10/16	150 8/16	3 5/16	2 8/16	3 10/16	2 13/16	3 15/16	3 2/16
11	49 6/16	48 1/16	47 13/16	157 8/16	3 7/16	2 9/16	3 13/16	2 15/16	4 2/16	3 5/16
11 8/16	51 10/16	50 4/16	49 15/16	164 8/16	3 10/16	2 11/16	3 15/16	3 1/16	4 5/16	3 7/16
12	53 14/16	52 7/16	52 2/16	171 8/16	3 12/16	2 13/16	4 2/16	3 3/16	4 8/16	3 9/16
13	58 6/16	56 13/16	56 8/16	185 8/16	4 1/16	3 1/16	4 8/16	3 8/16	4 14/16	3 14/16
14	62 14/16	61 3/16	60 13/16	199 8/16	4 6/16	3 5/16	4 13/16	3 12/16	5 4/16	4 3/16
15	67 6/16	65 9/16	65 3/16	213 8/16	4 11/16	3 9/16	5 3/16	4	5 10/16	4 8/16
16	71 13/16	69 15/16	69 8/16	227 8/16	5	3 12/16	5 8/16	4 4/16	6	4 12/16
17	76 5/16	74 5/16	73 14/16	241 8/16	5 5/16	4	5 14/16	4 9/16	6 6/16	5 1/16
18	80 13/16	78 11/16	78 3/16	255 8/16	5 10/16	4 4/16	6 3/16	4 13/16	6 12/16	5 6/16
19	85 5/16	83	82 9/16	269 8/16	5 15/16	4 8/16	6 9/16	5 1/16	7 2/16	5 11/16
20	89 13/16	87 6/16	86 14/16	283 8/16	6 4/16	4 11/16	6 14/16	5 6/16	7 8/16	6
21	94 5/16	91 12/16	91 4/16	297 8/16	6 9/16	4 15/16	7 4/16	5 10/16	7 14/16	6 4/16
22	98 12/16	96 2/16	95 9/16	311 8/16	6 14/16	5 3/16	7 9/16	5 14/16	8 4/16	6 9/16
23	103 4/16	100 8/16	99 15/16	325 8/16	7 3/16	5 7/16	7 15/16	6 2/16	8 10/16	6 14/16
24	107 12/16	104 14/16	104 4/16	339 8/16	7 8/16	5 10/16	8 4/16	6 7/16	9	7 3/16
25	112 4/16	109 4/16	108 10/16	353 8/16	7 13/16	5 14/16	8 10/16	6 11/16	9 6/16	7 7/16
26	116 12/16	113 10/16	112 15/16	367 8/16	8 2/16	6 2/16	8 15/16	6 15/16	9 12/16	7 12/16
27	121 4/16	118	117 5/16	381 8/16	8 7/16	6 6/16	9 5/16	7 3/16	10 2/16	8 1/16
28	125 12/16	122 6/16	121 10/16	395 8/16	8 12/16	6 9/16	9 10/16	7 8/16	10 8/16	8 6/16

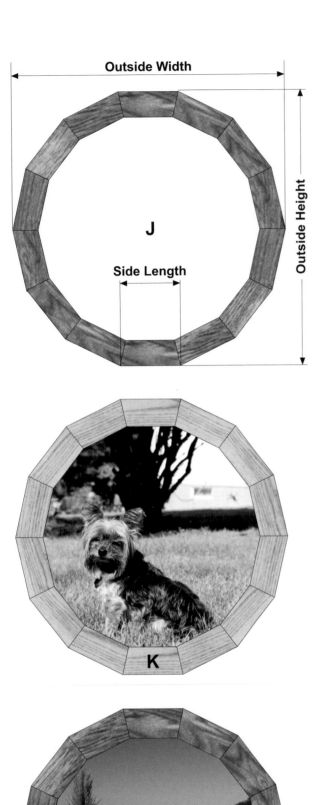

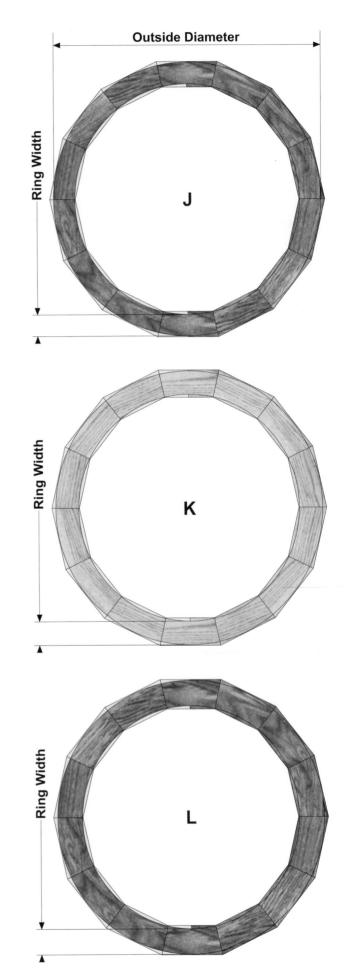

Outside Width

Outside Height

Side Length

J

Outside Diameter

Ring Width

J

Ring Width

K

K

L

Ring Width

L

Side Length	Frame Width	Frame Height	Ring Max. OD	Material Req'd.	J Side Width	J Ring Width	K Side Width	K Ring Width	L Side Width	L Ring Width
8/16	2 4/16	2 3/16	2 3/16	10 8/16	3/16	3/16	4/16	3/16	4/16	3/16
10/16	2 13/16	2 12/16	2 11/16	12 4/16	4/16	3/16	4/16	4/16	5/16	4/16
12/16	3 6/16	3 4/16	3 4/16	14	5/16	4/16	5/16	4/16	6/16	5/16
14/16	3 15/16	3 13/16	3 13/16	15 12/16	6/16	5/16	6/16	5/16	7/16	6/16
1	4 8/16	4 6/16	4 6/16	17 8/16	7/16	5/16	7/16	6/16	8/16	6/16
1 4/16	5 10/16	5 7/16	5 7/16	21	8/16	7/16	9/16	7/16	9/16	8/16
1 8/16	6 12/16	6 9/16	6 8/16	24 8/16	10/16	8/16	11/16	9/16	11/16	9/16
1 12/16	7 14/16	7 10/16	7 10/16	28	11/16	9/16	12/16	10/16	13/16	11/16
2	9	8 12/16	8 11/16	31 8/16	13/16	11/16	14/16	12/16	15/16	13/16
2 4/16	10 2/16	9 13/16	9 12/16	35	15/16	12/16	1	13/16	1 1/16	14/16
2 8/16	11 4/16	10 15/16	10 14/16	38 8/16	1	13/16	1 2/16	14/16	1 3/16	1
2 12/16	12 6/16	12	11 15/16	42	1 2/16	15/16	1 3/16	1	1 5/16	1 1/16
3	13 8/16	13 2/16	13 1/16	45 8/16	1 4/16	1	1 5/16	1 1/16	1 7/16	1 3/16
3 4/16	14 9/16	14 3/16	14 2/16	49	1 5/16	1 1/16	1 7/16	1 3/16	1 8/16	1 4/16
3 8/16	15 11/16	15 5/16	15 3/16	52 8/16	1 7/16	1 3/16	1 9/16	1 4/16	1 10/16	1 6/16
3 12/16	16 13/16	16 6/16	16 5/16	56	1 8/16	1 4/16	1 10/16	1 6/16	1 12/16	1 8/16
4	17 15/16	17 8/16	17 6/16	59 8/16	1 10/16	1 5/16	1 12/16	1 7/16	1 14/16	1 9/16
4 4/16	19 1/16	18 9/16	18 7/16	63	1 12/16	1 6/16	1 14/16	1 9/16	2	1 11/16
4 8/16	20 3/16	19 11/16	19 9/16	66 8/16	1 13/16	1 8/16	2	1 10/16	2 2/16	1 12/16
4 12/16	21 5/16	20 12/16	20 10/16	70	1 15/16	1 9/16	2 1/16	1 12/16	2 4/16	1 14/16
5	22 7/16	21 14/16	21 12/16	73 8/16	2 1/16	1 10/16	2 3/16	1 13/16	2 6/16	1 15/16
5 4/16	23 9/16	22 15/16	22 13/16	77	2 2/16	1 12/16	2 5/16	1 14/16	2 7/16	2 1/16
5 8/16	24 11/16	24 1/16	23 14/16	80 8/16	2 4/16	1 13/16	2 7/16	2	2 9/16	2 3/16
5 12/16	25 13/16	25 2/16	25	84	2 5/16	1 14/16	2 8/16	2 1/16	2 11/16	2 4/16
6	26 15/16	26 4/16	26 1/16	87 8/16	2 7/16	2	2 10/16	2 3/16	2 13/16	2 6/16
6 8/16	29 3/16	28 6/16	28 4/16	94 8/16	2 10/16	2 2/16	2 14/16	2 6/16	3 1/16	2 9/16
7	31 7/16	30 9/16	30 7/16	101 8/16	2 14/16	2 5/16	3 1/16	2 9/16	3 5/16	2 12/16
7 8/16	33 11/16	32 12/16	32 9/16	108 8/16	3 1/16	2 8/16	3 5/16	2 11/16	3 8/16	2 15/16
8	35 15/16	34 15/16	34 12/16	115 8/16	3 4/16	2 10/16	3 8/16	2 14/16	3 12/16	3 2/16
8 8/16	38 3/16	37 2/16	36 15/16	122 8/16	3 7/16	2 13/16	3 12/16	3 1/16	4	3 6/16
9	40 7/16	39 5/16	39 2/16	129 8/16	3 11/16	3	3 15/16	3 4/16	4 4/16	3 9/16
9 8/16	42 10/16	41 8/16	41 4/16	136 8/16	3 14/16	3 2/16	4 3/16	3 7/16	4 7/16	3 12/16
10	44 14/16	43 11/16	43 7/16	143 8/16	4 1/16	3 5/16	4 6/16	3 10/16	4 11/16	3 15/16
10 8/16	47 2/16	45 14/16	45 10/16	150 8/16	4 4/16	3 8/16	4 10/16	3 13/16	4 15/16	4 2/16
11	49 6/16	48 1/16	47 13/16	157 8/16	4 8/16	3 10/16	4 13/16	4	5 3/16	4 5/16
11 8/16	51 10/16	50 4/16	49 15/16	164 8/16	4 11/16	3 13/16	5 1/16	4 3/16	5 6/16	4 8/16
12	53 14/16	52 7/16	52 2/16	171 8/16	4 14/16	3 15/16	5 4/16	4 6/16	5 10/16	4 12/16
13	58 6/16	56 13/16	56 8/16	185 8/16	5 5/16	4 5/16	5 11/16	4 11/16	6 2/16	5 2/16
14	62 14/16	61 3/16	60 13/16	199 8/16	5 11/16	4 10/16	6 2/16	5 1/16	6 9/16	5 8/16
15	67 6/16	65 9/16	65 3/16	213 8/16	6 2/16	4 15/16	6 9/16	5 7/16	7 1/16	5 14/16
16	71 13/16	69 15/16	69 8/16	227 8/16	6 8/16	5 5/16	7	5 13/16	7 8/16	6 5/16
17	76 5/16	74 5/16	73 14/16	241 8/16	6 15/16	5 10/16	7 7/16	6 2/16	8	6 11/16
18	80 13/16	78 11/16	78 3/16	255 8/16	7 5/16	5 15/16	7 14/16	6 8/16	8 7/16	7 1/16
19	85 5/16	83	82 9/16	269 8/16	7 12/16	6 4/16	8 5/16	6 14/16	8 15/16	7 8/16
20	89 13/16	87 6/16	86 14/16	283 8/16	8 2/16	6 10/16	8 12/16	7 4/16	9 6/16	7 14/16
21	94 5/16	91 12/16	91 4/16	297 8/16	8 9/16	6 15/16	9 3/16	7 10/16	9 14/16	8 4/16
22	98 12/16	96 2/16	95 9/16	311 8/16	8 15/16	7 4/16	9 10/16	7 15/16	10 5/16	8 11/16
23	103 4/16	100 8/16	99 15/16	325 8/16	9 6/16	7 10/16	10 1/16	8 5/16	10 13/16	9 1/16
24	107 12/16	104 14/16	104 4/16	339 8/16	9 12/16	7 15/16	10 8/16	8 11/16	11 4/16	9 7/16
25	112 4/16	109 4/16	108 10/16	353 8/16	10 3/16	8 4/16	10 15/16	9 1/16	11 12/16	9 13/16
26	116 12/16	113 10/16	112 15/16	367 8/16	10 9/16	8 9/16	11 6/16	9 7/16	12 3/16	10 4/16
27	121 4/16	118	117 5/16	381 8/16	11	8 15/16	11 13/16	9 12/16	12 11/16	10 10/16
28	125 12/16	122 6/16	121 10/16	395 8/16	11 6/16	9 4/16	12 4/16	10 2/16	13 2/16	11

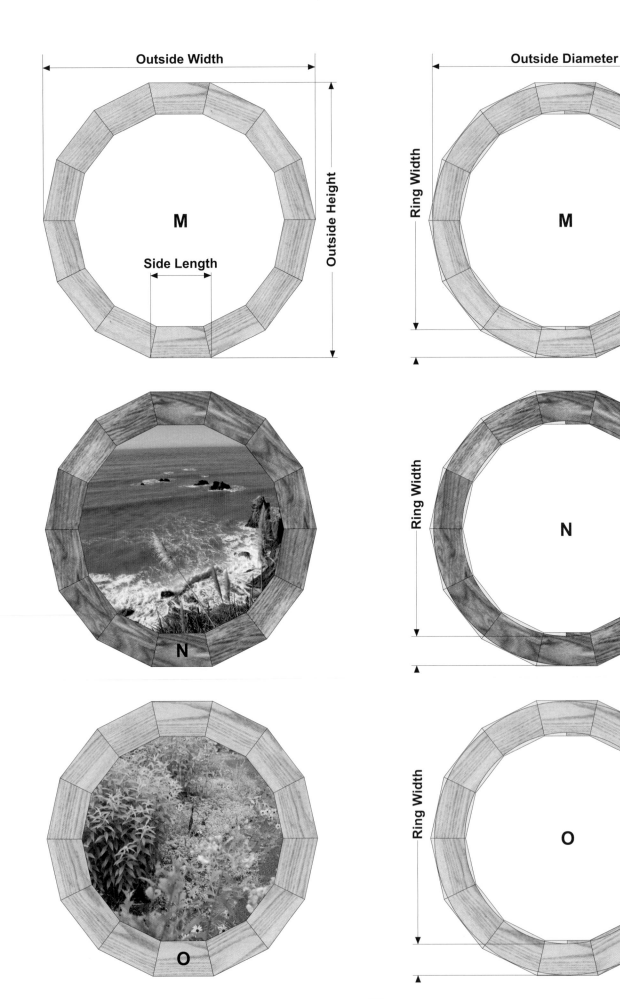

Side Length	Frame Width	Frame Height	Ring Max. OD	Material Req'd.	M Side Width	M Ring Width	N Side Width	N Ring Width	O Side Width	O Ring Width
8/16	2 4/16	2 3/16	2 3/16	10 8/16	4/16	3/16	4/16	4/16	5/16	4/16
10/16	2 13/16	2 12/16	2 11/16	12 4/16	5/16	4/16	5/16	5/16	6/16	5/16
12/16	3 6/16	3 4/16	3 4/16	14	6/16	5/16	6/16	5/16	7/16	6/16
14/16	3 15/16	3 13/16	3 13/16	15 12/16	7/16	6/16	7/16	6/16	8/16	7/16
1	4 8/16	4 6/16	4 6/16	17 8/16	8/16	7/16	9/16	7/16	9/16	8/16
1 4/16	5 10/16	5 7/16	5 7/16	21	10/16	9/16	11/16	9/16	11/16	10/16
1 8/16	6 12/16	6 9/16	6 8/16	24 8/16	12/16	10/16	13/16	11/16	14/16	12/16
1 12/16	7 14/16	7 10/16	7 10/16	28	14/16	12/16	15/16	13/16	1	14/16
2	9	8 12/16	8 11/16	31 8/16	1	14/16	1 1/16	15/16	1 2/16	1
2 4/16	10 2/16	9 13/16	9 12/16	35	1 2/16	15/16	1 3/16	1	1 4/16	1 2/16
2 8/16	11 4/16	10 15/16	10 14/16	38 8/16	1 4/16	1 1/16	1 5/16	1 2/16	1 7/16	1 4/16
2 12/16	12 6/16	12	11 15/16	42	1 6/16	1 3/16	1 7/16	1 4/16	1 9/16	1 5/16
3	13 8/16	13 2/16	13 1/16	45 8/16	1 8/16	1 4/16	1 10/16	1 6/16	1 11/16	1 7/16
3 4/16	14 9/16	14 3/16	14 2/16	49	1 10/16	1 6/16	1 12/16	1 8/16	1 13/16	1 9/16
3 8/16	15 11/16	15 5/16	15 3/16	52 8/16	1 12/16	1 8/16	1 14/16	1 10/16	2	1 11/16
3 12/16	16 13/16	16 6/16	16 5/16	56	1 14/16	1 10/16	2	1 11/16	2 2/16	1 13/16
4	17 15/16	17 8/16	17 6/16	59 8/16	2	1 11/16	2 2/16	1 13/16	2 4/16	1 15/16
4 4/16	19 1/16	18 9/16	18 7/16	63	2 2/16	1 13/16	2 4/16	1 15/16	2 6/16	2 1/16
4 8/16	20 3/16	19 11/16	19 9/16	66 8/16	2 4/16	1 15/16	2 6/16	2 1/16	2 9/16	2 3/16
4 12/16	21 5/16	20 12/16	20 10/16	70	2 6/16	2	2 8/16	2 3/16	2 11/16	2 5/16
5	22 7/16	21 14/16	21 12/16	73 8/16	2 8/16	2 2/16	2 11/16	2 5/16	2 13/16	2 7/16
5 4/16	23 9/16	22 15/16	22 13/16	77	2 10/16	2 4/16	2 13/16	2 6/16	2 15/16	2 9/16
5 8/16	24 11/16	24 1/16	23 14/16	80 8/16	2 12/16	2 5/16	2 15/16	2 8/16	3 2/16	2 11/16
5 12/16	25 13/16	25 2/16	25	84	2 14/16	2 7/16	3 1/16	2 10/16	3 4/16	2 13/16
6	26 15/16	26 4/16	26 1/16	87 8/16	3	2 9/16	3 3/16	2 12/16	3 6/16	2 15/16
6 8/16	29 3/16	28 6/16	28 4/16	94 8/16	3 4/16	2 12/16	3 7/16	3	3 11/16	3 3/16
7	31 7/16	30 9/16	30 7/16	101 8/16	3 8/16	3	3 12/16	3 3/16	3 15/16	3 7/16
7 8/16	33 11/16	32 12/16	32 9/16	108 8/16	3 12/16	3 3/16	4	3 7/16	4 4/16	3 11/16
8	35 15/16	34 15/16	34 12/16	115 8/16	4	3 6/16	4 4/16	3 11/16	4 8/16	3 15/16
8 8/16	38 3/16	37 2/16	36 15/16	122 8/16	4 4/16	3 10/16	4 8/16	3 14/16	4 13/16	4 2/16
9	40 7/16	39 5/16	39 2/16	129 8/16	4 8/16	3 13/16	4 13/16	4 2/16	5 1/16	4 6/16
9 8/16	42 10/16	41 8/16	41 4/16	136 8/16	4 12/16	4 1/16	5 1/16	4 5/16	5 6/16	4 10/16
10	44 14/16	43 11/16	43 7/16	143 8/16	5	4 4/16	5 5/16	4 9/16	5 10/16	4 14/16
10 8/16	47 2/16	45 14/16	45 10/16	150 8/16	5 4/16	4 7/16	5 9/16	4 13/16	5 15/16	5 2/16
11	49 6/16	48 1/16	47 13/16	157 8/16	5 8/16	4 11/16	5 14/16	5	6 3/16	5 6/16
11 8/16	51 10/16	50 4/16	49 15/16	164 8/16	5 12/16	4 14/16	6 2/16	5 4/16	6 8/16	5 10/16
12	53 14/16	52 7/16	52 2/16	171 8/16	6	5 2/16	6 6/16	5 8/16	6 12/16	5 14/16
13	58 6/16	56 13/16	56 8/16	185 8/16	6 8/16	5 8/16	6 15/16	5 15/16	7 5/16	6 6/16
14	62 14/16	61 3/16	60 13/16	199 8/16	7	5 15/16	7 7/16	6 6/16	7 14/16	6 13/16
15	67 6/16	65 9/16	65 3/16	213 8/16	7 8/16	6 6/16	8	6 14/16	8 7/16	7 5/16
16	71 13/16	69 15/16	69 8/16	227 8/16	8	6 13/16	8 8/16	7 5/16	9	7 13/16
17	76 5/16	74 5/16	73 14/16	241 8/16	8 8/16	7 4/16	9 1/16	7 12/16	9 9/16	8 5/16
18	80 13/16	78 11/16	78 3/16	255 8/16	9	7 10/16	9 9/16	8 4/16	10 2/16	8 13/16
19	85 5/16	83	82 9/16	269 8/16	9 8/16	8 1/16	10 2/16	8 11/16	10 11/16	9 5/16
20	89 13/16	87 6/16	86 14/16	283 8/16	10	8 8/16	10 10/16	9 2/16	11 4/16	9 12/16
21	94 5/16	91 12/16	91 4/16	297 8/16	10 8/16	8 15/16	11 3/16	9 10/16	11 13/16	10 4/16
22	98 12/16	96 2/16	95 9/16	311 8/16	11	9 6/16	11 11/16	10 1/16	12 6/16	10 12/16
23	103 4/16	100 8/16	99 15/16	325 8/16	11 8/16	9 13/16	12 4/16	10 8/16	12 15/16	11 4/16
24	107 12/16	104 14/16	104 4/16	339 8/16	12	10 3/16	12 12/16	11	13 8/16	11 12/16
25	112 4/16	109 4/16	108 10/16	353 8/16	12 8/16	10 10/16	13 5/16	11 7/16	14 1/16	12 3/16
26	116 12/16	113 10/16	112 15/16	367 8/16	13	11 1/16	13 13/16	11 14/16	14 10/16	12 11/16
27	121 4/16	118	117 5/16	381 8/16	13 8/16	11 8/16	14 6/16	12 5/16	15 3/16	13 3/16
28	125 12/16	122 6/16	121 10/16	395 8/16	14	11 15/16	14 14/16	12 13/16	15 12/16	13 11/16

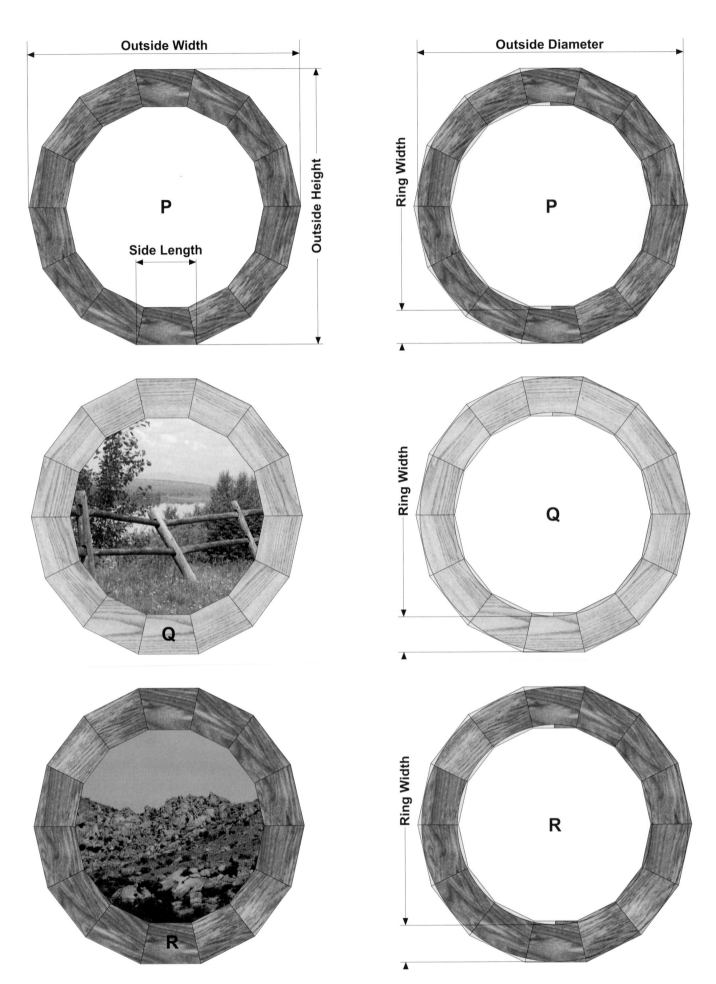

Side Length	Frame Width	Frame Height	Ring Max. OD	Material Req'd.	P Side Width	P Ring Width	Q Side Width	Q Ring Width	R Side Width	R Ring Width
8/16	2 4/16	2 3/16	2 3/16	10 8/16	5/16	4/16	5/16	4/16	5/16	5/16
10/16	2 13/16	2 12/16	2 11/16	12 4/16	6/16	5/16	6/16	6/16	7/16	6/16
12/16	3 6/16	3 4/16	3 4/16	14	7/16	6/16	8/16	7/16	8/16	7/16
14/16	3 15/16	3 13/16	3 13/16	15 12/16	8/16	7/16	9/16	8/16	9/16	8/16
1	4 8/16	4 6/16	4 6/16	17 8/16	10/16	8/16	10/16	9/16	11/16	9/16
1 4/16	5 10/16	5 7/16	5 7/16	21	12/16	10/16	13/16	11/16	13/16	12/16
1 8/16	6 12/16	6 9/16	6 8/16	24 8/16	14/16	12/16	15/16	13/16	1	14/16
1 12/16	7 14/16	7 10/16	7 10/16	28	1 1/16	15/16	1 2/16	15/16	1 2/16	1
2	9	8 12/16	8 11/16	31 8/16	1 3/16	1 1/16	1 4/16	1 2/16	1 5/16	1 3/16
2 4/16	10 2/16	9 13/16	9 12/16	35	1 5/16	1 3/16	1 7/16	1 4/16	1 8/16	1 5/16
2 8/16	11 4/16	10 15/16	10 14/16	38 8/16	1 8/16	1 5/16	1 9/16	1 6/16	1 10/16	1 7/16
2 12/16	12 6/16	12	11 15/16	42	1 10/16	1 7/16	1 12/16	1 8/16	1 13/16	1 10/16
3	13 8/16	13 2/16	13 1/16	45 8/16	1 13/16	1 9/16	1 14/16	1 10/16	2	1 12/16
3 4/16	14 9/16	14 3/16	14 2/16	49	1 15/16	1 11/16	2 1/16	1 13/16	2 2/16	1 14/16
3 8/16	15 11/16	15 5/16	15 3/16	52 8/16	2 1/16	1 13/16	2 3/16	1 15/16	2 5/16	2 1/16
3 12/16	16 13/16	16 6/16	16 5/16	56	2 4/16	1 15/16	2 6/16	2 1/16	2 7/16	2 3/16
4	17 15/16	17 8/16	17 6/16	59 8/16	2 6/16	2 1/16	2 8/16	2 3/16	2 10/16	2 5/16
4 4/16	19 1/16	18 9/16	18 7/16	63	2 8/16	2 3/16	2 11/16	2 6/16	2 13/16	2 8/16
4 8/16	20 3/16	19 11/16	19 9/16	66 8/16	2 11/16	2 5/16	2 13/16	2 8/16	2 15/16	2 10/16
4 12/16	21 5/16	20 12/16	20 10/16	70	2 13/16	2 8/16	3	2 10/16	3 2/16	2 12/16
5	22 7/16	21 14/16	21 12/16	73 8/16	3	2 10/16	3 2/16	2 12/16	3 5/16	2 15/16
5 4/16	23 9/16	22 15/16	22 13/16	77	3 2/16	2 12/16	3 5/16	2 14/16	3 7/16	3 1/16
5 8/16	24 11/16	24 1/16	23 14/16	80 8/16	3 4/16	2 14/16	3 7/16	3 1/16	3 10/16	3 3/16
5 12/16	25 13/16	25 2/16	25	84	3 7/16	3	3 10/16	3 3/16	3 12/16	3 6/16
6	26 15/16	26 4/16	26 1/16	87 8/16	3 9/16	3 2/16	3 12/16	3 5/16	3 15/16	3 8/16
6 8/16	29 3/16	28 6/16	28 4/16	94 8/16	3 14/16	3 6/16	4 1/16	3 9/16	4 4/16	3 13/16
7	31 7/16	30 9/16	30 7/16	101 8/16	4 3/16	3 10/16	4 6/16	3 14/16	4 10/16	4 1/16
7 8/16	33 11/16	32 12/16	32 9/16	108 8/16	4 7/16	3 14/16	4 11/16	4 2/16	4 15/16	4 6/16
8	35 15/16	34 15/16	34 12/16	115 8/16	4 12/16	4 3/16	5	4 7/16	5 4/16	4 11/16
8 8/16	38 3/16	37 2/16	36 15/16	122 8/16	5 1/16	4 7/16	5 5/16	4 11/16	5 9/16	4 15/16
9	40 7/16	39 5/16	39 2/16	129 8/16	5 6/16	4 11/16	5 10/16	4 15/16	5 15/16	5 4/16
9 8/16	42 10/16	41 8/16	41 4/16	136 8/16	5 10/16	4 15/16	5 15/16	5 4/16	6 4/16	5 9/16
10	44 14/16	43 11/16	43 7/16	143 8/16	5 15/16	5 3/16	6 4/16	5 8/16	6 9/16	5 13/16
10 8/16	47 2/16	45 14/16	45 10/16	150 8/16	6 4/16	5 7/16	6 9/16	5 13/16	6 14/16	6 2/16
11	49 6/16	48 1/16	47 13/16	157 8/16	6 9/16	5 12/16	6 14/16	6 1/16	7 4/16	6 7/16
11 8/16	51 10/16	50 4/16	49 15/16	164 8/16	6 13/16	6	7 3/16	6 6/16	7 9/16	6 11/16
12	53 14/16	52 7/16	52 2/16	171 8/16	7 2/16	6 4/16	7 8/16	6 10/16	7 14/16	7
13	58 6/16	56 13/16	56 8/16	185 8/16	7 12/16	6 12/16	8 2/16	7 3/16	8 9/16	7 9/16
14	62 14/16	61 3/16	60 13/16	199 8/16	8 5/16	7 5/16	8 12/16	7 12/16	9 3/16	8 3/16
15	67 6/16	65 9/16	65 3/16	213 8/16	8 15/16	7 13/16	9 6/16	8 4/16	9 14/16	8 12/16
16	71 13/16	69 15/16	69 8/16	227 8/16	9 8/16	8 5/16	10	8 13/16	10 8/16	9 5/16
17	76 5/16	74 5/16	73 14/16	241 8/16	10 2/16	8 14/16	10 10/16	9 6/16	11 3/16	9 15/16
18	80 13/16	78 11/16	78 3/16	255 8/16	10 11/16	9 6/16	11 4/16	9 15/16	11 13/16	10 8/16
19	85 5/16	83	82 9/16	269 8/16	11 5/16	9 14/16	11 14/16	10 8/16	12 8/16	11 1/16
20	89 13/16	87 6/16	86 14/16	283 8/16	11 14/16	10 6/16	12 8/16	11 1/16	13 2/16	11 11/16
21	94 5/16	91 12/16	91 4/16	297 8/16	12 8/16	10 15/16	13 2/16	11 9/16	13 13/16	12 4/16
22	98 12/16	96 2/16	95 9/16	311 8/16	13 1/16	11 7/16	13 12/16	12 2/16	14 7/16	12 13/16
23	103 4/16	100 8/16	99 15/16	325 8/16	13 11/16	11 15/16	14 6/16	12 11/16	15 2/16	13 7/16
24	107 12/16	104 14/16	104 4/16	339 8/16	14 4/16	12 8/16	15	13 4/16	15 12/16	14
25	112 4/16	109 4/16	108 10/16	353 8/16	14 14/16	13	15 10/16	13 13/16	16 7/16	14 9/16
26	116 12/16	113 10/16	112 15/16	367 8/16	15 7/16	13 8/16	16 4/16	14 6/16	17 1/16	15 3/16
27	121 4/16	118	117 5/16	381 8/16	16 1/16	14 1/16	16 14/16	14 14/16	17 12/16	15 12/16
28	125 12/16	122 6/16	121 10/16	395 8/16	16 10/16	14 9/16	17 8/16	15 7/16	18 6/16	16 5/16

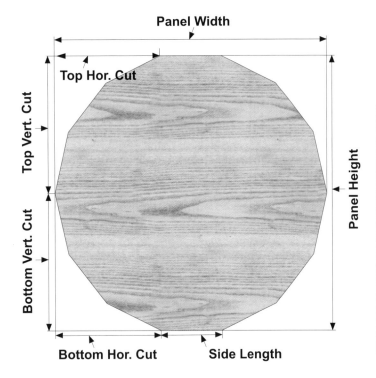

Panel Width

Top Hor. Cut

Top Vert. Cut

Bottom Vert. Cut

Panel Height

Bottom Hor. Cut **Side Length**

The Chart below shows the formulas that were used in the process of laying out the 14 sided shapes. These are included to assist you if you are designing a project to a size that is not illustrated in the Dimension Charts provided. We hope you find them helpful as you design your projects.

14 SIDED PANEL FORMULAS		
Panel Width =	Panel Height x	1.025
Panel Height =	Panel Width x	0.975
Side Length =	Panel Height x	0.223
Side Length =	Panel Width x	0.223
Top Hor. Cut =	Panel Width x	0.388
Bott. Hor. Cut =	Panel Width x	0.388
Top Vert. Cut =	Panel Width x	0.488
Bott.Vert. Cut =	Panel Width x	0.488

PANEL WIDTH	PANEL HEIGHT	SIDE LENGTH	TOP HOR. CUT	BOTTOM HOR. CUT	TOP VERT. CUT	BOTTOM VERT. CUT
12/16	12/16	3/16	5/16	5/16	6/16	6/16
1	1	3/16	6/16	6/16	8/16	8/16
1 4/16	1 4/16	3/16	8/16	8/16	10/16	10/16
1 8/16	1 7/16	5/16	9/16	9/16	12/16	12/16
1 12/16	1 11/16	6/16	11/16	11/16	14/16	14/16
2	1 15/16	7/16	12/16	12/16	1	1
2 4/16	2 3/16	8/16	14/16	14/16	1 2/16	1 2/16
2 8/16	2 7/16	9/16	1	1	1 4/16	1 4/16
2 12/16	2 11/16	10/16	1 1/16	1 1/16	1 5/16	1 5/16
3	2 15/16	11/16	1 3/16	1 3/16	1 7/16	1 7/16
3 4/16	3 3/16	12/16	1 4/16	1 4/16	1 9/16	1 9/16
3 8/16	3 7/16	12/16	1 6/16	1 6/16	1 11/16	1 11/16
3 12/16	3 11/16	13/16	1 7/16	1 7/16	1 13/16	1 13/16
4	3 14/16	14/16	1 9/16	1 9/16	1 15/16	1 15/16
4 4/16	4 2/16	15/16	1 10/16	1 10/16	2 1/16	2 1/16
4 8/16	4 6/16	1	1 12/16	1 12/16	2 3/16	2 3/16
4 12/16	4 10/16	1 1/16	1 13/16	1 13/16	2 5/16	2 5/16
5	4 14/16	1 2/16	1 15/16	1 15/16	2 7/16	2 7/16
5 4/16	5 2/16	1 3/16	2 1/16	2 1/16	2 9/16	2 9/16
5 8/16	5 6/16	1 4/16	2 2/16	2 2/16	2 11/16	2 11/16
5 12/16	5 10/16	1 5/16	2 4/16	2 4/16	2 13/16	2 13/16
6	5 14/16	1 5/16	2 5/16	2 5/16	2 15/16	2 15/16
6 4/16	6 2/16	1 6/16	2 7/16	2 7/16	3 1/16	3 1/16
6 8/16	6 5/16	1 7/16	2 8/16	2 8/16	3 3/16	3 3/16
6 12/16	6 9/16	1 8/16	2 10/16	2 10/16	3 5/16	3 5/16
7	6 13/16	1 9/16	2 11/16	2 11/16	3 7/16	3 7/16
7 4/16	7 1/16	1 10/16	2 13/16	2 13/16	3 9/16	3 9/16
7 8/16	7 5/16	1 11/16	2 15/16	2 15/16	3 11/16	3 11/16
7 12/16	7 9/16	1 12/16	3	3	3 13/16	3 13/16
8	7 13/16	1 13/16	3 2/16	3 2/16	3 14/16	3 14/16
8 4/16	8 1/16	1 13/16	3 3/16	3 3/16	4	4
8 8/16	8 5/16	1 14/16	3 5/16	3 5/16	4 2/16	4 2/16

PANEL WIDTH	PANEL HEIGHT	SIDE LENGTH	TOP HOR. CUT	BOTTOM HOR. CUT	TOP VERT. CUT	BOTTOM VERT. CUT
8 12/16	8 9/16	1 15/16	3 6/16	3 6/16	4 4/16	4 4/16
9	8 12/16	2	3 8/16	3 8/16	4 6/16	4 6/16
9 4/16	9	2 1/16	3 9/16	3 9/16	4 8/16	4 8/16
9 8/16	9 4/16	2 2/16	3 11/16	3 11/16	4 10/16	4 10/16
9 12/16	9 8/16	2 3/16	3 13/16	3 13/16	4 12/16	4 12/16
10	9 12/16	2 4/16	3 14/16	3 14/16	4 14/16	4 14/16
10 4/16	10	2 5/16	4	4	5	5
10 8/16	10 4/16	2 5/16	4 1/16	4 1/16	5 2/16	5 2/16
10 12/16	10 8/16	2 6/16	4 3/16	4 3/16	5 4/16	5 4/16
11	10 12/16	2 7/16	4 4/16	4 4/16	5 6/16	5 6/16
11 4/16	11	2 8/16	4 6/16	4 6/16	5 8/16	5 8/16
11 8/16	11 3/16	2 9/16	4 7/16	4 7/16	5 10/16	5 10/16
12	11 11/16	2 11/16	4 10/16	4 10/16	5 14/16	5 14/16
12 4/16	11 15/16	2 12/16	4 12/16	4 12/16	6	6
12 8/16	12 3/16	2 13/16	4 14/16	4 14/16	6 2/16	6 2/16
12 12/16	12 7/16	2 13/16	4 15/16	4 15/16	6 4/16	6 4/16
13	12 11/16	2 14/16	5 1/16	5 1/16	6 6/16	6 6/16
13 4/16	12 15/16	2 15/16	5 2/16	5 2/16	6 7/16	6 7/16
13 8/16	13 3/16	3	5 4/16	5 4/16	6 9/16	6 9/16
13 12/16	13 7/16	3 1/16	5 5/16	5 5/16	6 11/16	6 11/16
14	13 10/16	3 2/16	5 7/16	5 7/16	6 13/16	6 13/16
14 8/16	14 2/16	3 4/16	5 10/16	5 10/16	7 1/16	7 1/16
15	14 10/16	3 6/16	5 13/16	5 13/16	7 5/16	7 5/16
15 8/16	15 2/16	3 7/16	6	6	7 9/16	7 9/16
16	15 10/16	3 9/16	6 3/16	6 3/16	7 13/16	7 13/16
16 8/16	16 1/16	3 11/16	6 6/16	6 6/16	8 1/16	8 1/16
17	16 9/16	3 13/16	6 10/16	6 10/16	8 5/16	8 5/16
17 8/16	17 1/16	3 14/16	6 13/16	6 13/16	8 9/16	8 9/16
18	17 9/16	4	7	7	8 13/16	8 13/16
19	18 8/16	4 4/16	7 6/16	7 6/16	9 4/16	9 4/16
20	19 8/16	4 7/16	7 12/16	7 12/16	9 12/16	9 12/16
21	20 8/16	4 11/16	8 2/16	8 2/16	10 4/16	10 4/16
22	21 7/16	4 14/16	8 9/16	8 9/16	10 12/16	10 12/16
23	22 7/16	5 2/16	8 15/16	8 15/16	11 4/16	11 4/16
24	23 6/16	5 6/16	9 5/16	9 5/16	11 11/16	11 11/16
25	24 6/16	5 9/16	9 11/16	9 11/16	12 3/16	12 3/16
26	25 6/16	5 13/16	10 1/16	10 1/16	12 11/16	12 11/16
27	26 5/16	6	10 8/16	10 8/16	13 3/16	13 3/16
28	27 5/16	6 4/16	10 14/16	10 14/16	13 11/16	13 11/16
29	28 4/16	6 7/16	11 4/16	11 4/16	14 2/16	14 2/16
30	29 4/16	6 11/16	11 10/16	11 10/16	14 10/16	14 10/16
31	30 4/16	6 15/16	12	12	15 2/16	15 2/16
32	31 3/16	7 2/16	12 7/16	12 7/16	15 10/16	15 10/16
33	32 3/16	7 6/16	12 13/16	12 13/16	16 2/16	16 2/16
34	33 2/16	7 9/16	13 3/16	13 3/16	16 9/16	16 9/16
35	34 2/16	7 13/16	13 9/16	13 9/16	17 1/16	17 1/16
36	35 2/16	8	13 15/16	13 15/16	17 9/16	17 9/16
37	36 1/16	8 4/16	14 6/16	14 6/16	18 1/16	18 1/16
38	37 1/16	8 8/16	14 12/16	14 12/16	18 9/16	18 9/16
39	38	8 11/16	15 2/16	15 2/16	19 1/16	19 1/16
40	39	8 15/16	15 8/16	15 8/16	19 8/16	19 8/16
41	40	9 2/16	15 15/16	15 15/16	20	20
42	40 15/16	9 6/16	16 5/16	16 5/16	20 8/16	20 8/16

16 SIDED PROJECT INFORMATION

Geometric Name: Hexadecagon
Definition: A Polygon having 16 sides
Miter Angle: 11.25°
Angle Change / Adjoining Sides: 22.5°

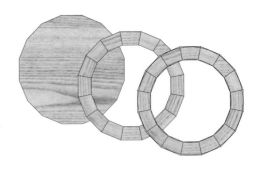

The 16 sided shape (Hexadecagon) is one of the "even numbered" shapes that's fairly easy to get creative with, because two pairs of parallel sides on the frame will be parallel to the 4 sides on a picture. The one thing that should be considered when using this shape (with sides of equal length) is that for most standard sizes of pictures, a lot of cropping will be required. However, the Hexadecagon is a fun frame to build using sides of different lengths for your frame.

The Illustrations to the right should give you an idea of the amount of cropping required by using a Hexadecagon (with equal length sides) as your choice of shape for a frame.

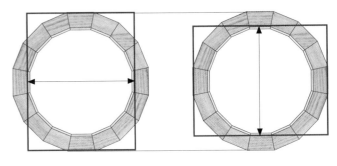

In the left Illustration, you see a scale (shown in red) 8" x 10" sheet in portrait format. The sheet border is slightly outside the rabbeted area (shown in yellow) of the frame. Note the amount of material that would need to be cropped off the sheet top and/or bottom.

In the right Illustration, you see the same size sheet, but rotated 90° into a landscape format. The same amount of material would need to be cropped off the sheet sides.

Portrait　　　　　**Landscape**

You should note that the frames are the same size. On a Hexadecagon, (with sides of equal length) the dimension between opposing sides is equal. Like the Octagon, pictures for these frames will start as squares, and are cropped at angles to fit the frame. In our **16 SIDED FRAME FORMULAS** below, you will be able to see that the dimensions for both formats for the pictures are identical.

If the project you are building is a frame for a specific size object, you should refer to the **16 SIDED FRAME FORMULAS** Chart below as a first step. On a Hexadecagon (with sides of equal length) the height will be identical to the width, so there is no controlling dimension for this shape of frame.

The Hexadecagon is one of the "medium difficulty" Polygons to get creative with. You can get creative and build a very pretty frame by using as few as 2 different lengths of sides for the frame for your picture.

16 SIDED FRAME FORMULAS		
WIDTH	**HEIGHT**	**SIDE LENGTH**
Width = Side Length x 5.02	Height = Side Length x 5.02	Side Length = Width x .199
Width = Height x 1.00	Height = Width x 1.00	Side Length = Height x .199

Though the information above is very helpful, one of the most time consuming (and frustrating) things about building frames is to try to cut to a dimension that is not measured on either the inside or outside edge of the molding. I like to cut miters from the inside to the outside edges of the molding. This not only allows me to eliminate tear out on the inside corners of the frame since I am cutting into the inside edge, I am also cutting with the grain of the molding. It also allows me to see the outside edge of the material as I cut it. To help you understand how easy it is to convert a dimension along the rabbeted edge into an outside measurement, I will explain how we can use some basic math to help us determine the outside length of our frame sides. The Illustration below should be helpful in showing you how we designed our **16 SIDED FRAME ADDED WIDTH AND LENGTH CHART** on the next page.

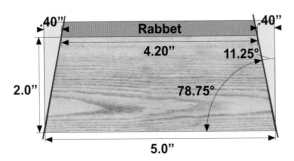

The Illustration to the left represents a piece of wood that is 5" long and 2" wide (to the edge of the rabbet). Note that on the right side that the end of the piece shows the miter angle for an Hexadecagon (11.25°) and the resulting angle of the cut (78.75°).

You should also note that at the rabbet, the 11.25° cuts shorten each end of the piece by .40". Since both ends of the piece are cut, this means that the length at the rabbet is 4.20", which is .80" shorter than the outside edge of the molding. What this tells us is that at an 11.25° cut, we will add .80" to the length at a 2" width. This is the basis of our formula.

If we divide the **Added Length** (.80") by the **Added Width** (2.0") we end up with .40 as our multiplier. In the event that you want to make a frame and need to work in fractions smaller than 1/16 increments, you would multiply the width of the molding outside the rabbet by .40. To determine the decimal equivalent of the fractions you need to use, refer to the **FRACTION TO DECIMAL CONVERSION CHART** provided.

If you are able to use 1/16" increments for the mathematics of your frames, you should use the **16 SIDED FRAME ADDED WIDTH AND LENGTH CHART** below.

Determine how wide you want the material to be (outside the rabbet). Refer to the Chart below to find this dimension in one of the yellow shaded columns. The added length for that width will be shown in the green shaded block to the right of it. Add this dimension to the side length determined in the first step. You should then add whatever waste you want to allow for each side. This total is then multiplied by 16 to determine how much material is needed to build your project.

16 SIDED FRAME ADDED WIDTH AND LENGTH CHART

Added Width	Added Length	Added Width	Added Length	Added Width	Added Length	Added Width	Added Length	Added Width	Added Length
1/16	0	1 1/16	7/16	2 1/16	13/16	3 1/16	1 4/16	4 1/16	1 10/16
2/16	1/16	1 2/16	7/16	2 2/16	14/16	3 2/16	1 4/16	4 2/16	1 10/16
3/16	1/16	1 3/16	8/16	2 3/16	14/16	3 3/16	1 4/16	4 3/16	1 11/16
4/16	2/16	1 4/16	8/16	2 4/16	14/16	3 4/16	1 5/16	4 4/16	1 11/16
5/16	2/16	1 5/16	8/16	2 5/16	15/16	3 5/16	1 5/16	4 5/16	1 12/16
6/16	2/16	1 6/16	9/16	2 6/16	15/16	3 6/16	1 6/16	4 6/16	1 12/16
7/16	3/16	1 7/16	9/16	2 7/16	1	3 7/16	1 6/16	4 7/16	1 12/16
8/16	3/16	1 8/16	10/16	2 8/16	1	3 8/16	1 6/16	4 8/16	1 13/16
9/16	4/16	1 9/16	10/16	2 9/16	1	3 9/16	1 7/16	4 9/16	1 13/16
10/16	4/16	1 10/16	10/16	2 10/16	1 1/16	3 10/16	1 7/16	4 10/16	1 14/16
11/16	4/16	1 11/16	11/16	2 11/16	1 1/16	3 11/16	1 8/16	4 11/16	1 14/16
12/16	5/16	1 12/16	11/16	2 12/16	1 2/16	3 12/16	1 8/16	4 12/16	1 14/16
13/16	5/16	1 13/16	12/16	2 13/16	1 2/16	3 13/16	1 8/16	4 13/16	1 15/16
14/16	6/16	1 14/16	12/16	2 14/16	1 2/16	3 14/16	1 9/16	4 14/16	1 15/16
15/16	6/16	1 15/16	12/16	2 15/16	1 3/16	3 15/16	1 9/16	4 15/16	2
1	6/16	2	13/16	3	1 3/16	4	1 10/16	5	2

The Chart below is provided to enable you to make 16 sided frames using the mathematics of most popular picture sizes. Note that the dimensions are identical in portrait and landscape format. This is because the picture for a Hexadecagon is a square with 2 (30°) crops on each 90° corner of the picture. In the Charts, the different colored columns represent the following information:

Red: The controlling dimension of the sheet size. (width in portrait, height in landscape)
Gray: The dimension of the sheet size that will need to be cropped.

White: The rabbet length for the frame sides.
Orange: The size of the opening in the direction the picture will need to be cropped.
Blue: The amount of material that will need to be cropped.

RABBET AREA DIMENSIONS FOR 16 SIDED FRAMES

FOR PORTRAIT FORMAT					FOR LANDSCAPE FORMAT				
Object Width	Object Height	Rabbet Length	Opening Height	Vertical Crop	Object Width	Object Height	Rabbet Length	Opening Width	Horizontal Crop
4	5	13/16	4 2/16	1	5	4	13/16	4 2/16	1
5	7	1	5 2/16	2	7	5	1	5 2/16	2
6	8	1 4/16	6 2/16	2	8	6	1 4/16	6 2/16	2
8	10	1 10/16	8 2/16	2	10	8	1 10/16	8 2/16	2
8 1/2	11	1 11/16	8 10/16	2 8/16	11	8 1/2	1 11/16	8 10/16	2 8/16
10	14	2	10 2/16	4	14	10	2	10 2/16	4
11	14	2 3/16	11 2/16	3	14	11	2 3/16	11 2/16	3
12	16	2 7/16	12 2/16	4	16	12	2 7/16	12 2/16	4
16	20	3 3/16	16 2/16	4	20	16	3 3/16	16 2/16	4
18	24	3 10/16	18 2/16	6	24	18	3 10/16	18 2/16	6
20	24	4	20 2/16	4	24	20	4	20 2/16	4
24	30	4 13/16	24 2/16	6	30	24	4 13/16	24 2/16	6

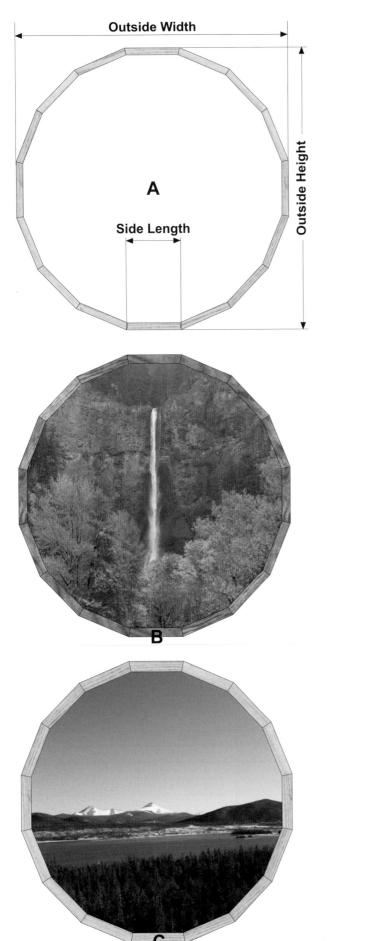

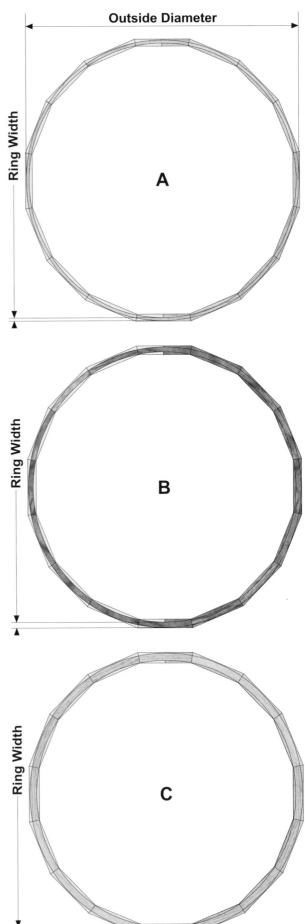

Side Length	Frame Width	Frame Height	Ring Max. OD	Material Req'd.	A Side Width	A Ring Width	B Side Width	B Ring Width	C Side Width	C Ring Width
8/16	2 8/16	2 8/16	2 8/16	12	1/16	0	1/16	1/16	2/16	1/16
10/16	3 2/16	3 2/16	3 2/16	14	1/16	1/16	2/16	1/16	2/16	1/16
12/16	3 12/16	3 12/16	3 12/16	16	2/16	1/16	2/16	1/16	2/16	1/16
14/16	4 6/16	4 6/16	4 6/16	18	2/16	1/16	2/16	1/16	3/16	2/16
1	5	5	5	20	2/16	1/16	3/16	1/16	3/16	2/16
1 4/16	6 4/16	6 4/16	6 4/16	24	3/16	1/16	3/16	2/16	4/16	2/16
1 8/16	7 8/16	7 8/16	7 8/16	28	3/16	1/16	4/16	2/16	5/16	3/16
1 12/16	8 13/16	8 13/16	8 12/16	32	4/16	1/16	4/16	2/16	5/16	3/16
2	10 1/16	10 1/16	10	36	4/16	2/16	5/16	3/16	6/16	4/16
2 4/16	11 5/16	11 5/16	11 4/16	40	5/16	2/16	6/16	3/16	7/16	4/16
2 8/16	12 9/16	12 9/16	12 8/16	44	5/16	2/16	6/16	3/16	8/16	5/16
2 12/16	13 13/16	13 13/16	13 12/16	48	6/16	2/16	7/16	4/16	8/16	5/16
3	15 1/16	15 1/16	15	52	6/16	3/16	8/16	4/16	9/16	6/16
3 4/16	16 5/16	16 5/16	16 4/16	56	7/16	3/16	8/16	4/16	10/16	6/16
3 8/16	17 9/16	17 9/16	17 8/16	60	7/16	3/16	9/16	5/16	11/16	7/16
3 12/16	18 13/16	18 13/16	18 12/16	64	8/16	3/16	9/16	5/16	11/16	7/16
4	20 1/16	20 1/16	20	68	8/16	3/16	10/16	5/16	12/16	8/16
4 4/16	21 5/16	21 5/16	21 4/16	72	9/16	4/16	11/16	6/16	13/16	8/16
4 8/16	22 9/16	22 9/16	22 8/16	76	9/16	4/16	11/16	6/16	14/16	8/16
4 12/16	23 14/16	23 14/16	23 11/16	80	10/16	4/16	12/16	6/16	14/16	9/16
5	25 2/16	25 2/16	24 15/16	84	10/16	4/16	13/16	7/16	15/16	9/16
5 4/16	26 6/16	26 6/16	26 3/16	88	11/16	4/16	13/16	7/16	1	10/16
5 8/16	27 10/16	27 10/16	27 7/16	92	11/16	5/16	14/16	8/16	1 1/16	10/16
5 12/16	28 14/16	28 14/16	28 11/16	96	12/16	5/16	14/16	8/16	1 1/16	11/16
6	30 2/16	30 2/16	29 15/16	100	12/16	5/16	15/16	8/16	1 2/16	11/16
6 8/16	32 10/16	32 10/16	32 7/16	108	13/16	6/16	1	9/16	1 4/16	12/16
7	35 2/16	35 2/16	34 15/16	116	14/16	6/16	1 2/16	10/16	1 5/16	13/16
7 8/16	37 10/16	37 10/16	37 7/16	124	15/16	6/16	1 3/16	10/16	1 7/16	14/16
8	40 3/16	40 3/16	39 15/16	132	1	7/16	1 4/16	11/16	1 8/16	15/16
8 8/16	42 11/16	42 11/16	42 7/16	140	1 1/16	7/16	1 5/16	12/16	1 10/16	1
9	45 3/16	45 3/16	44 15/16	148	1 2/16	8/16	1 7/16	12/16	1 11/16	1 1/16
9 8/16	47 11/16	47 11/16	47 7/16	156	1 3/16	8/16	1 8/16	13/16	1 13/16	1 2/16
10	50 3/16	50 3/16	49 15/16	164	1 4/16	8/16	1 9/16	14/16	1 14/16	1 3/16
10 8/16	52 11/16	52 11/16	52 7/16	172	1 5/16	9/16	1 10/16	14/16	2	1 4/16
11	55 4/16	55 4/16	54 15/16	180	1 6/16	9/16	1 12/16	15/16	2 1/16	1 5/16
11 8/16	57 12/16	57 12/16	57 7/16	188	1 7/16	10/16	1 13/16	1	2 3/16	1 6/16
12	60 4/16	60 4/16	59 15/16	196	1 8/16	10/16	1 14/16	1	2 4/16	1 7/16
13	65 4/16	65 4/16	64 15/16	212	1 10/16	11/16	2 1/16	1 2/16	2 7/16	1 9/16
14	70 4/16	70 4/16	69 15/16	228	1 12/16	12/16	2 3/16	1 3/16	2 10/16	1 10/16
15	75 5/16	75 5/16	74 14/16	244	1 14/16	13/16	2 6/16	1 4/16	2 13/16	1 12/16
16	80 5/16	80 5/16	79 14/16	260	2	14/16	2 8/16	1 6/16	3	1 14/16
17	85 5/16	85 5/16	84 14/16	276	2 2/16	14/16	2 11/16	1 7/16	3 3/16	2
18	90 6/16	90 6/16	89 14/16	292	2 4/16	15/16	2 13/16	1 9/16	3 6/16	2 2/16
19	95 6/16	95 6/16	94 14/16	308	2 6/16	1	3	1 10/16	3 9/16	2 4/16
20	100 6/16	100 6/16	99 14/16	324	2 8/16	1 1/16	3 2/16	1 11/16	3 12/16	2 6/16
21	105 7/16	105 7/16	104 14/16	340	2 10/16	1 2/16	3 5/16	1 13/16	3 15/16	2 8/16
22	110 7/16	110 7/16	109 14/16	356	2 12/16	1 3/16	3 7/16	1 14/16	4 2/16	2 9/16
23	115 7/16	115 7/16	114 14/16	372	2 14/16	1 3/16	3 10/16	1 15/16	4 5/16	2 11/16
24	120 8/16	120 8/16	119 13/16	388	3	1 4/16	3 12/16	2 1/16	4 8/16	2 13/16
25	125 8/16	125 8/16	124 13/16	404	3 2/16	1 5/16	3 15/16	2 2/16	4 11/16	2 15/16
26	130 8/16	130 8/16	129 13/16	420	3 4/16	1 6/16	4 1/16	2 4/16	4 14/16	3 1/16
27	135 9/16	135 9/16	134 13/16	436	3 6/16	1 7/16	4 4/16	2 5/16	5 1/16	3 3/16
28	140 9/16	140 9/16	139 13/16	452	3 8/16	1 8/16	4 6/16	2 6/16	5 4/16	3 5/16

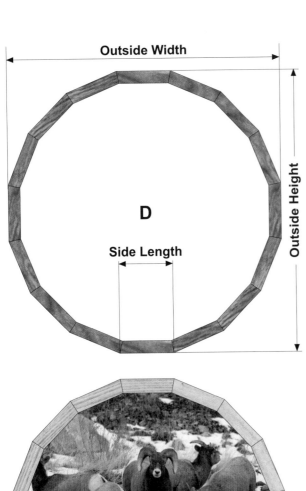

Outside Width

Outside Height

Side Length

D

E

F

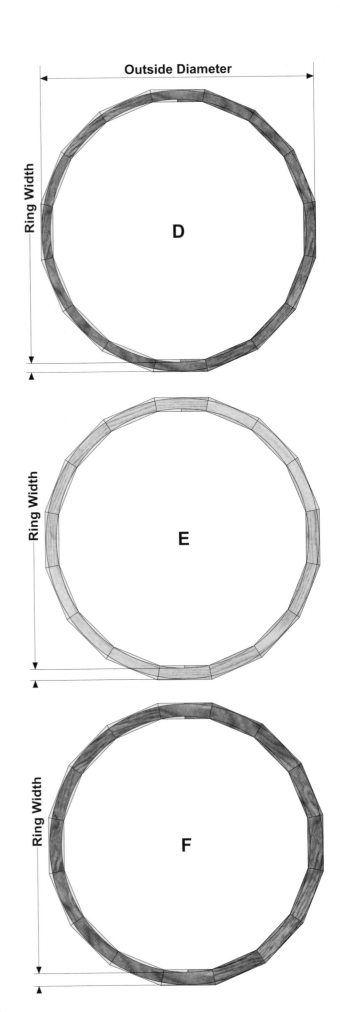

Outside Diameter

Ring Width

D

Ring Width

E

Ring Width

F

Outside Diameter

Side Length	Frame Width	Frame Height	Ring Max. OD	Material Req'd.	D Side Width	D Ring Width	E Side Width	E Ring Width	F Side Width	F Ring Width
8/16	2 8/16	2 8/16	2 8/16	12	2/16	1/16	2/16	1/16	2/16	2/16
10/16	3 2/16	3 2/16	3 2/16	14	2/16	2/16	3/16	2/16	3/16	2/16
12/16	3 12/16	3 12/16	3 12/16	16	3/16	2/16	3/16	2/16	3/16	3/16
14/16	4 6/16	4 6/16	4 6/16	18	3/16	2/16	4/16	3/16	4/16	3/16
1	5	5	5	20	4/16	2/16	4/16	3/16	5/16	3/16
1 4/16	6 4/16	6 4/16	6 4/16	24	4/16	3/16	5/16	4/16	6/16	4/16
1 8/16	7 8/16	7 8/16	7 8/16	28	5/16	4/16	6/16	4/16	7/16	5/16
1 12/16	8 13/16	8 13/16	8 12/16	32	6/16	4/16	7/16	5/16	8/16	6/16
2	10 1/16	10 1/16	10	36	7/16	5/16	8/16	6/16	9/16	7/16
2 4/16	11 5/16	11 5/16	11 4/16	40	8/16	5/16	9/16	7/16	10/16	8/16
2 8/16	12 9/16	12 9/16	12 8/16	44	9/16	6/16	10/16	7/16	11/16	9/16
2 12/16	13 13/16	13 13/16	13 12/16	48	10/16	7/16	11/16	8/16	12/16	9/16
3	15 1/16	15 1/16	15	52	11/16	7/16	12/16	9/16	14/16	10/16
3 4/16	16 5/16	16 5/16	16 4/16	56	11/16	8/16	13/16	10/16	15/16	11/16
3 8/16	17 9/16	17 9/16	17 8/16	60	12/16	8/16	14/16	10/16	1	12/16
3 12/16	18 13/16	18 13/16	18 12/16	64	13/16	9/16	15/16	11/16	1 1/16	13/16
4	20 1/16	20 1/16	20	68	14/16	10/16	1	12/16	1 2/16	14/16
4 4/16	21 5/16	21 5/16	21 4/16	72	15/16	10/16	1 1/16	12/16	1 3/16	15/16
4 8/16	22 9/16	22 9/16	22 8/16	76	1	11/16	1 2/16	13/16	1 4/16	15/16
4 12/16	23 14/16	23 14/16	23 11/16	80	1 1/16	11/16	1 3/16	14/16	1 5/16	1
5	25 2/16	25 2/16	24 15/16	84	1 2/16	12/16	1 4/16	15/16	1 7/16	1 1/16
5 4/16	26 6/16	26 6/16	26 3/16	88	1 2/16	13/16	1 5/16	15/16	1 8/16	1 2/16
5 8/16	27 10/16	27 10/16	27 7/16	92	1 3/16	13/16	1 6/16	1	1 9/16	1 3/16
5 12/16	28 14/16	28 14/16	28 11/16	96	1 4/16	14/16	1 7/16	1 1/16	1 10/16	1 4/16
6	30 2/16	30 2/16	29 15/16	100	1 5/16	14/16	1 8/16	1 2/16	1 11/16	1 5/16
6 8/16	32 10/16	32 10/16	32 7/16	108	1 7/16	1	1 10/16	1 3/16	1 13/16	1 6/16
7	35 2/16	35 2/16	34 15/16	116	1 9/16	1 1/16	1 12/16	1 4/16	2	1 8/16
7 8/16	37 10/16	37 10/16	37 7/16	124	1 10/16	1 2/16	1 14/16	1 6/16	2 2/16	1 10/16
8	40 3/16	40 3/16	39 15/16	132	1 12/16	1 3/16	2	1 7/16	2 4/16	1 12/16
8 8/16	42 11/16	42 11/16	42 7/16	140	1 14/16	1 4/16	2 2/16	1 9/16	2 6/16	1 13/16
9	45 3/16	45 3/16	44 15/16	148	2	1 6/16	2 4/16	1 10/16	2 9/16	1 15/16
9 8/16	47 11/16	47 11/16	47 7/16	156	2 1/16	1 7/16	2 6/16	1 12/16	2 11/16	2 1/16
10	50 3/16	50 3/16	49 15/16	164	2 3/16	1 8/16	2 8/16	1 13/16	2 13/16	2 2/16
10 8/16	52 11/16	52 11/16	52 7/16	172	2 5/16	1 9/16	2 10/16	1 15/16	2 15/16	2 4/16
11	55 4/16	55 4/16	54 15/16	180	2 7/16	1 10/16	2 12/16	2	3 2/16	2 6/16
11 8/16	57 12/16	57 12/16	57 7/16	188	2 8/16	1 12/16	2 14/16	2 2/16	3 4/16	2 8/16
12	60 4/16	60 4/16	59 15/16	196	2 10/16	1 13/16	3	2 3/16	3 6/16	2 9/16
13	65 4/16	65 4/16	64 15/16	212	2 14/16	1 15/16	3 4/16	2 6/16	3 11/16	2 13/16
14	70 4/16	70 4/16	69 15/16	228	3 1/16	2 2/16	3 8/16	2 9/16	3 15/16	3
15	75 5/16	75 5/16	74 14/16	244	3 5/16	2 4/16	3 12/16	2 12/16	4 4/16	3 4/16
16	80 5/16	80 5/16	79 14/16	260	3 8/16	2 6/16	4	2 15/16	4 8/16	3 7/16
17	85 5/16	85 5/16	84 14/16	276	3 12/16	2 9/16	4 4/16	3 2/16	4 13/16	3 11/16
18	90 6/16	90 6/16	89 14/16	292	3 15/16	2 11/16	4 8/16	3 5/16	5 1/16	3 14/16
19	95 6/16	95 6/16	94 14/16	308	4 3/16	2 14/16	4 12/16	3 8/16	5 6/16	4 1/16
20	100 6/16	100 6/16	99 14/16	324	4 6/16	3	5	3 10/16	5 10/16	4 5/16
21	105 7/16	105 7/16	104 14/16	340	4 10/16	3 3/16	5 4/16	3 13/16	5 15/16	4 8/16
22	110 7/16	110 7/16	109 14/16	356	4 13/16	3 5/16	5 8/16	4	6 3/16	4 12/16
23	115 7/16	115 7/16	114 14/16	372	5 1/16	3 7/16	5 12/16	4 3/16	6 8/16	4 15/16
24	120 8/16	120 8/16	119 13/16	388	5 4/16	3 10/16	6	4 6/16	6 12/16	5 3/16
25	125 8/16	125 8/16	124 13/16	404	5 8/16	3 12/16	6 4/16	4 9/16	7 1/16	5 6/16
26	130 8/16	130 8/16	129 13/16	420	5 11/16	3 15/16	6 8/16	4 12/16	7 5/16	5 10/16
27	135 9/16	135 9/16	134 13/16	436	5 15/16	4 1/16	6 12/16	4 15/16	7 10/16	5 13/16
28	140 9/16	140 9/16	139 13/16	452	6 2/16	4 3/16	7	5 2/16	7 14/16	6

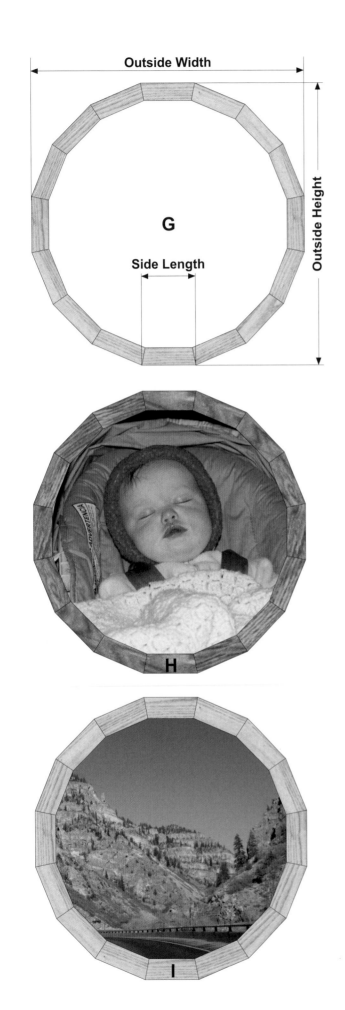

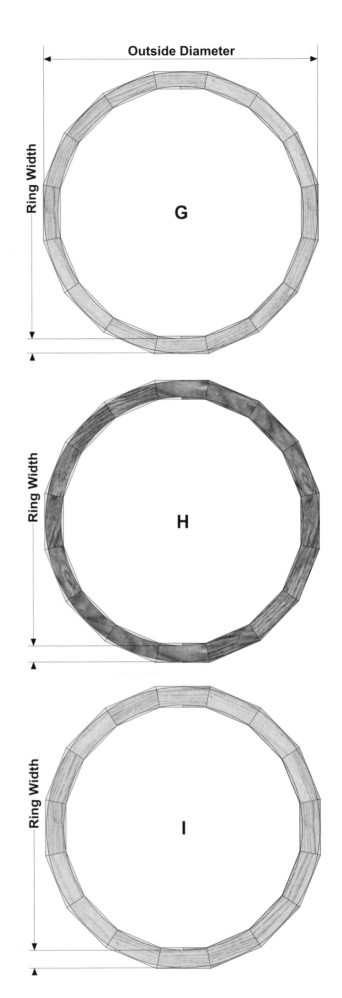

Side Length	Frame Width	Frame Height	Ring Max. OD	Material Req'd.	G Side Width	G Ring Width	H Side Width	H Ring Width	I Side Width	I Ring Width
8/16	2 8/16	2 8/16	2 8/16	12	3/16	2/16	3/16	2/16	3/16	3/16
10/16	3 2/16	3 2/16	3 2/16	14	3/16	2/16	3/16	3/16	4/16	3/16
12/16	3 12/16	3 12/16	3 12/16	16	4/16	3/16	4/16	3/16	5/16	4/16
14/16	4 6/16	4 6/16	4 6/16	18	4/16	3/16	5/16	4/16	5/16	4/16
1	5	5	5	20	5/16	4/16	6/16	4/16	6/16	5/16
1 4/16	6 4/16	6 4/16	6 4/16	24	6/16	5/16	7/16	6/16	8/16	6/16
1 8/16	7 8/16	7 8/16	7 8/16	28	8/16	6/16	8/16	7/16	9/16	8/16
1 12/16	8 13/16	8 13/16	8 12/16	32	9/16	7/16	10/16	8/16	11/16	9/16
2	10 1/16	10 1/16	10	36	10/16	8/16	11/16	9/16	12/16	10/16
2 4/16	11 5/16	11 5/16	11 4/16	40	11/16	9/16	12/16	10/16	14/16	11/16
2 8/16	12 9/16	12 9/16	12 8/16	44	13/16	10/16	14/16	11/16	15/16	13/16
2 12/16	13 13/16	13 13/16	13 12/16	48	14/16	11/16	15/16	12/16	1 1/16	14/16
3	15 1/16	15 1/16	15	52	15/16	12/16	1 1/16	13/16	1 2/16	15/16
3 4/16	16 5/16	16 5/16	16 4/16	56	1	13/16	1 2/16	15/16	1 4/16	1
3 8/16	17 9/16	17 9/16	17 8/16	60	1 2/16	14/16	1 3/16	1	1 5/16	1 2/16
3 12/16	18 13/16	18 13/16	18 12/16	64	1 3/16	15/16	1 5/16	1 1/16	1 7/16	1 3/16
4	20 1/16	20 1/16	20	68	1 4/16	1	1 6/16	1 2/16	1 8/16	1 4/16
4 4/16	21 5/16	21 5/16	21 4/16	72	1 5/16	1 1/16	1 7/16	1 3/16	1 10/16	1 5/16
4 8/16	22 9/16	22 9/16	22 8/16	76	1 7/16	1 2/16	1 9/16	1 4/16	1 11/16	1 7/16
4 12/16	23 14/16	23 14/16	23 11/16	80	1 8/16	1 3/16	1 10/16	1 5/16	1 13/16	1 8/16
5	25 2/16	25 2/16	24 15/16	84	1 9/16	1 4/16	1 12/16	1 6/16	1 14/16	1 9/16
5 4/16	26 6/16	26 6/16	26 3/16	88	1 10/16	1 5/16	1 13/16	1 8/16	2	1 10/16
5 8/16	27 10/16	27 10/16	27 7/16	92	1 12/16	1 6/16	1 14/16	1 9/16	2 1/16	1 12/16
5 12/16	28 14/16	28 14/16	28 11/16	96	1 13/16	1 7/16	2	1 10/16	2 3/16	1 13/16
6	30 2/16	30 2/16	29 15/16	100	1 14/16	1 8/16	2 1/16	1 11/16	2 4/16	1 14/16
6 8/16	32 10/16	32 10/16	32 7/16	108	2 1/16	1 10/16	2 4/16	1 13/16	2 7/16	2 1/16
7	35 2/16	35 2/16	34 15/16	116	2 3/16	1 12/16	2 7/16	1 15/16	2 10/16	2 3/16
7 8/16	37 10/16	37 10/16	37 7/16	124	2 6/16	1 14/16	2 9/16	2 2/16	2 13/16	2 6/16
8	40 3/16	40 3/16	39 15/16	132	2 8/16	2	2 12/16	2 4/16	3	2 8/16
8 8/16	42 11/16	42 11/16	42 7/16	140	2 11/16	2 2/16	2 15/16	2 6/16	3 3/16	2 11/16
9	45 3/16	45 3/16	44 15/16	148	2 13/16	2 4/16	3 2/16	2 8/16	3 6/16	2 13/16
9 8/16	47 11/16	47 11/16	47 7/16	156	3	2 6/16	3 4/16	2 11/16	3 9/16	3
10	50 3/16	50 3/16	49 15/16	164	3 2/16	2 8/16	3 7/16	2 13/16	3 12/16	3 2/16
10 8/16	52 11/16	52 11/16	52 7/16	172	3 5/16	2 10/16	3 10/16	2 15/16	3 15/16	3 5/16
11	55 4/16	55 4/16	54 15/16	180	3 7/16	2 12/16	3 13/16	3 1/16	4 2/16	3 7/16
11 8/16	57 12/16	57 12/16	57 7/16	188	3 10/16	2 14/16	3 15/16	3 4/16	4 5/16	3 10/16
12	60 4/16	60 4/16	59 15/16	196	3 12/16	3	4 2/16	3 6/16	4 8/16	3 12/16
13	65 4/16	65 4/16	64 15/16	212	4 1/16	3 4/16	4 8/16	3 10/16	4 14/16	4 1/16
14	70 4/16	70 4/16	69 15/16	228	4 6/16	3 7/16	4 13/16	3 15/16	5 4/16	4 6/16
15	75 5/16	75 5/16	74 14/16	244	4 11/16	3 11/16	5 3/16	4 3/16	5 10/16	4 11/16
16	80 5/16	80 5/16	79 14/16	260	5	3 15/16	5 8/16	4 8/16	6	5
17	85 5/16	85 5/16	84 14/16	276	5 5/16	4 3/16	5 14/16	4 12/16	6 6/16	5 5/16
18	90 6/16	90 6/16	89 14/16	292	5 10/16	4 7/16	6 3/16	5 1/16	6 12/16	5 10/16
19	95 6/16	95 6/16	94 14/16	308	5 15/16	4 11/16	6 9/16	5 5/16	7 2/16	5 15/16
20	100 6/16	100 6/16	99 14/16	324	6 4/16	4 15/16	6 14/16	5 10/16	7 8/16	6 4/16
21	105 7/16	105 7/16	104 14/16	340	6 9/16	5 3/16	7 4/16	5 14/16	7 14/16	6 9/16
22	110 7/16	110 7/16	109 14/16	356	6 14/16	5 7/16	7 9/16	6 3/16	8 4/16	6 14/16
23	115 7/16	115 7/16	114 14/16	372	7 3/16	5 11/16	7 15/16	6 7/16	8 10/16	7 3/16
24	120 8/16	120 8/16	119 13/16	388	7 8/16	5 15/16	8 4/16	6 12/16	9	7 8/16
25	125 8/16	125 8/16	124 13/16	404	7 13/16	6 3/16	8 10/16	7	9 6/16	7 13/16
26	130 8/16	130 8/16	129 13/16	420	8 2/16	6 7/16	8 15/16	7 5/16	9 12/16	8 2/16
27	135 9/16	135 9/16	134 13/16	436	8 7/16	6 11/16	9 5/16	7 9/16	10 2/16	8 7/16
28	140 9/16	140 9/16	139 13/16	452	8 12/16	6 15/16	9 10/16	7 13/16	10 8/16	8 12/16

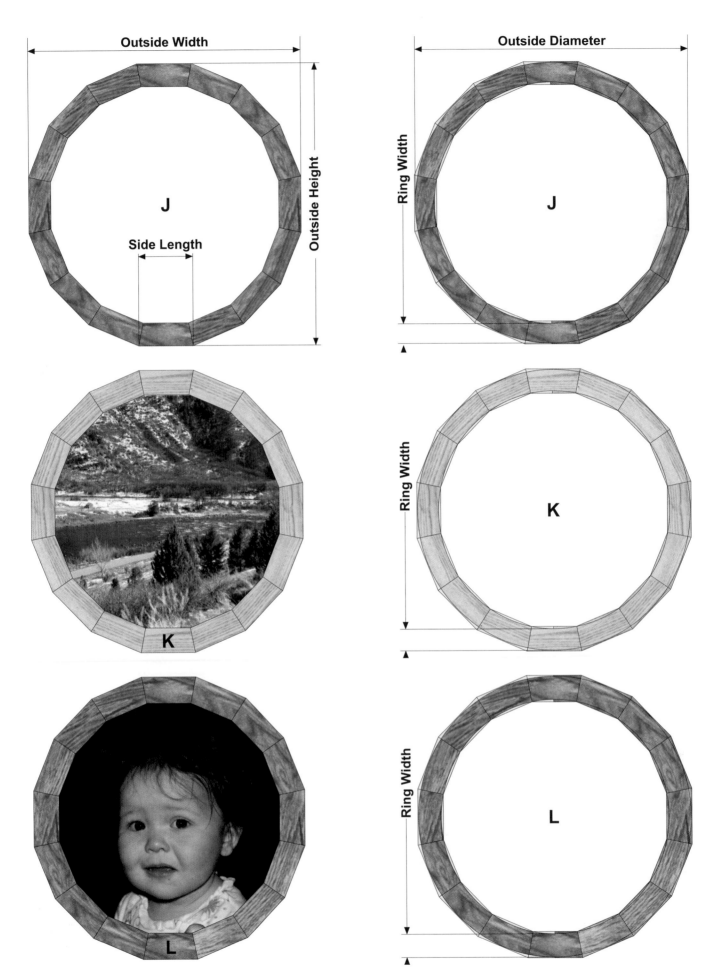

Side Length	Frame Width	Frame Height	Ring Max. OD	Material Req'd.	J Side Width	J Ring Width	K Side Width	K Ring Width	L Side Width	L Ring Width
8/16	2 8/16	2 8/16	2 8/16	12	3/16	3/16	4/16	3/16	4/16	3/16
10/16	3 2/16	3 2/16	3 2/16	14	4/16	3/16	4/16	4/16	5/16	4/16
12/16	3 12/16	3 12/16	3 12/16	16	5/16	4/16	5/16	5/16	6/16	5/16
14/16	4 6/16	4 6/16	4 6/16	18	6/16	5/16	6/16	5/16	7/16	6/16
1	5	5	5	20	7/16	6/16	7/16	6/16	8/16	7/16
1 4/16	6 4/16	6 4/16	6 4/16	24	8/16	7/16	9/16	8/16	9/16	8/16
1 8/16	7 8/16	7 8/16	7 8/16	28	10/16	8/16	11/16	9/16	11/16	10/16
1 12/16	8 13/16	8 13/16	8 12/16	32	11/16	10/16	12/16	11/16	13/16	11/16
2	10 1/16	10 1/16	10	36	13/16	11/16	14/16	12/16	15/16	13/16
2 4/16	11 5/16	11 5/16	11 4/16	40	15/16	12/16	1	14/16	1 1/16	15/16
2 8/16	12 9/16	12 9/16	12 8/16	44	1	14/16	1 2/16	15/16	1 3/16	1
2 12/16	13 13/16	13 13/16	13 12/16	48	1 2/16	15/16	1 3/16	1 1/16	1 5/16	1 2/16
3	15 1/16	15 1/16	15	52	1 4/16	1 1/16	1 5/16	1 2/16	1 7/16	1 4/16
3 4/16	16 5/16	16 5/16	16 4/16	56	1 5/16	1 2/16	1 7/16	1 4/16	1 8/16	1 5/16
3 8/16	17 9/16	17 9/16	17 8/16	60	1 7/16	1 3/16	1 9/16	1 5/16	1 10/16	1 7/16
3 12/16	18 13/16	18 13/16	18 12/16	64	1 8/16	1 5/16	1 10/16	1 7/16	1 12/16	1 9/16
4	20 1/16	20 1/16	20	68	1 10/16	1 6/16	1 12/16	1 8/16	1 14/16	1 10/16
4 4/16	21 5/16	21 5/16	21 4/16	72	1 12/16	1 7/16	1 14/16	1 10/16	2	1 12/16
4 8/16	22 9/16	22 9/16	22 8/16	76	1 13/16	1 9/16	2	1 11/16	2 2/16	1 14/16
4 12/16	23 14/16	23 14/16	23 11/16	80	1 15/16	1 10/16	2 1/16	1 13/16	2 4/16	1 15/16
5	25 2/16	25 2/16	24 15/16	84	2 1/16	1 12/16	2 3/16	1 14/16	2 6/16	2 1/16
5 4/16	26 6/16	26 6/16	26 3/16	88	2 2/16	1 13/16	2 5/16	2	2 7/16	2 2/16
5 8/16	27 10/16	27 10/16	27 7/16	92	2 4/16	1 14/16	2 7/16	2 1/16	2 9/16	2 4/16
5 12/16	28 14/16	28 14/16	28 11/16	96	2 5/16	2	2 8/16	2 3/16	2 11/16	2 6/16
6	30 2/16	30 2/16	29 15/16	100	2 7/16	2 1/16	2 10/16	2 4/16	2 13/16	2 7/16
6 8/16	32 10/16	32 10/16	32 7/16	108	2 10/16	2 4/16	2 14/16	2 7/16	3 1/16	2 11/16
7	35 2/16	35 2/16	34 15/16	116	2 14/16	2 7/16	3 1/16	2 10/16	3 5/16	2 14/16
7 8/16	37 10/16	37 10/16	37 7/16	124	3 1/16	2 9/16	3 5/16	2 13/16	3 8/16	3 1/16
8	40 3/16	40 3/16	39 15/16	132	3 4/16	2 12/16	3 8/16	3	3 12/16	3 5/16
8 8/16	42 11/16	42 11/16	42 7/16	140	3 7/16	2 15/16	3 12/16	3 3/16	4	3 8/16
9	45 3/16	45 3/16	44 15/16	148	3 11/16	3 2/16	3 15/16	3 6/16	4 4/16	3 11/16
9 8/16	47 11/16	47 11/16	47 7/16	156	3 14/16	3 4/16	4 3/16	3 9/16	4 7/16	3 14/16
10	50 3/16	50 3/16	49 15/16	164	4 1/16	3 7/16	4 6/16	3 12/16	4 11/16	4 2/16
10 8/16	52 11/16	52 11/16	52 7/16	172	4 4/16	3 10/16	4 10/16	3 15/16	4 15/16	4 5/16
11	55 4/16	55 4/16	54 15/16	180	4 8/16	3 13/16	4 13/16	4 2/16	5 3/16	4 8/16
11 8/16	57 12/16	57 12/16	57 7/16	188	4 11/16	4	5 1/16	4 6/16	5 6/16	4 11/16
12	60 4/16	60 4/16	59 15/16	196	4 14/16	4 2/16	5 4/16	4 9/16	5 10/16	4 15/16
13	65 4/16	65 4/16	64 15/16	212	5 5/16	4 8/16	5 11/16	4 15/16	6 2/16	5 5/16
14	70 4/16	70 4/16	69 15/16	228	5 11/16	4 13/16	6 2/16	5 5/16	6 9/16	5 12/16
15	75 5/16	75 5/16	74 14/16	244	6 2/16	5 3/16	6 9/16	5 11/16	7 1/16	6 2/16
16	80 5/16	80 5/16	79 14/16	260	6 8/16	5 8/16	7	6 1/16	7 8/16	6 9/16
17	85 5/16	85 5/16	84 14/16	276	6 15/16	5 14/16	7 7/16	6 7/16	8	7
18	90 6/16	90 6/16	89 14/16	292	7 5/16	6 3/16	7 14/16	6 13/16	8 7/16	7 6/16
19	95 6/16	95 6/16	94 14/16	308	7 12/16	6 9/16	8 5/16	7 3/16	8 15/16	7 13/16
20	100 6/16	100 6/16	99 14/16	324	8 2/16	6 14/16	8 12/16	7 9/16	9 6/16	8 3/16
21	105 7/16	105 7/16	104 14/16	340	8 9/16	7 4/16	9 3/16	7 15/16	9 14/16	8 10/16
22	110 7/16	110 7/16	109 14/16	356	8 15/16	7 10/16	9 10/16	8 5/16	10 5/16	9
23	115 7/16	115 7/16	114 14/16	372	9 6/16	7 15/16	10 1/16	8 11/16	10 13/16	9 7/16
24	120 8/16	120 8/16	119 13/16	388	9 12/16	8 5/16	10 8/16	9 1/16	11 4/16	9 14/16
25	125 8/16	125 8/16	124 13/16	404	10 3/16	8 10/16	10 15/16	9 7/16	11 12/16	10 4/16
26	130 8/16	130 8/16	129 13/16	420	10 9/16	9	11 6/16	9 13/16	12 3/16	10 11/16
27	135 9/16	135 9/16	134 13/16	436	11	9 5/16	11 13/16	10 3/16	12 11/16	11 1/16
28	140 9/16	140 9/16	139 13/16	452	11 6/16	9 11/16	12 4/16	10 9/16	13 2/16	11 8/16

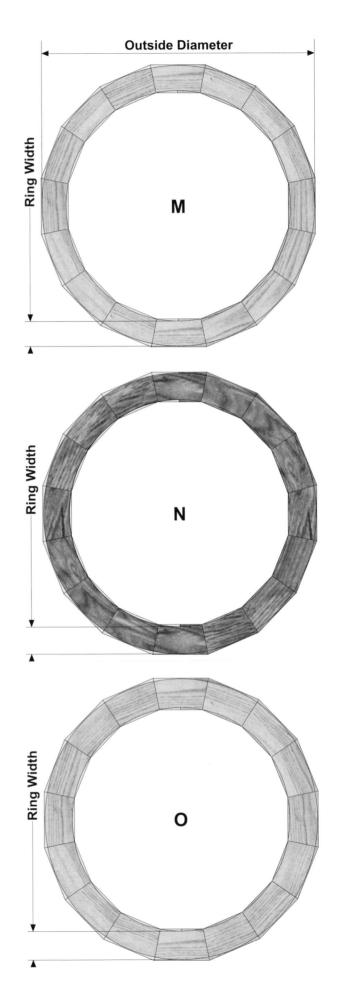

Side Length	Frame Width	Frame Height	Ring Max. OD	Material Req'd.	M Side Width	M Ring Width	N Side Width	N Ring Width	O Side Width	O Ring Width
8/16	2 8/16	2 8/16	2 8/16	12	4/16	4/16	4/16	4/16	5/16	4/16
10/16	3 2/16	3 2/16	3 2/16	14	5/16	4/16	5/16	5/16	6/16	5/16
12/16	3 12/16	3 12/16	3 12/16	16	6/16	5/16	6/16	6/16	7/16	6/16
14/16	4 6/16	4 6/16	4 6/16	18	7/16	6/16	7/16	7/16	8/16	7/16
1	5	5	5	20	8/16	7/16	9/16	8/16	9/16	8/16
1 4/16	6 4/16	6 4/16	6 4/16	24	10/16	9/16	11/16	10/16	11/16	10/16
1 8/16	7 8/16	7 8/16	7 8/16	28	12/16	11/16	13/16	11/16	14/16	12/16
1 12/16	8 13/16	8 13/16	8 12/16	32	14/16	12/16	15/16	13/16	1	14/16
2	10 1/16	10 1/16	10	36	1	14/16	1 1/16	15/16	1 2/16	1
2 4/16	11 5/16	11 5/16	11 4/16	40	1 2/16	1	1 3/16	1 1/16	1 4/16	1 2/16
2 8/16	12 9/16	12 9/16	12 8/16	44	1 4/16	1 2/16	1 5/16	1 3/16	1 7/16	1 4/16
2 12/16	13 13/16	13 13/16	13 12/16	48	1 6/16	1 3/16	1 7/16	1 5/16	1 9/16	1 6/16
3	15 1/16	15 1/16	15	52	1 8/16	1 5/16	1 10/16	1 7/16	1 11/16	1 8/16
3 4/16	16 5/16	16 5/16	16 4/16	56	1 10/16	1 7/16	1 12/16	1 9/16	1 13/16	1 10/16
3 8/16	17 9/16	17 9/16	17 8/16	60	1 12/16	1 9/16	1 14/16	1 11/16	2	1 12/16
3 12/16	18 13/16	18 13/16	18 12/16	64	1 14/16	1 11/16	2	1 13/16	2 2/16	1 14/16
4	20 1/16	20 1/16	20	68	2	1 12/16	2 2/16	1 14/16	2 4/16	2
4 4/16	21 5/16	21 5/16	21 4/16	72	2 2/16	1 14/16	2 4/16	2	2 6/16	2 3/16
4 8/16	22 9/16	22 9/16	22 8/16	76	2 4/16	2	2 6/16	2 2/16	2 9/16	2 5/16
4 12/16	23 14/16	23 14/16	23 11/16	80	2 6/16	2 2/16	2 8/16	2 4/16	2 11/16	2 7/16
5	25 2/16	25 2/16	24 15/16	84	2 8/16	2 3/16	2 11/16	2 6/16	2 13/16	2 9/16
5 4/16	26 6/16	26 6/16	26 3/16	88	2 10/16	2 5/16	2 13/16	2 8/16	2 15/16	2 11/16
5 8/16	27 10/16	27 10/16	27 7/16	92	2 12/16	2 7/16	2 15/16	2 10/16	3 2/16	2 13/16
5 12/16	28 14/16	28 14/16	28 11/16	96	2 14/16	2 9/16	3 1/16	2 12/16	3 4/16	2 15/16
6	30 2/16	30 2/16	29 15/16	100	3	2 10/16	3 3/16	2 14/16	3 6/16	3 1/16
6 8/16	32 10/16	32 10/16	32 7/16	108	3 4/16	2 14/16	3 7/16	3 1/16	3 11/16	3 5/16
7	35 2/16	35 2/16	34 15/16	116	3 8/16	3 2/16	3 12/16	3 5/16	3 15/16	3 9/16
7 8/16	37 10/16	37 10/16	37 7/16	124	3 12/16	3 5/16	4	3 9/16	4 4/16	3 13/16
8	40 3/16	40 3/16	39 15/16	132	4	3 9/16	4 4/16	3 13/16	4 8/16	4 1/16
8 8/16	42 11/16	42 11/16	42 7/16	140	4 4/16	3 12/16	4 8/16	4 1/16	4 13/16	4 5/16
9	45 3/16	45 3/16	44 15/16	148	4 8/16	4	4 13/16	4 4/16	5 1/16	4 9/16
9 8/16	47 11/16	47 11/16	47 7/16	156	4 12/16	4 3/16	5 1/16	4 8/16	5 6/16	4 13/16
10	50 3/16	50 3/16	49 15/16	164	5	4 7/16	5 5/16	4 12/16	5 10/16	5 1/16
10 8/16	52 11/16	52 11/16	52 7/16	172	5 4/16	4 10/16	5 9/16	5	5 15/16	5 5/16
11	55 4/16	55 4/16	54 15/16	180	5 8/16	4 14/16	5 14/16	5 4/16	6 3/16	5 9/16
11 8/16	57 12/16	57 12/16	57 7/16	188	5 12/16	5 1/16	6 2/16	5 7/16	6 8/16	5 13/16
12	60 4/16	60 4/16	59 15/16	196	6	5 5/16	6 6/16	5 11/16	6 12/16	6 1/16
13	65 4/16	65 4/16	64 15/16	212	6 8/16	5 12/16	6 15/16	6 3/16	7 5/16	6 10/16
14	70 4/16	70 4/16	69 15/16	228	7	6 3/16	7 7/16	6 10/16	7 14/16	7 2/16
15	75 5/16	75 5/16	74 14/16	244	7 8/16	6 10/16	8	7 2/16	8 7/16	7 10/16
16	80 5/16	80 5/16	79 14/16	260	8	7 1/16	8 8/16	7 10/16	9	8 2/16
17	85 5/16	85 5/16	84 14/16	276	8 8/16	7 8/16	9 1/16	8 1/16	9 9/16	8 10/16
18	90 6/16	90 6/16	89 14/16	292	9	7 15/16	9 9/16	8 9/16	10 2/16	9 2/16
19	95 6/16	95 6/16	94 14/16	308	9 8/16	8 7/16	10 2/16	9	10 11/16	9 10/16
20	100 6/16	100 6/16	99 14/16	324	10	8 14/16	10 10/16	9 8/16	11 4/16	10 2/16
21	105 7/16	105 7/16	104 14/16	340	10 8/16	9 5/16	11 3/16	10	11 13/16	10 11/16
22	110 7/16	110 7/16	109 14/16	356	11	9 12/16	11 11/16	10 7/16	12 6/16	11 3/16
23	115 7/16	115 7/16	114 14/16	372	11 8/16	10 3/16	12 4/16	10 15/16	12 15/16	11 11/16
24	120 8/16	120 8/16	119 13/16	388	12	10 10/16	12 12/16	11 6/16	13 8/16	12 3/16
25	125 8/16	125 8/16	124 13/16	404	12 8/16	11 1/16	13 5/16	11 14/16	14 1/16	12 11/16
26	130 8/16	130 8/16	129 13/16	420	13	11 8/16	13 13/16	12 6/16	14 10/16	13 3/16
27	135 9/16	135 9/16	134 13/16	436	13 8/16	11 15/16	14 6/16	12 13/16	15 3/16	13 11/16
28	140 9/16	140 9/16	139 13/16	452	14	12 6/16	14 14/16	13 5/16	15 12/16	14 3/16

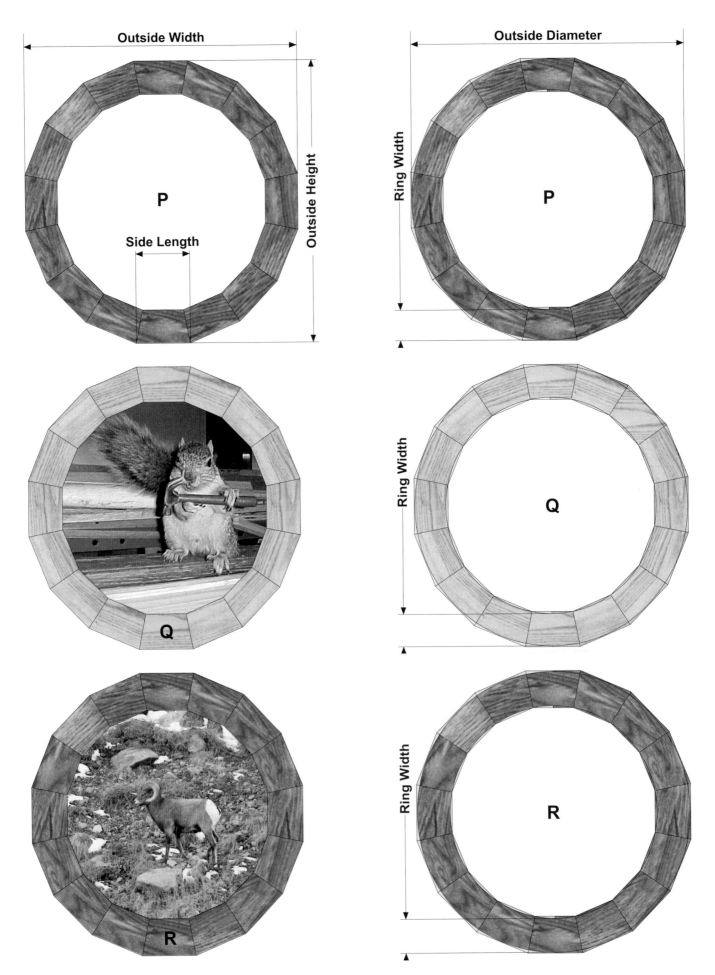

Side Length	Frame Width	Frame Height	Ring Max. OD	Material Req'd.	P Side Width	P Ring Width	Q Side Width	Q Ring Width	R Side Width	R Ring Width
8/16	2 8/16	2 8/16	2 8/16	12	5/16	4/16	5/16	5/16	5/16	5/16
10/16	3 2/16	3 2/16	3 2/16	14	6/16	5/16	6/16	6/16	7/16	6/16
12/16	3 12/16	3 12/16	3 12/16	16	7/16	6/16	8/16	7/16	8/16	7/16
14/16	4 6/16	4 6/16	4 6/16	18	8/16	8/16	9/16	8/16	9/16	8/16
1	5	5	5	20	10/16	9/16	10/16	9/16	11/16	10/16
1 4/16	6 4/16	6 4/16	6 4/16	24	12/16	11/16	13/16	11/16	13/16	12/16
1 8/16	7 8/16	7 8/16	7 8/16	28	14/16	13/16	15/16	14/16	1	15/16
1 12/16	8 13/16	8 13/16	8 12/16	32	1 1/16	15/16	1 2/16	1	1 2/16	1 1/16
2	10 1/16	10 1/16	10	36	1 3/16	1 1/16	1 4/16	1 2/16	1 5/16	1 3/16
2 4/16	11 5/16	11 5/16	11 4/16	40	1 5/16	1 3/16	1 7/16	1 5/16	1 8/16	1 6/16
2 8/16	12 9/16	12 9/16	12 8/16	44	1 8/16	1 6/16	1 9/16	1 7/16	1 10/16	1 8/16
2 12/16	13 13/16	13 13/16	13 12/16	48	1 10/16	1 8/16	1 12/16	1 9/16	1 13/16	1 11/16
3	15 1/16	15 1/16	15	52	1 13/16	1 10/16	1 14/16	1 11/16	2	1 13/16
3 4/16	16 5/16	16 5/16	16 4/16	56	1 15/16	1 12/16	2 1/16	1 14/16	2 2/16	1 15/16
3 8/16	17 9/16	17 9/16	17 8/16	60	2 1/16	1 14/16	2 3/16	2	2 5/16	2 2/16
3 12/16	18 13/16	18 13/16	18 12/16	64	2 4/16	2	2 6/16	2 2/16	2 7/16	2 4/16
4	20 1/16	20 1/16	20	68	2 6/16	2 3/16	2 8/16	2 5/16	2 10/16	2 7/16
4 4/16	21 5/16	21 5/16	21 4/16	72	2 8/16	2 5/16	2 11/16	2 7/16	2 13/16	2 9/16
4 8/16	22 9/16	22 9/16	22 8/16	76	2 11/16	2 7/16	2 13/16	2 9/16	2 15/16	2 12/16
4 12/16	23 14/16	23 14/16	23 11/16	80	2 13/16	2 9/16	3	2 12/16	3 2/16	2 14/16
5	25 2/16	25 2/16	24 15/16	84	3	2 11/16	3 2/16	2 14/16	3 5/16	3
5 4/16	26 6/16	26 6/16	26 3/16	88	3 2/16	2 13/16	3 5/16	3	3 7/16	3 3/16
5 8/16	27 10/16	27 10/16	27 7/16	92	3 4/16	3	3 7/16	3 2/16	3 10/16	3 5/16
5 12/16	28 14/16	28 14/16	28 11/16	96	3 7/16	3 2/16	3 10/16	3 5/16	3 12/16	3 8/16
6	30 2/16	30 2/16	29 15/16	100	3 9/16	3 4/16	3 12/16	3 7/16	3 15/16	3 10/16
6 8/16	32 10/16	32 10/16	32 7/16	108	3 14/16	3 8/16	4 1/16	3 12/16	4 4/16	3 15/16
7	35 2/16	35 2/16	34 15/16	116	4 3/16	3 12/16	4 6/16	4	4 10/16	4 4/16
7 8/16	37 10/16	37 10/16	37 7/16	124	4 7/16	4 1/16	4 11/16	4 5/16	4 15/16	4 9/16
8	40 3/16	40 3/16	39 15/16	132	4 12/16	4 5/16	5	4 9/16	5 4/16	4 13/16
8 8/16	42 11/16	42 11/16	42 7/16	140	5 1/16	4 9/16	5 5/16	4 14/16	5 9/16	5 2/16
9	45 3/16	45 3/16	44 15/16	148	5 6/16	4 14/16	5 10/16	5 2/16	5 15/16	5 7/16
9 8/16	47 11/16	47 11/16	47 7/16	156	5 10/16	5 2/16	5 15/16	5 7/16	6 4/16	5 12/16
10	50 3/16	50 3/16	49 15/16	164	5 15/16	5 6/16	6 4/16	5 12/16	6 9/16	6 1/16
10 8/16	52 11/16	52 11/16	52 7/16	172	6 4/16	5 11/16	6 9/16	6	6 14/16	6 6/16
11	55 4/16	55 4/16	54 15/16	180	6 9/16	5 15/16	6 14/16	6 5/16	7 4/16	6 10/16
11 8/16	57 12/16	57 12/16	57 7/16	188	6 13/16	6 3/16	7 3/16	6 9/16	7 9/16	6 15/16
12	60 4/16	60 4/16	59 15/16	196	7 2/16	6 8/16	7 8/16	6 14/16	7 14/16	7 4/16
13	65 4/16	65 4/16	64 15/16	212	7 12/16	7	8 2/16	7 7/16	8 9/16	7 14/16
14	70 4/16	70 4/16	69 15/16	228	8 5/16	7 9/16	8 12/16	8	9 3/16	8 8/16
15	75 5/16	75 5/16	74 14/16	244	8 15/16	8 2/16	9 6/16	8 9/16	9 14/16	9 1/16
16	80 5/16	80 5/16	79 14/16	260	9 8/16	8 10/16	10	9 3/16	10 8/16	9 11/16
17	85 5/16	85 5/16	84 14/16	276	10 2/16	9 3/16	10 10/16	9 12/16	11 3/16	10 5/16
18	90 6/16	90 6/16	89 14/16	292	10 11/16	9 12/16	11 4/16	10 5/16	11 13/16	10 14/16
19	95 6/16	95 6/16	94 14/16	308	11 5/16	10 4/16	11 14/16	10 14/16	12 8/16	11 8/16
20	100 6/16	100 6/16	99 14/16	324	11 14/16	10 13/16	12 8/16	11 7/16	13 2/16	12 2/16
21	105 7/16	105 7/16	104 14/16	340	12 8/16	11 5/16	13 2/16	12	13 13/16	12 11/16
22	110 7/16	110 7/16	109 14/16	356	13 1/16	11 14/16	13 12/16	12 10/16	14 7/16	13 5/16
23	115 7/16	115 7/16	114 14/16	372	13 11/16	12 7/16	14 6/16	13 3/16	15 2/16	13 15/16
24	120 8/16	120 8/16	119 13/16	388	14 4/16	12 15/16	15	13 12/16	15 12/16	14 8/16
25	125 8/16	125 8/16	124 13/16	404	14 14/16	13 8/16	15 10/16	14 5/16	16 7/16	15 2/16
26	130 8/16	130 8/16	129 13/16	420	15 7/16	14 1/16	16 4/16	14 14/16	17 1/16	15 12/16
27	135 9/16	135 9/16	134 13/16	436	16 1/16	14 9/16	16 14/16	15 7/16	17 12/16	16 5/16
28	140 9/16	140 9/16	139 13/16	452	16 10/16	15 2/16	17 8/16	16	18 6/16	16 15/16

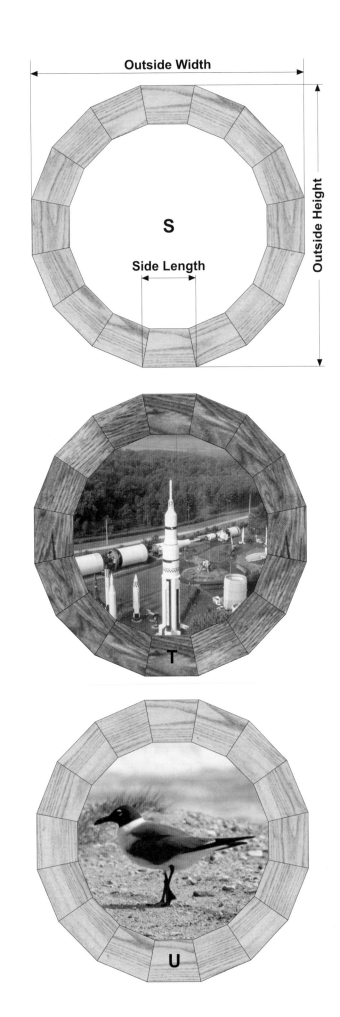
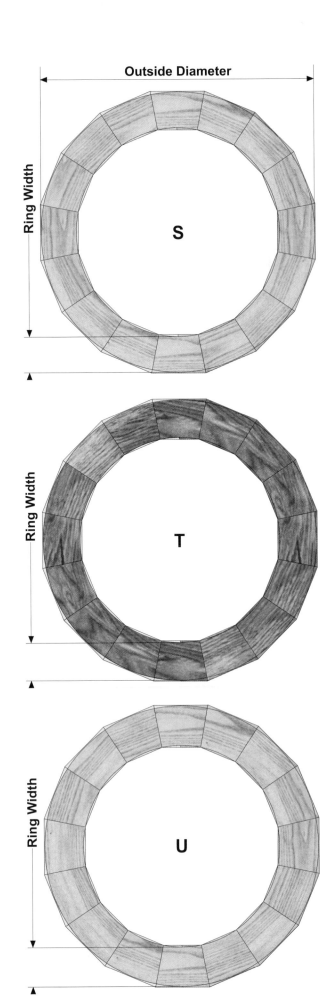

Side Length	Frame Width	Frame Height	Ring Max. OD	Material Req'd.	S Side Width	S Ring Width	T Side Width	T Ring Width	U Side Width	U Ring Width
8/16	2 8/16	2 8/16	2 8/16	12	6/16	5/16	6/16	5/16	6/16	6/16
10/16	3 2/16	3 2/16	3 2/16	14	7/16	6/16	7/16	7/16	8/16	7/16
12/16	3 12/16	3 12/16	3 12/16	16	8/16	8/16	9/16	8/16	9/16	8/16
14/16	4 6/16	4 6/16	4 6/16	18	10/16	9/16	10/16	9/16	11/16	10/16
1	5	5	5	20	11/16	10/16	12/16	11/16	12/16	11/16
1 4/16	6 4/16	6 4/16	6 4/16	24	14/16	13/16	14/16	13/16	15/16	14/16
1 8/16	7 8/16	7 8/16	7 8/16	28	1 1/16	15/16	1 1/16	1	1 2/16	1 1/16
1 12/16	8 13/16	8 13/16	8 12/16	32	1 3/16	1 2/16	1 4/16	1 3/16	1 5/16	1 4/16
2	10 1/16	10 1/16	10	36	1 6/16	1 4/16	1 7/16	1 5/16	1 8/16	1 6/16
2 4/16	11 5/16	11 5/16	11 4/16	40	1 9/16	1 7/16	1 10/16	1 8/16	1 11/16	1 9/16
2 8/16	12 9/16	12 9/16	12 8/16	44	1 12/16	1 9/16	1 13/16	1 11/16	1 14/16	1 12/16
2 12/16	13 13/16	13 13/16	13 12/16	48	1 14/16	1 12/16	2	1 13/16	2 1/16	1 15/16
3	15 1/16	15 1/16	15	52	2 1/16	1 15/16	2 3/16	2	2 4/16	2 2/16
3 4/16	16 5/16	16 5/16	16 4/16	56	2 4/16	2 1/16	2 5/16	2 3/16	2 7/16	2 5/16
3 8/16	17 9/16	17 9/16	17 8/16	60	2 7/16	2 4/16	2 8/16	2 6/16	2 10/16	2 7/16
3 12/16	18 13/16	18 13/16	18 12/16	64	2 9/16	2 6/16	2 11/16	2 8/16	2 13/16	2 10/16
4	20 1/16	20 1/16	20	68	2 12/16	2 9/16	2 14/16	2 11/16	3	2 13/16
4 4/16	21 5/16	21 5/16	21 4/16	72	2 15/16	2 11/16	3 1/16	2 14/16	3 3/16	3
4 8/16	22 9/16	22 9/16	22 8/16	76	3 2/16	2 14/16	3 4/16	3	3 6/16	3 3/16
4 12/16	23 14/16	23 14/16	23 11/16	80	3 4/16	3	3 7/16	3 3/16	3 9/16	3 5/16
5	25 2/16	25 2/16	24 15/16	84	3 7/16	3 3/16	3 10/16	3 6/16	3 12/16	3 8/16
5 4/16	26 6/16	26 6/16	26 3/16	88	3 10/16	3 6/16	3 12/16	3 8/16	3 15/16	3 11/16
5 8/16	27 10/16	27 10/16	27 7/16	92	3 13/16	3 8/16	3 15/16	3 11/16	4 2/16	3 14/16
5 12/16	28 14/16	28 14/16	28 11/16	96	3 15/16	3 11/16	4 2/16	3 14/16	4 5/16	4 1/16
6	30 2/16	30 2/16	29 15/16	100	4 2/16	3 13/16	4 5/16	4	4 8/16	4 3/16
6 8/16	32 10/16	32 10/16	32 7/16	108	4 8/16	4 2/16	4 11/16	4 6/16	4 14/16	4 9/16
7	35 2/16	35 2/16	34 15/16	116	4 13/16	4 7/16	5 1/16	4 11/16	5 4/16	4 15/16
7 8/16	37 10/16	37 10/16	37 7/16	124	5 3/16	4 12/16	5 6/16	5	5 10/16	5 4/16
8	40 3/16	40 3/16	39 15/16	132	5 8/16	5 2/16	5 12/16	5 6/16	6	5 10/16
8 8/16	42 11/16	42 11/16	42 7/16	140	5 14/16	5 7/16	6 2/16	5 11/16	6 6/16	6
9	45 3/16	45 3/16	44 15/16	148	6 3/16	5 12/16	6 8/16	6	6 12/16	6 5/16
9 8/16	47 11/16	47 11/16	47 7/16	156	6 9/16	6 1/16	6 13/16	6 6/16	7 2/16	6 11/16
10	50 3/16	50 3/16	49 15/16	164	6 14/16	6 6/16	7 3/16	6 11/16	7 8/16	7
10 8/16	52 11/16	52 11/16	52 7/16	172	7 4/16	6 11/16	7 9/16	7 1/16	7 14/16	7 6/16
11	55 4/16	55 4/16	54 15/16	180	7 9/16	7	7 15/16	7 6/16	8 4/16	7 12/16
11 8/16	57 12/16	57 12/16	57 7/16	188	7 15/16	7 5/16	8 4/16	7 11/16	8 10/16	8 1/16
12	60 4/16	60 4/16	59 15/16	196	8 4/16	7 10/16	8 10/16	8 1/16	9	8 7/16
13	65 4/16	65 4/16	64 15/16	212	8 15/16	8 5/16	9 6/16	8 11/16	9 12/16	9 2/16
14	70 4/16	70 4/16	69 15/16	228	9 10/16	8 15/16	10 1/16	9 6/16	10 8/16	9 13/16
15	75 5/16	75 5/16	74 14/16	244	10 5/16	9 9/16	10 13/16	10 1/16	11 4/16	10 9/16
16	80 5/16	80 5/16	79 14/16	260	11	10 3/16	11 8/16	10 11/16	12	11 4/16
17	85 5/16	85 5/16	84 14/16	276	11 11/16	10 13/16	12 4/16	11 6/16	12 12/16	11 15/16
18	90 6/16	90 6/16	89 14/16	292	12 6/16	11 8/16	12 15/16	12 1/16	13 8/16	12 10/16
19	95 6/16	95 6/16	94 14/16	308	13 1/16	12 2/16	13 11/16	12 12/16	14 4/16	13 6/16
20	100 6/16	100 6/16	99 14/16	324	13 12/16	12 12/16	14 6/16	13 6/16	15	14 1/16
21	105 7/16	105 7/16	104 14/16	340	14 7/16	13 6/16	15 2/16	14 1/16	15 12/16	14 12/16
22	110 7/16	110 7/16	109 14/16	356	15 2/16	14	15 13/16	14 12/16	16 8/16	15 7/16
23	115 7/16	115 7/16	114 14/16	372	15 13/16	14 11/16	16 9/16	15 7/16	17 4/16	16 2/16
24	120 8/16	120 8/16	119 13/16	388	16 8/16	15 5/16	17 4/16	16 1/16	18	16 14/16
25	125 8/16	125 8/16	124 13/16	404	17 3/16	15 15/16	18	16 12/16	18 12/16	17 9/16
26	130 8/16	130 8/16	129 13/16	420	17 14/16	16 9/16	18 11/16	17 7/16	19 8/16	18 4/16
27	135 9/16	135 9/16	134 13/16	436	18 9/16	17 3/16	19 7/16	18 1/16	20 4/16	18 15/16
28	140 9/16	140 9/16	139 13/16	452	19 4/16	17 14/16	20 2/16	18 12/16	21	19 11/16

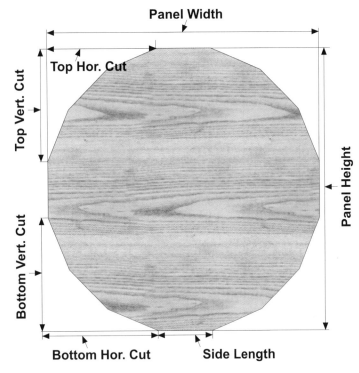

Panel Width

Top Hor. Cut

Top Vert. Cut

Bottom Vert. Cut

Bottom Hor. Cut

Side Length

Panel Height

The Chart below shows the formulas that were used in the process of laying out the 16 sided shapes. These are included to assist you if you are designing a project to a size that is not illustrated in the Dimension Charts provided. We hope you find them helpful as you design your projects.

16 SIDED PANEL FORMULAS		
Panel Width =	Panel Height x	1.000
Panel Height =	Panel Width x	1.000
Side Length =	Panel Height x	0.199
Side Length =	Panel Width x	0.199
Top Hor. Cut =	Panel Width x	0.400
Bott. Hor. Cut =	Panel Width x	0.400
Top Vert. Cut =	Panel Width x	0.400
Bott.Vert. Cut =	Panel Width x	0.400

PANEL WIDTH	PANEL HEIGHT	SIDE LENGTH	TOP HOR. CUT	BOTTOM HOR. CUT	TOP VERT. CUT	BOTTOM VERT. CUT
12/16	12/16	2/16	5/16	5/16	5/16	5/16
1	1	3/16	6/16	6/16	6/16	6/16
1 4/16	1 4/16	4/16	8/16	8/16	8/16	8/16
1 8/16	1 8/16	5/16	10/16	10/16	10/16	10/16
1 12/16	1 12/16	6/16	11/16	11/16	11/16	11/16
2	2	6/16	13/16	13/16	13/16	13/16
2 4/16	2 4/16	7/16	14/16	14/16	14/16	14/16
2 8/16	2 8/16	8/16	1	1	1	1
2 12/16	2 12/16	9/16	1 2/16	1 2/16	1 2/16	1 2/16
3	3	10/16	1 3/16	1 3/16	1 3/16	1 3/16
3 4/16	3 4/16	10/16	1 5/16	1 5/16	1 5/16	1 5/16
3 8/16	3 8/16	11/16	1 6/16	1 6/16	1 6/16	1 6/16
3 12/16	3 12/16	12/16	1 8/16	1 8/16	1 8/16	1 8/16
4	4	13/16	1 10/16	1 10/16	1 10/16	1 10/16
4 4/16	4 4/16	14/16	1 11/16	1 11/16	1 11/16	1 11/16
4 8/16	4 8/16	14/16	1 13/16	1 13/16	1 13/16	1 13/16
4 12/16	4 12/16	15/16	1 14/16	1 14/16	1 14/16	1 14/16
5	5	1	2	2	2	2
5 4/16	5 4/16	1 1/16	2 2/16	2 2/16	2 2/16	2 2/16
5 8/16	5 8/16	1 2/16	2 3/16	2 3/16	2 3/16	2 3/16
5 12/16	5 12/16	1 2/16	2 5/16	2 5/16	2 5/16	2 5/16
6	6	1 3/16	2 6/16	2 6/16	2 6/16	2 6/16
6 4/16	6 4/16	1 4/16	2 8/16	2 8/16	2 8/16	2 8/16
6 8/16	6 8/16	1 5/16	2 10/16	2 10/16	2 10/16	2 10/16
6 12/16	6 12/16	1 5/16	2 11/16	2 11/16	2 11/16	2 11/16
7	7	1 6/16	2 13/16	2 13/16	2 13/16	2 13/16
7 4/16	7 4/16	1 7/16	2 14/16	2 14/16	2 14/16	2 14/16
7 8/16	7 8/16	1 8/16	3	3	3	3
7 12/16	7 12/16	1 9/16	3 2/16	3 2/16	3 2/16	3 2/16
8	8	1 9/16	3 3/16	3 3/16	3 3/16	3 3/16
8 4/16	8 4/16	1 10/16	3 5/16	3 5/16	3 5/16	3 5/16
8 8/16	8 8/16	1 11/16	3 6/16	3 6/16	3 6/16	3 6/16

PANEL WIDTH	PANEL HEIGHT	SIDE LENGTH	TOP HOR. CUT	BOTTOM HOR. CUT	TOP VERT. CUT	BOTTOM VERT. CUT
8 12/16	8 12/16	1 12/16	3 8/16	3 8/16	3 8/16	3 8/16
9	9	1 13/16	3 10/16	3 10/16	3 10/16	3 10/16
9 4/16	9 4/16	1 13/16	3 11/16	3 11/16	3 11/16	3 11/16
9 8/16	9 8/16	1 14/16	3 13/16	3 13/16	3 13/16	3 13/16
9 12/16	9 12/16	1 15/16	3 14/16	3 14/16	3 14/16	3 14/16
10	10	2	4	4	4	4
10 4/16	10 4/16	2 1/16	4 2/16	4 2/16	4 2/16	4 2/16
10 8/16	10 8/16	2 1/16	4 3/16	4 3/16	4 3/16	4 3/16
10 12/16	10 12/16	2 2/16	4 5/16	4 5/16	4 5/16	4 5/16
11	11	2 3/16	4 6/16	4 6/16	4 6/16	4 6/16
11 4/16	11 4/16	2 4/16	4 8/16	4 8/16	4 8/16	4 8/16
11 8/16	11 8/16	2 5/16	4 10/16	4 10/16	4 10/16	4 10/16
12	12	2 6/16	4 13/16	4 13/16	4 13/16	4 13/16
12 4/16	12 4/16	2 7/16	4 14/16	4 14/16	4 14/16	4 14/16
12 8/16	12 8/16	2 8/16	5	5	5	5
12 12/16	12 12/16	2 9/16	5 2/16	5 2/16	5 2/16	5 2/16
13	13	2 9/16	5 3/16	5 3/16	5 3/16	5 3/16
13 4/16	13 4/16	2 10/16	5 5/16	5 5/16	5 5/16	5 5/16
13 8/16	13 8/16	2 11/16	5 6/16	5 6/16	5 6/16	5 6/16
13 12/16	13 12/16	2 12/16	5 8/16	5 8/16	5 8/16	5 8/16
14	14	2 13/16	5 10/16	5 10/16	5 10/16	5 10/16
14 8/16	14 8/16	2 14/16	5 13/16	5 13/16	5 13/16	5 13/16
15	15	3	6	6	6	6
15 8/16	15 8/16	3 1/16	6 3/16	6 3/16	6 3/16	6 3/16
16	16	3 3/16	6 6/16	6 6/16	6 6/16	6 6/16
16 8/16	16 8/16	3 5/16	6 10/16	6 10/16	6 10/16	6 10/16
17	17	3 6/16	6 13/16	6 13/16	6 13/16	6 13/16
17 8/16	17 8/16	3 8/16	7	7	7	7
18	18	3 9/16	7 3/16	7 3/16	7 3/16	7 3/16
19	19	3 12/16	7 10/16	7 10/16	7 10/16	7 10/16
20	20	4	8	8	8	8
21	21	4 3/16	8 6/16	8 6/16	8 6/16	8 6/16
22	22	4 6/16	8 13/16	8 13/16	8 13/16	8 13/16
23	23	4 9/16	9 3/16	9 3/16	9 3/16	9 3/16
24	24	4 12/16	9 10/16	9 10/16	9 10/16	9 10/16
25	25	5	10	10	10	10
26	26	5 3/16	10 6/16	10 6/16	10 6/16	10 6/16
27	27	5 6/16	10 13/16	10 13/16	10 13/16	10 13/16
28	28	5 9/16	11 3/16	11 3/16	11 3/16	11 3/16
29	29	5 12/16	11 10/16	11 10/16	11 10/16	11 10/16
30	30	6	12	12	12	12
31	31	6 3/16	12 6/16	12 6/16	12 6/16	12 6/16
32	32	6 6/16	12 13/16	12 13/16	12 13/16	12 13/16
33	33	6 9/16	13 3/16	13 3/16	13 3/16	13 3/16
34	34	6 12/16	13 10/16	13 10/16	13 10/16	13 10/16
35	35	6 15/16	14	14	14	14
36	36	7 3/16	14 6/16	14 6/16	14 6/16	14 6/16
37	37	7 6/16	14 13/16	14 13/16	14 13/16	14 13/16
38	38	7 9/16	15 3/16	15 3/16	15 3/16	15 3/16
39	39	7 12/16	15 10/16	15 10/16	15 10/16	15 10/16
40	40	7 15/16	16	16	16	16
41	41	8 3/16	16 6/16	16 6/16	16 6/16	16 6/16
42	42	8 6/16	16 13/16	16 13/16	16 13/16	16 13/16

PROJECT WORKSHEETS

If you build a project that you really like, and would like to save the information on it so the next time you build it you won't need to recalculate the measurements required, the following project forms are provided. We have tried to include all of the "data blocks" that you need (in each form) to make the project as simple as possible. To help you understand the information you need, the first one of each of the worksheets is filled in as an example.

We will say that you would like to build the Octagonal Frame illustrated in the "**EXAMPLE OF GETTING CREATIVE (WITH AN 8 SIDED FRAME)** article, where 3 different side lengths were need for the frame. Since there are quite a few calculations that need to be made, I would recommend that you first use the **PROJECT MATERIAL CALCULATIONS** form as a first step so that you can make the calculations for the project easier.

The first thing I recommend is that you enter all the information about the frame in the top 2 rows of the form. Note that the "**Side Crop**" measurement is 4", because on the Illustration we are cropping 2" in both directions on the corners of the picture. This is why the rabbet lengths on sides 1 and 2 are 4" smaller than the object dimensions.

The **Rabbet Length** for **Side 3** (the 4 short frame sides) was determined by multiplying the side crop (4") by .705, as found in the **CREATIVE 8 SIDED FRAME FORMULAS. (4 X .705 = 2.82)** The **Side Length** for all 3 sides was determined by adding their **Rabbet Length** and **Added Length**. These numbers were then moved to the 2 **Side Material** rows to determine the total material needed for each group of sides, and added together (including waste) to determine the total amount of material needed. I would then transfer the information to one of the **PROJECT MATERIAL CUT LIST** forms to make it easier to find.

PROJECT MATERIAL CALCULATIONS

Project:		Type: ☐Regular ☐Creative	Object Size: " x "
Molding Width: "	Rabbet Width: "	Width Outside the Rabbet: "	Side Crop: "

Side 1: Rabbet Length: "	Added Length = ____ x ____ = ____ " (Width Outside Rabbet) (Multiplier) (Added Length)	Side Length: " (Rabbet Length + Added Length)
Side 2: Rabbet Length: "	Added Length = ____ x ____ = ____ " (Width Outside Rabbet) (Multiplier) (Added Length)	Side Length: " (Rabbet Length + Added Length)
Side 3: Rabbet Length: "	Added Length = ____ x ____ = ____ " (Width Outside Rabbet) (Multiplier) (Added Length)	Side Length: " (Rabbet Length + Added Length)
Side 4: Rabbet Length: "	Added Length = ____ x ____ = ____ " (Width Outside Rabbet) (Multiplier) (Added Length)	Side Length: " (Rabbet Length + Added Length)

Side 1 Material: ____ x ____ = ____ " (Outside Length) (Number of Sides) (Total Material Side 1)	Side 2 Material: ____ x ____ = ____ " (Outside Length) (Number of Sides) (Total Material Side 2)
Side 3 Material: ____ x ____ = ____ " (Outside Length) (Number of Sides) (Total Material Side 3)	Side 4 Material: ____ x ____ = ____ " (Outside Length) (Number of Sides) (Total Material Side 4)

Total Material Required: ____ + ____ + ____ + ____ + ____ = ____
(Total Material Side 1) (Total Material Side 2) (Total Material Side 3) (Total Material Side 4) (Waste Allowance) (Total Material)

PROJECT MATERIAL "CUT LIST"

Project:		Type: ☐Regular ☐Creative	Object Size: " x "
Molding Width: "	Rabbet Width: "	Width Outside the Rabbet: "	Side Crop:
Side 1: ( ) pcs. Outside Side Length: "		Side 2: ( ) pcs. Outside Side Length: "	
Side 3: ( ) pcs. Outside Side Length: "		Side 4: ( ) pcs. Outside Side Length: "	
Total amount of material needed: "		Material used on project:	
Shop Notes:			

PROJECT MATERIAL "CUT LIST"

Project:		Type: ☐Regular ☐Creative	Object Size: " x "
Molding Width: "	Rabbet Width: "	Width Outside the Rabbet: "	Side Lengths:
Side 1: ( ) pcs. Outside Side Length: "		Side 2: ( ) pcs. Outside Side Length: "	
Side 3: ( ) pcs. Outside Side Length: "		Side 4: ( ) pcs. Outside Side Length: "	
Total amount of material needed: "		Material used on project:	
Shop Notes:			

Project:		Type: ☐Regular ☐Creative	Object Size: " x "
Molding Width: "	Rabbet Width: "	Width Outside the Rabbet: "	Side Lengths:
Side 1: ( ) pcs. Outside Side Length: "		Side 2: ( ) pcs. Outside Side Length: "	
Side 3: ( ) pcs. Outside Side Length: "		Side 4: ( ) pcs. Outside Side Length: "	
Total amount of material needed: "		Material used on project:	
Shop Notes:			

Project:		Type: ☐Regular ☐Creative	Object Size: " x "
Molding Width: "	Rabbet Width: "	Width Outside the Rabbet: "	Side Lengths:
Side 1: ( ) pcs. Outside Side Length: "		Side 2: ( ) pcs. Outside Side Length: "	
Side 3: ( ) pcs. Outside Side Length: "		Side 4: ( ) pcs. Outside Side Length: "	
Total amount of material needed: "		Material used on project:	
Shop Notes:			

PROJECT MATERIAL "CALCULATIONS"

Project: | **Type:** ☐Regular ☐Creative | **Object Size:** ___ " x ___ "

Molding Width: ___ " | **Rabbet Width:** ___ " | **Width Outside the Rabbet:** ___ " | **Side Crop:** ___ "

Side 1: Rabbet Length: ___ " | **Added Length =** _____ x _____ = _____ "
(Width Outside Rabbet) (Multiplier) (Added Length) | **Outside Length:** ___ "
(Rabbet Length + Added Length)

Side 2: Rabbet Length: ___ " | **Added Length =** _____ x _____ = _____ "
(Width Outside Rabbet) (Multiplier) (Added Length) | **Outside Length:** ___ "
(Rabbet Length + Added Length)

Side 3: Rabbet Length: ___ " | **Added Length =** _____ x _____ = _____ "
(Width Outside Rabbet) (Multiplier) (Added Length) | **Outside Length:** ___ "
(Rabbet Length + Added Length)

Side 4: Rabbet Length: ___ " | **Added Length =** _____ x _____ = _____ "
(Width Outside Rabbet) (Multiplier) (Added Length) | **Outside Length:** ___ "
(Rabbet Length + Added Length)

Side 1 Material: _____ x _____ = _____ "
(Outside Length) (Number of Sides) (Total Material Side 1) | **Side 2 Material:** _____ x _____ = _____ "
(Outside Length) (Number of Sides) (Total Material Side 2)

Side 3 Material: _____ x _____ = _____ "
(Outside Length) (Number of Sides) (Total Material Side 3) | **Side 4 Material:** _____ x _____ = _____ "
(Outside Length) (Number of Sides) (Total Material Side 4)

Total Material Required: _____ + _____ + _____ + _____ + _____ = _____
(Total Material Side 1) (Total Material Side 2) (Total Material Side 3) (Total Material Side 4) (Waste Allowance) (Total Material)

Project: | **Type:** ☐Regular ☐Creative | **Object Size:** ___ " x ___ "

Molding Width: ___ " | **Rabbet Width:** ___ " | **Width Outside the Rabbet:** ___ " | **Side Crop:** ___ "

Side 1: Rabbet Length: ___ " | **Added Length =** _____ x _____ = _____ "
(Width Outside Rabbet) (Multiplier) (Added Length) | **Outside Length:** ___ "
(Rabbet Length + Added Length)

Side 2: Rabbet Length: ___ " | **Added Length =** _____ x _____ = _____ "
(Width Outside Rabbet) (Multiplier) (Added Length) | **Outside Length:** ___ "
(Rabbet Length + Added Length)

Side 3: Rabbet Length: ___ " | **Added Length =** _____ x _____ = _____ "
(Width Outside Rabbet) (Multiplier) (Added Length) | **Outside Length:** ___ "
(Rabbet Length + Added Length)

Side 4: Rabbet Length: ___ " | **Added Length =** _____ x _____ = _____ "
(Width Outside Rabbet) (Multiplier) (Added Length) | **Outside Length:** ___ "
(Rabbet Length + Added Length)

Side 1 Material: _____ x _____ = _____ "
(Outside Length) (Number of Sides) (Total Material Side 1) | **Side 2 Material:** _____ x _____ = _____ "
(Outside Length) (Number of Sides) (Total Material Side 2)

Side 3 Material: _____ x _____ = _____ "
(Outside Length) (Number of Sides) (Total Material Side 3) | **Side 4 Material:** _____ x _____ = _____ "
(Outside Length) (Number of Sides) (Total Material Side 4)

Total Material Required: _____ + _____ + _____ + _____ + _____ = _____
(Total Material Side 1) (Total Material Side 2) (Total Material Side 3) (Total Material Side 4) (Waste Allowance) (Total Material)

Project: | **Type:** ☐Regular ☐Creative | **Object Size:** ___ " x ___ "

Molding Width: ___ " | **Rabbet Width:** ___ " | **Width Outside the Rabbet:** ___ " | **Side Crop:** ___ "

Side 1: Rabbet Length: ___ " | **Added Length =** _____ x _____ = _____ "
(Width Outside Rabbet) (Multiplier) (Added Length) | **Outside Length:** ___ "
(Rabbet Length + Added Length)

Side 2: Rabbet Length: ___ " | **Added Length =** _____ x _____ = _____ "
(Width Outside Rabbet) (Multiplier) (Added Length) | **Outside Length:** ___ "
(Rabbet Length + Added Length)

Side 3: Rabbet Length: ___ " | **Added Length =** _____ x _____ = _____ "
(Width Outside Rabbet) (Multiplier) (Added Length) | **Outside Length:** ___ "
(Rabbet Length + Added Length)

Side 4: Rabbet Length: ___ " | **Added Length =** _____ x _____ = _____ "
(Width Outside Rabbet) (Multiplier) (Added Length) | **Outside Length:** ___ "
(Rabbet Length + Added Length)

Side 1 Material: _____ x _____ = _____ "
(Outside Length) (Number of Sides) (Total Material Side 1) | **Side 2 Material:** _____ x _____ = _____ "
(Outside Length) (Number of Sides) (Total Material Side 2)

Side 3 Material: _____ x _____ = _____ "
(Outside Length) (Number of Sides) (Total Material Side 3) | **Side 4 Material:** _____ x _____ = _____ "
(Outside Length) (Number of Sides) (Total Material Side 4)

Total Material Required: _____ + _____ + _____ + _____ + _____ = _____
(Total Material Side 1) (Total Material Side 2) (Total Material Side 3) (Total Material Side 4) (Waste Allowance) (Total Material)